MW01628619

Morality
for Catholic Students

Written by Thomas J. Centrella

With Sidebars and Edits by Seton Staff

Seton Press
Front Royal, VA

Nihil Obstat: Reverend Paul F. deLadurantaye, S.T.D.
Censor Librorum

Imprimatur: + Most Reverend Michael F. Burbidge
Bishop of Arlington
March 19, 2018

The *Nihil obstat* and *Imprimatur* are official declarations that a book or pamphlet is free of doctrinal or moral error. No implication is contained therein that those who have granted the *Nihil obstat* and *Imprimatur* agree with the contents, opinions, or statements expressed.

Executive Editor: Dr. Mary Kay Clark
Editors: Seton Staff

First Edition
Printed in the United States of America

Seton Press
1350 Progress Drive
Front Royal, VA 22630

Phone: (540) 636-9990
Fax: (540) 636-1602

For more information, visit us on the web at www.setonpress.com.
Contact us by e-mail at info@setonpress.com.

ISBN: 978-1-60704-154-2

Cover: Interior of Saint Peter's Basilica
Back Cover: Exterior of Saint Peter's Basilica, Vatican City

Dedicated to the Sacred Heart of Jesus

Christ the King (Russian Icon)

Preface by the Author

This book aims to present an authentically Catholic understanding of morality, not only for Catholic high school students, but for all people of good will. The book is divided into three main sections and has a total of 16 chapters. There are three different levels of headings to help organize the material. Each chapter title and first-level heading is followed by a quote from Sacred Scripture. Each second-level heading is followed by a quote from the *Catechism of the Catholic Church*. To highlight the beginning of a new section, the first paragraph in that section is not indented. Each chapter ends with a Chapter Review. Please be sure to answer all the questions in the Chapter Review after you finish studying the chapter.

The book also has a Glossary and an Index. Finally, there is a Bibliography at the end of the book. Please note that the quotations in the book do not necessarily follow Seton's guidelines for capitalization and punctuation, but rather maintain the capitalization and punctuation given in the original sources.

Along with Sacred Scripture and the *Catechism of the Catholic Church*, Father John Laux's *Catholic Morality: A Course in Religion, Book III* (Rockford, Ill.: TAN Books and Publishing, Inc., 1990) has been a primary resource from which I have drawn extensively and gained many insights for this book. I'd like to express my appreciation and esteem for Fr. Laux's excellent treatment of the subject.

I'd also like to express my gratitude to the faculty at the Notre Dame Graduate School of Christendom College, where I completed my theological studies, and, in particular, to the late Dr. William E. May, my instructor in moral theology.

I humbly submit everything in this book to the sure judgment of the Magisterium of the Catholic Church. In writing this book, my sincere intention, from beginning to end, has always been to teach the truth about morality, to the best of my ability and understanding. If I have succeeded in meeting this goal, I praise God for the grace to do so. I pray that God will use this book as one of His instruments for the glory of His Holy Name, the salvation of souls, the honor of the Church, and the Christian renewal of this nation.

> "And if you be unwilling to serve the Lord, choose this day whom you will serve … but as for me and my house, we will serve the Lord" (Joshua 24:15).

May God, Our Father, bless everyone who reads this book. May our hearts and minds be guided by the Holy Spirit, the Spirit of Truth. May the Blessed Virgin Mary, St. Joseph, and all the angels and saints pray for us and help us. May we always remain faithful to Our Lord and Savior Jesus Christ and His Holy Church, no matter what may come. Jesus Christ is Lord!

Table of Contents

SECTION II: THE TEN COMMANDMENTS

Section I: Foundations of Morality

Introduction

> "Behold, I am coming soon, bringing my recompense, to repay everyone for what he has done. I am the Alpha and the Omega, the first and the last, the beginning and the end. Blessed are those who wash their robes, that they may have the right to the tree of life and that they may enter the city by the gates" (Revelation 22:12-14).

HOW DO WE KNOW what is right and wrong? Are there objective rules of morality, or are good and evil relative to place and time? What is morality? What is the basis of morality? What is the role of conscience in the moral life? How are we to understand moral evil and sin? How can we effectively resist temptation? What conditions must be met for an act to be morally good?

These are just a few of the questions that will be answered in this book. Our Lord has made it clear that our actions will have eternal consequences. Therefore, the subject of this book is of the utmost importance, so that we may know how to live good, morally upright lives that are pleasing to God.

> For he will render to every man according to his works: to those who by patience in well-doing seek for glory and honor and immortality, he will give eternal life; but for those who are factious and do not obey the truth, but obey wickedness, there will be wrath and fury (Romans 2:6-8).

This book is divided into three main sections. This first section discusses the foundations of morality: the truths and principles that support a sound approach to morality based on right reason and the teachings of the Catholic Church.

The second section of the book focuses on the Ten Commandments—the foundation of the Moral Law revealed by God—as well as many important conclusions that follow from these Commandments.

The third section emphasizes Christian perfection. This section includes an effective strategy to resist temptation, as well as a discussion on Christian charity and the Beatitudes—the ideal of the Christian moral life, as modeled by Our Lord Jesus Christ. Through His life and teachings, Jesus has shown us how to perfectly follow God's Law, and He calls us to be His disciples.

This first section is organized as follows:

- Chapter 1 explains the basis of morality.
- Chapter 2 discusses the standard of morality, along with the ultimate goal of morality.
- Chapter 3 focuses on God's Law and man's participation in His Authority.
- Chapter 4 describes the role of conscience in the moral life.
- Chapter 5 explains the three elements that determine the morality of every human act, and the conditions that must be met for an act to be morally good.
- Chapter 6 discusses moral good and virtue.
- Chapter 7 examines the problem of sin and moral evil.

Chapter 1. The Basis of Morality

The Lord hates all abominations, and they are not loved by those who fear him. It was he who created man in the beginning, and he left him in the power of his own inclination. If you will, you can keep the commandments, and to act faithfully is a matter of your own choice (Sirach 15:13-15).

What is morality, and what makes morality possible for human beings? **Morality** is the measure of the good or evil of concrete human acts. Morality concerns what is right versus what is wrong, what is good versus what is evil. The **basis of morality** is freedom—or, more precisely, *free will.* **It is free will that makes morality possible for human beings.**

The Seven Archangels in Adoration of the Trinity, by Federico Zuccaro

God created *man* (male and female) in His image and likeness (Genesis 1:27). God has given every human being a *rational soul.* A **rational soul** is the spiritual principle that animates the body of a human being, and that enables him to think and reason, to understand and know, and to decide what he will believe and what he will do. Every **human being** is an individual person who is the union of a body and a soul.

The **intellect** is the faculty of our rational soul through which we think, reason, understand, and know. The **will** is the faculty of our rational soul through which we decide what we will believe and what we will do.

Because we have a rational soul, we can use our intellect to learn and know truth, and we can use our will to freely decide whether to accept or reject that truth. On the basis of what we decide to believe, we can further use our will to decide what we will do.

Free will is our ability to decide what we will believe and what we will do. Because we have free will, we are able to make our own free choices about our actions. With choices come *responsibilities.* Since God has given us the freedom to make our own choices, He holds us accountable for those choices.

> Freedom is the power, rooted in reason and will, to act or not to act, to do this or that, and so to perform deliberate actions on one's own responsibility. By free will one shapes one's own life (*Catechism of the Catholic Church*, 2nd ed., trans. United States Catholic Conference, Inc. [Citta del Vaticano: Libreria Editrice Vaticana, 1997], no. 1731).

Evidence of Free Will

> "I call heaven and earth to witness against you this day, that I have set before you life and death, blessing and cursing; therefore choose life, that you and your descendants may live, loving the Lord your God, obeying his voice, and cleaving to him…" (Deuteronomy 30:19-20).

To deny that human beings have *free will*, and thus are responsible for their actions, would be to completely ignore Sacred Scripture, Church teaching, the basis of all human laws and legal trials, and all of human experience. All of these clearly indicate that human beings have free will (Fr. John Laux, *Catholic Morality*: *A Course in Religion, Book III* [Rockford, Ill.: TAN Books and Publishing, Inc., 1990], pp. 6, 8).

Free Will in Sacred Scripture

> God created man in his image and established him in his friendship. A spiritual creature, man can live this friendship only in free submission to God (*Catechism*, 396).

Sacred Scripture clearly affirms that human beings have free will. If man did not have free will, God would not have told Adam and Eve that they must obey His command (Genesis 2:16-17; 3:3), and He would have been unjust in punishing them for transgressing that command (Genesis 3:16-19).

If man did not have free will, God would not have given Moses the Ten Commandments (Exodus 20:2-17, Deuteronomy 5:6-21). How could man obey any Commandment whatsoever without the *freedom* to obey?

The fact is that man *does* have free will, and therefore God holds him accountable for his actions. Without free will, it would be impossible for man to make rational choices. In telling man to "choose life" (Deuteronomy 30:19), God shows that man is indeed capable of making rational choices.

We need God's grace to perform any good act (John 15:1-6). However, this grace does not take away our free will, but rather gives us the assistance we need to make the right decisions. As the Gospels show, Our Lord, far from denying man's free will, affirmed it by placing even greater demands on His followers than the demands of the Old Covenant:

> "But I say to you that hear, love your enemies, do good to those who hate you, bless those who curse you, pray for those who abuse you. To him who strikes you on the cheek, offer the other also; and from him who takes away your cloak do not withhold your coat as well" (Luke 6:27-29).

Without free will (and God's grace), man could never love his enemies. Man has a natural inclination to despise, not love, those who hate him. Loving our enemies requires a determined, free act of the will to do what Our Lord has commanded, no matter how difficult it may be.

The rest of the New Testament attests to man's free will as well. Indeed, there are so many examples that one would need to quote practically the entire Bible to cite all the evidence.

Free Will in Church Teaching

> By virtue of his soul and his spiritual powers of intellect and will, man is endowed with freedom, an "outstanding manifestation of the divine image" (*Catechism*, 1705).

The Council of Trent, called by the Catholic Church in the 16th century, clearly affirmed the truth of man's free will (Council of Trent, Session VI, *Decree on Justification*, Jan. 13, 1547, Canons on Justification, Canon 4). Justification is a free gift from God, but, to access this gift, man must freely cooperate with God's grace. This cooperation requires free will, through which man freely chooses to accept God's call to follow Him.

The Second Vatican Council (Vatican II) also affirmed the truth of man's free will:

> Man's dignity therefore requires him to act out of conscious and free choice, as moved and drawn in a personal way from within, and not by blind impulses in himself or by mere external constraint. Man gains such dignity when, ridding himself of all slavery to the passions, he presses forward towards his goal by freely choosing what is good, and, by his diligence and skill, effectively secures for himself the means suited to this end (The Second Vatican Council, *Gaudium et Spes* [Pastoral Constitution on the Church in the Modern World], December 7, 1965, no. 17).

Human beings have the ability to make free moral choices. **Unlike animals, human beings are not merely ruled by instincts, emotions, and impulses.** We can *freely decide* what we are going to do. When we struggle against our **passions** (emotions and physical impulses) and choose what is good, we gain a dignity that is not shared by any other creature in the visible universe.

The Catholic Church has always affirmed the existence of free will in human beings. This free will is an intrinsic part of our dignity as men and women created in the image and likeness of God.

Free Will in Law

> God created man a rational being, conferring on him the dignity of a person who can initiate and control his own actions (*Catechism*, 1730).

In every age, from the beginning of time to the present, laws have been made which presuppose that human beings have free will and thus may be held accountable for their actions. The reason there are no laws telling animals what they may or may not do is that animals do *not* have free will. The law of nature that God has established *makes* animals be the creatures they are and act according to the instincts that God has given them. However, there are many laws telling humans what we may and may not do, because we *do* have free will.

William Blackstone, by Thomas Gainsborough

Moreover, there has always been some form of *legal trial*. Such trials would be meaningless—indeed, cruel—if man were not endowed by his Creator with the ability to freely choose his actions (Fr. Laux, p. 8).

In his famous *Commentaries*, Sir William Blackstone, a widely recognized and respected 18th-century English legal scholar, affirmed that, along with reason, free will is the basis for the laws governing man's behavior:

> But laws, in their more confined sense … denote the rules, not of action in general, but of human action or conduct: that is, the precepts by which man, the noblest of all sublunary beings, a creature endowed with both reason and freewill, is commanded to make use of those faculties in the general regulation of his behavior (Sir William Blackstone, *Commentaries on the Laws of England*, 1765-1769 [online ed. by Lonang Inst., 2014], Introduction, Section 2; www.lonang.com/exlibris/blackstone/bla-002.htm).

It is precisely because man has free will that he can be held accountable for his behavior. This principle is the very foundation of law itself, and of all legal trials.

Free Will in Human Experience

> Endowed with a spiritual soul, with intellect and with free will, the human person is from his very conception ordered to God and destined for eternal beatitude. He pursues his perfection in "seeking and loving what is true and good" (*Catechism*, 1711).

Besides Sacred Scripture, Church teaching, and law, human experience also attests that human beings have free will.

In literature, what plot would be possible if the protagonist and antagonist did not have free will? In scientific inquiry, how could scientists decide what to study or which conclusions to draw if they did not have free will? In business, how could managers decide whom to hire or fire, where to invest their resources, or how to run their enterprises, without free will?

Indeed, the entire scope of human experience, as well as common sense itself, affirms that human beings have free will. To say otherwise would be to deny reality. Therefore, any religious or philosophical system claiming that man does not have free will, or is not responsible for his actions, is fundamentally flawed.

The Role of Motives

> "For where your treasure is, there will your heart be also" (Matthew 6:21).

It is clear that human beings have free will, and that this free will enables us to choose what we will believe and what we will do. Because of this, we are responsible for our own behavior, and we must answer to God for it. However, *why* do we make the particular choices we make? What are our *motives* for making these choices? What drives one person to make one choice, and another person to choose differently about the same thing?

The answer is that, by God's plan, **human beings are drawn toward the good**. Our reason for making a particular moral choice is always to obtain or maintain something that we *see* as, or believe to be, *good*.

The problem is that our judgment is far from perfect. We have different perceptions about what is good. We see one thing as good, while another person sees something else as good. Also, what we *see* as good might not actually be as good as we think it is, or, worse, it might even be evil. However, because we do not see it as evil, we are drawn toward it. Even the person who does grave evil is motivated by a disordered attachment to something which he *sees* as a good that he would like to possess. So, he pursues this apparent (but *false*) good at the expense of everything else, even the *true* good.

Thus, free will involves choosing one set of motives over another, which means choosing one set of goods over another. These "goods" may be apparent goods or true goods. If we had no motives, then we would have no basis for making free rational choices. Free choice without motives is impossible. At least some motive, however simple or subtle, is behind every freely chosen human act. Likewise, if there were only one possible option for us to choose, then we could not truly make a free rational choice (Fr. Laux, p. 5).

Animals are not capable of making rational choices, but rather must follow their instincts, coupled with some very basic, but intense, emotions and drives (anger, hunger, fear, affection, and so forth). If an animal is angry, it *must* act on that anger. It cannot do anything else, unless some other emotion or drive (fear, for example) is strong enough to make it change its course. However, if a human being is angry, he can *decide* to forgive rather than act on his anger. The emotion may persist, but **it is his free will that determines his actions**.

The Role of Knowledge

> "Everyone to whom much is given, of him will much be required; and of him to whom men commit much they will demand the more" (Luke 12:48).

In order to be held responsible for our actions, we must know what we are doing and be capable of controlling our actions. **Morality depends on knowledge, as well as freedom.**

Both the intellect and the will are involved when we make moral decisions. Our intellect provides the knowledge we need in order to make judgments about what to do. Our will uses that knowledge to decide how to act according to those judgments.

St. Augustine, by Cornelis de Vos

Influence of Our Will on Our Intellect

> By deviating from the moral law man violates his own freedom, becomes imprisoned within himself, disrupts neighborly fellowship, and rebels against divine truth (*Catechism*, 1740).

God created man so that he can use his intellect to know and understand truth, and use his will to accept truth and decide what to do on the basis of that truth. In many instances, however, **our will influences our intellect** (Fr. Laux, p. 6). We use our will to decide what we want to do, and therefore what we want to believe. Then we filter out what we don't want our intellect to focus on. We tend to believe only what we want to believe. By the actions of our will, we can hinder our knowledge or understanding by keeping our intellect in ignorance of the truth.

This tendency is evident in those who deny the existence of God. As St. Augustine aptly put it, "He who denies the existence of God has some reason for *wishing* that God did not exist" (quoted by Fr. Laux, p. 6).

Maturity and Awareness

> Freedom makes man *responsible* for his acts to the extent that they are voluntary (*Catechism*, 1734).

Several factors can affect our knowledge, and consequently our ability to make free rational

A Saint by God's Grace

When we cooperate with God's grace, it is never too late to turn our life around and become a true disciple of Jesus Christ. This is abundantly clear from the life of St. Augustine.

Augustine was born in 354 A.D., in North Africa. He was very gifted intellectually. He did well in his education, and he became a skilled public speaker. However, he fell into sins of impurity and pride, and his great mind was darkened by a strange heresy called Manicheism.

In some ways, Manicheism was a precursor to the modern New Age movement. It claimed to be a synthesis of all the religions at that time, but in reality it was very anti-Christian. Manicheism denied the truth that there is one, infinitely good, all-powerful God. The Manichean heresy also taught that the human soul was good, but the human body was evil; therefore, people were not responsible for the sins of the body. This appealed to Augustine, because it seemed to give him permission to continue committing sins of impurity.

Augustine's mother, St. Monica, prayed for years that her son would turn his life around. She often followed him during his travels and pleaded with him. For a long time, Augustine put her off. However, by the grace of God, he began listening to sermons of St. Ambrose, the bishop of Milan. Augustine was struck by what he heard, and he came to realize that Christianity was the one true religion.

Augustine rejected the Manichean heresy, and he tried to turn his life around. But his attachment to his sins of impurity made it very difficult for him to break away. Finally, he repented of his sins and committed his life to Jesus Christ. He was baptized into the Catholic Church in 387, and he became a priest in 391. In 396, he became the bishop of Hippo, Africa, where he lived until his death in 430.

St. Augustine was a prolific writer. His best-known works are *Confessions* and *The City of God.* He also refuted several great heresies in his day, including the Manichean heresy and another terrible heresy, called Pelagianism.

Pelagianism claimed that free will alone was sufficient for people to gain Heaven. St. Augustine, more than anyone, knew this was not true. Free will is essential, but it is not enough. We also need God's grace to bring us to conversion, sustain us throughout our life, and protect us at the moment of our death.

Through God's grace, St. Augustine was converted from a great sinner to a great priest, bishop, and saint. He is now honored as one of the greatest Doctors of the Church.

choices. One such factor is *maturity.* A child who has not reached the age of reason must still be taught responsibility for his actions, through our good example and appropriate consequences and rewards. However, he cannot be held responsible for what he does not know.

An infant cannot be held responsible for being too demanding. A three-year-old cannot be held responsible for repeating whatever she hears (hence, the importance of careful discretion in our use of radio, television, and so forth).

Another factor that can affect our freedom is our *level of awareness*. No one, adult or child, may be held responsible for anything he does while he is asleep, unconscious, mentally incapacitated, or insane (Fr. Laux, p. 5). If we are not aware of what we are doing, or cannot control what we are doing, then we are not free. If we are not free, then we are not morally responsible for our actions. **Freedom is necessary to make moral choices.**

However, if it is our own fault that we are not aware of, or cannot control, what we are doing, then we *are* responsible for those actions. For example, if a person deliberately abuses drugs or alcohol, then he is morally responsible for that abuse, as well as everything he does while under their influence.

Ignorance

> *Unintentional ignorance* can diminish or even remove the imputability of a grave offense. But no one is deemed to be ignorant of the principles of the moral law, which are written in the conscience of every man (*Catechism*, 1860).

Even when someone is mature, awake, and fully in command of his senses, his knowledge may be incomplete or flawed. If someone offers to sell me a stolen coat for $50, but I do not know the coat is stolen, my lack of knowledge may hinder my ability to make the right moral decision. I have no guilt, as long as I truly do not know or suspect that the coat is stolen.

Ignorance of the truth makes it impossible for us to act on that truth. Even if someone did something evil, he would not be guilty of sin if, through no fault of his own, he truly did not know that it was evil. If someone has not actually *consented* to evil, he cannot be held responsible for that evil.

However, sometimes a person's ignorance is due to carelessness or **hardness of heart** (an obstinate refusal to obey the Word of God or to accept good counsel). In such cases, the person is still responsible for any evil he commits as a result of this ignorance, because *he should have known better*.

Even if I only *suspect* that something is morally wrong, I must not perform that action; if I do, I sin. In the case described above, if I realize that the seller is a thief and he is selling the coat for far less than it's worth, I should know better than to buy it from him. If I ignore these concerns and buy the coat anyway, I sin.

If I am merely *pretending* not to know (which is called **feigned ignorance**), I am sinning as well. In fact, my sin is even greater, because I am effectively trying to deceive God. **Feigned ignorance and hardness of heart increase, not decrease, one's guilt for sin** (*Catechism*, 1859).

A person may be able to deceive others, but he will never be able to deceive God, Who knows all things. God searches our hearts and knows us even more intimately than we know ourselves (Psalm 139).

Forces against Freedom

> Jesus answered them, "Truly, truly, I say to you, everyone who commits sin is a slave to sin. The slave does not continue in the house forever; the son continues forever. So if the Son makes you free, you will be free indeed" (John 8:34-36).

Our free will is a priceless treasure given to us by God. He has not given this gift to any other creature in the visible universe—only man, whom He created in His own image and likeness. God expects us to properly use and develop this gift. If we do not, our freedom will suffer. The more we properly use our free will by choosing good rather than giving in to our passions, the stronger we become. The more we sacrifice our free will for the sake of our passions, the weaker we become.

> The more one does what is good, the freer one becomes. There is no true freedom except in the service of what is good and just. The choice to disobey and do evil is an abuse of freedom and leads to "the slavery of sin" (*Catechism*, 1733).

It is critical that we do what we know we ought to do, even when it is difficult or painful. Every time we act according to **right reason** (clear, rational thinking that leads to sound judgment), we strengthen the mastery of our will over our passions, and we become *more free*. Every time we act contrary to right reason, following our passions and seeking only to please ourselves, we become *less free*.

Concupiscence

> Because man is a *composite being, spirit and body*, there already exists a certain tension in him; a certain struggle of tendencies between "spirit" and "flesh" develops. But in fact this struggle belongs to the heritage of sin. It is a consequence of sin and at the same time a confirmation of it (*Catechism*, 2516).

One of the greatest forces against our freedom is **concupiscence**, an inclination to sin due to disordered physical appetites and desires. Concupiscence is a direct consequence of Original Sin. Although Baptism removes the state of Original Sin from our soul, our *inclination* to sin (concupiscence) remains.

The result is that our flesh tends to be at war with our spirit and pulls us like a magnet toward sin. We find ourselves drawn toward those things that we should not look at, listen to, say, think, desire, or do. The inclinations themselves are not sins, but they draw us toward sin.

As long as we do not give our consent, we do not sin. However, if we consent to follow these inclinations, we not only sin but also make these tendencies more powerful in the future. Consequently, we will find it more difficult to resist them, even if deep down we really do not want to go along with them. The end result is that we will become a slave to these inclinations and to the sins they lead us to commit.

> For I know that nothing good dwells within me, that is, in my flesh. I can will what is right, but I cannot do it. For I do not do the good I want, but the evil I do not want is what I do.... For I delight in the law of God, in my inmost self, but I see in my members another law at war with the law of my mind and making me captive to the law of sin which dwells in my members (Romans 7:18-19, 22-23).

Because concupiscence wars against our freedom, our responsibility for sinful actions can be lessened in some instances. However, if we intentionally excite our passions, our responsibility *increases*, not decreases. We cannot use concupiscence as an excuse for sin. With all our might, we must strive against the pull of these inclinations, just as if we were striving against falling down a great mountain. At the same time, we need the grace of God, Who can free us from our slavery to sin.

> Jesus then said to the Jews who had believed in him, "If you continue in my word, you are truly my disciples, and you will know the truth, and the truth will make you free" (John 8:31-32).

When we live as faithful disciples of Jesus Christ, He abides in us, and we in Him. The more fully we know Him, the more fully we know the truth, because He *is* the Truth (John 14:6), and the truth sets us free.

Emotions

> The promptings of feelings and passions can also diminish the voluntary and free character of the offense, as can external pressures or pathological disorders (*Catechism*, 1860).

Joan of Arc's Death at the Stake, by Hermann Anton Stilke

In addition to concupiscence, emotions can strongly influence our freedom. A person enduring intense emotional suffering may find it very difficult to think clearly enough to make sound moral decisions. It is important to avoid acting when we are experiencing such intense emotions. We must always try to make decisions **according to right reason**, rather than according to our emotions. We should try to wait until we are in a calmer state of mind before acting or making any serious decisions.

One of the strongest emotions that can directly challenge our freedom is fear. Whether it concerns something in the present or in the future, fear can exert a powerful influence over us.

Fear can lessen our responsibility in proportion to its intensity. Nevertheless, unless fear actually drives us to temporary insanity, in which we truly do not know what we are doing, it cannot completely take away our freedom. We are still at least partly responsible for any sins we commit as a result of fear or any other emotion.

Ultimately, we are called to develop *self-mastery* over our emotions and other passions by consistently acting according to right reason and persevering in virtue. Until we develop this self-mastery, we may find ourselves constantly giving in to intense emotions such as fear and anger, leading us to commit one sin after another. We should pray for this self-mastery and ask for God's help to attain it. If we act according to our emotions, our reason will suffer. If we act according to right reason, our emotions will eventually follow.

Violence

> *Imputability* and responsibility for an action can be diminished or even nullified by ignorance, inadvertence, duress, fear… (*Catechism*, 1735).

Freedom can also be affected by violence or threats of violence, whether against ourselves or against those we hold dear. If we consent to sinful acts in such cases, we still incur at least some guilt, but not as much as someone who sins without being subjected to such conditions. Those who deny Our Lord under torture are guilty of sin, but not as much as someone who denies Him without having suffered any violence.

If we are physically *forced* to do something without our consent, then we bear no moral responsibility for that act. For example, if we were physically forced to consume a large quantity of alcohol by someone literally pouring it down our throat without our consent, and we became drunk, we would not be guilty of sin. **There can be no sin without consent.**

Moreover, no one—neither human beings nor evil spirits—can force the *human will* to give consent to any act. A person's freedom may be thwarted or diminished by many factors, such as concupiscence, emotions, and violence. He may even be physically forced to do something that he does not want to do. However, **his will cannot be touched**. As Father John Laux states: "The will is an inviolable shrine" (Fr. Laux, p. 10).

Habits and Natural Tendencies

> It is not easy for man, wounded by sin, to maintain moral balance. Christ's gift of salvation offers us the grace necessary to persevere in the pursuit of the virtues. Everyone should always ask for this grace of light and strength, frequent the sacraments, cooperate with the Holy Spirit, and follow his calls to love what is good and shun evil (*Catechism*, 1811).

Some of the most powerful hindrances to freedom are sinful habits. Performing the same action several times will likely form a habit. If the action is good, we will develop a morally good habit, or *virtue*. If the action is bad, we will develop a morally bad habit, or *vice*.

The force of a sinful habit can be very powerful, and can greatly affect our freedom. Our moral responsibility for committing such sins may be diminished, **but only if we are seriously trying to resist giving in to them**. However, we are still morally responsible for falling into the sinful habit in the first place. Part of our serious attempts to conquer such habits should be to confess them in the Sacrament of Penance (Confession).

Sometimes people "inherit" natural tendencies toward one vice or another; these tendencies can also be powerful hindrances to freedom (Fr. Laux, p. 10). Perhaps we have a tendency toward intense anger—a bad temper. Whether this tendency is the result of some genetic hereditary factor or years of being exposed to a bad example can be debated. However, the end result is the same: we have a tendency toward some particular sin that we seem to have "inherited" in some way. If the tendency has already developed into a vice, our struggle against it will be more difficult.

Saint Anthony of Padua
(Polish, c. 19th century, artist unknown)

"Inherited" tendencies may lessen the degree to which our behavior is voluntary, and hence our culpability for sin. However, we are still responsible for our own actions. We must not blame our parents or anyone else for our sins. Rather, we must resist those tendencies all the more fervently. **The more we resist temptation, the more we grow in the opposite virtue.** In fact, the saints encourage us to *intentionally practice* the opposite virtue, out of our love for Christ.

Chapter 1 Review

Matching: For each statement, select the letter of the best term from the list below. There are more terms listed than there are statements, and no term can be used more than once.

A. intellect	E. rational soul	I. knowledge	M. right reason
B. free will	F. morality	J. luck	N. emotions
C. senses	G. synderesis	K. good	O. instincts
D. passions	H. concupiscence	L. easy	P. human being

1. The measure of the good or evil of concrete human acts: ________.
2. Every ________ is an individual person who is the union of a body and a soul.
3. Our reason for making a particular moral choice is always to obtain or maintain something that we see as ________.
4. The faculty of our rational soul through which we think, reason, understand, and know: ________.
5. An inclination to sin due to disordered physical appetites and desires: ________.
6. Emotions and physical impulses: ________.
7. Our ability to decide what we will believe and what we will do: ________.
8. Morality depends on ________, as well as freedom.
9. Clear, rational thinking that leads to sound judgment: ________.
10. The spiritual principle that animates the body of a human being, and that enables him to think and reason, to understand and know, and to decide what he will believe and what he will do: ________.

True or False: Write *True* or *False* for the following statements.

________ 11. Without free will, man could still make rational choices, but it would be far more difficult.

________ 12. The more we resist temptation, the more we grow in the opposite virtue.

________ 13. The Catholic Church has not yet officially affirmed the existence of free will in human beings, so it remains an open question.

________ 14. Neither human beings nor evil spirits can force the human will to give consent to any act.

________ 15. If someone does something evil, he is guilty of sin, whether or not he knows it is evil.

________ 16. Human beings cannot freely decide what they are going to do, because, like animals, they are merely ruled by instincts, emotions, and impulses.

_________ 17. Even the person who does grave evil is motivated by a disordered attachment to something which he sees as a good that he would like to possess.

_________ 18. If we are physically forced to do something without our consent, then we bear no moral responsibility for that act.

_________ 19. Our intellect is an inviolable shrine; therefore, our will cannot influence it.

_________ 20. Every time we act contrary to right reason, following our passions and seeking only to please ourselves, we become less free.

Multiple Choice: Write the letter of the best answer in the space provided.

21. Our knowledge may be affected by _________.
    A. Ignorance
    B. Maturity
    C. Level of awareness
    D. Our will influencing our intellect
    E. All of the above

22. The existence of free will in man is affirmed by _________.
    A. Sacred Scripture
    B. Church teaching
    C. Law
    D. Human experience
    E. All of the above

23. Which of the following may *not* decrease our responsibility for sin? _________
    A. Violence
    B. Emotions
    C. Feigned ignorance
    D. Habits and natural propensities
    E. All of the above

24. Which of the following statements regarding concupiscence is correct? _________
    A. Concupiscence is a direct consequence of Original Sin.
    B. Baptism removes concupiscence, along with the state of Original Sin.
    C. Our inclinations toward sinful acts are sins themselves.
    D. All of the above
    E. None of the above

25. Which of the following is *not* likely to increase our freedom? _________
    A. Knowing the truth
    B. Following our emotions
    C. Living according to right reason
    D. Developing self-mastery over our passions
    E. None of the above. All of these are likely to increase our freedom.

Chapter 2. The Standard of Morality

> "Not everyone who says to me, 'Lord, Lord,' shall enter the kingdom of heaven, but he who does the will of my Father who is in heaven" (Matthew 7:21).

Living a morally good life and doing God's Will are inseparable. The **moral life** is the path by which we walk toward God or walk away from God. If we sin, we walk away from God. If we repent and follow His commands, we walk toward God. In Him, and only in Him, can we find true fulfillment and happiness.

> The desire for God is written in the human heart, because man is created by God and for God; and God never ceases to draw man to himself. Only in God will he find the truth and happiness he never stops searching for (*Catechism*, 27).

If we claim that we want to do God's Will, yet we are not obedient to His Commandments, we cannot be in fellowship with Him. Our Lord said, "I have called you friends, for all that I have heard from my Father I have made known to you" (John 15:15). However, this friendship is *not* unconditional; we are his friends *only* if we are *obedient* to Him: "You are my friends if you do what I command you" (John 15:14).

All our actions should be directed toward doing the Will of God. Every action in which we are obedient to the Will of God is a good action; every action in which we are not obedient to the Will of God is a bad action. If we are not accustomed to following God's Commandments, then doing so may seem burdensome to us at first. However, the more faithful we are, the more we will eventually become like His Son, Jesus Christ, and the more joy we will find in doing His Will.

The One Thing Necessary

> But the Lord answered her, "Martha, Martha, you are anxious and troubled about many things; one thing is needful. Mary has chosen the good portion, which shall not be taken away from her" (Luke 10:41-42).

The **standard of morality** by which moral good and evil are measured is the Will of God, and ultimately God Himself. God is Goodness itself, Truth itself, and Love itself. **God does not change**: "Jesus Christ is the same yesterday and today and forever" (Hebrews 13:8). Therefore, the standard for what is morally good versus morally evil is **absolute** (unchanging and universal), *not* **relative** (changing according to the situation).

Moral good and evil are **objective** (universally the same for all persons, times, places, and cultures). Moral good and evil are *not* **subjective** (relative to one's own personal preferences or philosophy, the historical period in which one lives, the part of the world where one lives, one's culture, and so on).

> Human acts, that is, acts that are freely chosen in consequence of a judgment of conscience, can be morally evaluated. They are either good or evil (*Catechism*, 1749).

Doing the Will of God is the "one thing necessary" (Luke 10:42). It is the **guiding principle of the moral life**. By following this principle, we will, by God's grace, attain the **ultimate goal of morality**: happiness through union with God in Heaven.

The Ultimate Goal of Morality

"These things I have spoken to you, that my joy may be in you, and that your joy may be full" (John 15:11).

All people, regardless of their situation, agree on one thing: they want to be happy. However, there is great disagreement on *how* to attain this happiness. Many people fall into sin because they try to find their happiness apart from God. When they do, the result is always the same: misery and *unhappiness*.

God created us, and we are meant to live and act in fellowship with Him. That's how we are designed. That's who we are. It is impossible for us to be happy if we are not united with God. Fish are meant to be in water, plants are meant to be in the ground, and human beings are meant to be in fellowship with God.

Christ in the House of Martha and Mary, by Jacopo Tintoretto

The ultimate goal of morality is happiness through union with God in Heaven. If we remain in fellowship with God, we will ultimately be happy with Him in Heaven. If we do not remain in fellowship with God, we will not be happy. **True happiness comes only from union with God.** God wants us to succeed, and He gives us the grace we need. In order to remain in fellowship with Him, we must cooperate with this grace and live a morally good life.

The Meaning and Purpose of Life

So God created man in his own image, in the image of God he created him; male and female he created them (Genesis 1:27).

Because God created man to be in fellowship with Him, the ultimate **meaning and purpose of life** is to know, love, and serve God, so that we may be happy with Him in Heaven. We must strive, with God's help, to fulfill this purpose above all else.

God created man to be free and happy. When man uses his freedom to seek the truth and do good, he enjoys more freedom and greater happiness. When man abuses his freedom and seeks his happiness apart from God, he ends up losing both, and he becomes a slave to sin. In order to fulfill the purpose of our existence, we must surrender ourselves completely to God and His perfect Will.

Man's search to understand the meaning and purpose of life can find its answer only in God. He created us. We are the work of His hands. We belong to Him. We are here to do His Will. Until we make a genuine commitment to obey the Will of God in all things, we will never truly be happy. **Only in faithfully doing God's Will can we find true meaning and happiness in our life.**

The Perfect Model: A Faithful Son

> "This is my beloved Son, with whom I am well pleased" (Matthew 3:17).

In the Gospel, we see the perfect model of one who is completely faithful to the Will of God: Jesus Christ. His obedience to the Will of the Father is not the servile obedience of a hired hand. It is the willing obedience of a faithful Son, Who truly *knows* the Father and *wants* to do His Will.

> Jesus said to them, "My food is to do the will of him who sent me, and to accomplish his work" (John 4:34).

Jesus Christ is both God and Man. He is one Person, a divine Person, but He has two natures: human and divine. Therefore, He has *two* wills: His human will and His divine Will.

As God, He is one substance with the Father and coequal to Him. As Man, He has completely surrendered His human will to the divine Will.

> And he withdrew from them about a stone's throw, and knelt down and prayed, "Father, if thou art willing, remove this cup from me; nevertheless not my will, but thine, be done" (Luke 22:41-42).

As a faithful Son, Jesus Christ perfectly fulfills the Will of the Father and gives glory to His Name.

> "I glorified thee on earth, having accomplished the work which thou gavest me to do; and now, Father, glorify thou me in thy own presence with the glory which I had with thee before the world was made" (John 17:4-5).

The more we become like Jesus, the more we too, as adopted sons and daughters of God in Christ, can surrender our will to the Father and give glory to His Name.

> He who believes in Christ becomes a son of God. This filial adoption transforms him by giving him the ability to follow the example of Christ. It makes him capable of acting rightly and doing good. In union with his Savior, the disciple attains the perfection of charity which is holiness. Having matured in grace, the moral life blossoms into eternal life in the glory of heaven (*Catechism*, 1709).

Just as living a morally good life is inseparable from doing the Will of God, **the spiritual life is inseparable from the moral life.** If we think we are "spiritual," yet we do not obey God's Commandments, we are fooling ourselves, and we are not truly in fellowship with Him.

Jesus Christ is the Son of God, the Second Person of the Holy Trinity, yet He came down from Heaven and was obedient to the Father in all things. If we, mere human beings, wish to attain happiness, we too must humble ourselves and be obedient to the Father in all things.

> Have this mind among yourselves, which was in Christ Jesus, who, though he was in the form of God, did not count equality with God a thing to be grasped, but emptied himself, taking the form of a servant, being born in the likeness of men. And being found in human form he humbled himself and became obedient unto death, even death on a cross (Philippians 2:5-8).

The saints in Heaven, through their prayers and the example of their holy lives, can greatly help us in our efforts to be faithful sons and daughters of God. In particular, Our Blessed Mother can help us to live a morally good life in fellowship with the Holy Spirit. Through her perfect example of obedience and charity, her powerful intercession, and her maternal love, Mary can show us how to humbly accept the Will of the Father in all things and be like her Son, Jesus Christ.

The Faithful Son

One of the parables of Jesus concerns two sons who are asked to work in their father's vineyard (Matthew 21:28-32). The one son says that he will go right away, but then never follows through with the work. The second son at first states that he will not go, but then thinks better of his decision and decides to do the will of his father.

There is a story in the Bible about the prophet Jonah that is similar to the story of the second son in this parable (Jonah 1–4). When God told Jonah to preach repentance to the people of Nineveh, Jonah did not want to go. In fact, he set out in the opposite direction, west toward the seacoast, rather than east toward Nineveh! However, God stopped Jonah in his tracks by means of a large sea creature. After that ordeal, Jonah reversed course and completed a successful mission to the great city of Nineveh, in faithfulness to the Father.

We may draw hope from this account of Jonah. If we are not heading in the right direction, it is not too late to turn our life around. Like Jonah and the second son in the parable, we can change our direction and begin to do the Will of Our Father.

Jonah Thrown into the Sea, by Peter Paul Rubens

Chapter 2 Review

Matching: For each statement, select the letter of the best term from the list below. There are more terms listed than there are statements, and no term can be used more than once.

A. Will of God	E. natures	I. Jesus Christ	M. will of the majority
B. happiness	F. persons	J. moral life	N. meaning and purpose of life
C. absolute	G. bad	K. the world	O. freedom from morality
D. subjective	H. man	L. autonomy	P. standard of morality

1. The ________ by which moral good and evil are measured is the Will of God, and ultimately God Himself.
2. The ultimate goal of morality is ________ through union with God in Heaven.
3. The standard for what is morally good is ________, not relative.
4. The perfect model of one who is completely faithful to the Will of God: ________.
5. The ________ is the path by which we either walk toward God or walk away from God.
6. The ________ is to know, love, and serve God, so that we may be happy with Him in Heaven.
7. Doing the ________ is the guiding principle of the moral life.
8. Our Lord Jesus Christ has two ________: human and divine.
9. Every action in which we are not obedient to the Will of God is a ________ action.
10. Moral good and evil are objective, *not* ________.

True or False: Write *True* or *False* for the following statements.

________ 11. Through her perfect example of obedience and charity, her powerful intercession, and her maternal love, Our Blessed Mother can show us how to humbly accept the Will of the Father in all things and be like her Son, Jesus Christ.

________ 12. To be in fellowship with God, we do not necessarily have to obey *all* of His Commandments, but we must have faith in Him.

________ 13. True happiness comes only from doing what makes us feel good about ourselves.

________ 14. The one thing necessary to fulfill the meaning and purpose of our life is to follow our dreams with all our heart.

________ 15. Our Lord Jesus Christ has one will that is both human and divine.

________ 16. The moral life and the spiritual life are two separate, unrelated ways through which we may be in fellowship with God.

________ 17. Only in faithfully doing God's Will can we find true meaning and happiness in our life.

Multiple Choice: Write the letter of the best answer in the space provided.

18. God is ________.
    A. Goodness itself
    B. Truth itself
    C. Love itself
    D. All of the Above
    E. None of the Above

19. If we wish to find meaning in our life and the happiness we are searching for, we must ________.
    A. Be financially successful
    B. Make a name for ourselves in the world
    C. Eat right, stay fit, and have three square meals a day
    D. Have a rewarding career
    E. Faithfully do the Will of God in all things

20. Living a morally good life and doing the Will of God are ________.
    A. Mutually exclusive
    B. Relative to the times
    C. Optional
    D. Inseparable
    E. All of the above

21. Like Our Lord Jesus Christ, we too must ________.
    A. Be poor
    B. Lead others
    C. Humble ourselves and be obedient to the Father in all things
    D. Perform miracles
    E. All of the above

22. When man uses his freedom to ________, he enjoys more freedom and greater happiness.
    A. Build up his self-esteem
    B. Seek the truth and do good
    C. Have fun
    D. Work
    E. Do whatever he feels like

Jonah Cast Up by the Whale, by Claude-Joseph Vernet

23. The standard of morality is all of the following, *except* ________.
    A. Relative
    B. Universal
    C. Unchanging
    D. Objective
    E. Absolute

24. Jesus Christ said that we are His friends ________.
    A. If we do what He commands us
    B. Unconditionally
    C. Only when we get to Heaven
    D. Never
    E. None of the above

25. Jesus Christ ________.
    A. Has two natures and two wills
    B. Is the Son of God
    C. Is both God and Man
    D. All except A
    E. All of the above

Chapter 3. God's Law

> The law of the Lord is perfect, reviving the soul; the testimony of the Lord is sure, making wise the simple; the precepts of the Lord are right, rejoicing the heart; the commandment of the Lord is pure, enlightening the eyes; the fear of the Lord is clean, enduring forever; the ordinances of the Lord are true, and righteous altogether (Psalm 19:7-9).

THE BASIS OF MORALITY is freedom. The standard of morality is the Will of God. If we follow the Will of God, we will attain the ultimate goal of morality: happiness through union with God in Heaven. However, in order to follow the Will of God, we must first know what His Will is. God makes His Will known to us through His Law.

God's Law is called the *Divine Law*. The **Divine Law**, or *Eternal Law*, is God's eternal, objective, and universal plan through which He orders, directs, and governs the entire universe in love and wisdom. It is the highest **norm** (rule of conduct) for human behavior; it applies to all people, in all circumstances, in all places, and at all times. It is absolute and universal.

The Holy Trinity as Mercy Seat (Austrian, c. 1470, artist unknown)

God manifests His Divine Law to us in two ways: Natural Law and Revealed Law. Human laws are just only if they are in harmony with the Divine Law, and hence with both the Natural Law and Revealed Law.

The Natural Law

> For it is not the hearers of the law who are righteous before God, but the doers of the law who will be justified. When the Gentiles who have not the law do by nature what the law requires, they are a law to themselves, even though they do not have the law. They show that what the law requires is written on their hearts, while their conscience also bears witness and their conflicting thoughts accuse or perhaps excuse them on that day when, according to my gospel, God judges the secrets of men by Christ Jesus (Romans 2:13-16).

Within the heart of man is a law directing him to do what is good and avoid what is evil. This law is called the Natural Law. The **Natural Law** is the Divine Law inscribed in the soul of man, so that man may know right from wrong. Through the light of natural reason, man comes to better understand who he is, and he discerns the principles of the Natural Law that God has placed in his heart.

The Structure of the Natural Law

> The natural law expresses the original moral sense which enables man to discern by reason the good and the evil, the truth and the lie (*Catechism*, 1954).

The Divine Law is manifested through the Natural Law in three distinct grades:

1. the primary precepts of morality,
2. the proximate conclusions of morality, and
3. the remote conclusions of morality.

Through the Natural Law, every person who has attained the age of reason can know the primary precepts and proximate conclusions of morality. However, the remote conclusions of morality can be known only through study and discernment.

Grade 1: Primary Precepts of Morality. These are the most fundamental moral principles of the Natural Law. Included in this group are precepts such as the following (adapted from William E. May, *An Introduction to Moral Theology*, 2nd ed. [Huntington, Ind.: Our Sunday Visitor Publishing, 2003], p. 77):

- We must do good and avoid evil.
- We must not do evil to any human being.
- We are not to offend those with whom we must live.
- Human life is good and so must be protected and preserved.
- We are to pursue knowledge of the truth.
- We must do to others what we would want them to do to us.
- We must not do to others what we would not want them to do to us.
- We are to overcome ignorance.
- We need to control our **sense appetite** (the physical drives and tendencies within us that draw us toward what is perceived as desirable, and away from what is perceived as undesirable).
- We must love and worship God.
- We must love our neighbor.
- We are to honor our father and mother.

These are precepts that every normal, sane person who has attained the age of reason can readily know, though perhaps expressed in somewhat different words.

Notice that one of these precepts is the love and worship of God. The truth that God exists may be known with absolute certainty through the light of natural reason. **St. Thomas Aquinas**, who is known as the Angelic Doctor, proved the existence of God in five different ways (St. Thomas Aquinas, *Summa Theologica* [online ed. by Kevin Knight, New Advent, 2016], I, q. 2, a. 3; www.newadvent.org/summa).

Refusing to believe in God is not only an indication of a lack of faith; it is also a denial of reality. We believe that Jesus Christ is the Son of God through faith in God's revelation, but we know that God exists through the light of natural reason. Once we know that God exists, it is immediately obvious that we are to love and worship Him.

Grade 2. Proximate Conclusions of Morality. These precepts can easily be known with a minimal amount of thought, because they immediately follow from the primary precepts of morality. Included in this category are all of the Ten Commandments except the Third Commandment ["Remember the Sabbath day, to keep it holy"] (May, p. 78).

Anyone of average intelligence can readily reach these obvious conclusions. However, because of sin, it is possible for us to misunderstand or distort their meaning. Therefore, God gave us the Ten Commandments so that we would explicitly know these precepts through divine revelation.

This brings us to an important point: The acts forbidden by the Ten Commandments (murder, adultery, stealing, etc.) are evil *not only* because God has given us the Commandments forbidding them. Rather, God has given us the Commandments forbidding them *because* these acts *are* evil.

Grade 3. Remote Conclusions of Morality. Included in this group are precepts such as the Catholic Church's *just war doctrine* and the *principle of double effect* (which we will discuss in later chapters), as well as some moral issues involving scientific research.

Unlike the first two grades of moral precepts, many of the remote conclusions of morality are not easy to discern by the average person. This does not mean they are outside the scope of the Natural Law. However, without the aid of God's revelation, these remote conclusions can be determined only by those who have perfected the virtue of prudence (May, p. 80). Among those who do not know God's revelation and the teachings of the Catholic Church, ignorance of these precepts is possible and might be excusable.

The Natural Law Is Binding on All

> The natural law, present in the heart of each man and established by reason, is universal in its precepts and its authority extends to all men. It expresses the dignity of the person and determines the basis for his fundamental rights and duties (*Catechism*, 1956).

The Natural Law is the Divine Law inscribed in the soul of man. Therefore, like the Divine Law, the Natural Law is binding on all people, in all circumstances, in all places, and at all times. The precepts of the Natural Law are absolute and universal. Every human law that contradicts the Natural Law is, by definition, unjust and must not be obeyed.

The Natural Law Is Unchangeable

> The natural law, the Creator's very good work, provides the solid foundation on which man can build the structure of moral rules to guide his choices (*Catechism*, 1959).

The Natural Law is the very good work of God. However, since God can do all things, could He change the Natural Law if He wanted to do so?

One of the greatest *errors* that is prevalent today is the notion that God could change what is morally good versus morally evil. This error leads to a denial of the Natural Law and to a false division between morals and reason, between morality and objective reality. The result is the widespread perversion of fundamental laws of nature and the promotion of false man-made moral precepts in place of God's Law.

The truth is that **God could never change the Natural Law**. God could never change what is morally good versus morally evil. In order to do so, He would have to contradict Himself. God is all-knowing, all-powerful, and all-good. God does not make mistakes. His Divine Law is perfect, and the Natural Law is the Divine Law inscribed in the soul of man. Like the Divine Law, the Natural Law is unchangeable, even by God Himself.

Revealed Law

> And he gave to Moses, when he had made an end of speaking with him upon Mount Sinai, the two tablets of the testimony, tables of stone, written with the finger of God (Exodus 31:18).

Man is capable of discerning many of the principles of the Natural Law through natural reason. However, our ability to reason is often clouded by disordered passions and desires. Therefore, God has conveyed what He requires of man through **supernatural revelation** (God's communication to man about Who He is and what He requires). God's supernatural revelation of the Divine Law is called **Revealed Law**, or *Positive Divine Law*.

God gave this Revealed Law to man in stages, as recorded in Sacred Scripture. The first stage of Revealed Law was the **Old Law**, recorded in the Old Testament. The Old Law is contained primarily in the first five books of the Bible. The Prophets and the other books of the Old Testament complete the Old Law and "set its course toward the New Covenant and the Kingdom of heaven" (*Catechism*, 1964). The Old Law included both the *Patriarchal Laws* and the *Law of Moses*.

The Patriarchal Laws

> To obey (from the Latin *ob-audire*, to "hear and listen to") in faith is to submit freely to the word that has been heard, because its truth is guaranteed by God, who is Truth itself. Abraham is the model of such obedience offered us by Sacred Scripture. The Virgin Mary is its most perfect embodiment (*Catechism*, 144).

God began to reveal the Old Law through the Patriarchal Laws. The **Patriarchal Laws** comprise those commands that God gave to (1) Adam and Eve; (2) Noah; and (3) Abraham, Isaac, and Jacob.

The first Patriarchal Laws were those that God gave to man at the beginning of time. Central among them was the command that God gave to Adam and Eve (Genesis 3:3) regarding the tree of the knowledge of good and evil:

> And the Lord God commanded the man, saying, "You may freely eat of every tree of the garden; but of the tree of the knowledge of good and evil you shall not eat, for in the day that you eat of it you shall die" (Genesis 2:16-17).

God also simultaneously blessed and commanded mankind to "be fruitful and multiply, and fill the earth and subdue it," while giving them dominion over the visible creation (Genesis 1:28). In addition, He gave them specific instructions about the type of food they were to eat.

The second set of Patriarchal Laws was given by God to Noah and his descendants after the Flood (Genesis 9:1-7).

The third set of Patriarchal Laws included all the commands that God gave to Abraham, Isaac, and Jacob, beginning in Genesis 12. Included in this set of laws was the *Law of Circumcision*. The **Law of Circumcision** was the Patriarchal Law in which God commanded that Abraham, as well as every male among him and his descendants, be circumcised, as the sign of the *covenant* between God and His

People. A **covenant** is a sacred agreement and bond between God and one or more persons, or between two persons or groups under God.

> And God said to Abraham, "As for you, you shall keep my covenant, you and your descendants after you throughout their generations. This is my covenant, which you shall keep, between me and you and your descendants after you: Every male among you shall be circumcised" (Genesis 17:9-10).

The **Old Covenant** was the sacred agreement and bond between God and the people of Israel. In this covenant, the people of Israel agreed to obey God's Law, as revealed in the *Old Law*. The Patriarchal Laws recorded in Sacred Scripture represent the beginning of God's revelation to man about His Law. However, the vast majority of the Old Law was contained in an immense body of Revealed Law known as the *Law of Moses*.

Moses, by Valentin de Boulogne

The Law of Moses

> God, our Creator and Redeemer, chose Israel for himself to be his people and revealed his Law to them, thus preparing for the coming of Christ. The Law of Moses expresses many truths naturally accessible to reason. These are stated and authenticated within the covenant of salvation (*Catechism*, 1961).

God revealed the vast majority of the Old Law to His Chosen People through His servant Moses. This large body of Revealed Law is known as the **Law of Moses**, or the *Mosaic Law*.

The Law of Moses had three main parts:

- Judicial
- Ceremonial
- Moral

The **Judicial Law** included various precepts and ordinances to regulate the civil government of Israel. The **Ceremonial Law** prescribed the system of worship that Israel was to follow.

The *Moral Law* consisted of commands given for the moral life, including the Ten Commandments and certain other moral precepts. Unlike the Judicial and Ceremonial Laws, the Moral Law still remains in force today.

The Moral Law

> The moral law is the work of divine Wisdom.... It prescribes for man the ways, the rules of conduct that lead to the promised beatitude; it proscribes the ways of evil which turn him away from God and his love. It is at once firm in its precepts and, in its promises, worthy of love (*Catechism*, 1950).

The **Moral Law** encompasses all the moral principles of the Divine Law governing human behavior. This includes both those moral principles known through the Natural Law and those that God has communicated through Revealed Law.

The foundation of the Moral Law is the *Decalogue*, or **Ten Commandments**, which God Himself inscribed on tablets of stone for His servant Moses (Exodus 31:18).

> The precepts of the Decalogue lay the foundations for the vocation of man fashioned in the image of God; they prohibit what is contrary to the love of God and neighbor and prescribe what is essential to it. The Decalogue is a light offered to the conscience of every man to make God's call and ways known to him and to protect him against evil (*Catechism*, 1962).

In addition to revealing moral requirements, the Ten Commandments protect us from evil. Just as we are commanded not to harm our neighbor, so our neighbor is commanded not to harm us. The precept that commands me not to steal from my neighbor is the same precept that protects me from being robbed by my neighbor. **The Ten Commandments are the foundation of equal rights for all mankind, the weak and the strong alike.**

Just as freedom is the basis of morality, **the Moral Law is the guardian of freedom**. All people are obliged to follow the Moral Law, and are meant to be *protected* by it. Any nation that departs from the objective truths of the Moral Law will fall into tyranny, replacing God's Law with whatever those in power *say* is the law of the land. The inevitable result will be the corruption of justice, the oppression of the weak, and the persecution of the innocent.

The New Law

> The New Law or the Law of the Gospel is the perfection here on earth of the divine law, natural and revealed. It is the work of Christ and is expressed particularly in the Sermon on the Mount. It is also the work of the Holy Spirit and through him it becomes the interior law of charity (*Catechism*, 1965).

The final stage of Revealed Law is the **New Law**, which is also called the *Law of the Gospel.* God has given this New Law to all mankind through His Son, Jesus Christ.

Once God established this New Law, the Judicial and Ceremonial Laws under the Old Law ceased to be binding. However, Our Lord confirmed the Moral Law, and He further perfected it, insisting on a righteousness that come from the heart (Matthew 5:21-7:27).

> "Think not that I have come to abolish the law and the prophets; I have come not to abolish them but to fulfill them. For truly, I say to you, till heaven and earth pass away, not an iota, not a dot, will pass from the law until all is accomplished" (Matthew 5:17-18).

In addition to correcting false interpretations of the Moral Law that were prevalent at the time, Our Lord gave the two Great Commandments of loving God and loving our neighbor new emphasis, highlighted by His own suffering and crucifixion for all mankind.

He also expanded the requirements of the Moral Law by revealing new truths and instituting the seven sacraments. We are morally obligated to believe these truths, and to do what He has commanded. We must believe in the Holy Trinity, the Incarnation, the Crucifixion, the Resurrection, and all the other articles of our Catholic Faith. We are morally obligated to receive the sacraments of Baptism, the Holy Eucharist, Confirmation, Penance, and the other sacraments according to our vocation or situation.

Our Lord made it clear that the Moral Law applies, not only to Israel, but to the entire world. **The entire Moral Law is binding on all.**

Man's Participation in God's Authority

> Let every person be subject to the governing authorities. For there is no authority except from God, and those that exist have been instituted by God (Romans 13:1).

As part of His wise and loving plan, God has given man a participation in His authority as the Divine Lawgiver. This participation is manifested in three main areas: the *Church*, the *State*, and the *family*.

Authority in the Church

> The power to "bind and loose" connotes the authority to absolve sins, to pronounce doctrinal judgments, and to make disciplinary decisions in the Church. Jesus entrusted this authority to the Church through the ministry of the apostles and in particular through the ministry of Peter, the only one to whom he specifically entrusted the keys of the kingdom (*Catechism*, 553).

The Lord Jesus Christ spoke with many people, but He specifically appointed twelve Apostles and gave them authority to speak in His Name (Mark 3:14-19). Jesus gave the Apostles authority to make laws that would be binding on all people in matters concerning faith and morals, declaring: "Whatever you bind on earth shall be bound in heaven, and whatever you loose on earth shall be loosed in heaven" (Matthew 18:18).

The Calling of St. Peter and St. Andrew, by Federico Barocci

Jesus gave the Apostles the authority, not only to make new laws, but also to free ("loose") people from old laws. During a council in Jerusalem (Acts 15:1-31), the Apostles addressed a controversy concerning whether new converts would have to be circumcised and follow the Law of Moses. Acting in the Name of the Holy Spirit, the Apostles listed the few "necessary things" from the Old Law that would be required of the people, effectively freeing them from the Law of Circumcision, the Ceremonial Law, and the Judicial Law of the Old Covenant.

However, the Apostles did not, and *could not*, free the people from the Moral Law. God Himself had revealed the foundation of the Moral Law, the Ten Commandments, to Moses, along with certain other moral precepts. Furthermore, as part of the Natural Law, the Moral Law was already in effect *before* the Law of Moses. Therefore, it would continue after the Law of Moses was superseded by the New Law. Neither the Apostles nor their successors could ever free anyone from the Moral Law. As Our Lord Jesus Christ had already confirmed (Matthew 5:17-20), the Moral Law would remain.

Although Jesus gave the authority of loosing and binding to all the Apostles, it was to St. Peter alone that He gave "the keys of the Kingdom of Heaven":

> "And I say to thee: That thou art Peter; and upon this rock I will build my church, and the gates of hell shall not prevail against it. And I will give to thee the keys of the kingdom of heaven. And whatsoever thou shalt bind upon earth, it shall be bound also in heaven: and whatsoever thou shalt loose on earth, it shall be loosed also in heaven" (Matthew 16:18-19).

The King's Good Servant

St. Thomas More possessed the keenest legal mind in England, and he had a distinguished career in law and politics. Eventually, he was even named Lord Chancellor, making him one of the most powerful men in England. Throughout his career, he was a steadfast supporter and friend of King Henry VIII. Trouble between them arose only when the king began pressuring his officials to support his efforts to have his marriage to Catherine of Aragon annulled. For a few years, St. Thomas used every legal trick at his disposal to avoid this issue.

Meanwhile, Henry grew more exasperated with the Catholic Church and eventually took the fateful step of declaring himself the head of the Church in England. St. Thomas More was practically alone among the king's high officials in not expressing his approval for this unlawful title.

Even then, because of their personal friendship and the high regard Henry had for St. Thomas, the king did not press him too closely. However, certain supporters of the king began to lay false charges against St. Thomas. These were enough to deprive St. Thomas of his offices and finally to bring him to imprisonment in the Tower of London. Convicted of treason because of his Catholic allegiance, St. Thomas was beheaded. Just prior to his execution, he declared that he was "the king's good servant, but God's first."

St. Peter was the first pope. Jesus placed him over the household of God, in charge of all that belongs to His Kingdom, the Church (*Catechism*, 553). The office given to St. Peter has been passed down from one pope to another, right down to the pope today. Likewise, the offices of the Apostles have been passed down to the current bishops. This passing down of authority from St. Peter and the Apostles to the pope and the bishops is called **Apostolic Succession**.

Apostolic Succession is rooted in Sacred Scripture (Acts 1:15-26), and is evident from the writings of the early Fathers of the Church. For example, toward the end of the 2nd century, St. Irenaeus listed all the popes from St. Peter to the pope in his own day (St. Irenaeus, *Against Heresies*, [3, 3, 3], inter 180/199 A.D., in *Faith of the Early Fathers*, vol. 1, trans. William A. Jurgens [Collegeville, Minn.: Liturgical Press, 1970], no. 211, p. 90).

The **Magisterium** (from the Latin *magister*, meaning "master") is the teaching authority of the Catholic Church. This authority is vested in either the pope acting alone or all the bishops acting in union with the pope, when teaching, sanctifying, or governing the faithful on issues concerning faith or morals.

> To the apostles and their successors Christ has entrusted the office of teaching, sanctifying, and governing in his name and by his power (*Catechism*, 873).

The Magisterium was established by Our Lord Jesus Christ as a sure guide for the faithful, and it is protected from error by the Holy Spirit, Who leads the Catholic Church to all truth (John 16:13-15). The faithful are morally obligated to accept and obey all the teachings

Sir Thomas More, by Hans Holbein the Younger

of the Magisterium of the Catholic Church on faith and morals.

Authority in the State

> Every human community needs an authority to govern it. The foundation of such authority lies in human nature. It is necessary for the unity of the state. Its role is to ensure as far as possible the common good of the society (*Catechism*, 1898).

God has allowed man to participate in His authority in order to ensure the just rule of law. This authority is manifested in organized human political systems, each exercising influence over the affairs of the people under its care. The degree of this influence can vary widely, depending on the *type* of political regime and the specific government.

The **State** refers to an organized political community or territory governed by a political regime, and to the authorities in power within that regime. The Scriptures clearly affirm the rightful authority of the State and man's obligation to submit to that authority, within just limits.

When the Blessed Virgin Mary was with Child, she and St. Joseph were obedient to the decree of the Emperor Augustus that everyone must participate in the census. When a question was posed to Our Lord about paying taxes, He responded, "Render therefore to Caesar the things that are Caesar's, and to God the things that are God's" (Matthew 22:21). Finally, toward the end of His earthly life, when He was being questioned by Pontius Pilate, Jesus clearly indicated that Pilate's authority was from God:

> Jesus answered him, "You would have no power over me unless it had been given you from above; therefore he who delivered me to you has the greater sin" (John 19:11).

The Church has always taught that the authority of the State is part of God's Providence. We must obey that authority, as long as what the State commands is just (*Catechism*, 2238). However, if the State commands something that is contrary to the Natural Law (and hence the Divine Law), we must refuse to obey that directive.

> The citizen is obliged in conscience not to follow the directives of civil authorities when they are contrary to the demands of the moral order, to the fundamental rights of persons or the teachings of the Gospel. *Refusing obedience* to civil authorities, when their demands are contrary to those of an upright conscience, finds its justification in the distinction between serving God and serving the political community (*Catechism*, 2242).

The principle behind this teaching is simple: we must obey the lawful authority above us unless the directives of that authority contradict those of a higher lawful authority. We must *not* obey the political authorities of the State—even the president or the Supreme Court—if they direct us to do something that is forbidden by God, Whose Authority is greater than any other authority.

Authority in the Family

> A man and a woman united in marriage, together with their children, form a family. This institution is prior to any recognition by public authority, which has an obligation to recognize it. It should be considered the normal reference point by which the different forms of family relationship are to be evaluated (*Catechism*, 2202).

The Fourth Commandment, "Honor your father and your mother," makes it clear that God has given parents authority over their children. The **scope of this authority** includes every aspect of the child's life, including all his bodily, intellectual, emotional, and spiritual needs. The **object of this authority** is the entire welfare of the child, both temporal and eternal.

The State must respect the dignity of the **family** as the lifelong union of one man and one woman under God, along with their children. Parents and children are members of a family, not merely subjects of the State. When the State ignores the dignity of the family and the authority of parents over their children, the State abuses its own authority. The authority of parents over their children *precedes* the State's authority over those entrusted to its care, not the other way around.

St. Joseph in His Workshop, by Gerrit van Honthorst

Chapter 3 Review

Matching: For each statement, select the letter of the best term from the list below. There are more terms listed than there are statements, and no term can be used more than once.

A. Moral Law	E. Natural Law	I. covenant	M. Laws of Abraham
B. Law of David	F. Revealed Law	J. Ceremonial Law	N. New Law
C. Old Law	G. Divine Law	K. Human Law	O. Magisterial Law
D. Federal Law	H. Law of Moses	L. Judicial Law	P. Patriarchal Laws

1. The ________ is God's eternal, objective, and universal plan through which He orders, directs, and governs all mankind, as well as the entire universe, in love and wisdom.
2. The Law of Circumcision was the Patriarchal Law in which God commanded that Abraham, as well as every male among him and his descendants, be circumcised, as the sign of the ________ between God and His People.
3. The ________ comprise those commands that God gave to (1) Adam and Eve; (2) Noah; and (3) Abraham, Isaac, and Jacob.
4. God's supernatural revelation of the Divine Law is called ________.
5. The ________ included various precepts and ordinances to regulate the civil government of Israel.
6. The ________ prescribed the system of worship that Israel was to follow.
7. The first stage of Revealed Law was the ________, as recorded in the Old Testament. It included both the Patriarchal Laws and the Mosaic Law.
8. The ________ encompasses all the moral principles of the Divine Law governing human behavior. This includes both those moral principles known through the Natural Law and those that God has communicated through Revealed Law.
9. The vast majority of the Old Law was given by God to His Chosen People, Israel, in what is known as the ________.
10. The ________ is the Divine Law inscribed in the soul of man, so that man may know right from wrong.

Matching II: For each statement, select the letter of the best term from the list below. There are more terms listed than there are statements, and no term can be used more than once.

A. St. Peter	E. St. Irenaeus	I. World Court
B. family	F. St. Thomas Aquinas	J. Apostolic Succession
C. parish	G. Magisterium	K. Counsels of Perfection
D. State	H. Ten Commandments	L. consensus of theologians

11. The teaching authority of the Catholic Church: ________.
12. The ________ refers to an organized political community or territory governed by a political regime, and to the authorities in power within that regime.
13. The foundation of the Moral Law: ________.
14. Using natural reason, ________ proved the existence of God in five different ways.
15. The passing down of authority from St. Peter and the Apostles to the pope and the bishops: ________.

True or False: Write *True* or *False* for the following statements.

________ 16. The Natural Law is binding on all people, in all circumstances, in all places, and at all times.

________ 17. Since God can do all things, He could change the Natural Law.

________ 18. Just as freedom is the basis of morality, the Moral Law is the guardian of freedom.

________ 19. The scope of the authority of parents over their children is limited to those areas specifically designated by the State.

Multiple Choice: Write the letter of the best answer in the space provided.

20. The first grade of the Natural Law consists of the ________ of morality, which are the most fundamental moral principles of the Natural Law.
    A. Proximate conclusions
    B. Remote conclusions
    C. Primary precepts
    D. Secondary precepts
    E. None of the above

21. The ________ of morality, which include all of the Ten Commandments except the Third Commandment, can easily be known with a minimal amount of thought.
    A. Proximate conclusions
    B. Remote conclusions
    C. Primary precepts
    D. Secondary precepts
    E. None of the above

22. The third grade of the Natural Law consists of the ________ of morality. Without the aid of God's revelation, these precepts can be determined only by those who have perfected the virtue of prudence.
    A. Proximate conclusions
    B. Remote conclusions
    C. Primary precepts
    D. Secondary precepts
    E. None of the above

23. Included in the Patriarchal Laws was the ________, which was the sign of the covenant between God and His People.
    A. Ceremonial Law
    B. Law of the Gospel
    C. Law of Circumcision
    D. Decalogue
    E. All of the above

24. Which of the following statements is correct? ________
    A. Murder, adultery, and stealing are evil *only because* God has given us the Commandments forbidding them.
    B. Murder, adultery, and stealing are *not* evil.
    C. God has not given us any Commandments forbidding murder, adultery, or stealing; however, such acts *are* evil.
    D. God has given us the Commandments forbidding murder, adultery, and stealing *because* murder, adultery, and stealing *are* evil.
    E. None of the above

25. The foundation of equal rights for all mankind: ________.
    A. The State
    B. The United Nations
    C. The U.S. Supreme Court
    D. The Ten Commandments
    E. All of the above

The Good Shepherd, by Philippe de Champaigne

Chapter 4. The Judgment of Conscience

For our boast is this, the testimony of our conscience that we have behaved in the world, and still more toward you, with holiness and godly sincerity, not by earthly wisdom but by the grace of God (2 Corinthians 1:12).

God makes His Will known to us through His Divine Law. To reach our ultimate goal, union with God in Heaven, we must follow this Law in our individual lives. Therefore, God has given each person an internal guide, known as a *conscience*.

Conscience is a judgment of reason by which we apply the Divine Law to our acts (thoughts, words, and deeds) and recognize whether those acts are morally good or evil (*Catechism*, 1778). Conscience evaluates three types of acts: those we are thinking of doing, those we are in the process of doing, and those we have already done.

The ultimate source of a true, well-formed conscience is God. As the Divine Lawgiver,

Adoration of the Trinity, by Albrecht Durer

God tells us what we must do and what we must not do. As the Divine Judge, He convicts us through the voice of our conscience when we have sinned, and He gives us peace when we have done what is right. In fact, conscience is sometimes referred to as the "voice of God" in our soul. God manifests Himself to us in our soul and, through our conscience, He makes His judgments known to us.

> Deep within his conscience man discovers a law which he has not laid upon himself but which he must obey. Its voice, ever calling him to love and to do what is good and to avoid evil, tells him inwardly at the right moment: do this, shun that. For man has in his heart a law inscribed by God. His dignity lies in observing this law, and by it he will be judged (*Gaudium et Spes*, no. 16).

Everyone who has attained the age of reason knows he has a conscience. This knowledge is one of the reasons that people try to justify the sins they commit. It may also be one of the reasons that those who are wicked seek to change human laws to gain approval for their behavior. Deep down, they know their actions are wrong, but they refuse to admit it. Instead, they try to silence the voices of all those who disapprove, by working for unjust laws that will suit their purposes. However, they will never be able to completely silence the voice of their own conscience.

How We Apply Our Conscience

> So I always take pains to have a clear conscience toward God and toward men (Acts 24:16).

Conscience is not a matter of how we feel or what we want, but of the *recognition* of right or wrong. Conscience is an act, not of the emotions or the will, but of the *intellect*. The **intellect** is the faculty of our rational soul through which we think, reason, understand, and know. Through our intellect, we understand the Divine Law. Our conscience applies this understanding to our acts in order to judge whether those acts are morally good or evil.

For example, let's say we have an extra bag of garbage that we forgot to put outside our house for collection. We notice an area in the back of our neighbor's yard that is somewhat remote. The thought enters our mind that we could drop our smelly garbage in this hidden area when our neighbor is not at home.

However, our mind also recalls the principle of the Natural Law that we are to treat others the way we want them to treat us. Our conscience applies this principle to the present situation. We would not want our neighbor to throw his garbage in our yard, so we should not put our garbage in his yard. Recognizing the voice of our conscience, we decide not to throw our garbage in our neighbor's yard. Instead, we find the closest trash disposal facility, and we drop it off there.

When the case in question is a matter of obeying a positive precept such as a specific law of the Church, our mind simply recalls this precept, and our conscience instructs us to obey it. For instance, we know that the Church commands that we receive Holy Communion at least once during each Easter season and that we confess our sins at least once each year. Our conscience instructs us to act accordingly.

Conscience is "the connecting link between law and particular acts" (Fr. Laux, p. 17). Conscience applies the Divine Law to our thoughts, words, and deeds. We recognize the principles of this Law, and our conscience applies these principles to particular situations.

Different Kinds of Conscience

> I am not aware of anything against myself, but I am not thereby acquitted. It is the Lord who judges me (1 Corinthians 4:4).

Because man is imperfect and beset by many emotions, desires, and temptations, it is not always easy for him to know whether particular acts are morally good or evil. Moreover, if he has accepted ideas or opinions that are false, his conscience may make an erroneous judgment.

There are four main kinds of conscience:

- A true conscience
- An erroneous conscience
- A certain conscience
- A doubtful conscience

A True Conscience

> The truth about the moral good, stated in the law of reason, is recognized practically and concretely by the *prudent judgment* of conscience. We call that man prudent who chooses in conformity with this judgment (*Catechism*, 1780).

A **true conscience** is one that consistently makes correct judgments about what is morally good and evil. When a person has a true conscience, the voice of his conscience is like an echo of the voice of God in his soul (Fr. Laux, p. 19).

We have a *moral obligation* to form our conscience. The following practices can help us cultivate a true conscience.

Pray and Ask God for a True Conscience. The first step in cultivating a true conscience is to sincerely ask God for the grace to have one. God will surely grant this petition, because He *wants* us to have a true conscience.

Study Church Teachings and Sacred Scripture. Because our conscience can make mistakes, it is not, by itself, a perfectly reliable guide to lead us to Heaven. God has given us the Magisterium of the Catholic Church, so that we can be sure that the judgments of our conscience are correct. **The Magisterium of the Catholic Church is a sure guide for our conscience, and its teachings are an anchor for our soul.** As long as we hold firmly to all of the Magisterium's teachings on faith and morals, we will be safe and secure in the truth.

Studying the teachings of the Catholic Church is essential to the formation of our conscience. We will learn not only the fundamental principles of the Natural Law and the proximate conclusions of those principles, but even the remote conclusions of the Natural Law. This will help us to better form our conscience, so that we can correctly apply those principles in our lives.

> Conscience must be informed and moral judgment enlightened.... The education of conscience is indispensable for human beings who are subjected to negative influences and tempted by sin to prefer their own judgment and to reject authoritative teachings (*Catechism*, 1783).

One of the best ways to learn the teachings of the Catholic Church is to carefully read the *Baltimore Catechism* and the *Catechism of the Catholic Church*. (Make sure you have the Second Edition of the latter, because it includes important changes that were made in the final version of the official Latin text.) The more deeply we understand the Church's teachings, the more fortified our conscience will be.

Regularly studying Sacred Scripture can also be extremely beneficial to forming our conscience. Sacred Scripture is the living Word of God, and the Lord will instruct us and convict us when we read His Word.

> For the word of God is living and active, sharper than any two-edged sword, piercing to the division of soul and spirit, of joints and marrow, and discerning the thoughts and intentions of the heart. And before him no creature is hidden, but all are open and laid bare to the eyes of him with whom we have to do (Hebrews 4:12-13).

Studying Sacred Scripture and studying the teachings of the Catholic Church go hand in hand. By studying Sacred Scripture, we can truly hear the Word of God and receive it in our heart. By studying the teachings of the Catholic Church, we can make sure we have a proper understanding of this Word and correctly apply it in our lives. God gave us the Church, and God gave us the Bible *through* the Church.

Those who study the Bible without studying the teachings of the Catholic Church can easily fall into error. In the early days of the Church, there was a man named Apollos who was "well versed in the scriptures" (Acts 18:24). However, when he began teaching the Gospel, Apollos was not in the company of the Apostles, and there were some serious deficiencies in his teaching. Apollos was a good man and a sincere Christian, and he was able to teach "accurately the things concerning Jesus" (Acts 18:25), but he was apparently was not even aware of the Third Person of the Holy Trinity. When St. Paul asked the disciples of Apollos if they had received the Holy Spirit, they answered, "No, we have never even heard that there is a Holy Spirit" (Acts 19:2). Sacred Scripture alone is not enough. We need the Catholic Church to guide us and to help us understand the Scriptures correctly (Acts 8:27-31).

Those who study the teachings of the Catholic Church without studying Sacred Scripture are actually not following *all* the teachings of the Catholic Church. The Magisterium specifically exhorts the faithful to read the Scriptures frequently (*Catechism*, 133) and describes the Word of God as "a light for our path":

> The Word of God is a light for our path. We must assimilate it in faith and prayer and put it into practice. This is how moral conscience is formed (*Catechism*, 1802).

The Holy Spirit speaks to us through both Sacred Scripture and the teachings of the Catholic Church. Studying Sacred Scripture while also studying the Church's teachings will open our heart to the Word of God—the "light for our path"—and help us to understand this Word correctly. The Holy Spirit will use this light to guide us in forming our conscience and to help us to become more like Jesus Christ.

Always Be Truthful. We must *always* be truthful, without exception. This does not mean we should be blunt or say things that are better left unsaid. We should still be sensitive to the feelings of others, and remaining silent is sometimes the best course of action. However, we must *never* lie.

If a person lies even once, his resolve to tell the truth in the future will be weakened, and he will be more likely to lie again. If he does lie again, his resolve will be weakened even further. Unless he repents, he will lie more and more, until lying becomes second nature to him. He may even begin to lie without thinking about it.

Once the habit of lying is established, it becomes far easier to lie to oneself. Besides being sinful, lying can damage our conscience. It is impossible to have a true conscience if we believe our own lies. If our lying is chronic, so will be the damage to our conscience; we will be like someone lost in the woods without a reliable compass.

If, on the other hand, we are always truthful, **truth will be a way of life for us**. We will grow to *love* the truth, and we will desire with all our heart that our conscience be true.

Reject Temptations. We must **reject all temptations**. We must be especially vigilant regarding those passions that tend to stifle, block, or drown out the voice of conscience. Among the sins that can particularly harm a person's conscience are those related to pride, impurity, and anger.

Pride is the capital sin in which a person has an inflated self-image and an inordinate desire to be honored above everyone else. Sins related to *pride* can stifle a person's conscience by opposing anything that challenges his inflated self-image.

Jesus Tempted, by Carl Bloch

The prideful person rejects all counsel except praise. He will ignore even the counsel of his own conscience if it causes him to feel criticized, restricted, or insulted. Sins of pride can lead to spiritual corruption and hardness of heart.

> Pride goes before destruction, and a haughty spirit before a fall (Proverbs 16:18).

Sins related to *impurity* tend to block everything standing in their way, including one's conscience. If a person given over to impurity hears his conscience at all, he will quickly dismiss it as so-called "Catholic guilt" or some other cliché. Sins of impurity can lead to spiritual blindness.

> Do not follow your base desires, but restrain your appetites. If you allow your soul to take pleasure in base desire, it will make you the laughingstock of your enemies (Sirach 18:30-31).

Sins related to *anger* can drown out the voice of conscience until the anger subsides. Sometimes, anger lasts only for a moment. However, even in that brief moment, the degree to which anger can drown out the voice of conscience is so great that it can place the person and those around him in grave danger. Whereas sins of pride can lead to spiritual corruption and hardness of heart, and sins of impurity can lead to spiritual blindness, sins of anger can lead to spiritual madness. It is critical, therefore, that we control our anger and not allow it to sabotage our ability to reason.

> Let every man be quick to hear, slow to speak, slow to anger, for the anger of man does not work the righteousness of God (James 1:19-20).

If we do not win the battle against these temptations, and we let ourselves be controlled by our passions, we will find it very difficult to correctly form our conscience. However, if we strongly resist these and all other temptations, and we control our passions, our conscience will not need to compete with these loud, obnoxious "voices" in order to get our attention. We will be in fellowship with God, and we will hear *His* voice.

Regularly Examine Our Conscience. We need to examine our conscience on a regular basis. For example, we could examine our conscience every night before we go to bed. If we have a long drive to work or school, we could also examine our conscience during that time—as long we can still focus on the road.

We should always examine our conscience before going to Holy Communion. It is also beneficial to examine our conscience before the Cross of Our Lord Jesus Christ. By regularly examining our conscience, we will grow more sensitive to its gentle voice and develop the habit of carefully listening to it.

Go to Confession Frequently. Frequent reception of the Sacrament of Penance is an excellent way to develop our conscience. If a person goes to Confession only occasionally, it will be easier for him to hang on to his "favorite sins" and ignore his conscience. When someone ignores a true conscience for long enough, he may begin to believe what is false rather than what is true. The result will be an erroneous conscience.

If, on the other hand, someone frequently receives the Sacrament of Penance, he will continually learn more about what he may and may not do, and he can form his conscience accordingly. The happy result will be a true, refined conscience.

Seek Good Counsel. We should seek counsel only from those who are completely faithful to the Catholic Church and are living morally upright lives. If the person in which we confide is not living a morally upright life, how can we expect to grow closer to God? Despite his or her good intentions, that person will damage our conscience and lead us away from God.

The Sinner, by John Collier

Our truest friends are those who always tell us the truth. However, if they themselves do not know the truth, it will be impossible for them to impart truth to us. We must be very careful, therefore, in choosing whom we will confide in and seek counsel from.

Let those that are at peace with you be many, but let your advisors be one in a thousand (Sirach 6:6).

If our closest friends or mentors disagree with *any* of the teachings of the Catholic Church, our conscience could be seriously harmed. However, if they are godly persons who are faithful to all the teachings of the Catholic Church, their advice could be a great help to us.

Spend Time in Silent Reflection. Our conscience can benefit from occasional retreats from our everyday lives, in which we spend some time in silent reflection. This can help us become more receptive to the voice of our conscience. A formal retreat can serve this purpose, provided there are extended periods of silence. Some "retreats" are actually a series of talks without much time for silence. These retreats may also benefit our conscience, but they will not serve the purpose of setting aside time for silent reflection.

The simplest way to take a retreat from our everyday lives and spend time with God in silence is through Eucharistic Adoration. Spending time in the presence of the Holy Eucharist can help us to be completely honest with ourselves. We will be face to face with Our Lord, Who knows our thoughts and desires even before we do.

Blessings of a True Conscience. By following these practices, we can cultivate a true conscience, whose judgment is always in accord with the Will of God. The result will be peace and serenity, with an increase in moral strength and a resolve to always live according to the truth.

Along with a true conscience, we will have a **watchful conscience**. We will be able to more readily discern the right path from all the wrong paths placed before us. Regardless of what disguise evil assumes, it will not fool us. We will, so to speak, "smell" evil with our conscience. We will also be blessed with a **tender conscience**. We will have a heightened sense of awareness of even the slightest offense against God, and we will grow in our determination to never offend Him. Finally, we will be blessed with profound peace in our soul—the peace of being in fellowship with God.

An Erroneous Conscience

> Faced with a moral choice, conscience can make either a right judgment in accordance with reason and the divine law or, on the contrary, an erroneous judgment that departs from them (*Catechism*, 1786).

An **erroneous conscience** is one that judges as right something that is actually wrong, or judges as wrong something that is actually right. An erroneous conscience is a conscience that judges falsely. In the extreme, an erroneous conscience could actually see good as evil, and see evil as good. A conscience may be *culpably* or *inculpably* erroneous.

A Culpably Erroneous Conscience. A conscience that judges falsely because of the person's own fault is a **culpably erroneous conscience**. If our conscience is erroneous, we have a moral obligation to try to correct it, using all the reasonable means available to us. We should pray to God and ask Him to help us. We should study Sacred Scripture and the teachings of the Catholic Church, and strive to live by them. We should make a commitment to be truthful and to reject all temptations. We should examine our conscience regularly and go to Confession frequently. We should seek good counsel from a godly person. We should spend time in silent reflection and Eucharistic Adoration.

If, after all this, we still cannot overcome our ignorance, then we are not responsible for this ignorance; we have an *inculpably erroneous* conscience. However, if we do not bother to take any of these steps, then we are **culpable** (morally responsible) for our ignorance, and we have a *culpably erroneous* conscience.

Two Consciences Awakened

Even in the early Church, there were some Christians who were lukewarm in their faith. In the fourth century, there lived in Rome a young woman named Aglae, who was the wealthy daughter of a senator. Aglae was rather frivolous, much given to parties and amusements. She and her steward, Boniface, led a publicly disorderly life, while still both professing the Catholic Faith. The scandal was becoming very serious. Finally, Christians in Rome prevailed upon Aglae to renounce her sins. She repented and began to live her life as a Christian should. She eventually convinced Boniface to mend his ways as well. Together, they embarked on a life of penance, almsgiving, and prayer.

Eventually, her conversion inspired Aglae to pursue the worthy project of obtaining some relics of Christian martyrs and building a church to house them. A fierce persecution was then raging in St. Paul's city of Tarsus. So, she asked Boniface to go there with the mission of obtaining the body of a Christian martyr. Several companions accompanied him on the journey.

Upon his arrival in Tarsus, Boniface was faced with the spectacle of twenty Christians being brutally tortured in the public marketplace before their execution. Boniface felt a sudden urge to join them. Rushing toward them, he began to exhort them to persevere because their eternal reward would be glorious. Of course, he was immediately arrested, and he was sent before the governor to explain himself. Boniface proudly proclaimed himself a Christian, whereupon the governor had him tortured and beheaded.

His companions obtained the body of Boniface and brought it back to Rome, where Aglae placed it in a tomb. Aglae then built a beautiful chapel over the tomb of her former steward, who was now a Christian martyr for the Faith.

In today's society, the easiest way to develop an erroneous conscience is to do nothing. The "spiritual gravity" of a depraved culture naturally tends to pull people down. It takes effort to be countercultural and to refuse to go along with the crowd. That doesn't mean we must reject everything in the world. However, we need to make a decision about whether Jesus Christ will be first in our life, or whether we will allow some created good to come before Him.

"And if you be unwilling to serve the Lord, choose this day whom you will serve ... but as for me and my house, we will serve the Lord" (Joshua 24:15).

If a person does nothing, he will naturally gravitate toward the "ways of the world," and away from the Way of the Lord. If a person fills up his mind with books, movies, television shows, and websites that promote beliefs contrary to the Catholic Faith, then his downward slide will be even faster. He will not want to listen to the remnants of his once true conscience nagging him about the compromises he is making every day. Instead, he will shut out his conscience and lose the little good he once had (Matthew 13:12).

In its place, he will develop an erroneous conscience, just as an idolater devises a false god in place of the One True God. In doing so, he will be responsible for all the errors that follow from his erroneous conscience (*Catechism*, 1791).

A Hardened Conscience. In extreme cases, someone with a erroneous conscience may actually see evil as good, and see good as evil. This could happen if someone has had an erroneous conscience for a long time, and it turns into a *hardened conscience*, which is the opposite of a *tender conscience*. A **hardened conscience** is one that is closed to the Word of God, and therefore to good counsel. A person with a hardened conscience will repeatedly and stubbornly reject God's decrees, even when they are made clear to him.

When a person is in fellowship with God, his conscience is like a quiet, gentle voice, and the temptations of the devil are like loud, obnoxious sounds. When a person is given over to evil, the temptations of the devil are in his heart, and it is God Who must act in a dramatic way in order to get the person's attention.

> Transgression speaks to the wicked deep in his heart; there is no fear of God before his eyes (Psalm 36:1).

When someone reaches this point, he is obviously at a very dangerous place. If his conscience is evil, then his acts will also be evil.

> "The eye is the lamp of the body. So, if your eye is sound, your whole body will be full of light; but if your eye is not sound, your whole body will be full of darkness. If then the light in you is darkness, how great is the darkness!" (Matthew 6:22-23)

The process that leads to a hardened conscience is usually gradual, but with some critical turning points along the way. Initially, the person may drift away from God slowly, making countless little compromises regarding what he wears, listens to, watches, and reads. He may be further corrupted by the friends he chooses and the places where he decides to go. Then, at some point, he will be tempted to commit a more serious sin. If he rejects this temptation, he may turn his life around. If he does not, he will drift even further away from God.

Unless he repents, this process will continue. He will keep drifting further away from God, and he will keep committing increasingly serious sins. The more he sins, the weaker he will become. Over time, his conscience will become hardened. To justify his behavior, he may scoff at those who stand up for truth and righteousness. Eventually, he may even call good what is actually evil, and call evil what is actually good.

> Woe to those who call evil good and good evil, who put darkness for light and light for darkness, who put bitter for sweet and sweet for bitter! (Isaiah 5:20)

As tragic and devastating as this process is, however, there is still a glimmer of hope. At each step in the process, but particularly when the person is tempted to commit a more serious sin, there is a chance that he will not only reject this temptation, but also repent of all his previous sins. At any point, God may break through the darkness in unexpected ways and call to him. It will not be easy, but with God's help, this person could turn his life around. Others have done so.

If he does repent, Our Lord Jesus Christ, in His amazing mercy, will take him back and forgive him. For Jesus is the Good Shepherd, and He longs for His lost sheep to return to Him. When a sinner repents, God will welcome him home with open arms, and there will be much rejoicing in Heaven. Just ask the Prodigal Son (Luke 15:11-32).

An Inculpably Erroneous Conscience. A conscience that judges falsely through no fault of the person is an **inculpably erroneous conscience**. An example of an inculpably erroneous conscience is that of a young adult whose parents taught him, whether by word or example, serious errors throughout his childhood regarding what is morally good and evil. There still may be times when the light of conscience shines through for this young adult. However, there will also likely be times when he unknowingly accepts what is false as true, and what is true as false.

This is tragic, and the grave errors that he commits because of his erroneous conscience will still be evil. However, if he honestly acts according to what his conscience is telling him, **he will not be guilty of sin**. God is just and merciful, and He will not condemn someone for doing something that he could not have known was sinful.

Such a person's ignorance is sometimes said to be "invincible" (*Catechism*, 1793), but it is "invincible" only to the person himself. **Nothing is invincible to God.** If there is no human way for someone to overcome his ignorance, then he is not responsible for it. However, God can help this person to overcome his ignorance if he humbly comes to Him. For, "with God all things are possible" (Matthew 19:26).

A Scrupulous Conscience. One of the ways an erroneous conscience can manifest itself is in a **scrupulous conscience**, which is a conscience that is affected by a disorder known as *scrupulosity*. **Scrupulosity** is a disorder of the soul characterized by excessive worry that some act is a sin which truly isn't, or that some act is a mortal sin when it is actually only a venial sin or an imperfection. A scrupulous conscience usually is *inculpably* erroneous. However, once a person becomes aware of a tendency toward scrupulosity, he is morally obligated to try to correct his erroneous conscience.

One danger of scrupulosity is that it can cause someone to focus so much on one area of morality that he blinds his conscience from other areas where he actually *is* sinning. Scrupulosity can also expose a person to near occasions of sin. A person who keeps worrying about some specific temptation that he has experienced is constantly placing himself in a near occasion of sin by keeping his mind focused on that temptation. Because of his scrupulosity, he is *still being tempted* to commit that sin.

There are three excellent practices that can help cure a scrupulous conscience. First, the person should find a good, wise confessor who is faithful to the teachings of the Catholic Church. A **confessor** is a priest to whom one regularly goes to receive the Sacrament of Penance (Confession). The person must trust and *be obedient to* this confessor. The faithfulness of the confessor should ease this person's mind and give him confidence that **when his confessor says something is not a sin, it really isn't.**

Second, when this person worries that he may have consented to a sin, he should acknowledge to God that he was tempted, admit his uncertainty, say an Act of Contrition, and move on. If this situation comes into his mind during his next Confession, he may confess it as a "doubtful sin"; that is, he may explain that he is not sure whether it was a sin. However, **he must trust what his confessor says to him about it**. If his confessor says it is not a sin, then he must accept that it is not a sin. If his confessor says that it is a sin, then he must accept that it is a sin. In this way, the person's conscience will be better formed to avoid scrupulosity in the future.

Third, the person should receive the Holy Eucharist often. A problem that sometimes accompanies scrupulosity is hesitation in receiving the sacraments, especially the Holy Eucharist. It may help to bear in mind that Jesus commanded us to receive Him in Holy Communion: "Truly, truly, I say to you, unless you eat the flesh of the Son of man and drink his blood, you have no life in you" (John 6:53). A scrupulous person should think of this verse often.

The Last Supper, by Juan Ribalta

No person is ever fully worthy to receive the Holy Eucharist, but we are all commanded to do so. **As long as we are in a state of grace, we should receive the Holy Eucharist often** (daily, if possible). If we are not in a state of grace, then we must first confess our sins in the Sacrament of Penance. Receiving Holy Communion daily is one of the best remedies for a scrupulous conscience.

If we see someone acting in a way that is scrupulous, we should be compassionate. People who suffer from scrupulosity are in a form of spiritual torment. They sincerely desire to do what is right and are often deeply committed to the Church, yet they have doubts that are extremely difficult to overcome. In certain cases, they truly may not know whether they've committed a sin, and their doubts may grieve them terribly. In other cases, they may experience intense fear that they have committed a mortal sin, even though they actually haven't sinned at all or have committed only a venial sin.

Gently give them the advice above and pray for them. God knows their fragility, and He loves them. He will not break their spirit; nor should we. He desires to *heal* them, not crush them: "A bruised reed he will not break, and a dimly burning wick he will not quench; he will faithfully bring forth justice" (Isaiah 42:3).

A Certain Conscience

> A human being must always obey the certain judgment of his conscience. If he were deliberately to act against it, he would condemn himself (*Catechism*, 1790).

A **certain conscience** judges with assurance and conviction, and without any doubt or suspicion of error. If we have a certain conscience, we are morally obligated to follow it. The firm conclusions of our conscience about what we may and may not do are called the **dictates of conscience**. If we do not follow the dictates of our conscience, we sin.

> Happy is he who has no reason to judge himself for what he approves (Romans 14:22).

A person with a certain conscience may have either a true conscience or an erroneous conscience; God will judge that person accordingly. God will not hold someone accountable for ignorance through no fault of his own. When God judges our actions, He takes into account the type of conscience we have and our efforts to form it, as well as our knowledge of the truth and our efforts to live in accordance with that truth:

- If someone has both a *certain* and a *true* conscience, then he has been given much, and much will be expected of him.
- If someone has both a *certain* and a ***culpably*** *erroneous* conscience, then much will be expected of him as well, because **he should have known better**.

- If someone has both a *certain* and an ***inculpably*** *erroneous* conscience, then Our Lord will judge him only according to what he knows.

Because everyone is obliged to follow the dictates of a certain conscience, no one should be forced to act contrary to those dictates.

> No authority, ecclesiastical or civil, can make it lawful for us to do what our conscience condemns as *certainly wicked* (Fr. Laux, p. 19).

The Catholic Church is the one true Church founded by Jesus Christ. We have a fundamental right and duty to evangelize all the nations of the world and to *invite* all people to embrace the Catholic Faith (Matthew 28:16-20). The Church does not ask us to force our religion on anyone, nor should anyone try to force his religion (or lack of religion) on us. We must respect the conscience of others, and others must respect our conscience.

> Man has the right to act in conscience and in freedom so as personally to make moral decisions. "He must not be forced to act contrary to his conscience. Nor must he be prevented from acting according to his conscience, especially in religious matters" (*Catechism*, 1782).

A Doubtful Conscience

> Man is sometimes confronted by situations that make moral judgments less assured and decision difficult. But he must always seriously seek what is right and good and discern the will of God expressed in divine law (*Catechism*, 1787).

A **doubtful conscience** is one that is not certain about what is right or wrong, and therefore about what the person ought to do. As long as this uncertainty continues, the person's conscience is unable to function. He must try to clear up this doubt before taking any action.

The person with a doubtful conscience really does not know what to do. It is not merely a scrupulous worry; it is a genuine lack of knowledge about what he ought to do. Before acting, this person must first acquire the knowledge he needs to make an informed decision. Once he has acquired this knowledge, he should act accordingly.

Here again we see the importance of the Magisterium for the formation of conscience. The best way to heal a doubtful conscience is to look to the true and certain "conscience" of the Catholic Church, which is the Magisterium. By accepting all the teachings of the Magisterium on faith and morals and applying them in our life, we can adopt this true and certain conscience as our own.

We must also be aware of certain fundamental rules that apply in every situation (*Catechism*, 1789):

1. "One may never do evil so that good may result from it."
2. "The Golden Rule: 'Whatever you wish that men would do to you, do so to them.'"
3. "Charity always proceeds by way of respect for one's neighbor and his conscience ... Therefore 'it is right not to ... do anything that makes your brother stumble.'"

By judging acts according to these three rules, we can more easily recognize whether those acts are morally acceptable.

One case in which we may have doubts about how to proceed is when we are faced with two laws or levels of authority that seem to be in conflict. Suppose a teenager's parents tell him to lie when someone calls for them on the phone, saying: "Tell them we're not home." Should the teenager obey his parents in this case?

God has established parents as a lawful authority whom children must obey, and in the Fourth Commandment He directs us to honor our father and our mother. **All children, including teenagers, must be obedient to their parents in all things, as long as what their parents ask is not sinful.** However, lying *is* sinful, and hence is forbidden by an Authority that is higher than one's parents: God Himself. In this case, the teenager not only *may* refuse to obey his parents; he *must* refuse to obey them.

This does not mean that he should just hand the phone to one of his parents or express his refusal in a disrespectful manner. He can respond in a way that tactfully avoids lying. For example, he can quickly ask who is calling, and say, "OK. I'll let them know you called," and then end the conversation. Better yet, if his parents allow it, he can simply not answer the phone at all and let their voicemail take the call instead.

A more serious conflict arises when the State or some other authority demands that we do something forbidden by the Church. If the matter concerns faith or morals, the authority of the Church is higher than that of the State, as well as every other human authority. Therefore, we must obey the Church.

The Holy Family and Saint John the Baptist,
by Willem van Mieris

In the early Church, the Sanhedrin, the Jewish authority for religious matters in Israel, commanded the Apostles to stop preaching about Jesus. However, the Lord Jesus Christ, clearly a higher Authority, had commanded the Apostles to spread the Gospel. Therefore, St. Peter and the Apostles rightly responded: "We must obey God rather than men" (Acts 5:29).

Once again, the **principle regarding obedience to authority** is that we must obey the lawful authority above us unless the directives of that authority contradict those of a higher lawful authority. The key lies in understanding which authority is higher in each situation, and then obeying that authority. The following rules apply (adapted, in part, from Fr. Laux, pp. 15-22):

1. **God is the highest Authority, and His Divine Law is higher than any other law.** We must never obey any law that directs us to do anything contrary to God's Law. **Obedience to lawful authority is never an excuse for sin.**
2. **The salvation of one's soul is more important than one's health, well-being, or life.** We must never sin, even to save our life. The Christian martyrs are witnesses to the priceless value of the soul over all other possessions, including life itself. We must be willing to publicly confess our faith that "Jesus is Lord" (Romans 10:9), rather than reject Him, even if our life is threatened. **Sin is never the solution.**
3. **The authority of the Magisterium is higher than that of the State and that of parents in matters pertaining to faith and morals.** The State does not have the right to command Catholic

health insurance plans to offer free contraception. I do not have the right to skip Mass on Sunday so that I can go to my child's soccer game, nor do I have the right to give my child permission to do so.

4. **The duties of one's vocation take precedence over leisure, or even religious activities.** If my young child is sick with a stomach virus, I must stay home with him, even if that unfortunately means missing Mass on Sunday. If my spouse and I can alternate watching our child while the other attends Mass at a different time, then that is what we must do. However, if it is literally impossible to go to Mass without either leaving my sick child home alone or taking him to church, where he will endanger others, then I must stay home with my sick child.
5. **The authority of parents is higher than that of the State in matters concerning the training, education, and upbringing of their children.** The State does not have the right to order parents to send their children to public school or to any other specific type of school. Parents have a fundamental right to educate their children however they see fit, whether through private school, homeschooling, or some other means.
6. **The authority of the State or an employer is higher than one's own personal preferences.** I may not feel like stopping at every red light, but I am obliged to do so. You may not feel like doing the work that your boss tells you to do, but you are obliged to do so, provided it is not sinful.
7. **The authority of a certain conscience is higher than the authority of the State or of one's employer.** If I am a nurse, I must refuse to participate in any procedure that is intended to cause the death of an innocent human being. If the State commands a priest or deacon to preside over a so-called "wedding" ceremony that is contrary to the Natural Law, he must refuse to do so.
8. **Obedience is greater than sacrifice.** If parents command their child to immediately go to bed, then that child must not stay up, even to do a kind service for his brother or sister.
9. **The obligations of justice are higher than the claims of charity.** Paying my debts must take precedence over giving money to the poor. However, if I am able to both pay my debts and give money to the poor, then I am morally obligated to do so.
10. **The duties of those in life-saving professions (police officers, doctors, firefighters, etc.) take precedence over their personal duties to maintain their own health and well-being.** A firefighter may be called to go into a burning building to save others. As long as he wishes to work in this profession, he is morally obligated to perform this life-saving duty, even at the risk of losing his own life.

Keeping these rules in mind can help us to more clearly discern how to act in situations when our various duties and responsibilities seem to conflict. As with every decision we make, we should begin by praying to God and asking for His wisdom, so that we may act according to His perfect Will, with a true and upright conscience.

Chapter 4 Review

Matching: For each statement, select the letter of the best term from the list below. There are more terms listed than there are statements, and no term can be used more than once.

A. intentions	E. tender	I. inculpably	M. conscience
B. will	F. certain	J. confessor	N. scrupulosity
C. intellect	G. hardened	K. watchful	O. dictates
D. emotions	H. culpably	L. doubtful	P. guilt

1. A judgment of reason by which we apply the Divine Law to our acts and recognize whether those acts are morally good or evil: ________.
2. A ________ conscience is one that is closed to the Word of God, and therefore to good counsel.
3. A disorder of the soul characterized by excessive worry that some act is a sin which truly isn't, or that some act is a mortal sin when it is actually only a venial sin or an imperfection: ________.
4. A person with a ________ conscience will more quickly discern the right path from all the wrong paths placed before him. Regardless of what disguise evil assumes, it will not fool him.
5. A conscience that judges falsely through no fault of the person is ________ erroneous.
6. A priest to whom one regularly goes to receive the Sacrament of Penance: ________.
7. A person with a ________ conscience will have a heightened sense of awareness of even the slightest offense against God, and will grow in his determination to never offend Him.
8. The ________ of conscience are the firm conclusions of our conscience about what we may and may not do.
9. A conscience that judges falsely because of the person's own fault is ________ erroneous.
10. Conscience is an act of the ________.

True or False: Write *True* or *False* for the following statements.

________ 11. God is the Highest Authority, and His Divine Law is higher than any other law.

________ 12. The duties of one's vocation take precedence over leisure, but not over religious activities, which must always be given top priority.

________ 13. The authority of parents is higher than that of the Magisterium in all things pertaining to their children, until those children become adults.

________ 14. The authority of a certain conscience is higher than the authority of the State or of one's employer.

_________ 15. In order to ensure effective development of its human resources and maintain an adequate level of competitiveness, the State has the right to determine which schools all children must attend.

_________ 16. The salvation of one's soul is more important than one's health, well-being, or even life.

_________ 17. Obedience to lawful authority is never an excuse for sin.

_________ 18. Sacrifice is greater than obedience. God doesn't care about rules and regulations; He cares only about loving service from the heart.

_________ 19. The claims of charity are higher than the obligations of justice.

_________ 20. There is never a case in which the authority of the State is greater than one's own personal preferences.

_________ 21. The duties of those in life-saving professions take precedence over their personal duties to maintain their own health and well-being.

_________ 22. It is sometimes permissible to do evil for the sake of a greater good.

_________ 23. The Magisterium of the Catholic Church is a sure guide for our conscience, and its teachings are an anchor for our soul.

Multiple Choice: Write the letter of the best answer in the space provided.

24. A conscience that judges as right something that is actually wrong, or judges as wrong something that is actually right: _________.
    - A. True conscience
    - B. Erroneous conscience
    - C. Certain conscience
    - D. Doubtful conscience
    - E. Tender conscience

25. A conscience that judges with assurance and conviction, and without any doubt or suspicion of error: _________.
    - A. True conscience
    - B. Erroneous conscience
    - C. Certain conscience
    - D. Doubtful conscience
    - E. Scrupulous conscience

26. A conscience that consistently makes correct judgments about what is morally good and evil: ________.
    A. True conscience
    B. Erroneous conscience
    C. Certain conscience
    D. Doubtful conscience
    E. Hardened conscience

27. A conscience that is not certain about what is right or wrong, and therefore about what the person ought to do: ________.
    A. True conscience
    B. Erroneous conscience
    C. Certain conscience
    D. Doubtful conscience
    E. Watchful conscience

28. We are morally obligated to form our conscience. Which of the following practices can help us cultivate a true conscience? ________
    A. Pray and ask God for a true conscience, always be truthful, and seek good counsel.
    B. Study the teachings of the Catholic Church and Sacred Scripture, and spend time in silent reflection and Eucharistic Adoration.
    C. Reject all temptations.
    D. Regularly examine our conscience, and go to Confession frequently.
    E. All of the above

29. The principle regarding obedience to authority is as follows: ________.
    A. We must be obedient to all lawful authority, no matter what.
    B. We are meant to be free, so we do not need to be obedient to any authority.
    C. We must be obedient to the State in all things, for the good of the masses.
    D. We must obey the lawful authority above us unless the directives of that authority contradict those of a higher lawful authority.
    E. There is no principle regarding obedience to authority.

30. Which of the following is correct? ________
    A. If someone has both a certain and a true conscience, then he has been given much, and much will be expected of him.
    B. If someone has both a certain and a culpably erroneous conscience, then little will be expected of him.
    C. If someone has both a certain and an inculpably erroneous conscience, then Our Lord will judge him only according to what he knows.
    D. Both A and C
    E. All of the above

Chapter 5. The Elements of Morality

> Beloved, do not imitate evil but imitate good. He who does good is of God; he who does evil has not seen God (3 John 1:11).

WHAT IS MORALLY GOOD, and what is morally evil? **Moral good** is any freely chosen act that is in accordance with the Will of God. **Moral evil** is any freely chosen act that is contrary to the Will of God. In order to evaluate whether a particular act is in accordance with the Will of God, we must examine three elements of that act: the object, the intention (or end), and the circumstances. These three **elements of morality** are also called *sources of morality*, since together they determine the morality of every human act.

The **object** is *what* a person deliberately decides to do in performing an act. For example, if someone gives money to a family in need, the object is giving money to a family in need. If someone tells a lie, the object is telling a lie. **The object is the act itself, apart from any intentions or circumstances surrounding the act.**

The **intention** (or **end**) is the reason, or motive, for performing an act. The object is something toward which the will directs itself

The Betrayal by Judas, by Valentin de Boulogne

and decides to do. The intention is *why* the act is done; the intention is *inside* the person. Any given act may have just one intention, or there may be several intentions.

The **circumstances** are all the conditions surrounding an act, including its consequences: *who*, *what kind*, *when*, *where*, *how*, *how much*, etc. The circumstances include everything about the act other than the object and the intentions. The following examples illustrate some of these different circumstances:

- *Who*—a man or a woman, a child or an adult, a Catholic priest or an escaped convict, an elderly lady or a middle-aged man
- *What kind*—a magazine or the Bible, an alcoholic beverage or milk
- *When*—during the week or on Sunday, right after being fired from one's job or right after winning an election
- *Where*—a fast-food restaurant or a church, in one's home or at a park
- *How*—with chalk or with paint, using a rolled-up newspaper or using a club
- *How much*—a nickel or a thousand dollars, a few envelopes or an entire supply cabinet

The Primary Element of Morality

> My son, do not forget my teaching, but let your heart keep my commandments; for length of days and years of life and abundant welfare will they give you. Let not loyalty and faithfulness forsake you; bind them about your neck, write them on the tablet of your heart. So you will find favor and good repute in the sight of God and man (Proverbs 3:1-4).

The moral good or evil of a human act is called its **moral quality**. The *object* is the *primary* element for determining the moral quality of a human act. Thus, **the object is the primary element for determining whether a human act is morally good or evil**.

> The morality of the human act depends primarily and fundamentally on the "object" rationally chosen by the deliberate will, as is borne out by the insightful analysis, still valid today, made by Saint Thomas (Pope John Paul II, *Veritatis Splendor* [Encyclical on the Splendor of Truth], Aug. 6, 1993, no. 78.1).

If the object is evil, then the act is evil, regardless of the intentions and the circumstances. If the object is good, then the act is good, as long as both the intentions and the circumstances are also good; if either of these are evil, then the act is also evil.

Conditions for an Act to Be Morally Good

> "And now, Israel, what does the Lord your God require of you, but to fear the Lord your God, to walk in all his ways, to love him, to serve the Lord your God with all your heart and with all your soul, and to keep the commandments and statutes of the Lord, which I command you this day for your good?" (Deuteronomy 10:12-13)

Neither the intentions nor the circumstances can make a morally evil act become good. However, either the intentions or the circumstances can make a morally good act become evil. **For an act to be morally good, all three elements of morality—the object, the intentions, and the circumstances—must be good.** If even one of these three elements is bad, the act is morally bad.

Giving money to the poor is good in itself. However, under some circumstances, the act could be bad. For example, the act would be bad if it were obvious that the person receiving the money would use it for drugs. The act would also be bad if it were done with a bad intention—for example, to gain control over someone by giving him money.

> A morally good act requires the goodness of its object, of its end, and of its circumstances together (*Catechism*, 1760).

A common error today is to overemphasize the *intentions* when trying to assess whether an act is morally good or evil. Good intentions are not enough for an act to be morally good; the object and the circumstances must also be good. A good intention (or *end*) cannot justify using evil *means* to attain that end. If the object is evil, a good intention cannot make the act good. However, even if the object is morally good, a bad intention would still make the act bad.

> A good intention (for example, that of helping one's neighbor) does not make a behavior that is intrinsically disordered, such as lying or calumny, good or just. The end does not justify the means.... On the other hand, an added bad intention (such as vainglory) makes an act evil that, in and of itself, can be good (such as almsgiving) (*Catechism*, 1753).

Another common error is to assume that everything depends on the circumstances. However, the circumstances cannot make an act morally good that is itself morally bad.

The circumstances can affect the *degree*, or amount, of the moral good or evil of an act: stealing a candy bar from a store is not as evil as stealing someone's car. The circumstances can also affect how *culpable* (morally responsible) a person is for an act: saying an unkind word to your boss for telling you to stop being late for work is more sinful than saying an unkind word to your boss because he fired you for refusing to do something against your conscience. However, the circumstances cannot make an act become good that is itself evil.

Object Changed by Circumstances

> Circumstances of themselves cannot change the moral quality of acts themselves; they can make neither good nor right an action that is in itself evil (*Catechism*, 1754).

The circumstances cannot make a morally evil act become a morally good act. However, for *some* types of acts, the circumstances can change *the object* of the act, and this in turn can affect the moral good or evil of the act. In other words, the circumstances can change the object such that the act itself is altered and *becomes a different act*.

For example, as a general principle, we are morally required to keep our promises; breaking one's promises is a serious matter. **We must keep our promises, even if doing so could lead to our own harm** (Psalm 15:4). However, if, for a particular promise, *both* of the following conditions are met, we are not only permitted, but morally obligated, to *break* our promise:

1. *Breaking* this promise would not itself be an evil act: for example, it would not break any Commandment of God or the Church.
2. *Keeping* this promise would very likely result in a grave evil.

A distinction must be drawn between the general object of breaking one's promises (which is morally bad) and the specific object of breaking a particular promise for which both of the conditions above are met.

We *cannot* assume that *all* promises may be broken. **There are many promises that absolutely may never be broken under any circumstances,** because doing so would not meet the conditions listed above. An example is the promise of fidelity that a husband and wife make to each other in their wedding vows. Breaking this promise would clearly be an evil

Saint John the Baptist Reproaching King Herod, by Antoine Ansiaux

act; it would break the Sixth Commandment ("You shall not commit adultery"). The first condition listed above would not be met. A man and a woman validly married in the Sacrament of Holy Matrimony must keep their promise of fidelity to each other as long as they both shall live.

An example of a promise that should *not* have been kept is the rash promise made by Herod that led to the beheading of St. John the Baptist:

> When Herod's birthday came, the daughter of Herodias danced before the company, and pleased Herod, so that he promised with an oath to give her whatever she might ask. Prompted by her mother, she said, "Give me the head of John the Baptist here on a platter." And the king was sorry; but because of his oaths and his guests he commanded it to be given; he sent and had John beheaded (Matthew 14:6-10).

Herod never should have made such an open-ended promise in the first place. Making a promise or an oath is a very serious matter. Yet, he foolishly did make this promise. If the daughter of Herodias had asked for something that was not sinful, Herod would have been bound to keep his promise.

In this case, however, because of the evil he was asked to do, Herod should *not* have kept his promise. Both of the conditions listed above would have been met: *breaking* this promise would not itself have been an evil act, and *keeping* this promise would clearly result in a grave evil. Thus, the circumstances changed the object (and hence the act itself) from the general object of *breaking one's promises* to the more specific object of *breaking this particular promise, for which both of the conditions above were met.*

Unfortunately, Herod placed more importance on upholding his reputation than on upholding justice and respecting human life, and he kept his rash promise. The result was the martyrdom of St. John the Baptist.

We must be very careful about making promises. If we develop the habit of making too many promises, some of which we cannot keep, we could put ourselves in danger of breaking a promise that we have no right to break, possibly even committing a serious sin. Furthermore, if we break even *one* promise to someone, we will seriously harm that person's trust in anything we say in the future. This is true even if the conditions above are met and we have a moral obligation to break the promise.

Therefore, it is best not to make any promises except those that we *know* we will never be morally obligated to break. This is the only way to avoid falling into the trap in which Herod caught himself. **We should not make a promise unless we are absolutely certain that we will always be able and willing to keep that promise, no matter what.** Our word must be our bond.

> O Lord, who shall sojourn in thy tent? Who shall dwell on thy holy hill? He who walks blamelessly, and does what is right, and speaks truth from his heart … who swears to his own hurt and does not change… (Psalm 15).

Returning to the example above, does it follow that the circumstances can make a morally evil act become morally good? The answer is *no.* In such cases, the circumstances do *not* change the moral quality of the act from good to evil. Rather, the circumstances change the *object* of the act—*and hence the act itself*—and this new object in turn affects the moral quality of the new act. **The circumstances cannot directly make what is morally evil become morally good.**

Furthermore, it is a *grave error* to assume that, for *all* human acts, there are some circumstances that can alter the act by changing its object, such that the act becomes morally good. **There are some acts that cannot be altered by the circumstances in any way, even indirectly, that could ever make them good**. These acts are called intrinsically evil acts.

Intrinsically Evil Acts

> There are concrete acts that it is always wrong to choose, because their choice entails a disorder of the will, i.e., a moral evil (*Catechism*, 1761).

An **intrinsically evil act** is an act that is evil always, everywhere, and in all cases, because of its very nature. If an act is intrinsically evil, there are absolutely no circumstances that could ever alter the act such that it could become morally good. **Intrinsically evil acts are always evil.**

> Do you not know that the unrighteous will not inherit the kingdom of God? Do not be deceived; neither the immoral, nor idolaters, nor adulterers … will inherit the kingdom of God (1 Corinthians 6:9-10).

The commandments forbidding intrinsically evil acts are examples of *moral absolutes*. A **moral absolute** is a moral precept that applies always, everywhere, and in all cases, with no exceptions. Moral absolutes include all the precepts stated in the Ten Commandments, as well as several other moral precepts given in Sacred Scripture or taught by the Church.

Some of these precepts (for example, "Honor your father and your mother") are stated positively, commanding good acts to be done. Others (such as "You shall not kill") are stated negatively, forbidding intrinsically evil acts from being done.

Besides the acts that are *explicitly* forbidden, there are other intrinsically evil acts that are *implicitly* forbidden by the Ten Commandments. Many of these acts are also condemned elsewhere in Sacred Scripture or by the Church.

Examples of intrinsically evil acts include abortion, adultery, blasphemy, contraception, euthanasia, human cloning, idolatry, infanticide, murder, sacrilege, sins of impurity, stealing, and suicide. These acts are evil always, everywhere, and in all cases. Nothing whatsoever, including the intentions or the circumstances, could ever make an intrinsically evil act become morally good.

> Reason attests that there are objects of the human act which are by their nature "incapable of being ordered" to God, because they radically contradict the good of the person made in his image. These are the acts which, in the Church's moral tradition, have been termed "intrinsically evil"... (*Veritatis Splendor*, no. 80.1).

Embryonic stem cell research is another example of an act that is intrinsically evil, because it destroys a **human embryo** (a human being in the earliest stage of development). Even if millions of people could be saved from terminal illnesses or other serious diseases through this research, it still would not be morally permissible. Nothing can justify the intentional killing of an innocent human being. **The end does not justify the means.**

> Since it must be treated from conception as a person, the embryo must be defended in its integrity, cared for, and healed, as far as possible, like any other human being (*Catechism*, 2274).

Embryonic stem cell research is against God's Law, and it should be forbidden by all human laws as well. The intentional killing of an innocent human being, born or preborn, is never morally permissible. It is an intrinsically evil act.

The Principle of Double Effect

> Search me, O God, and know my heart! Try me and know my thoughts! ... and lead me in the way everlasting! (Psalm 139:23-24)

What if an act, which is neither forbidden nor required by a moral absolute, has two consequences (or *effects*), one good and one bad? Is it morally permissible to perform that act? The **principle of double effect** states that such an act is morally permissible *only if* all of the following conditions are met:

1. The object of the act (apart from the effects, or consequences) must be good, or at least morally neutral.
2. The bad effect must *not* be the *means* of attaining the good effect. The good effect must be caused by the act itself, *not* the bad effect.
3. The intentions of the act must be good. The bad effect must *not* be *intended*, only allowed.
4. There must be a grave reason for allowing the bad effect. The good effect must be at least as important as the bad effect.

This principle is an example of a *remote conclusion of morality* in the Natural Law. Without the aid of the Catholic Church, it would be very difficult to understand this principle and apply it properly.

The principle of double effect does not apply to intrinsically evil acts or moral absolutes. We must obey the Ten Commandments, and all other moral absolutes, always and everywhere, regardless of what grave evils we believe could result from our doing so. Furthermore, **the principle of double effect cannot be used to justify an evil moral object or an evil intention**. The conditions for an act to be morally good still apply: all three elements of morality—the object, the intentions,

St. Gianna Molla

and the circumstances—must be good in order for the act to be morally good. If any *one* of these elements is evil, then the act is evil.

An example in which the principle of double effect would apply is when a preborn baby tragically dies as an *unintended* consequence of saving the life of the mother during a pregnancy. If a pregnant woman has an aggressive, life-threatening form of uterine cancer, it may be necessary to remove her uterus (and hence everything in it, including the baby) as soon as possible, in order to stop the cancer from spreading to the rest of her body. If this is done during the early stages of a pregnancy, the baby will not be able to survive when he is removed from his mother's body. If this is not done, both the woman and the baby may die.

Even in such cases, it would *not* be morally permissible to *intentionally kill* the baby through abortion. Neither the circumstances leading to the pregnancy, nor the health of the mother, nor even the life of the mother, could ever justify *intentionally killing* a preborn baby.

However, it would be morally permissible to remove the cancerous uterus, and therefore the baby, from the woman's body—*without intending to kill the baby*—provided this is done with as much gentleness and care as possible to safeguard to the fullest extent possible the baby's life, integrity, and dignity.

If, at some time in the future, advances in medicine make it possible to keep such a baby alive after he has been removed from his mother's body, then there would be a moral obligation to do so. However, until that time, it is still permissible to perform this operation, even though doing so will tragically lead to the baby's death.

Let us now evaluate this example more closely, according to the five conditions that must be met for the principle of double effect to apply:

1. The object of the act (apart from the effects, or consequences) must be good, or at least morally neutral. **The object of this act is to save the mother's life by removing her uterus (and hence everything in it, including the baby), in order to stop cancer from spreading to the rest of her body. The baby is removed with as much gentleness and care as possible to safeguard to the fullest extent possible his life, integrity, and dignity.—Condition met.**
2. The bad effect must *not* be the *means* of attaining the good effect. The good effect must be caused by the act itself, *not* the bad effect. **The life of the mother is saved because her cancerous uterus is removed, not because the baby dies.—Condition met.**
3. The intentions of the act must be good. The bad effect must *not* be *intended*, only allowed. **Saving the mother's life is intended; the death of the baby is not.—Condition met.**
4. There must be a grave reason for allowing the bad effect. The good effect must be at least as important as the bad effect. **Saving the mother's life is a grave reason, which is equally as important as saving the baby's life, and which outweighs allowing both the mother and the baby to die.—Condition met.**

A Heroic Wife and Mother

St. Gianna Francesca Beretta was born in Magenta, Italy, in 1922, the tenth of thirteen children in her family. She studied in Milan, and became a pediatric physician. In 1955, she married Pietro Molla. They had three children from 1956 to 1959, then Gianna had two miscarriages.

In 1961, she became pregnant for the sixth time. However, she developed a tumor, which endangered both her and her baby. She was given three options: an abortion, removal of the part of her reproductive system that contained the tumor, or removal of only the tumor. Gianna knew that having an abortion would be a grave sin, against the Catholic Church's teachings. It would kill her innocent little baby! She firmly rejected that course of action.

The second option, removing part of her reproductive system, would safeguard Gianna's life, but it would have the unintended consequence of leading to her baby's death. The Church would allow this procedure in such a grave situation. All the conditions for the principle of double effect would be met. Gianna could have chosen this option without sinning, but she didn't.

The third option would preserve the baby's life, but it would put Gianna's life in grave danger. Gianna firmly and heroically chose this option. The tumor was removed, and her baby's life was spared. There were further complications throughout the pregnancy, but Gianna did not waver in her resolve. She told her family: "This time, it will be a difficult delivery, and they may have to save one or the other: I want them to save my baby." On April 21, 1962 (which was Holy Saturday that year), her baby was born. Seven days later, St. Gianna Molla died.

A wife and a mother, as well as a physician, St. Gianna Molla heroically chose to save her preborn baby's life over her own. Forty-two years later, on May 16, 2004, Gianna Francesca Molla was canonized a saint. Among those attending the ceremony was the daughter whose life she had saved: Dr. Gianna Emanuela Molla.

Doing everything possible to meet all four of the conditions above with the express purpose of saving a woman's life is a far cry from direct abortion, the object of which is always to *kill* a preborn baby—an intrinsically evil act, which is never morally permissible.

The principle of double effect does *not* apply to intrinsically evil acts or moral absolutes, nor may this principle be used to justify an evil moral object or an evil intention. This principle applies only in a few limited cases. Therefore, before performing any actions on the basis of this principle, it is advisable to consult with a confessor who is completely faithful to the teachings of the Catholic Church. In fact, one of the reasons we discuss the principle of double effect in this book is that this principle is sometimes misapplied to justify behavior that does not meet the conditions above, and thus is not morally permissible.

Chapter 5 Review

Matching: For each statement, select the letter of the best term from the list below. There are more terms listed than there are statements, and no term can be used more than once.

A. moral quality	E. object	I. secondary	M. elements of morality
B. moral absolute	F. goal	J. intention	N. conditionally bad act
C. circumstances	G. primary	K. moral good	O. intrinsically evil act
D. moral measure	H. only	L. moral evil	P. consequences of morality

1. Any freely chosen act that is in accordance with the Will of God: ________.
2. The three ________, which are also called sources of morality, together determine the morality of every human act.
3. The ________ is what a person deliberately decides to do in performing an act.
4. A moral precept that applies always, everywhere, and in all cases, with no exceptions: ________.
5. Any freely chosen act that is contrary to the Will of God: ________.
6. The ________ are all the conditions surrounding an act, including its consequences.
7. The moral good or evil of a human act: ________.
8. An act that is evil always, everywhere, and in all cases, because of its very nature: ________.
9. The ________ is the reason, or motive, for performing an act.
10. The object is the ________ element for determining whether a human act is morally good or evil.

True or False: Write *True* or *False* for the following statements.

________ 11. There are no moral absolutes. Everything depends on the circumstances.

________ 12. One must make allowances for unforeseen complexities when making moral decisions. Sometimes, a noble end can justify using whatever means are necessary to attain that end.

________ 13. The main thing to consider when evaluating the moral good or evil of a particular human act is the person's intentions. If the person's intentions are good, then his actions cannot really be considered evil, just perhaps somewhat less than ideal.

________ 14. The principle of double effect cannot be used to justify an evil moral object or an evil intention.

________ 15. If the object is good, then the act is good in every case.

________ 16. If the object is evil, then the act is evil in every case.

_________ 17. Neither the circumstances leading to the pregnancy, nor the health of the mother, nor even the life of the mother, could ever justify intentionally killing a preborn baby through abortion.

_________ 18. The object is the act itself, apart from any intentions or circumstances surrounding the act.

_________ 19. The principle of double effect is a universal norm that applies to all human acts, in all circumstances, in all places, and at all times.

_________ 20. The end does *not* justify the means.

_________ 21. Nothing whatsoever, including the intentions or the circumstances, could ever make an intrinsically evil act become morally good.

_________ 22. An example in which the principle of double effect would apply is when a preborn baby tragically dies as an *unintended* consequence of saving the life of the mother during a pregnancy.

_________ 23. The only intrinsically evil acts are those explicitly forbidden by the Ten Commandments.

Multiple Choice: Write the letter of the best answer in the space provided.

24. For an act to be morally good, the following must also be good: _________.
    A. The object
    B. The intentions
    C. The circumstances
    D. All of the above
    E. None of the above

25. Which of the following is correct? _________
    A. We should not make a promise unless we are absolutely certain that we will always be able and willing to keep that promise, no matter what. Our word must be our bond.
    B. There are many promises that absolutely may never be broken under any circumstances whatsoever.
    C. We are not only permitted, but morally obligated, to break a promise if both of the following apply: (1) breaking this promise would not itself be an evil act, and (2) keeping this promise would very likely result in a grave evil.
    D. We may break any promise whatsoever if we believe that doing so will increase the happiness of ourselves or our loved ones.
    E. All except D

26. Which of the following is an intrinsically evil act? _________
    A. Euthanasia
    B. Contraception
    C. Human cloning
    D. All of the above
    E. None of the above

27. When would embryonic stem cell research, which causes a human embryo to die, be morally permissible? ________
    A. Always
    B. Never; it is an intrinsically evil act.
    C. It depends on the circumstances.
    D. When it is certain that this research will lead to a greater good, such as saving millions of human lives.
    E. None of the above

28. A man and a woman who are validly married in the Sacrament of Holy Matrimony must keep their promise of fidelity to each other: ________.
    A. As long as they both shall live
    B. Unless doing so would likely result in a grave evil
    C. As long as they still love each other
    D. Both B and C
    E. None of the above

29. Which of the following is correct? ________
    A. The circumstances can affect the degree, or amount, of the moral good or evil of an act.
    B. The circumstances can affect how culpable someone is for an act.
    C. The circumstances can directly make what is morally evil become morally good.
    D. For *all* human acts, there are some circumstances that can alter the act by changing its object, such that the act becomes morally good.
    E. Both A and B

30. According to the *principle of double effect*: if an act, which is neither forbidden nor required by a moral absolute, has two consequences (or *effects*), one good and one bad, the act is morally permissible *only if* which of the following conditions are met? ________
    A. The object of the act (apart from the effects, or consequences) must be good, or at least morally neutral.
    B. The bad effect must *not* be the *means* of attaining the good effect. The good effect must be caused by the act itself, *not* the bad effect.
    C. The intentions of the act must be good. The bad effect must *not* be *intended*, only allowed.
    D. There must be a grave reason for allowing the bad effect. The good effect must be at least as important as the bad effect.
    E. All of the above
    F. No conditions need to be met. The principle of double effect is a universal principle, so it always applies.

Chapter 6. Moral Good and Virtue

> He has showed you, O man, what is good; and what does the Lord require of you but to do justice, and to love kindness, and to walk humbly with your God? (Micah 6:8)

EVERY MORAL DECISION we make affects who we are. Although our free will enables us to decide what we will do, our moral choices shape the kind of person we become, and this in turn influences what we are likely to do in the future. Our **character**, or moral identity, is the net effect of all our moral choices, good and bad. Our character defines who we are and influences how we act.

A person of *good character* habitually does what is right. His character is upright and pleasing to God. This person is trustworthy, honest, pure, merciful, just, gentle, modest, chaste, humble, and honorable.

The Good Samaritan, by Julius Schnorr von Carolsfeld

A person of *bad character* habitually does what is evil. His character is offensive to God. This person is unfaithful, dishonest, impure, cruel, unjust, violent, immodest, perverse, prideful, and dishonorable.

Over time, we *become* what we *do*. A person who always speaks the truth becomes a *truthful person*. A person who habitually lies becomes a *liar*. A person who steals becomes a *thief*. A person who lavishes his riches on the poor becomes a *generous person*.

The good news is that people can change for the better. A liar who decides never to lie again and who begins telling only the truth will improve his moral character. If he persists in refusing to lie, he will become a truthful person.

The bad news is that people can change for the worse. A truthful person who allows himself to lie even once will find his moral character changing for the worse. In time, he may even become a habitual liar.

Left unchecked, small sins can multiply and grow into greater sins. Conversely, through persistence, a person can gradually advance from performing small acts of goodness to performing great acts of goodness.

A person who *consistently* does what is good is **virtuous**. A person who does *not* consistently do what is good is *not* virtuous. A **virtue** is a firm and habitual disposition to do good. In other words, a virtue is a morally good habit. Conversely, a *vice* is a morally bad habit.

> A virtue ... allows the person not only to perform good acts, but to give the best of himself. The virtuous person tends toward the good with all his sensory and spiritual powers; he pursues the good and chooses it in concrete actions (*Catechism*, 1803).

Over time, our virtues make it easier for us to do what is right. The virtuous person loves doing what is good and hates doing what is evil. The ultimate goal of morality is happiness through union with God in Heaven. Our joy will be complete only when we are in Heaven. However, even in this life, we can experience much joy and peace by living a virtuous life.

There are two main *categories of virtues in terms of their source*: natural and supernatural. There are three main *categories of virtues in terms of their type*: intellectual virtues, moral virtues, and theological virtues.

Natural virtues are those virtues that are acquired through repeated good actions. Acquiring natural virtues is like developing muscles through weightlifting. The more we persist in doing good, the more virtuous we become. Everyone is capable of acquiring natural virtues.

Supernatural virtues are those virtues resulting from God acting on our soul in some way. At Baptism, God infuses virtues into our soul, along with His sanctifying grace. Just like the seeds in our garden, the seeds of virtue that God infuses in our soul require effort on our part to help them grow. We must *cooperate* with God's grace.

By continually giving us grace, God also purifies and elevates our natural virtues. Consequently, all the virtues possessed by a baptized Christian in a state of grace are also supernatural virtues (Fr. Laux, p. 27).

Thus, natural and supernatural virtues are not completely mutually exclusive. Generally, only baptized Christians receive supernatural virtues, whereas anyone can develop natural virtues. However, for a Christian in a state of grace, God purifies and elevates the natural virtues, so that they become supernatural virtues.

Intellectual Virtues

> The beginning of wisdom is this: Get wisdom, and whatever you get, get insight (Proverbs 4:7).

The **intellectual virtues** are those virtues that perfect the intellect in its grasp of the truth.

They include the following:

- **Wisdom.** The virtue of wisdom perfects the intellect to grasp the highest causes of everything that exists.
- **Understanding.** The virtue of understanding perfects the intellect in its comprehension of **first principles** (the fundamental self-evident truths that are at the root of human knowledge).
- **Science.** The virtue of science perfects the intellect in its grasp of scientific matters. This virtue primarily perfects our work, not our character or moral life. In order to make morally upright decisions about scientific matters, we need other virtues as well.
- **Art.** The virtue of art perfects the intellect in its knowledge of how to make things. This virtue helps a carpenter to make a table and helps a painter to produce a painting. As with the virtue of science, the virtue of art primarily perfects our work, not our character or moral life. In order to make morally upright decisions about artistic matters, we need other virtues as well.
- **Prudence.** The virtue of prudence perfects the intellect in its use of reason. Prudence is also a moral virtue and has a profound effect on our character and moral life.

Moral Virtues

> Finally, brethren, whatever is true, whatever is honorable, whatever is just, whatever is pure, whatever is lovely, whatever is gracious, if there is any excellence, if there is anything worthy of praise, think about these things. What you have learned and received and heard and seen in me, do; and the God of peace will be with you (Philippians 4:8-9).

The **moral virtues** are those virtues that regulate our moral life. Examples include chastity, modesty, humility, honesty, integrity, faithfulness, truthfulness, sincerity, magnanimity, courage, kindness, clemency, meekness, mildness, patience, perseverance, obedience, simplicity, and love of the truth.

> The moral virtues are acquired by human effort. They are the fruit and seed of morally good acts; they dispose all the powers of the human being for communion with divine love (*Catechism*, 1804).

There are four principal moral virtues, around which all the other moral virtues are grouped: *prudence*, *justice*, *fortitude*, and *temperance* (*Catechism*, 1805). These four virtues are called **cardinal virtues** (from the Latin *cardo*, meaning "hinge"). Just as a door opens on its hinges, our moral life hinges on the cardinal virtues.

Prudence

> Prudence immediately guides the judgment of conscience. The prudent man determines and directs his conduct in accordance with this judgment. With the help of this virtue we apply moral principles to particular cases without error and overcome doubts about the good to achieve and the evil to avoid (*Catechism*, 1806).

The cardinal virtue of **prudence** perfects our intellect in its use of reason, so that we discern the true good in every circumstance and the right means to achieve it. Prudence regulates our intellect—specifically, our **reason** (the ability to think logically, make judgments, and draw conclusions). Prudence helps us to know what is right and how to attain it, and what is wrong and how to avoid it.

Prudence is the mother and "charioteer of the virtues" (*Catechism*, 1806). It is the compass and map of the moral life. Without the virtue of prudence, a person's life will be like a ship without a rudder or compass, lost in the middle of a vast ocean without direction. With the virtue of prudence, a person will consistently keep his last end (Heaven) in mind and recognize the best way to attain this last end.

Justice

> The just man, often mentioned in the Sacred Scriptures, is distinguished by habitual right thinking and the uprightness of his conduct toward his neighbor (*Catechism*, 1807).

The cardinal virtue of **justice** disposes our will to always give God and our neighbor their due. Without the virtue of justice, a person will not do what is right, but rather what is evil. With the virtue of justice, a person will do what is right and just at all times.

> The way of the wicked is an abomination to the Lord, but He loves him who pursues righteousness (Proverbs 15:9).

Justice regulates our will. Whereas prudence helps us to *know* what is right and how to attain it, justice helps us to *do* what is right and in the right way.

If we fully practice the virtue of justice, we will observe the entire Moral Law, including all the moral virtues. We owe God gratitude and obedience for all the blessings He has given us—including our very life, well-being, and salvation! If we truly are just, we will strive to love God with all our mind, all our heart, all our soul, and all our strength, and to love our neighbor as ourselves, just as He has commanded us. We will be loving, humble, truthful, reverent, pious, grateful, obedient, kind, gentle, clement, meek, modest, pure, generous, diligent, courageous, faithful, honest, and fair.

Justice also requires that we be merciful to others, just as God has been merciful to us. From the Cross, Our Lord Jesus Christ forgave us for our sins; He even forgave those who crucified Him, saying, "Father, forgive them; for they know not what they do" (Luke 23:34). Justice does not preclude mercy; justice *demands* mercy.

Christ on the Cross, by Carl Bloch

At the same time, we need to make sure we are being merciful to *everyone*, not only to those who have done something wrong. We must also be merciful to the *victims* of those wrongs—especially people who are suffering because they or their loved ones have been unjustly subjected to grave evil. Failing to provide sufficient punishment for crimes is not only unjust; it is also *unmerciful* to the victims of those crimes.

> Legitimate public authority has the right and duty to inflict punishment proportionate to the gravity of the offense. Punishment has the primary aim of redressing the disorder introduced by the offense. When it is willingly accepted by the guilty party, it assumes the value of expiation (*Catechism*, 2266).

The Saintly King

In the middle of the 13th century, there lived a king who exemplified a life of virtue. His name was Louis IX, King of France. Born in 1214, he became king at the young age of twelve. His mother, Blanche of Castille, acted as regent, ruling on his behalf, until he was an adult.

When Louis was a boy, Blanche kept young Louis close to her and made sure he was raised as a good Catholic. She taught him that being a good Catholic was more important than anything else. "I love you, my dear son, as much as a mother can love her child. But I would rather see you dead at my feet than that you should ever commit a mortal sin." Louis always remembered those words. When he was king, he was known to spend many hours in prayer, fasting, and penance.

When Louis was twenty, he married a virtuous woman named Margaret, whom he loved very much. In the years that followed, they had 11 children together.

In 1235, Louis began to rule France. As king, he was very generous and fair, and he served the poor in many ways. In fact, he would invite them to dine at the castle every day. He also set up a house for poor women who had turned in desperation to a life of sin. He called them daughters of God. He washed the feet of the poor, in imitation of Christ. He provided funds to establish a Catholic university in Paris, called the Sorbonne, for the poor. St. Albert the Great, St. Bonaventure, and St. Thomas Aquinas all taught there.

King Louis loved justice, and he would never allow himself to be bribed or coerced into doing anything that would offend God. He liked to sit by a tree and hear cases himself. Whenever there was a case between a poor person and a rich person, he would listen to both sides, but he would listen more carefully to the poor. The rich, he said, had plenty of people to listen to them already.

Once, King Louis tried a case against a count who had killed three children for hunting foxes on his land. The count was sentenced to death. However, King Louis changed the sentence to life imprisonment, along with an enormous fine. The fine was so large that it drained practically all of the count's possessions. King Louis ordered that the money be given to the poor.

St. Louis also went on two Crusades to rescue the Holy Land from the hands of the Muslims. On his second Crusade, he fell ill and died in 1270. His memory lives on as a testimony of what it means to be a great leader. St. Louis, King of France, teaches us to love God above all else; to always act with justice; to live virtuously; and to love and serve the poor, the weak, and the vulnerable.

Justice demands that we treat our neighbor fairly, just as we want our neighbor to treat us fairly. Likewise, justice demands that we respect our neighbor's rights, just as we want our rights to be respected. No one has a right to be *unjust.* Every human being has been created by God in His image, and therefore has fundamental rights that must be respected, beginning with the right to life itself. Any law that attempts to deny any of these fundamental rights is gravely evil and unjust.

The Virgin and Child Adored by Saint Louis, King of France, by Claudio Coello

People sometimes have a tendency to demand justice for themselves, yet neglect it for others. The roots of this tendency often include pride, ingratitude, and selfishness. The remedy is the virtue of justice, seasoned with the virtues of humility, gratitude, selflessness, and charity.

The virtue of justice disposes us to give God all that we owe Him. The specific moral virtue by which we practice justice toward God is known as the virtue of **religion**.

Fortitude

> Fortitude is the moral virtue that ensures firmness in difficulties and constancy in the pursuit of the good. It strengthens the resolve to resist temptations and to overcome obstacles in the moral life (*Catechism*, 1808).

The cardinal virtue of **fortitude** regulates the *irascible passions* of our *sense appetite* so that we remain firm and constant in doing what is right, despite difficulties, hardships, or dangers. The

irascible passions pertain to what is perceived as a difficult good or a threatening difficulty or danger. These passions include daring, fear, and anger.

The **sense appetite** refers to the physical drives and tendencies within us that draw us toward what is perceived as desirable, and away from what is perceived as undesirable. The sense appetite includes both the *irascible passions* and the *concupiscible passions* (which are discussed in the next section). The sense appetite is not part of the human soul; it is part of the body (including the brain). However, the virtue of fortitude itself is the work of the soul, as are all virtues.

Whereas prudence helps us to *know* what is right and how to attain it, and justice helps us to *do* what is right and in the right way, fortitude helps us to *persist in doing* what is right, no matter how difficult or dangerous it is.

> The virtue of fortitude enables one to conquer fear, even fear of death, and to face trials and persecutions. It disposes one even to renounce and sacrifice his life in defense of a just cause (*Catechism*, 1806).

Without the virtue of fortitude, a person will allow his emotions to guide his actions. He will be unable to resist temptation, because he will be living "according to the flesh." With the virtue of fortitude, a person will "live according to the Spirit." He will be responsive to the promptings of the Holy Spirit, and he will live his life accordingly.

> But I say, walk by the Spirit, and do not gratify the desires of the flesh. For the desires of the flesh are against the Spirit, and the desires of the Spirit are against the flesh; for these are opposed to each other, to prevent you from doing what you would (Galatians 5:16-17).

The witness of the martyrs throughout the history of the Church is an excellent testimony to the virtue of fortitude in the Christian moral life.

Three moral virtues that are related to the virtue of fortitude are patience, perseverance, and magnanimity. **Patience** is the virtue by which a person, out of love for God, endures suffering or hardship without being unreasonably saddened or agitated. **Perseverance** is the virtue by which a person firmly strives for the good, regardless of the obstacles involved or the time required. **Magnanimity**, or *greatness of soul*, is the virtue that enables a person to perform heroic acts of virtue.

The virtues of meekness and clemency are also related to fortitude. **Meekness** is the virtue by which a person restrains his anger. **Clemency** is the virtue by which a person seeks to moderate the punishment of others so that this punishment remains within the limits of right reason. These virtues are related to the cardinal virtue of temperance as well.

Temperance

> The temperate person directs the sensitive appetites toward what is good and maintains a healthy discretion (*Catechism*, 1809).

The cardinal virtue of **temperance** regulates the *concupiscible passions* of our sense appetite so that we keep our emotions, desires, and attractions within reasonable limits, and we maintain balance in our treatment of created goods. The **concupiscible passions** pertain to what is perceived as good (that is, whatever attracts us). These passions include desire, aversion, like, dislike, joy, and sadness. The virtue of temperance moderates these passions and desires so that we keep them within the bounds of right reason.

All of creation can be divided into two types of beings: persons and things. (A **being** simply means anyone or anything that exists.) A **person** is an individual being, existing in and of himself, who has a *rational* nature, and thus can know and love God. A **thing** is a being that is not rational, and thus cannot truly know or love God.

Persons are to be loved and respected; things may be owned or used. Spirits and human beings are *persons*. All other beings in creation (animals, trees, plants, rocks, and so on) are *things*. Some are living things, and others are nonliving things, but they are all things. God has given human beings dominion over the entire visible creation, including all living and nonliving things.

> God created everything for man, but man in turn was created to serve and love God and to offer all creation back to him (*Catechism*, 358).

Every human being is a unique person with immeasurable intrinsic value, whom God knows personally by name, and for whom Jesus Christ died on the Cross. Human life is sacred, and each and every human being possesses a dignity that nothing else in the entire visible creation could ever possess.

> Of all visible creatures only man is "able to know and love his creator." He is "the only creature on earth that God has willed for its own sake," and he alone is called to share, by knowledge and love, in God's own life. It was for this end that he was created, and this is the fundamental reason for his dignity" (*Catechism*, 356).

The virtue of temperance helps us to *use things* according to right reason, and to *love persons* rather than use them. Temperance helps us to avoid doing what is wrong, or to avoid doing something in the wrong way, because of a disordered attachment to a created good (whether a person or a thing).

As with someone who lacks fortitude, the person who lacks temperance lives "according to the flesh" (though in a different way) rather than "according to the Spirit."

Without the virtue of temperance, a person will be controlled by his physical impulses and desires. Such a person is in grave danger of becoming a slave to the sins of the flesh, especially sins of impurity. With the virtue of temperance, a person will keep everything in its proper place. He will refrain from impurity. His treatment of created goods will be in accordance with right reason. He will treat all people, including himself, as persons to love and respect, and not as things to own or use.

Temperance is related to several other moral virtues, including chastity, humility, and modesty. **Chastity** is the virtue by which a person regulates his procreative instincts and abilities according to his state in life, and moderates his related passions according to right reason. **Humility** is the virtue by which a person moderates his estimation of his own importance, and acknowledges his limitations and imperfections. **Modesty** is the virtue by which a person maintains a proper amount of reserve in his conduct and manner of dressing. Modesty is closely related to both chastity and humility.

Meekness and *clemency*, are two virtues that are related to both temperance and fortitude. Since both temperance and fortitude concern the sense appetite, they are closely connected.

The Mutual Dependence of the Four Cardinal Virtues

> The human virtues are stable dispositions of the intellect and the will that govern our acts, order our passions, and guide our conduct in accordance with reason and faith. They can be grouped around the four cardinal virtues: prudence, justice, fortitude, and temperance (*Catechism*, 1834).

The cardinal virtues enable us to live a morally good life in fellowship with God. All other moral virtues are related in some way to these four virtues. The cardinal virtues themselves do not stand alone, but are joined together like links in a chain.

If one of the links in this chain is missing, the entire chain is broken, and every effort must be made to repair that link as soon as possible. If all four links are strong, whole, and intact, then we will wear this glorious chain as a witness that we belong to Jesus Christ, the Son of God.

Theological Virtues

> So faith, hope, love abide, these three; but the greatest of these is love (1 Corinthians 13:13).

The **theological virtues** are those virtues that relate directly to God and dispose us to have a personal relationship with Him. God infuses these virtues in our soul at Baptism so that we can live as His children and merit eternal life.

> The theological virtues are the foundation of Christian moral activity; they animate it and give it its special character. They inform and give life to all the moral virtues (*Catechism*, 1813).

The three theological virtues are faith, hope, and charity. It is primarily through the theological virtues that we surrender ourselves completely to God.

Faith

> By faith "man freely commits his entire life to God." For this reason the believer seeks to know and do God's will (*Catechism*, 1814).

Faith is the theological virtue by which we believe in God, and we accept everything He has revealed to us, as well as everything His Church teaches that we are to believe (*Catechism*, 1814).

> Now faith is the assurance of things hoped for, the conviction of things not seen (Hebrews 11:1).

One sure way to strengthen our faith is to accept, and always remember, a simple but important truth: **nothing is impossible with God** (Luke 1:37). Once we firmly believe this truth, our faith will have a sure foundation, upon which all the other truths of our Catholic Faith may be firmly fixed.

> Nothing tends more to confirm our faith and animate our hope than a deep conviction that all things are possible to God; for whatever may be afterwards proposed as an object of faith, however great, however wonderful, however raised above the natural order, is easily and without hesitation believed, once the mind has grasped the knowledge of the omnipotence of God (*The Catechism of the Council of Trent*, 1566, ed. St. Charles Borromeo, trans. John A. McHugh and Charles J. Callan [reprint, Rockford, Ill.: TAN Books and Publishers, Inc., 1982], Article I, p. 25).

Our faith must be a *living faith* in order to bear fruit that will last. It is not sufficient to simply say that we believe.

> You see that a man is justified by works and not by faith alone.... For as the body apart from the spirit is dead, so faith apart from works is dead (James 2:24,26).

Faith is *necessary* for salvation, but it is *not* enough. **We are not saved by faith alone.** We must put our faith into practice by living a morally good life in fellowship with Our Lord Jesus Christ.

Hope

> The virtue of hope responds to the aspiration to happiness which God has placed in the heart of every man; it takes up the hopes that inspire men's activities and purifies them so as to order them to the Kingdom of heaven; it keeps man from discouragement; it sustains him during times of abandonment; it opens up his heart in expectation of eternal beatitude (*Catechism*, 1818).

Hope is the theological virtue by which we desire the happiness of eternal life with God in Heaven, and we trust in His promises and rely on His grace to lead us there (*Catechism*, 1817).

Every person wants to be happy. The theological virtue of hope assures us that we truly *can* be happy if we trust in Jesus Christ and, through the grace of the Holy Spirit, live a life in obedience to the Father. As with faith, hope is strengthened by the firm belief that nothing is impossible with God.

> And should we expect any favor from heaven, we are not discouraged by the greatness of the desired benefit, but are cheered and confirmed by frequently considering that there is nothing which an omnipotent God cannot effect (*The Catechism of the Council of Trent*, Article I, p. 25).

The theological virtue of hope is a strong anchor for the moral virtue of fortitude. Our hope in salvation and eternal life is like a bright light upon which the Christian fixes his gaze. This great theological virtue, the "helmet of salvation" (Ephesians 6:17), is an essential part of the spiritual Armor of God, through which we may "withstand in the evil day, and having done all, to stand" (Ephesians 6:13).

Charity

> The practice of all the virtues is animated and inspired by charity, which "binds everything together in perfect harmony"; it is the *form of the virtues*; it articulates and orders them among themselves; it is the source and the goal of their Christian practice (*Catechism*, 1827).

In the end, faith, hope, and love will remain, "but the greatest of these is love" (1 Corinthians 13:13). There are different *types of love*. There is the love between family members, the love between friends, and the special love between a man and a woman. The highest form of love (***agape***, in Greek) is the self-giving love that truly seeks the good of another. This love is even greater than faith and hope. It is the selfless love that Jesus Christ has for His Church, and it is the love that God calls us to have for our neighbor. This love is called *charity*.

Parable of the Good Samaritan, by Domenico Fetti

Charity is the theological virtue by which we love God above all else for His own sake, and we love our neighbor as ourselves for the sake of God (*Catechism*, 1822). Without charity, our faith will avail us nothing, and everything we say, no matter how impressive we think it is, will be but "a noisy gong or a clanging cymbal" (1 Corinthians 13:1). With charity, we will please God by acting like His beloved Son.

Both the Old and New Testaments affirm God's Commandments that we are to love Him with all our heart, all our soul, all our mind, and all our strength, and love our neighbor as ourselves. **To truly fulfill these two Great Commandments, we must obey all the other Commandments.**

> The commandments, "You shall not commit adultery, You shall not kill, You shall not steal, You shall not covet," and any other commandment, are summed up in this sentence, "You shall love your neighbor as yourself." Love does no wrong to a neighbor; therefore love is the fulfilling of the law (Romans 13:10).

By dying on the Cross for us, Jesus Christ gave a new, definitive meaning to the Commandment that we must love our neighbor as ourselves: **we must love others as Jesus has loved us.**

> "This is my commandment, that you love one another as I have loved you. Greater love has no man than this, that a man lay down his life for his friends" (John 15:12-13).

We must love, not only with the love that one brother has for another, but with *agape*: with true Christian charity. This is not easy to do. It requires being in union with God, Who lives within us, so that *He* may love others through us.

> Charity upholds and purifies our human ability to love, and raises it to the supernatural perfection of divine love (*Catechism*, 1827).

All the moral virtues are related in some way to charity. A careful reading of 1 Corinthians 13:4-7 will point to several: patience, kindness, modesty, chastity, humility, mildness, gentleness, selflessness, temperance, good will, meekness, mercy, clemency, justice, honesty, love of the truth, perseverance, prudence, magnanimity, and fortitude.

There are three main **fruits of charity**: peace, joy, and mercy (*Catechism*, 1829). Through the theological virtue of charity, we love the Lord our God with all our heart, all our soul, all our mind, and all our strength, and we love our neighbor as ourselves. By God's grace, we can truly act as God's sons and daughters, and we can love one another as He has loved us.

Gifts and Fruits of the Holy Spirit

> "A new heart I will give you, and a new spirit I will put within you; and I will take out of your flesh the heart of stone and give you a heart of flesh. And I will put my spirit within you, and cause you to walk in my statutes and be careful to observe my ordinances" (Ezekiel 36:26-27).

Along with the virtues, we are also blessed with the seven **gifts of the Holy Spirit**: wisdom, understanding, counsel, fortitude, knowledge, piety, and fear of the Lord. These gifts are permanent dispositions in our soul that perfect and complete the virtues. A few of them have the same names as some of the intellectual or moral virtues.

The Holy Spirit infuses these gifts in our soul when we receive the Sacrament of Baptism, and He further showers them upon us in the Sacrament of Confirmation.

> The seven *gifts* of the Holy Spirit ... complete and perfect the virtues of those who receive them. They make the faithful docile in readily obeying divine inspirations (*Catechism*, 1831).

When we humble ourselves before God and strive with all our heart to please Him, the Holy Spirit continually cultivates these gifts in us, and transforms us so that we become more like Jesus Christ (Romans 12:2). Then the twelve **fruits of the Holy Spirit** are manifested in our lives: charity, joy, peace, patience, kindness, goodness, generosity, gentleness, faithfulness, modesty, self-control, and chastity. These are "perfections that the Holy Spirit forms in us as the first fruits of eternal glory" (*Catechism*, 2832).

The ultimate goal of morality is happiness through union with God in Heaven. The gifts and fruits of the Holy Spirit are like so many lights along the way, leading us home.

Chapter 6 Review

Matching: For each statement, select the letter of the best term from the list below. There are more terms listed than there are statements, and no term can be used more than once.

A. virtue	E. faith	I. fortitude	M. temperance
B. clemency	F. hope	J. intellectual	N. magnanimity
C. character	G. joy	K. person	O. thing
D. justice	H. charity	L. prudence	P. natural

1. Our moral identity, which is the net effect of all our moral choices, good and bad: ________.
2. The cardinal virtue of ________ helps us to remain firm and constant in doing what is right, despite difficulties, hardships, or dangers.
3. Theological virtue by which we desire the happiness of eternal life with God in Heaven, and we trust in His promises and rely on His grace to lead us there: ________.
4. The cardinal virtue of ________ perfects our intellect in its use of reason, so that we discern the true good in every circumstance and the right means to achieve it.
5. A firm and habitual disposition to do good: ________.
6. The cardinal virtue of ________ regulates the concupiscible passions of our sense appetite so that we keep our emotions, desires, and attractions within the limits of right reason, and we maintain balance in our treatment of created goods.
7. Virtue that enables a person to perform heroic acts of virtue: ________.
8. Theological virtue by which we believe in God, and we accept everything He has revealed to us, as well as everything His Church teaches that we are to believe: ________.
9. An individual being, existing in and of himself, who has a *rational* nature, and thus can know and love God: ________.
10. The cardinal virtue of ________ disposes our will to always give God and our neighbor their due.
11. Theological virtue by which we love God above all else for His own sake, and we love our neighbor as ourselves for the sake of God: ________.
12. The ________ virtues are those virtues that perfect the intellect in its grasp of the truth.

Matching II: For each statement, select the letter of the best term from the list below. There are more terms listed than there are statements, and no term can be used more than once.

A. living thing	E. patience	I. irascible	M. acts of the Holy Spirit
B. humility	F. kindness	J. concupiscible	N. gifts of the Holy Spirit
C. modesty	G. chastity	K. perseverance	O. sense appetite
D. clemency	H. religion	L. human being	P. fruits of the Holy Spirit

13. Moral virtue by which we practice justice toward God: ________.
14. Virtue by which a person, out of love for God, endures suffering or hardship without being unreasonably saddened or agitated: ________.
15. The ________ passions pertain to what is perceived as a difficult good or a threatening difficulty or danger.
16. The ________ refers to the physical drives and tendencies within us that draw us toward what is perceived as desirable, and away from what is perceived as undesirable.
17. Virtue by which a person maintains a proper amount of reserve in his conduct and manner of dressing: ________.
18. Virtue by which a person seeks to moderate the punishment of others so that this punishment remains within the limits of right reason: ________.
19. Virtue by which a person moderates his estimation of his own importance, and acknowledges his limitations and imperfections: ________.
20. The seven ________, which perfect and complete the virtues, are wisdom, understanding, counsel, fortitude, knowledge, piety, and fear of the Lord.
21. Virtue by which a person firmly strives for the good, regardless of the obstacles involved or the time required: ________.
22. The ________ passions pertain to what is perceived as good (that is, whatever attracts us).
23. Virtue by which a person regulates his procreative instincts and abilities according to his state in life, and moderates his related passions according to right reason: ________.
24. The twelve ________ are charity, joy, peace, patience, kindness, goodness, generosity, gentleness, faithfulness, modesty, self-control, and chastity.
25. Every ________ is a unique person with immeasurable intrinsic value, whom God knows personally by name, and for whom Jesus Christ died on the Cross.

True or False: Write *True* or *False* for the following statements.

________ 26. All the virtues possessed by a baptized Christian in a state of grace are natural virtues.

________ 27. To truly fulfill the Great Commandments to love God and love our neighbor, we must obey all the other Commandments.

________ 28. The fruits of charity are peace, joy, and mercy.

________ 29. We are saved by faith alone.

________ 30. Supernatural virtues are those virtues resulting from God acting on our soul in some way.

Multiple Choice: Write the letter of the best answer in the space provided.

31. Which of the following is *not* correct? ________
    A. If we fully practice the virtue of justice, we will observe the entire Moral Law.
    B. Failing to provide sufficient punishment for crimes is not only unjust; it is also unmerciful to the victims of those crimes.
    C. No one has a right to be unjust.
    D. It is impossible to have both justice and mercy at the same time; justice precludes mercy, and mercy precludes justice.
    E. None of the above. They are all correct.

32. The principal moral virtues, around which all the other moral virtues are grouped: ________.
    A. Theological virtues
    B. Intellectual virtues
    C. Cardinal virtues
    D. Natural virtues
    E. None of the above

33. Faith, hope, and charity are ________.
    A. Theological virtues
    B. Intellectual virtues
    C. Cardinal virtues
    D. Moral virtues
    E. None of the above

34. Virtues that can be acquired by all people (including those not baptized as Christians) through repeated good actions: ________.
    A. Theological virtues
    B. Supernatural virtues
    C. Gifts and fruits of the Holy Spirit
    D. Natural virtues
    E. None of the above

35. The virtue of prudence regulates our ________.
    A. Will
    B. Intellect
    C. Concupiscible passions
    D. Irascible passions
    E. None of the above

36. The virtue of justice regulates our ________.
    A. Will
    B. Intellect
    C. Concupiscible passions
    D. Irascible passions
    E. None of the above

37. The virtue of fortitude regulates our ________.
    A. Will
    B. Intellect
    C. Concupiscible passions
    D. Irascible passions
    E. None of the above

38. The virtue of temperance regulates our ________.
    A. Will
    B. Intellect
    C. Concupiscible passions
    D. Irascible passions
    E. None of the above

39. Which of the following is *both* an intellectual virtue and a moral virtue? ________
    A. Understanding
    B. Prudence
    C. Justice
    D. Fortitude
    E. Temperance

40. All of creation can be divided into two groups: persons and things. Persons are to be loved and respected; things may be owned or used. Which of the following are persons? ________
    A. Apes
    B. Baseballs
    C. Cats
    D. Dogs
    E. Eucalyptus trees
    F. Ferns
    G. Giraffes
    H. Human beings
    I. "Intelligent" computer systems
    J. June bugs
    K. Kangaroos
    L. Lemon trees
    M. Most of the above
    N. None of the above
    O. Only those who are declared to be persons by the U.S. Supreme Court

Chapter 7. Sin and Moral Evil

There is a way which seems right to a man, but its end is the way to death (Proverbs 16:25).

GOD CREATED EVERY human being to know, love, and serve Him, and ultimately to be happy with Him in Heaven. Sin opposes God's loving plan and purpose for man by leading him along a way that in reality leads to death.

Whereas **moral good** is any freely chosen act that is in accordance with the Will of God, **moral evil** is any freely chosen act that is contrary to the Will of God. Every time we deliberately decide to do something that is morally evil, we *sin*.

What Is Sin?

Everyone who commits sin is guilty of lawlessness; sin is lawlessness (1 John 3:4).

Sin is any thought, word, deed, or omission that is contrary to God's Law. In Sacred Scripture, one of the Hebrew words used for sin (*pasha*) means to transgress or overstep the limits set by God, or to rebel against His authority. The Greek word used in Scripture for sin (*hamartia*) means "missing the mark." Another Hebrew word used for sin, *chata*, also has this sense.

Fundamentally, **sin is disobedience to God**. When we sin, we place more importance on doing what *we* want to do than on pleasing God and obeying His commands. Sin arises from an attachment to some good that we place before our true good, God Himself. If we sin

Expulsion from the Garden of Eden, by Thomas Cole

repeatedly in some particular way, we develop a vice. A **vice** is a morally bad habit due to repeated sins in a particular moral area.

When we do something that God has forbidden (stealing or lying, for example) we are guilty of a **sin of commission**. When we neglect to do something that God has commanded (honoring our parents, going to Mass on Sunday, etc.) we are guilty of a **sin of omission**.

Sin is contrary to faith in God, because if we truly believe in God and trust what He says, we will never want to do anything that offends Him. The knowledge that God is all-powerful and "can destroy both soul and body in hell" (Matthew 10:28) should be enough to instill in us a healthy fear of ever offending Him. "It is a fearful thing to fall into the hands of the living God" (Hebrews 10:31).

Sin is a lack of trust in God and His goodness. When we sin, we show that we doubt or have forgotten about God's goodness and what He has commanded. **Sin is rebellion against God.** We know God wants us to be good, yet we sin by doing what we know He does *not* want us to do, or by neglecting to do what we know He *does* want us to do. **Sin is an insult against God**, for it is contrary to the honor we owe our loving Creator and Redeemer. **Sin is an act of ingratitude**, for we owe God everything, including our life (Fr. Laux, pp. 41-42).

Sin is also contrary to right reason, for three reasons. First, man was created in the image and likeness of God (Genesis 1:27). Our nature is good, even sublime. Just as we were created in God's image, we are also called to reflect this image by our acts. Sin corrupts our nature and degrades our dignity.

Second, sin disturbs the moral order that God created. **At the root of every sin is a denial of truth and reality.** The truth is that God is good, and man was created to be good. When man sins, he denies or ignores God's goodness, as well as his own obligation to be good. Instead, he chooses to believe in a delusion, which ultimately can lead him to treat something other than God as his "god."

Third, when we sin, we often injure our neighbor, and we always injure ourselves. Sin endangers the end for which God created us: happiness through union with God in Heaven. Sin harms our soul by degrading our moral character and jeopardizing both our temporal and eternal welfare. If a person does not repent of serious sin, it will even deprive him of eternal happiness. Sin also robs us of true interior peace and freedom. As Our Lord declared, "everyone who commits sin is a slave to sin" (John 8:34).

Why Does Moral Evil Exist?

> And God saw everything that he had made, and behold, it was very good (Genesis 1:31).

Since God is all-powerful and all-good, why does He allow moral evil to exist? This question has been asked many times through the centuries, and it is still asked today. St. Augustine tried to shed some light on this "mystery of lawlessness" (2 Thessalonians 2:7) by explaining that God would never allow an evil to occur unless He could bring some good from that evil. Remember, God is all-powerful; He can do anything. He can even bring good from evil.

God hates evil, and He never *wants* it to occur; nor should we. However, He *permits* that which He does not want to occur, and then somehow uses it to bring about good. In some cases, we may not see this good until God reveals it to us in Heaven, when He makes His entire plan known to us.

In the beginning, everything that God created was good (Genesis 1:31); God created a universe *without* moral evil. However, because of the sinful rebellion of the devil and his followers (Isaiah 14:12), moral evil began to exist in creation. Then, because of the sin of Adam and Eve (Genesis 3:6), moral evil began to exist in the *visible* creation.

God's creation includes both *physical beings* (those in the visible universe) and *nonphysical beings*. A **spirit** is a rational being that is not physical, and thus is invisible. All the spirits were created good, and the first man and woman were created good. However, one of the spirits that God had created, Lucifer, used his free will to rebel against God, and some of the other spirits followed. The result was a cataclysmic upheaval in Heaven itself.

St. Michael the Archangel (the Prince of the Heavenly Host) and the other angels who remained loyal to God battled against Lucifer and his followers (Revelation 12:7-9). In that battle, St. Michael and the angels with him defeated Lucifer and the other spirits who refused to serve God, casting them out of Heaven forever (Luke 10:18).

The decision of Lucifer and his followers to rebel against God was definitive and irrevocable, and therefore unforgivable. As St. John Damascene explained, "There is no repentance for the angels after their fall, just as there is no repentance for men after death" (St. John Damascene, *De Fide Orthodoxa* 2, 4, in *Catechism*, 393). From then on, they were no longer **angels** (spirits who are servants and messengers of God), but rather **demons** (spirits who are enemies of God).

Notice, once again, that **the root and basis of morality is freedom**. It was freedom that made Lucifer and the other spirits who followed him *capable* of deciding to act against God, and thus to *do evil* for the first time. It was freedom that made St. Michael and the angels with him capable of deciding to remain loyal to their Creator, and thus to *do good*.

Likewise, it is freedom that makes man capable of deciding to do good or evil. God has given man a rational soul with an intellect and a free will, so that he can discern right from wrong and freely decide to do what is right. God does not condone sin; there are still consequences for our actions. However, God respects the natural order that He created, including the reality of man's free will. Therefore, rather than take away that free will, God permits man even to sin.

God wants us to *freely* decide to love Him and our neighbor. This freedom is part of our dignity as human beings. Our first parents, Adam and Eve, faced with their first moral test, used their freedom to disobey their Creator.

Thus, **moral evil exists because** (1) God created spirits and human beings to be free; (2) some of the spirits used their freedom to rebel against God, thereby introducing moral evil into creation; and (3) Adam and Eve, tempted by the devil, used their freedom to rebel against God, thereby introducing moral evil into the *visible* creation. God hates evil, and He certainly does *not* need evil in order to carry out His Will. However, He allows it and somehow mysteriously brings good from it.

Original Sin

And the Lord God commanded the man, saying, "You may freely eat of every tree of the garden; but of the tree of the knowledge of good and evil you shall not eat, for in the day that you eat of it you shall die" (Genesis 2:16-17).

But the serpent said to the woman, "You will not die. For God knows that when you eat of it your eyes will be opened, and you will be like God, knowing good and evil." So … she took of its fruit and ate; and she also gave some to her husband, and he ate" (Genesis 3:4-6).

Angel Guard, by Juan de Juanes

Adam and **Eve** were the first man and woman in all of creation. God created the body of Adam from the dust of the Earth (Genesis 2:7), and He created the body of Eve from the side of Adam (Genesis 2:21-22). God created their souls (and likewise creates the soul of every other human being) directly, out of nothing (Genesis 2:7). Both Adam and Eve were created good (Genesis 1:27). However, when they used their free will to disobey God's command, they introduced sin and moral evil into the visible creation.

> The account of the fall in Genesis 3 uses figurative language, but affirms a primeval event, a deed that took place *at the beginning of the history of man.* Revelation gives us the certainty of faith that the whole of human history is marked by the original fault freely committed by our first parents (*Catechism*, 390).

Paradise, by Jan Brueghel the Younger

Original Sin refers to (1) this first (original) sin of Adam, in cooperation with Eve, at the beginning of the history of man, and (2) the resulting state of separation from God that mankind inherited because of this sin. This inherited state, called the **state of Original Sin**, is the absence of God's sanctifying grace in the soul.

Sanctifying grace is the supernatural gift of God's presence in a person's soul, by which that person shares in the Divine Life of the Holy Trinity. A person who has sanctifying grace in his soul is in a **state of grace**. Every person who is in a state of grace is in fellowship with God. Every person who is not in a state of grace is not in fellowship with God.

The consequences of the sin of Adam and Eve have been tragic:

- Moral evil was introduced into the visible creation, and countless sins have been committed since then (Genesis 4:8, 6:5).
- Death entered the world (Genesis 5:5-31, 6:3; Romans 6:23).
- Man lost the original holiness and justice that he had received from God (*Catechism*, 416). Rather than being conceived in a state of sanctifying grace, now man is conceived in the state of Original Sin, in which his soul is separated from God and His Divine Life.
- Man is plagued by **concupiscence** (an inclination to sin due to disordered physical appetites and desires), and his soul is in turmoil, battling between what he wills to do and what his flesh incites him to do (Romans 7:14-25).
- Strife and domination endanger the lifelong union of a man and a woman in marriage (Genesis 3:16) which God always intended (Mark 10:6-12).

- The harmony that man had originally enjoyed with the rest of creation has been damaged (Genesis 3:17-19).
- Man's understanding of the Natural Law is often obscured, and it is only with much difficulty that he arrives at truth (*Catechism*, 1960).

However, God's love is stronger than death (Song of Solomon 8:6). In His love for us, God sent us a Redeemer. God's only Son, the Second Person of the Holy Trinity, "became flesh and dwelt among us" (John 1:14), and died on the Cross to save us (John 3:16-17).

> The doctrine of original sin is, so to speak, the "reverse side" of the Good News that Jesus is the Savior of all men, that all need salvation, and that salvation is offered to all through Christ. The Church, which has the mind of Christ, knows very well that we cannot tamper with the revelation of original sin without undermining the mystery of Christ (*Catechism*, 389).

The mystery of salvation is intrinsically tied to God's revelation regarding Original Sin. This revelation and doctrine must be guarded zealously.

Temptation

> Let no one say when he is tempted, "I am tempted by God"; for God cannot be tempted with evil and he himself tempts no one; but each person is tempted when he is lured and enticed by his own desire. Then desire when it has conceived gives birth to sin; and sin when it is full-grown brings forth death. Do not be deceived, my beloved brethren (James 1:13-16).

Temptation is an incitement to act contrary to God's Law, and thus to commit sin. Temptation comes from three sources: the world, the flesh, and the devil.

Three Aspects of Temptation

> For all that is in the world, the *lust of the flesh* and the *lust of the eyes* and the *pride of life*, is not of the Father but is of the world. And the world passes away, and the lust of it; but he who does the will of God abides forever (1 John 2:16, emphasis added).

At the root of every sin, is a *lack of trust* in God and *disobedience* toward Him. This can be seen from the original sin of our first parents, Adam and Eve. Rather than trusting in God, they allowed themselves to listen to the lies of the devil. Doubting the goodness of God, they disobeyed His command.

> Man, tempted by the devil, let his trust in his Creator die in his heart and, abusing his freedom, disobeyed God's command. This is what man's first sin consisted of. All subsequent sin would be disobedience toward God and lack of trust in his goodness (*Catechism*, 397).

Once Adam and Eve allowed their trust in God to waver, they began to turn their focus away from God and toward the fruit that He had commanded them not to eat, and they were enticed. Deceived by the devil, they saw as good that which God had forbidden:

> So when the woman saw that the tree was *good for food*, and that it was a *delight to the eyes*, and that the tree was *to be desired to make one wise*, she took of its fruit and ate; and she also gave some to her husband, and he ate (Genesis 3:6, emphasis added).

The apparent goods of satisfying the *lust of the flesh* ("good for food"), succumbing to the *lust of the eyes* ("a delight to the eyes"), and relishing the *pride of life* ("to be desired to make one wise") became more important to Eve than the true good of obeying God. So, she disobeyed God's command, and Adam, her husband, followed. **This is the nature of all sin**: a person has a disordered attachment to some apparent good, and he places that apparent good before God and His commands.

One or more of these same **three aspects of temptation** (the lust of the flesh, the lust of the eyes, and the pride of life) have been behind all the sins ever committed since this first sin of Adam and Eve. All **three sources of temptation** (the world, the flesh, and the devil) are tied in some way to these three aspects of temptation.

Lust of the Flesh. We have a disordered desire for pleasure, which can entice us in several ways. One of the most powerful ways in which this desire is manifested is in temptations against purity. As the lust of the flesh incites us from within, the world lures us from without, and the devil waits for an opportunity to entice us to sin. If a person gives the devil that opportunity by opening his heart to sin, the devil will try to drag him down even further, from impurity to unnatural lust, to perversity and other grave evils.

Lust of the Eyes. We are tempted with a consuming desire for everything we don't have: "Hell and destruction are never filled: so the eyes of man are never satisfied" (Proverbs 27:20). We want money; we want riches; we want luxury; we want many things. Once again, the world, with all its empty promises, is a willing accomplice. This is especially true in our modern culture, where we are bombarded with countless images, many of them inciting the lust of the flesh as well.

If a person begins succumbing to the lust of the eyes, the devil will try to lead him from one sin to another, until he is so infatuated with what he covets that he practically worships it as an idol.

The Expulsion of Adam and Eve from Paradise, by Benjamin West

> But those who desire to be rich fall into temptation, into a snare, into many senseless and hurtful desires that plunge men into ruin and destruction. For the love of money is the root of all evils; it is through this craving that some have wandered away from the faith and pierced their hearts with many pangs. But as for you, man of God, shun all this; aim at righteousness, godliness, faith, love, steadfastness, gentleness (1 Timothy 6:9-11).

Pride of Life. We are beset from within and from without with the lure of power, fame, and self-promotion. It is easy to give in to these enticements and to seek to be praised and esteemed by others. The world feeds our pride by promising that we can be the greatest, the richest, the smartest, the most successful, and the most beautiful if we just follow our dreams and buy what the world is selling.

It was out of pride and envy that the devil refused to serve God. The devil even tried to tempt the Lord Jesus Christ to adore him (Matthew 4:9)—which, of course, Our Lord immediately refused to do, rebuking him instead (Matthew 4:10). It is also out of pride that the devil hates the thought of *anyone* serving God rather than him.

If a person succumbs to the pride of life, the devil will try to "puff him up" with further temptations. He will tempt him to put down others in order to make himself look better. He will incite him to engage in gossip and slander. He will try to burden him with envy. The more the person gives in to these temptations, the more self-centered he will become. He will want to be served rather than serve others, and he will be easily offended when he is not served. Ultimately, he will be driven to destroy anyone who makes him look bad or stands in his way.

Three Stages of Temptation

> The way of perfection passes by way of the Cross. There is no holiness without renunciation and spiritual battle (*Catechism*, 2015).

Every temptation typically has **three stages**: the occasion, the conflict, and the resolution (Fr. Laux, pp. 44-45).

The **occasion of temptation** is the person, place, or thing that arouses a desire in us to commit sin. We may be tempted through something external to us, or we may be tempted through something within us, such as emotions or physical impulses. Often, we are tempted from within and from without at the same time. In any case, some set of passions within us is aroused. These passions can be very intense. However, we are just being tempted; we have not sinned.

The **conflict of temptation** is the internal struggle we experience when we recognize that we cannot fulfill the desire with which we are being tempted, without compromising our morals. In this struggle, our own passions ensnare us, tempting us to do something that we know is sinful. As our conscience warns us not to proceed further, these passions may increase, and our mind may be bombarded with many deceitful arguments in favor of the temptation. At this point, it would appear, the devil has entered the battle. We still have not sinned.

Finally, the **resolution of temptation** is the point at which we make a decision for or against committing the sin that we are being tempted to commit. If we give in to the temptation, we sin. If we do not give in to the temptation, we do not sin.

Sometimes a person makes a resolution against one temptation but gives in to another. For example, we may experience a feeling of pleasure during certain temptations. As long as we do not *will* to experience this pleasure, we are not sinning; we are merely being tempted. However, if we *willfully* take pleasure in a temptation, then we have already begun to sin by freely consenting to take pleasure in something evil. This is the case even if we eventually reject a related temptation to commit a more serious sin.

The bottom line is that unless we make some resolution with our will, we have not sinned. However, once there is resolution, we are liable to judgment.

If we honestly do not know whether we have given in to a temptation, then we probably have not sinned. The best way to proceed in such cases is to acknowledge our uncertainty to God, express to Him that if we have sinned we are sorry, and then focus on something else. Otherwise, we will only prolong the temptation, exposing our soul to greater danger.

Temptations can be very powerful, and the more we allow ourselves to dwell on them, the more difficult they will be to shake off. Therefore, **we should always reject temptations immediately and not dwell on them.**

Experiencing temptations can be very unsettling, especially to a sensitive soul trying to live a morally upright life. However, we must remember that **temptations are not sins**. As long as we have not given consent with our will, we have not sinned, regardless of how strong, long, or terrible the temptation may be.

> Blessed is the man who endures trial, for when he has stood the test he will receive the crown of life which God has promised to those who love him (James 1:12).

Let us take heart from the counsel and witness of the saints: the more we resist temptation, the more we will grow in the opposite virtue, and the Lord God will bless us.

Types of Sin

> If anyone sees his brother committing what is not a mortal sin, he will ask, and God will give him life for those whose sin is not mortal. There is sin which is mortal; I do not say that one is to pray for that. (1 John 5:16).

There are two *types of sin*: actual sin and Original Sin. **Actual sin** is any sinful act of the will. **Original Sin** refers to (1) the first sin committed by Adam, in cooperation with Eve, and (2) the state of separation from God resulting from this sin. For Adam and Eve, this first (original) sin was indeed actual sin. However, for the rest of us, Original Sin is *not* an act of the will, but rather an inherited state of the soul. Thus, all sin is actual sin, except for the state of Original Sin, which mankind inherited from Adam.

There are two *categories of actual sin*: mortal sin and venial sin. In addition, certain sins are called **capital sins**, because they are the chief sources of other sins, which they engender. The seven capital sins are pride, greed (or avarice), envy, anger (or wrath), lust, gluttony, and sloth.

Finally, **there are some sins that are so offensive to God that they cry to Heaven for justice**. These include "the blood of Abel"; "the sin of the Sodomites"; "the cry of the people oppressed in Egypt"; "the cry of the foreigner, the widow, and the orphan"; and "injustice to the wage earner" (*Catechism*, 1867).

Mortal Sin

> *Mortal sin* destroys charity in the heart of man by a grave violation of God's law; it turns man away from God, who is his ultimate end and his beatitude, by preferring an inferior good to Him (*Catechism*, 1855).

There is nothing more evil in the world than mortal sin. It is a greater evil than the worst tornadoes and hurricanes, the most violent earthquakes and typhoons, and the most horrific fires. It is a greater evil than all the tragedies of disease, pestilence, hunger, sickness, and death. *Moral evil* is even worse than *physical evil* (anything that causes suffering or harm to people), and mortal sin is the worst possible moral evil.

Mortal sin is any morally evil act that is grave (serious) in nature, undertaken with full knowledge, and committed with complete consent. Mortal sin causes the loss of sanctifying grace in the soul. A person who lacks sanctifying grace in his soul because of one or more mortal sins he has committed for which he has not repented is in a **state of mortal sin**.

All sin offends God, and therefore all sin is evil. However, the Magisterium of the Catholic Church has always taught that there is a distinction between *mortal sin* and *venial sin*. Sacred Scripture also distinguishes between sins that bring death to the soul (mortal sins), and sins that offend God but do not bring death to the soul (venial sins):

> All wrongdoing is sin, but there is sin which is not mortal (1 John 5:17).

Not all sins are of equal gravity; some sins are more serious than others. Our Lord clearly affirmed this when He told Pontius Pilate, "He who delivered Me to you has the greater sin" (John 19:11).

The distinction between mortal and venial sin is also clear from natural reason. Saying an unkind word to one's neighbor is obviously less sinful than spreading terrible lies about one's neighbor. Eating too much ice cream is obviously far less sinful than committing adultery. It is common sense to recognize that, although all sins are bad, some are worse than others.

There are also differences in the *gravity of mortal sins*. Robbing a bank is a grave sin, but killing an innocent human being is even worse. The same can be said of venial sins. However, the worst venial sin is still far less evil than the least serious mortal sin, because mortal sins and venial sins differ in their very **essence** (what they are).

Jesus Is Condemned to Death, by Benjamin Stahl

The **effects of mortal sin** are devastating:

- total separation from God;
- the complete loss of sanctifying grace in the soul;
- spiritual death to the soul;
- the complete loss of charity in the soul;
- dramatically increased vulnerability to attacks from the devil (mortal sin destroys a person's spiritual immune system);
- an increased likelihood to commit other mortal sins; and
- eternal punishment in Hell if the person does not repent and return to God.

There are three conditions for a sin to be mortal (*Catechism*, 1857-1859):

- Grave matter
- Full knowledge
- Complete consent

We will now examine these three conditions more closely.

Grave Matter. Recall that three elements determine the morality of every human act: the object, the intention, and the circumstances. Every act in which the object is gravely evil constitutes grave matter, regardless of the intentions or the circumstances. **Grave matter** refers to any morally evil act that is serious in nature. **All grave sins are mortal sins if they are committed with full knowledge and complete consent.**

Most intrinsically evil acts involve grave matter. An **intrinsically evil act** is an act that is evil always, everywhere, and in all cases, because of its very nature. **Intrinsically evil acts that always involve grave matter** include abortion, adultery, blasphemy, contraception, embryonic stem cell research, euthanasia, human cloning, idolatry, infanticide, murder, sacrilege, sins of impurity, suicide, and others.

The gravity of some sins, however, depends on the degree to which the sin violates justice or injures charity. Stealing and lying are intrinsically evil acts, so they are *always sinful*. However, they do not always constitute grave matter, because their object is not always *gravely* evil. Stealing a candy bar is not grave, but stealing a car is. Lying to avoid hurting someone's feelings is not grave, but lying to destroy someone's reputation is.

> The gravity of sins is more or less great: murder is graver than theft. One must also take into account who is wronged: violence against parents is in itself graver than violence against a stranger (*Catechism*, 1858).

Certain acts can become gravely sinful because of the circumstances or intentions. Gambling is not in itself sinful. However, a man failing to provide for his family because he gambles away his paycheck not only sins, but *gravely* sins.

The opposite is *not* true: if the object is gravely evil, then neither the intentions nor the circumstances can lessen the gravity of the sin, although they can affect the person's culpability.

Full Knowledge. For an act to be a mortal sin, it must be done with **full knowledge**: there must be sufficient knowledge about the *moral quality* (moral good or evil) and *gravity* of the act. If a person truly does not know that something is a serious sin, then he is not guilty of mortal sin. If a person *pretends* not to know, however, his guilt is even greater, because he is effectively trying to deceive God.

Complete Consent. The final condition for an act to be a mortal sin is **complete consent**, which is consent that is deliberate enough to be a personal choice, meaning the person has freely and deliberately decided to perform the act. If someone is coerced into committing a sin, the voluntary nature of the sin is lessened. Depending on the level of coercion, the sin might no longer be considered mortal. If the coercion is mild, the sin would most likely remain mortal. If the coercion is grave, such as a threat of serious violence, then it is more likely that the sin would be venial. If no consent is given at all, there is no responsibility for sin.

Venial Sin

> Venial sin weakens charity; it manifests a disordered affection for created goods; it impedes the soul's progress in the exercise of the virtues and the practice of the moral good; it merits temporal punishment (*Catechism*, 1863).

Any actual sin that does not meet the threefold criteria for a mortal sin is a venial sin. A **venial sin** is any morally evil act that does not separate our soul from God, but that wounds our relationship with Him.

There are two main categories of venial sin:

- sins that do not constitute grave matter, and
- sins that constitute grave matter but that are not done with sufficient knowledge or consent to be mortal sins.

Many sins are venial because they are not serious enough to be mortal sins. For example, overeating is a sin, but it is generally venial, not mortal.

Some sins are venial because, although they involve grave matter, they are not done with sufficient knowledge or consent to be mortal sins. Such venial sins are still likely to have serious *natural consequences*, though, because they are gravely contrary to the Divine Law.

For example, the abuse of alcohol is grave matter, but if someone abuses alcohol because of intense emotional problems that significantly hinder his freedom, he might not be guilty of mortal sin. However, his actions will still likely hurt others, especially his own family—possibly quite seriously. He could even end up accidentally killing someone while driving under the influence of alcohol.

We must not have a cavalier attitude about venial sin. If we allow ourselves to continually commit venial sins without repenting of them, we will become more susceptible to falling into mortal sin. Venial sins weaken our will and make us more comfortable with committing sin. We must not give sin any foothold in our life. God wants us to love Him with our *all* of our heart, soul, mind, and strength.

> Deliberate and unrepented venial sin disposes us little by little to commit mortal sin (*Catechism*, 1863).

We should do our very best to avoid *all* sin. Then, if we fail, we will most likely have committed only a venial sin. By immediately repenting of every venial sin and continually striving to avoid all sin, we will decrease the likelihood of ever falling into mortal sin—the worst of *all* evils.

Punishment for Sin

> For the wages of sin is death, but the free gift of God is eternal life in Christ Jesus our Lord (Romans 6:23).

When a person works, he generally receives some wage, or payment, for that work. The wages for the "work" of venial sin is a *wound to the soul*. The wages for the "work" of mortal sin is *death to the soul*.

> For if God did not spare the angels when they sinned, but cast them into hell and committed them to pits of nether gloom to be kept until the judgment; if he did not spare the ancient world, but preserved Noah, a herald of righteousness, with seven other persons, when he brought a flood upon the world of the ungodly ... then the Lord knows how to rescue the godly from trial, and to keep the unrighteous under punishment until the day of judgment, and especially those who indulge in the lust of defiling passion and despise authority (2 Peter 2:4-10).

All sins, mortal and venial, incur some **temporal punishment** (punishment that does not last forever). Any unrepented mortal sin that a person has committed incurs **eternal punishment** (punishment that lasts for all eternity).

Temporal Punishment

> All who die in God's grace and friendship, but still imperfectly purified, are indeed assured of their eternal salvation; but after death they undergo purification, so as to achieve the holiness necessary to enter the joy of heaven (*Catechism*, 1030).

Temporal punishment is remedial; it helps purify us so that we may one day stand in the presence of God. The Sacrament of Penance does not remove all the temporal punishment due to sin. Some punishment remains for a time, just as some scars remain for a time after a person has been healed from a wound to the body.

The temporal punishment for our sins may take place on Earth or in Purgatory. The Church also offers us other means to lessen temporal punishment, including indulgences and, more recently, the Feast of Divine Mercy.

Eternal Punishment

> To die in mortal sin without repenting and accepting God's merciful love means remaining separated from him forever by our own free choice. This state of definitive self-exclusion from communion with God and the blessed is called "hell" (*Catechism*, 1033).

There is a Heaven, and there is a Hell. Anyone who dies in a *state of grace* will ultimately go to Heaven, although he may first need to be purified in Purgatory. Anyone who dies in a *state of mortal sin* will experience eternal punishment in Hell.

> The message of the Last Judgment calls men to conversion while God is still giving them "the acceptable time, … the day of salvation." It inspires a holy fear of God and commits them to the justice of the Kingdom of God (*Catechism*, 1041).

The gravity of mortal sin is evident from the Catholic Church's constant teachings. It is also evident from the witness of the saints, who did everything they could to avoid committing sin—many even dying a cruel death rather than sinning. As the young St. Dominic Savio proclaimed: "Death rather than sin!" **Death to the body, rather than death to the soul through sin!**

Remedy for Sin

> For if while we were enemies we were reconciled to God by the death of his Son, much more, now that we are reconciled, shall we be saved by his life. Not only so, but we also rejoice in God through our Lord Jesus Christ, through whom we have now received our reconciliation (Romans 5:10-11).

Despite all the warnings God has given us, and all the graces and gifts He has bestowed upon us, we still fall into sin. We still offend God. However, despite our sinfulness, God still remains merciful to us.

> But God shows his love for us in that while we were yet sinners Christ died for us. Since, therefore, we are now justified by his blood, much more shall we be saved by him from the wrath of God (Romans 5:8-9).

Our Lord Jesus Christ came upon this Earth to "bear witness to the truth" (John 18:37), to save our souls (John 3:16-17), to free us from the slavery of sin (John 8:31-36), and to establish His Kingdom (2 Samuel 7:12-13; Mark 1:14-15). He Himself is the Remedy for sin; there is no other. He Himself is the Way to the Father, the Gate through which His sheep enter His sheepfold (John 10:7-18, 14:6); there is no other. He Himself is "the Lamb of God, who takes away the sin of the world" (John 1:29); there is no other.

Weeping for Our Sins

St. John-Marie Vianney is honored as the patron saint of parish priests. He was born in Dardilly, France, in 1786, the fourth of six children.

St. John Vianney was not a good student, and he struggled greatly in the seminary. However, since there was a great shortage of priests after the French Revolution, he was permitted to remain in the seminary. He was ordained to the sacred priesthood in 1815. Because of his perceived deficiencies, he was assigned to a small, out-of-the-way parish in a little town called Ars, France. For this reason, he is often called the "Curė d'Ars," which means the Pastor of Ars.

In Ars, the saintliness of Father Vianney became evident to all. Soon, he was well-known as a holy confessor, and he often spent as many as 17 hours a day hearing confessions. People came from as far away as the United States to have Father Vianney hear their confessions and give them spiritual advice.

St. John Vianney would often weep while hearing confessions. One day, he was asked why he wept. He said he wept because the penitents did not weep for their sins. He also had the gift of reading souls. If a penitent did not remember all of his sins, or if he tried to hide some of them, St. John Vianney would know. He would then bring out the truth, and try to help the sinner to have true contrition for his sins and to make a good, holy confession.

St. John Vianney was very devoted to St. Philomena, and he had a shrine built in her honor. He also had great devotion to the Blessed Virgin Mary.

In His mercy, God has provided a way for the sons and daughters of Adam to be reconciled to Him. Through His suffering and death on the Cross and His Resurrection, Jesus Christ has won for us an incredible, precious gift: eternal life.

To receive this gift, we must believe in Him and be baptized, just as He commanded:

> "He who believes and is baptized will be saved; but he who does not believe will be condemned" (Mark 16:16).

Through the **Sacrament of Baptism**, we are freed from Original Sin, and we receive sanctifying grace in our soul. Whoever is baptized in the Name of the Father, and of the Son, and of the Holy Spirit is born again "in water and the Spirit" (John 3:5) and enters the *Church*, which is "the seed and beginning" of the Kingdom of Heaven on Earth (*Catechism*, 541). Through Baptism, he becomes an adopted son of God, dying to sin and rising to new life in Christ Jesus.

Baptism removes Original Sin. However, it does not remove our *inclination* to sin (concupiscence). To resist this inclination and remain in fellowship with God, we need to continually receive His grace through the Mass and the other sacraments, and cooperate with this grace by living a morally good life in obedience to God's Law.

> He who believes in Christ has new life in the Holy Spirit. The moral life, increased and brought to maturity in grace, is to reach its fulfillment in the glory of heaven (*Catechism*, 1715).

If a person commits a mortal sin after receiving the Sacrament of Baptism, he loses the gift of sanctifying grace in his soul—and therefore the gift of eternal life. However, God in His mercy has provided a further remedy: the **Sacrament of Penance**. When that person repents of his sins and makes a valid confession in the Sacrament of Penance, Our Lord and Savior Jesus Christ restores sanctifying grace to his soul. Through the Sacrament of Penance, he is reconciled to God and the Church, and he once again receives the gift of eternal life.

Jesus calls sinners to repentance, and He teaches us to pray for the Father's forgiveness and to forgive others (Matthew 6:9-15). Those who humble themselves before Him will obtain His mercy (Luke 18:9-14).

When Jesus died on the Cross, He offered Himself up as a loving Sacrifice to the Father in atonement for our sins, and He made it possible for us to be saved. To receive all the benefits of this Sacrifice, we must be united with Him in the sacraments, beginning with the Sacrament of Baptism, and continuing with the Sacrament of Penance, the Holy Eucharist, Confirmation, and the other sacraments according to our situation or state in life.

Jesus Christ is the **New Adam** (1 Corinthians 15:45). Unlike the first Adam, Jesus remained obedient to the Father in all things. If we are to please the Father, we must become like His beloved Son by living a morally good life in obedience to the Commandments, through the grace and fellowship of the Holy Spirit, Who sanctifies us (John 15:26).

The Confession, by Giuseppe Molteni

Likewise, the Blessed Virgin Mary is the **New Eve**. Just as the first Eve cooperated in the sin of the first Adam, Mary has cooperated in the work of Redemption of her Son, Jesus Christ, the New Adam.

Chapter 7 Review

Matching: For each statement, select the letter of the best term from the list below. There are more terms listed than there are statements, and no term can be used more than once.

A. angels	E. temptation	I. mortal sin	M. sin of omission
B. prophets	F. vice	J. grave matter	N. sanctifying grace
C. concupiscence	G. attraction	K. capital sin	O. original sin
D. demons	H. sin	L. venial sin	P. sin of commission

1. Any thought, word, deed, or omission that is contrary to God's Law: ________.
2. The first sin of Adam, in cooperation with Eve, at the beginning of the history of man: ________.
3. Spirits who are servants and messengers of God: ________.
4. An incitement to act contrary to God's Law, and thus to commit sin: ________.
5. The supernatural gift of God's presence in a person's soul, by which that person shares in the Divine Life of the Holy Trinity: ________.
6. A morally bad habit due to repeated sins in a particular moral area: ________.
7. A sin in which we neglect to do something that God has commanded: ________.
8. Spirits who are enemies of God: ________.
9. Any morally evil act that does not separate our soul from God, but that wounds our relationship with Him: ________.
10. Any morally evil act that is grave in nature, undertaken with full knowledge, and committed with complete consent: ________.

True or False: Write *True* or *False* for the following statements.

________ 11. There is no further remedy for a person who has committed a mortal sin after receiving the Sacrament of Baptism.

________ 12. Baptism removes Original Sin, as well as our inclination to sin.

________ 13. Unless we make some resolution with our will, we have not sinned.

________ 14. Even if someone dies in a state of mortal sin, he will not go to Hell, as long as he has faith in Jesus Christ.

________ 15. The Blessed Virgin Mary is the New Eve.

________ 16. Anyone who dies in a state of grace will ultimately go to Heaven.

________ 17. Willfully taking pleasure in a temptation is not sinful unless we act on that temptation in some external way.

________ 18. There is nothing more evil in the world than mortal sin.

________ 19. At the root of every sin is a lack of trust in God and disobedience toward Him.

Multiple Choice: Write the letter of the best answer in the space provided.

20. Moral evil exists because of which of the following? ________
    A. God created spirits and human beings to be free.
    B. Some of the spirits used their freedom to rebel against God, thereby introducing moral evil into creation.
    C. Adam and Eve, tempted by the devil, used their freedom to rebel against God, thereby introducing moral evil into the *visible* creation.
    D. All of the above
    E. None of the above

21. Sin is ________.
    A. Contrary to right reason
    B. Contrary to faith in God
    C. A lack of trust in God and His goodness
    D. An act of ingratitude
    E. All of the above

22. The effects of mortal sin include ________.
    A. Total separation from God
    B. The complete loss of sanctifying grace and charity in the soul
    C. Spiritual death to the soul
    D. Both A and B
    E. All of the above

23. Our Lord Jesus Christ came upon this Earth to ________.
    A. Bear witness to the truth
    B. Save our souls and free us from the slavery of sin
    C. Establish His Kingdom
    D. All of the above
    E. None of the above

24. Adam ________.
    A. Was the first man in all of creation
    B. Is the name used by Sacred Scripture to represent the first clan of human beings on Earth
    C. Was one of many human beings who roamed the Earth in ancient times, but the first with whom God directly communicated
    D. Is a symbolic term representing, not any specific person, but all mankind
    E. All of the above

25. The *soul* of Eve _________.
   A. Was taken from the side of Adam
   B. Evolved over billions of years
   C. Was created directly by God, out of nothing
   D. Was conceived in a state of Original Sin
   E Both A and D

26. _________ battled against Lucifer and cast him out of Heaven forever.
   A. Adam and Eve
   B. St. Michael the Archangel
   C. Our Blessed Mother
   D. St. Peter
   E. All of the above

27. The seven _________ are the chief sources of other sins.
   A. Actual sins
   B. Original sins
   C. Capital sins
   D. Mortal sins
   E. Venial sins

28. *Any* sinful act of the will: _________.
   A. Actual sin
   B. Original Sin
   C. Capital sin
   D. Mortal sin
   E. Venial sin

29. The state of _________ was inherited from Adam.
   A. Actual sin
   B. Original Sin
   C. Capital sin
   D. Mortal sin
   E. Venial sin

30. Sins that cry to Heaven for justice include _________.
   A. The blood of Abel, the sin of the Sodomites, and the cry of the people oppressed in Egypt
   B. The cry of the foreigner, the widow, and the orphan
   C. Injustice to the wage earner
   D. All of the above
   E. None of the above

31. Which of the following conditions *must* be met for a sin to be mortal: ________.
    A. Grave matter
    B. Full knowledge and complete consent
    C. It must be an intrinsically evil act.
    D. Both A and B
    E. All of the above

32. The ________ is the internal struggle we experience when we recognize that we cannot fulfill the desire with which we are being tempted, without compromising our morals.
    A. Occasion of temptation
    B. Conflict of temptation
    C. Resolution of temptation
    D. Aftermath of temptation
    E. None of the above

33. The ________ is the point at which we make a decision for or against committing the sin that we are being tempted to commit.
    A. Occasion of temptation
    B. Conflict of temptation
    C. Resolution of temptation
    D. Aftermath of temptation
    E. None of the above

34. The ________ is the person, place, or thing that arouses a desire in us to commit sin.
    A. Occasion of temptation
    B. Conflict of temptation
    C. Resolution of temptation
    D. Aftermath of temptation
    E. None of the above

35. The New Adam is ________.
    A. Jesus Christ
    B. All mankind
    C. The pope
    D. A symbolic term representing the new species into which the human race will have evolved, billions of years from now
    E. All of the above

36. Which of the following statements is correct? ________
    A. Some sins are venial because they do not constitute grave matter.
    B. Some sins are venial because, although they constitute grave matter, they are not done with sufficient knowledge or consent.
    C. Venial sins do not separate us from God, but they wound our relationship with Him.
    D. All of the above
    E. None of the above

37. One or more of the following three aspects of temptation have been behind all the sins ever committed since the first sin of Adam and Eve: ________.
    A. Sloth, ignorance, and gluttony
    B. Concupiscence, temperance, and uncertainty
    C. The lust of the flesh, the lust of the eyes, and the pride of life
    D. All of the above
    E. None of the above

38. Which of the following is a source of temptation? ________
    A. The world
    B. The flesh
    C. The devil
    D. All of the above
    E. None of the above

39. The temporal punishment for our sins may take place ________.
    A. In Heaven or Hell
    B. On Earth or in Purgatory
    C. Only if we have never received the Sacrament of Penance
    D. All of the above
    E. There is no temporal punishment for sin.

40. When a person receives the Sacrament of Baptism: ________.
    A. He dies to sin and rises to new life in Christ Jesus
    B. He receives sanctifying grace in his soul
    C. He is born again in water and the Spirit, and becomes an adopted son of God
    D. He enters the Church
    E. All of the above

Moses Presenting the Tablets of the Law, by Philippe de Champaigne

Section II: The Ten Commandments

Introduction

"You shall love the Lord your God with all your heart, and with all your soul, and with all your mind. This is the great and first commandment. And a second is like it, you shall love your neighbor as yourself. On these two commandments depend all the law and the prophets" (Matthew 22:37-40).

The foundation of the Moral Law is the *Ten Commandments.* God inscribed these Commandments on tablets of stone for His servant Moses. All moral precepts follow, either directly or indirectly, from the Ten Commandments.

Besides revealing moral requirements, the Ten Commandments protect us from evil. Just as we are commanded not to harm our neighbor, so our neighbor is commanded not to harm us. The Ten Commandments are the foundation of equal rights for all mankind.

This second section focuses on the Ten Commandments, along with several important conclusions that follow from them:

- Chapters 8 and 9 focus on the First Commandment.
- Chapter 10 discusses the Second and Third Commandments.
- Chapter 11 examines the Fourth Commandment.
- Chapter 12 discusses the Fifth Commandment.
- Chapter 13 discusses the Sixth and Ninth Commandments.
- Chapter 14 addresses the Seventh, Eighth, and Tenth Commandments.

The entire Moral Law, including the Ten Commandments, is summed up in the two Great Commandments of love: we must love the Lord our God with all our heart, all our soul, all our mind, and all our strength, and we must love our neighbor as ourselves. In order to truly fulfill these two Great Commandments, we must obey all the other Commandments. The first three Commandments focus on the love of God. The last seven Commandments focus on the love of neighbor.

Moses with the Tablets of the Law, by Guido Reni

Chapter 8. Faith, Hope, and Charity: The First Commandment

> "I am the Lord your God, who brought you out of the land of Egypt, out of the house of bondage. You shall have no other gods before me" (Exodus 20:2-3).

In the First Commandment, God reveals Himself as a loving, all-powerful, personal God. The first demand He makes is that we adore and serve Him *alone*. God created us, and He sustains us. It is right and just that we adore and serve only God, and that we have no other gods before Him (Deuteronomy 6:13-14).

In order to fulfill the requirements of the First Commandment, we must practice the theological virtues of faith, hope, and charity, and the moral virtue of religion.

Faith

> "Father, the hour has come; glorify thy Son that the Son may glorify thee, since thou hast given him power over all flesh, to give eternal life to all whom thou hast given him. And this is eternal life, that they know thee the only true God, and Jesus Christ whom thou hast sent" (John 17:1-3).

Our first step in serving and adoring God is to have *faith* in Him. **Faith is necessary for salvation.** For, "without faith it is impossible to please him" (Hebrews 11:6). **Faith** is the theological virtue by which we believe in God, and we accept everything He has revealed to us, as well as everything His Church teaches that we are to believe. God infuses the seeds of faith in us at Baptism. Faith comes from God and leads to God. It is the work of God's grace in us. At the same time, it is the fruit of our cooperation with this grace.

Qualities and Duties Concerning Faith

> "In faith, the human intellect and will cooperate with divine grace" (*Catechism*, 155).

Faith is not the same as knowledge. Our faith *rests on* the knowledge of God and the truths revealed to us for our salvation. However, knowledge is not enough. We must *decide* to accept the gift of faith and to believe in, trust, love, and obey God.

Our Lady the Spinner, by Feliks Cichocki-Nałęcz

Faith demands that we believe everything God has revealed to us, and live our lives accordingly. The **obedience of faith** (Romans 16:26) is man's free submission of himself, through faith, to the Authority of God, leading him to accept His Word, obey His Commandments, and remain faithful to His Church.

Our Lord Jesus Christ gives us the grace to respond to God with the obedience of faith, so that, like Him, we will please the Father in all things. To maintain, nourish, and strengthen our faith, we must cooperate with this grace and fervently hold onto the fear of the Lord. The **fear of the Lord** is the gift of the Holy Spirit that instills in us a fervent zeal to put God before all else, attentively listen to Him, and obey His commands.

We must put our faith into practice, and trust God above all else. We must also perform *acts of faith* and good deeds expressing our trust in God. Our faith in Him must be firm, steadfast, and unwavering.

> Faith by its specific nature is an encounter with the living God—an encounter opening up new horizons extending beyond the sphere of reason. But it is also a purifying force for reason itself.... Faith enables reason to do its work more effectively and to see its proper object more clearly (Pope Benedict XVI, *Deus Caritas Est* [Encyclical on Christian Love], December 25, 2005, no. 28a).

Whenever the glory of God, the salvation of souls, or the honor of the Church requires us to do so, **we must profess our faith** openly and honestly, regardless of the consequences (Fr. Laux, p. 55).

> If you confess with your lips that Jesus is Lord and believe in your heart that God raised him from the dead, you will be saved (Romans 10:9).

Sins against Faith

> The first commandment requires us to nourish and protect our faith with prudence and vigilance, and to reject everything that is opposed to it (*Catechism*, 2088).

There are several sins against the virtue of faith and the First Commandment. They include doubt, heresy, schism, apostasy, and infidelity.

Doubt. Faith is incompatible with doubt, just as light is incompatible with darkness. However, there is a difference between *voluntary* doubt and *involuntary* doubt (*Catechism*, 2088). **Voluntary doubt** is the willful rejection of a truth that God has revealed or that the Catholic Church teaches. **Involuntary doubt** is hesitation or difficulty in believing a truth that God has revealed or that the Catholic Church teaches.

Voluntary doubt is always gravely sinful. Involuntary doubt is generally not sinful or is a venial sin, depending on whether we have consented to it and the degree to which we are responsible for it (for example, if it is due to sloth or some other sin). However, it is a grave sin to deliberately or carelessly cultivate involuntary doubt—for example, by reading literature or watching movies that attack the Catholic Faith. We also sin if we fail to take the necessary steps to safeguard our faith and, when necessary, to combat such doubts.

If we experience an involuntary doubt, we should calmly confront it by making an act of faith affirming our belief in the truth that we are having difficulty with, and then move on. The inability to understand, or reconcile with other information we have, a truth that we accept in faith is a **difficulty**, not a voluntary doubt. We should not dwell on this difficulty or allow it to shake our faith. Voluntary doubts are sinful; difficulties are *not* sinful.

> "Ten thousand difficulties do not make one doubt" (Blessed John Henry Cardinal Newman, *Apologia pro Vita Sua*, 239, in *Catechism*, 157).

As long as we do not consent to this involuntary doubt, and we continue to accept the truth that we are having difficulty with, we are not sinning. However, if, because of our difficulty, we willfully reject this truth, then we have crossed over from a *difficulty* to a *voluntary doubt*, and we sin.

Heresy, Schism, and Apostasy. The fruit of voluntary doubt is the sin of **incredulity**, which is "the neglect of revealed truth or the willful refusal to assent to it" (*Catechism*, 2089). Incredulity manifests itself in three different ways: heresy, schism, and apostasy.

Heresy is "the obstinate post-baptismal denial of some truth which must be believed with divine and catholic faith" or "an obstinate doubt concerning the same" (*Catechism*, 2089). The Church distinguishes between two kinds of heresy: *material* and *formal.*

If a person is unaware that his position on some issue is contrary to the Catholic Faith, he commits **material heresy**. A person who holds such a position is still in a state of heresy, but he is not necessarily guilty of sin. Many Christians have been raised in a different tradition, and they do not know the Catholic Church's teachings. If, *through no fault of their own*, they hold beliefs contrary to these teachings, they have fallen into *material* heresy, but they are not guilty of sin because of this heresy. If, on the other hand, a person knows that his position on some issue is contrary to the Catholic Faith, but he embraces that position anyway, he commits **formal heresy**. Formal heresy is a grave sin.

Schism is the refusal to submit to the pope or to be in communion with the members of the Church who are subject to him (*Catechism*, 2089). It is a sin of *disobedience* to the authority that God has established.

Apostasy is the total rejection of Christianity by a person who has been baptized. It is a revolt against the Lord Jesus Christ Himself and His Church. Apostasy is the worst evil that a person can inflict upon himself, because he is rejecting the only Way there is to Heaven: Jesus Christ (Fr. Laux, p. 56).

Denying one's faith under torture, although still sinful, is *not* apostasy if the person continues to believe in his heart. *Concealing* one's faith for grave reasons is also not apostasy; in fact, it is not sinful at all. The early Christians hiding in the catacombs to avoid being put to death by the Romans were *not* sinning; they were being prudent.

Infidelity. An unbaptized person who does not believe in the Gospel of Jesus Christ is in a state of **infidelity**. Those in this state include all unbaptized persons who are **atheists** (who deny the existence of God), **agnostics** (who claim not to know whether God exists), or **Deists** (who believe in God, but reject His Providence in creation), as well as all other unbaptized persons who do not profess faith in Jesus Christ as the Son of God.

Pagans and **idolaters** (those who worship false gods) are also in a state of infidelity. **Polytheism** (belief in many gods) is a grave sin against the First Commandment. When the Israelites first inhabited the Promised Land, the people were commanded **not to even mention the names of false gods**:

> "Therefore be very steadfast to keep and do all that is written in the book of the law of Moses, turning aside from it neither to the right hand nor to the left, that you may not be mixed with these nations left here among you, or make mention of the names of their gods, or swear by them, or serve them, or bow down yourselves to them, but cleave to the Lord your God as you have done to this day" (Joshua 23:6-8).

The **New Age** movement purports to combine elements from different religions with Christianity. This religious movement effectively denies that there is one God, one Lord, and one Church. It is *not* compatible with Christianity, and it is very dangerous to the virtue of faith.

There are some religions that may appear to be Christian, but in reality are not, because they deny fundamental truths about Jesus Christ. For example, Mormons, Seventh Day Adventists, and Jehovah's Witnesses deny the fundamental truth that Jesus Christ is the Only Begotten Son of God, coeternal with the Father. "In the beginning was the Word, and the Word was with God, and the Word was God" (John 1:1).

Not everyone in a state of infidelity is guilty of mortal sin. Good people, without realizing it, can fall into serious errors regarding religious beliefs. One of the conditions for a sin to be mortal is *full knowledge*. Those who do not believe in the Gospel because they have never heard it are in a state of **negative infidelity**, and are not guilty of mortal sin. Those who hear and understand the Gospel but *refuse* to accept it are in a state of **positive infidelity**, and are guilty of mortal sin.

Dangers to Our Faith

> The Church, "the pillar and bulwark of the truth," faithfully guards "the faith which was once for all delivered to the saints"... (*Catechism*, 171).

The Catholic Faith is a gift from God. We must carefully guard our soul and avoid anything that can draw us away from this precious gift.

Temptations of Doubt. We should avoid anything that tempts us to entertain doubts about Catholic teaching or Sacred Scripture. Many versions of the Bible include comments. These comments are *not* part of Scripture itself, and are not guaranteed to be in accordance with the Magisterium, even if they claim to be "Catholic." They are simply the comments of that translation's editors. Some commentaries, such as the one in the Rev. Fr. Geo Leo Haydock edition of the Douay-Rheims Version of the Bible, are excellent because they are faithful to the teachings of the Church Fathers. Others can be very dangerous to souls, because they tend to plant seeds of doubt that can draw Catholics away from their trust in God, His Holy Word, and His Holy Church.

St. Jerome in His Study, by Domenico Ghirlandaio

Non-Catholic Religious Services. According to St. Alphonsus Liguori (in *Theologia Moralis*), we must not be present at the religious services of non-Catholics in such a way that **we would appear to be in communion with them** (Fr. Thomas Crean, "Praying with Non-Catholics – Is It Possible?" Feb. 8, 2009, in *Christendom Awake*; www.christendom-awake.org). The Church permits *passive* attendance (just being present) at weddings or funerals of non-Catholics. However, the Church could never sanction any activity that endangers or compromises our faith or Catholic identity.

Even *passive* attendance at a religious service outside the Catholic Church is sinful in some cases. For example, if a *Catholic* is married outside the Catholic Church without the proper dispensation from the Church, we are not permitted to attend. Our attendance would cause scandal by implying that we approve of an act of public disobedience to the Church. Therefore, we should always check with our confessor before attending any wedding or other religious service outside the Catholic Church.

Freemasonry. Even more dangerous to our faith is **freemasonry**, an anti-Christian system of morality and religion, upheld by a secret society organized into a federation of fraternal lodges. The Catholic Church forbids Catholics from supporting or participating in freemasonry, or any other society that has the following characteristics (Fr. Laux, p. 58):

- **Complete Secrecy.** Members must swear that they will never reveal the teachings or rituals of the lodge.
- **Oaths Promising Blind Obedience.** All must take a series of oaths, under pain of death, swearing, among other things, to blindly obey the leaders of the society.
- **Opposition to the Catholic Church.** Although the society often disguises its actual teachings in public, and even to lower-level members, a closer look at those teachings reveals an anti-Christian agenda.
- **Its Own "Religious" Worship.** The society uses Christian terminology to deceive lower-level members and the public, but the meanings that it assigns to those terms are actually the *opposite* of Christianity.

Knowingly supporting or participating in freemasonry, or belonging to any of the lodges or organizations affiliated with it, is a sin against the First Commandment.

Hope

> For thou, O Lord, art my hope, my trust, O Lord, from my youth. Upon thee I have leaned from my birth; thou art he who took me from my mother's womb. My praise is continually of thee (Psalm 71:5-6).

Our next step in serving and adoring God is to have *hope* in Him. **Hope** is the theological virtue by which we desire the happiness of eternal life with God in Heaven, and we trust in His promises and rely on His grace to lead us there. **Hope is necessary for salvation.** We must acknowledge God as the source of all good, and have confidence that He can help us attain that good. "I can do all things in him who strengthens me" (Philippians 4:13).

Hope always accompanies faith. If we truly believe that God is all-good, all-knowing, and all-loving, then we will place our hope in Him for our happiness. Through the virtue of hope, we approach everything from the perspective of our ultimate goal: happiness through union with God in Heaven.

> "Therefore do not be anxious, saying, 'What shall we eat?' or 'What shall we drink?' or 'What shall we wear?' For the Gentiles seek all these things; and your heavenly Father knows that you need them all. But seek first his kingdom and his righteousness, and all these things shall be yours as well" (Matthew 6:31-33).

Hope is "a sure and steadfast anchor of the soul" (Hebrews 6:19) and the "helmet of salvation" (1 Thessalonians 5:8).

Qualities and Duties Concerning Hope

> Hope is the confident expectation of divine blessing and the beatific vision of God; it is also the fear of offending God's love and of incurring punishment (*Catechism*, 2090).

The seeds of hope are infused in our soul at Baptism. We must cooperate with God's grace to maintain, nourish, and strengthen this hope in us. God knows and cares about each of us *personally*. If we are to draw close to Him, we must place our hope in Him, trusting that in His goodness He will reward us for seeking Him. "For whoever would draw near to God must believe that He exists and that He rewards those who seek him" (Hebrews 11:6).

As with faith, our hope must be a **living hope** (Fr. Laux, p. 60). We must express our hope by the way we live our life. God gives us hope so that we will keep our eyes fixed on the things of Heaven rather than on the things of this world.

> If then you have been raised with Christ, seek the things that are above, where Christ is, seated at the right hand of God. Set your minds on things that are above, not on things that are on earth (Colossians 3:1-2).

We must have a **firm and unwavering hope** (Fr. Laux, p. 60). We must strive with all our strength to persevere in faith and hope to the end, so that we may attain the salvation that Our Lord Jesus Christ won for us by His death on the Cross and Resurrection.

> Therefore, my beloved, as you have always obeyed, so now, not only as in my presence but much more in my absence, work out your own salvation with fear and trembling; for God is at work in you, both to will and to work for his good pleasure (Philippians 2:12-13).

When we have hope, we can rejoice even in the midst of suffering, knowing that He Who began a good work in us "will bring it to completion at the day of Jesus Christ" (Philippians 1:6).

> Rejoice in your hope, be patient in tribulation, be constant in prayer (Romans 12:12).

Our hope must be an **authentic hope**. Our confidence must be in God, not in ourselves. We need to guard our way by firmly holding onto the fear of the Lord and cultivating the virtue of humility. We must acknowledge that we need Our Lord and Savior Jesus Christ in order to get to Heaven. With His help, we can persevere in our hope, no matter what trials we face.

Sins against Hope

> The first commandment is also concerned with sins against hope, namely, despair and presumption (*Catechism*, 2091).

The two main sins against hope are despair and presumption. We must have trust in God and His mercy, and not give into *excessive* fear that we won't make it to Heaven. At the same time, we should have *sufficient* concern about the punishment for sin, to avoid being *overconfident* that we will go to Heaven. The happy medium is the virtue of hope.

Despair. When a person falls into **despair**, he no longer trusts in God for his salvation or for the forgiveness of his sins (*Catechism*, 2091). Despair is a grave sin because it denies God's goodness and justice, "for the Lord is faithful to his promises—and to his mercy" (*Catechism*, 2091).

The effects of despair can be devastating. Despair can lead to sadness in the soul, an abandonment of prayer, self-indulgence, and vulnerability to every vice. When someone gives into despair, the devil attacks him like a lion pouncing on a maimed animal. The result is spiritual disaster.

St. Maximilian Kolbe

Sometimes, people give up hope regarding some aspect of their earthly life. This type of despair is not as serious as despairing of one's salvation. However, failing to trust in God's Providence is still sinful and can lead to other sins and disorders.

The best way to avoid the sin of despair is to devote oneself to daily prayer, frequent reception of the sacraments, and meditation on the mercy of Our Lord Jesus Christ.

Presumption. When a person is overconfident about his salvation, he commits the sin of **presumption**. Presumption is a grave sin, and it is very dangerous. Whereas the person given over to despair is overcome with fear that he will never get to Heaven, the presumptuous person isn't really worried about it at all. He is sure that he will end up in Heaven. Such overconfidence can lead to carelessness in the spiritual life and a failure to avoid the near occasions of sin. The sin of presumption may take different forms, including the following:

- **Having Excessive Confidence in Oneself.** A person who thinks or acts as if he does not need God for his salvation is guilty of this type of presumption.
- **Presuming on God's Mercy.** God is merciful and forgiving, but we must not *presume* on His mercy and assume that He will overlook all our sins. "Do not be so confident of atonement that you add sin to sin" (Sirach 5:5).
- **Presuming on God's Power.** We must not be careless regarding the near occasions of sin and then assume that God will rescue us.
- **Intentionally Deferring Repentance.** Some people know they are sinning, but they don't want to give up their sins *just yet*. This is very foolish and dangerous. "Do not delay to turn to the Lord, nor postpone it from day to day; for suddenly the wrath of the Lord will go forth, and at the time of punishment you will perish" (Sirach 5:7).

Some Christians profess that once a person is "saved," he can be perfectly certain that he will go to Heaven, no matter what: "once saved, always saved." This teaching substitutes presumption for hope. The Catholic Church, as well as Sacred Scripture, firmly rejects this false teaching.

"Note then the kindness and the severity of God: severity toward those who have fallen, but God's kindness to you, provided you continue in his kindness; otherwise you too will be cut off" (Romans 11:22).

No Greater Love

"Greater love has no man than this, that a man lay down his life for his friends" (John 15:13). St. Maximilian Kolbe was a holy Franciscan priest who had a very large, successful publishing ministry in Europe and as far afield as Japan. St. Maximilian cultivated charity in his every act, making it the bedrock of his spiritual life. When the Nazis took over Poland, St. Maximilian became active in hiding persecuted Jews and helping them to safety. He and his fellow friars often hid refugees in their monastery.

St. Maximilian was also quite outspoken in his opposition to Nazi atrocities. Before long, he was arrested and sent to the notorious Auschwitz concentration camp, where more than a million innocent victims would lose their lives. As best as he could in this extremely difficult situation, St. Maximilian kept up his priestly ministry in service to his fellow inmates.

After an escape by several prisoners, the guards decided to execute ten random victims in retaliation. One of those chosen was a stranger to St. Maximilian by the name of Franciszek Gajowniczek. When this man heard his name called for execution, he cried out, "My wife! My children!" St. Maximilian was moved with pity for this husband and father. With amazing courage, the holy priest stepped forward and offered to stand in the place of Gajowniczek.

Placed in a bunker with nine others and left to starve to death, St. Maximilian was heard leading the others in constant hymns and prayers. After two weeks of starvation and dehydration, St. Maximilian was put to death by the Nazis through a lethal injection of carbolic acid.

Years later, Franciszek Gajowniczek, the man whose life was spared by St. Maximilian's heroic act, was present at the canonization ceremony of his rescuer. In honor of his heroic sacrifice, St. Maximilian Kolbe was designated by Pope John Paul II as a "martyr for charity."

The best remedies for the sin of presumption include the virtues of humility and obedience, steadfastness in the fear of the Lord, daily prayer, frequent Confession, and continued fellowship with the Lord Jesus Christ and His Holy Church.

Charity

"Hear, O Israel: The Lord our God is one Lord; and you shall love the Lord your God with all your heart, and with all your soul, and with all your might" (Deuteronomy 6:4-5).

The First Commandment also requires us to practice the virtue of *charity*. **Charity** is the theological virtue by which we love God above all else for His own sake, and we love our neighbor as ourselves for the sake of God. Without charity, it is impossible to please God. **Charity is necessary for salvation.**

Our charity may be perfect or imperfect. **Perfect charity** is loving God for His own sake because of Who He is. **Imperfect charity** is loving God because of what He has done for us or what we hope He will do for us. Either perfect charity or imperfect charity is sufficient to fulfill the First Commandment. However, perfect charity is a strong indication that a person is in union with God, Who is Love itself (1 John 4:8).

view of reality. The real face of pride is evident in all its ugliness when it drives a person to hate even God Himself.

Sometimes, persons experiencing great suffering express anger at God. This is not the same as hatred of God. A person experiencing serious emotional stress is likely to have limited freedom, making him less culpable for his sins. True hatred of God is not an emotional reaction, but rather a deliberate act of the will. It is a very grievous sin against the First Commandment.

We should make reparation for this grievous sin, and for all other offenses against the Sacred Heart of Jesus and the Immaculate Heart of Mary, by fervently expressing our **love for God** in all that we think, say, and do.

Apparition of Christ to the Virgin, by Filippo Lippi

Chapter 8 Review

Matching: For each statement, select the letter of the best term from the list below. There are more terms listed than there are statements, and no term can be used more than once.

A. faith	E. hope	I. charity	M. theoretical indifference
B. polytheism	F. formal	J. material	N. difficulty
C. agnostic	G. atheist	K. idolater	O. New Age
D. Deist	H. fear	L. hatred of God	P. practical indifference

1. Virtue by which we desire the happiness of eternal life with God in Heaven, and we trust in His promises and rely on His grace to lead us there: ________.
2. Belief in many gods, a grave sin against the First Commandment: ________.
3. Sin in which a person *believes* that it doesn't matter which religion one chooses: ________.
4. Someone who denies the existence of God: ________.
5. Sin in which a person *acts* as if his faith or religion doesn't matter, or he neglects to put them into practice in his life: ________.
6. Someone who claims not to know whether God exists: ________.
7. Virtue by which we believe in God and accept everything He has revealed to us, as well as everything His Church teaches that we are to believe: ________.
8. A ________ believes in God, but he rejects His Providence in creation.
9. If a person is unaware that his position on some issue is contrary to the Catholic Faith, he commits ________ heresy.
10. Someone who worships a false god: ________.
11. The ________ movement purports to combine elements from different religions with Christianity.
12. If a person knows that his position on some issue is contrary to the Catholic Faith, but he embraces that position anyway, he commits ________ heresy.
13. The inability to understand, or reconcile with other information we have, a truth that we accept in faith is a ________, not a voluntary doubt.
14. Extremely grave sin in which a person wishes harm to God Himself: ________.
15. The greatest of all the virtues: ________.

Matching II: For each statement, select the letter of the best term from the list below. There are more terms listed than there are statements, and no term can be used more than once.

A. apostasy	E. schism	I. infidelity	M. involuntary doubt
B. acedia	F. freemasonry	J. imperfect	N. fear of the Lord
C. lukewarmness	G. ingratitude	K. presumption	O. perfect
D. despair	H. heresy	L. indifference	P. voluntary doubt

16. The obstinate post-baptismal denial of some truth which must be believed with divine and Catholic faith, or an obstinate doubt concerning the same: ________.
17. Insufficient concern or conviction about one's faith or religion: ________.
18 Refusal to submit to the pope or to be in communion with the members of the Church who are subject to him: ________.
19. An anti-Christian system of morality and religion, upheld by a secret society organized into a federation of fraternal lodges: ________.
20. The total rejection of Christianity by a person who has been baptized: ________.
21. ________ charity is loving God because of what He has done for us or what we hope He will do for us.
22. Carelessness of heart, spiritual laxness, and insufficient vigilance in the spiritual life, leading to a type of spiritual depression: ________.
23. Sin in which a person is not sufficiently grateful to God for all the gifts and blessings that he has received from Him: ________.
24. An unbaptized person who does not believe in Jesus Christ and the doctrines of Christianity is in a state of ________.
25. Practical indifference is closely related to ________, which is a lack of zeal regarding serving God and obeying His Commandments.
26. Hesitation or difficulty in believing a truth that God has revealed or that the Catholic Church teaches: ________.
27. Sin in which a person no longer trusts in God for his salvation or for the forgiveness of his sins: ________.
28. Willful rejection of a truth that God has revealed or that the Catholic Church teaches: ________.
29. Sin in which a person is overconfident about his salvation: ________.
30. ________ charity is loving God for His own sake because of Who He is.

True or False: Write *True* or *False* for the following statements.

________ 31. Faith demands that we believe everything God has revealed to us, and live our lives accordingly.

________ 32. Venial sin destroys charity in a person's soul.

________ 33. Faith, hope, and charity are all necessary for salvation.

________ 34. The Catholic Church teaches that once a person is saved, he can be perfectly certain that he will go to Heaven.

________ 35. Only perfect charity fulfills the requirement for charity given by the First Commandment.

Multiple Choice: Write the letter of the best answer in the space provided.

36. Which of the following statements concerning doubts about the Catholic Faith is correct? ________
    A. All doubts, whether voluntary or involuntary, are gravely sinful.
    B. No doubts are sinful.
    C. All voluntary doubts are sinful.
    D. No doubts are gravely sinful.
    E. None of the above

37. ________ is the opposite of the zeal that accompanies the fear of the Lord.
    A. Lukewarmness
    B. Heresy
    C. Involuntary doubt
    D Schism
    E. All of the above

38. Knowingly supporting or participating in ________ is a sin against the First Commandment.
    A. Any lodge or organization affiliated with freemasonry
    B. Any society that has the following characteristics: complete secrecy, oaths promising blind obedience, opposition to the Catholic Church, and its own "religious" worship
    C. Any secular organization
    D. Both A and B
    E. None of the above

39. Which of the following is *permitted* by the Church? ________
    A. Participating in the religious services of non-Catholics, even if doing so endangers or compromises our faith or Catholic identity
    B. Passive attendance (just being present) at weddings or funerals of non-Catholics
    C. Being present at the religious services of non-Catholics in such a way that we would appear to be in communion with them
    D. Passive attendance at the wedding of a Catholic who is married outside the Catholic Church without the proper dispensation from the Church
    E. All of the above

40. Our charity must be ________.
    A. Complete
    B. Active
    C. Constant
    D. Generous
    E. All of the above

Chapter 9. The Virtue of Religion: The First Commandment

> "I am the Lord your God, who brought you out of the land of Egypt, out of the house of bondage. You shall have no other gods before me. You shall not make for yourself a graven image, or any likeness of anything that is in heaven above, or that is on the earth beneath, or that is in the water under the earth; you shall not bow down to them or serve them" (Deuteronomy 5:6-8).

The First Commandment requires us to adore God alone. Through the virtue of religion, we recognize God as the Supreme Being, Who has dominion over our life and eternal destiny, and we freely subject ourselves to Him through frequent acts of *worship*. **Religion** is the moral virtue by which we practice justice toward God. **It is the greatest of all the moral virtues** (*Summa*, II-II, q. 81, a. 6).

> The theological virtues of faith, hope, and charity inform and give life to the moral virtues. Thus charity leads us to render to God what we as creatures owe him in all justice. The *virtue of religion* disposes us to have this attitude (*Catechism*, 2095).

The **motives of religion** include our complete dependence on God, our debt of gratitude to Him, and our recognition of His glory and perfection as God (Fr. Laux, p. 65).

Acts of Religion

> "And now, Israel, what does the Lord your God require of you, but to fear the Lord your God, to walk in all his ways, to love him, to serve the Lord your God with all your heart and with all your soul, and to keep the commandments and statutes of the Lord...?" (Deuteronomy 10:12-13)

The **acts of religion** are the ways we practice the virtue of religion. They include adoration, penance, fasting, prayer, almsgiving, vows, and oaths.

Adoration

> Adoration is the first act of the virtue of religion. To adore God is to acknowledge him as God, as the Creator and Savior, the Lord and Master of everything that exists, as infinite and merciful Love (*Catechism*, 2096).

The first act of religion is adoration. **Adoration** (***latria***) is the highest form of worship, in which we submit ourselves completely to God, giving

Adoration of the Magi, by Hans von Kulmbach

our love and homage to the Supreme Being Who created us and upon Whom we depend entirely. **Only God may be the object of adoration.**

The Blessed Virgin Mary, the angels, and the saints may *not* be the object of adoration, because they are not God. However, in view of their intimate relationship with God, along with their goodness and holiness, it is fitting that they be the object of **veneration** (profound respect, honor, and devotion).

Our worship of God is *direct* when we adore and honor God Himself. Our worship of God is *indirect* when we honor Him by honoring the Blessed Virgin Mary, the angels, or the saints.

The veneration given to the angels and the saints is called ***dulia***. The angels and saints are servants of God, and Jesus affirmed that those who serve Him will be honored by His Father (John 12:26). When we honor them, we honor God, Who works through them. Asking for their help and prayers is a sign of humility. Just as we ask those on Earth to pray for us, we should ask the angels and saints in Heaven to pray for us. The best way to honor the angels and saints is to imitate them. By imitating God's servants, we grow in holiness and serve Him more faithfully.

The highest form of veneration, ***hyperdulia***, is reserved for the Blessed Virgin Mary. By embracing her unique, singular privilege of being the Mother of God, she cooperated with the work of our Redemption. Everything said about the angels and saints applies more so to Mary. Even Jesus was obedient to her when He was a child. By honoring Mary, we honor God.

We honor Mary, the angels, and the saints for the sake of God, but **we honor God for His own sake**. To God alone do we give adoration. We have a *duty* to adore God. He is our Creator, our Lawgiver, our Lord, our Redeemer, our Sanctifier, and our Savior.

Our worship of God must not be a mechanical process; it must come from the heart. At the same time, it must be expressed through external actions. Remember, every human being is the union of a body and a soul. Therefore, **it is fitting that we worship God with both our body and our soul.**

> I appeal to you therefore, brethren, by the mercies of God, to present your bodies as a living sacrifice, holy and acceptable to God, which is your spiritual worship (Romans 12:1).

Lex orandi, lex credendi. This is an ancient Latin saying, meaning "the law of prayer is the law of faith." The way we pray and adore God is not only an expression of our faith; it also *affects* our faith. When we adore God by kneeling or bowing down before Him, we express our faith that He is God, and at the same time we strengthen this faith. Knowing our human nature, Our Lord instituted the Mass and the sacraments, making it obligatory for everyone to worship God externally, as well as internally.

Penance and Fasting

> Jesus' call to conversion and penance, like that of the prophets before him, does not aim first at outward works, "sackcloth and ashes," fasting and mortification, but at the *conversion of the heart, interior conversion*. Without this, such penances remain sterile and false; however, interior conversion urges expression in visible signs, gestures and works of penance (*Catechism*, 1430).

Penance and fasting are important acts of religion as well. **Penance** is an interior conversion of the heart to God, expressed through acts of charity, sacrifice, and mercy. Whatever external sacrifices we make in performing acts of penance should be motivated by this interior conversion of the heart. "The sacrifice acceptable to God is a broken

Saint Teresa of Jesus, by Jose de Ribera

spirit; a broken and contrite heart, O God, thou wilt not despise" (Psalm 51:17). Among the expressions of this interior conversion of heart, three are absolutely necessary: *prayer*, *fasting*, and *almsgiving*, each of which is also an act of religion.

The most pleasing sacrifice to God is the Holy Sacrifice of His Son, Jesus Christ, on the Cross. If we unite our penances to this Sacrifice, they will be pleasing to God as well.

> The only perfect sacrifice is the one that Christ offered on the cross as a total offering to the Father's love and for our salvation. By uniting ourselves with his sacrifice we can make our lives a sacrifice to God (*Catechism*, 2100).

We must observe all the penances that the Church prescribes, including the days of fasting and abstinence, as well as any penances assigned to us during the Sacrament of Penance (Confession). We should also perform *voluntary* acts of self-denial, especially in those areas that can serve as near occasions of sin in our life.

> "Yet even now," says the Lord, "return to me with all your heart, with fasting, with weeping, and with mourning; and rend your hearts and not your garments." Return to the Lord, your God, for he is gracious and merciful, slow to anger, and abounding in steadfast love (Joel 2:12-13).

Penance is an essential part of being a follower of Our Lord Jesus Christ. Before we perform any significant voluntary act of self-denial, however, we should consult with our confessor, so that he can help us choose the most suitable penance for our situation and make sure we avoid doing anything that could be harmful to us.

Prayer

> *Prayer is a vital necessity*.... "Those who pray are certainly saved; those who do not pray are certainly damned" (*Catechism*, 2744).

Another essential act of religion is **prayer**, which is raising our mind and heart to God. **Prayer is necessary for salvation.** Prayer includes both *private prayer* and *public prayer*.

The three main **expressions of prayer** (ways of praying) are vocal prayer, mental prayer, and contemplative prayer. **Vocal prayer** is conversing with God. **Mental prayer** is meditating on God, and on the truths He has revealed through His Holy Word and His Holy Church. **Contemplative prayer** is quietly resting in the presence of the Lord.

The four main **acts of prayer** are adoration, thanksgiving, contrition, and petition. In **adoration**, we give worship, honor, and praise to God. In **thanksgiving**, we express our gratitude to God. In **contrition**, we express our sorrow to God for our sins, and we resolve not to sin again. In **petition**, we request favors from God.

> Out of the depths I cry to thee, O Lord! Lord, hear my voice! Let thy ears be attentive to the voice of my supplications! If thou, O Lord, shouldst mark iniquities, Lord, who could stand? But there is forgiveness with thee, that thou mayest be feared. I wait for the Lord, my soul waits, and in his word I hope; my soul waits for the Lord more than watchmen for the morning, more than watchmen for the morning (Psalm 130:1-6).

Some try to argue, for one reason or another, that prayer is not useful or worthwhile, but the Church rejects such false notions. These notions generally fall into two main categories: *chance* and *fate*. **Chance** claims that prayer is useless because everything in the world happens without any direction from a Supreme Being. **Fate** claims that prayer is useless because the outcome of everything in the universe is rigidly predetermined. Neither extreme is correct. God is Provident, and the entire universe is directed by Him. However, He also gives man a free will, so that he can freely decide what he will do. God knows our desires even before we express them, but He still wants us to use our free will to turn to Him in prayer.

There are two main reasons why we must pray: (1) because God wills that we pray; and (2) so that we may remain in fellowship with Him, upon Whom we depend for our salvation. It is impossible to have a relationship with God without spending time with Him. Jesus said we "ought always to pray and not lose heart" (Luke 18:1), and Sacred Scripture tells us to "pray constantly" (1 Thessalonians 5:17). We can do this by making our entire life a prayer to God, every day offering up to Him all our work, joys, trials, and suffering.

According to St. Augustine, "we may pray for whatever we may lawfully desire" (quoted by Fr. Laux, p. 69). We can ask for spiritual or temporal favors. We should also pray for our neighbor. Jesus even tells us to pray for our enemies (Matthew 5:44).

We should always try to pray with devotion, attentiveness, fervor, confidence, humility, obedience, and gratitude. Finally, we should pray in the Name of Jesus—the obedient, beloved Son, with Whom the Father is well-pleased.

Almsgiving

> "Every action done so as to cling to God in communion of holiness, and thus achieve blessedness, is a true sacrifice" (*Catechism*, 2099).

Just as God has been merciful to us, we must be merciful to others. This includes acting with compassion and charity toward those in need. The virtue of religion demands **almsgiving** (giving to the poor or others in need) and other *works of mercy*.

> Religion that is pure and undefiled before God and the Father is this: to visit orphans and widows in their affliction, and to keep oneself unstained from the world (James 1:27).

We have a duty to express our love for Jesus Christ by caring for the bodily and spiritual needs of our neighbor. The main ways in which we fulfill this duty are the *corporal works of mercy* and the *spiritual works of mercy*.

Corporal Works of Mercy. The seven **corporal works of mercy** are feeding the hungry, giving drink to the thirsty, clothing the naked, sheltering the homeless, visiting the sick, visiting the imprisoned, and burying the dead. When we serve others, we serve Jesus Christ in them. Every corporal work of mercy we perform is accepted by Jesus as an act of mercy done to Him. Every corporal work of mercy that we neglect to do will be treated by Jesus as something that we neglected to do for Him.

> "Then the King will say to those at his right hand, 'Come, O blessed of my Father, inherit the kingdom prepared for you from the foundation of the world; for I was hungry and you gave me food, I was thirsty and you gave me drink, I was a stranger and you welcomed me, I was naked and you clothed me, I was sick and you visited me, I was in prison and you came to me ... Truly, I say to you, as you did it to one of the least of these my brethren, you did it to me'" (Matthew 25:34-40).

Our works of mercy must be guided by prudence (Fr. Laux, pp. 123-125). For example, it generally would not be wise to invite a homeless man to live in our home. A more prudent way to provide for the homeless would be to support a homeless shelter in our community or perhaps to start an outreach in our church. We must not put our own family in danger in order to perform a work of mercy for someone else.

True Christian charity is not simply giving people what they want. For example, if a young woman wants money for an abortion or asks for a ride to an abortion facility, we must refuse her request, no matter what emotions our answer may evoke. Instead, we could offer to take her to the nearest pregnancy help center, where both she and her baby can receive true compassionate care. No matter how compassionate we may *feel*, if we depart from objective truth and goodness, our actions are not charity, but rather the opposite of charity. Our charity cannot be blind; it must be informed by truth and right reason. **Truth and love cannot be separated.**

St. Elizabeth of Hungary, by Hans Holbein the Elder

Spiritual Works of Mercy. The seven **spiritual works of mercy** are admonishing the sinner, instructing the ignorant, counseling the doubtful, comforting the sorrowful, bearing wrongs patiently, forgiving injuries, and praying for the living and the dead.

One of the spiritual works of mercy, admonishing the sinner, must sometimes be expressed through **fraternal correction**: an act of charity in which we warn our neighbor to turn away from some particular sin. Those in authority *must* practice fraternal correction toward those under their care. For example, parents must admonish their children, and bishops must admonish priests in their diocese. In all other cases, **we are to practice fraternal correction only when it is likely to profit our neighbor's soul** (Fr. Laux, p. 129).

> My brethren, if anyone among you wanders from the truth and someone brings him back, let him know that whoever brings back a sinner from the error of his way will save his soul from death and will cover a multitude of sins (James 5:19-20).

As with the corporal works of mercy, the spiritual works of mercy must be guided by prudence. In all cases, we must protect our soul from falling into sin. If performing a certain work of mercy is a near occasion of sin for us, then we are not the person that Christ wants to perform that particular work of mercy.

Tithes and Free-Will Offerings. Under the Old Law, the Israelites were required to pay tithes to God (Deuteronomy 14:22). The **tithe** was 10 percent of all "income," which was typically in the form of flocks or produce. The Israelites were also expected to make **free-will offerings** to God, voluntary offerings above and beyond the tithe (Exodus 36:3-4). Under the New Law, we are not required to devote any precise percentage of our income to almsgiving. However, **we are still required to provide for the Church, promote social justice, and give to the poor, according to our means**.

How much should we give? Frankly, the best rule of thumb is to *tithe* (give 10 percent of our income), if we are able. For those who would like to give more than 10 percent, they are free to do so. We should also remain open to making donations in addition to our tithe—that is, *free-will offerings*.

> The point is this: he who sows sparingly will also reap sparingly, and he who sows bountifully will also reap bountifully. Each one must do as he has made up his mind, not reluctantly or under compulsion, for God loves a cheerful giver. And God is able to provide you with every blessing in abundance, so that you may always have enough of everything and may provide in abundance for every good work (2 Corinthians 9:6-8).

Rules of Charity. The following rules can help guide our charity (Fr. Laux, pp. 125-126). First, in order to truly be able to love our neighbor, we must love our own soul. This is our *first duty* as a person created in the image and likeness of God. **We must never do anything, even in the name of charity, that would endanger the salvation of our soul.**

Second, we must not neglect the duties of our vocation in order to practice charity toward others. We should not ignore the needs of those outside our own family, but we must not neglect our family to save the world. "Charity begins at home."

> If anyone does not provide for his relatives, and especially for his own family, he has disowned the faith and is worse than an unbeliever (1 Timothy 5:8).

Third, we must provide for the needs of those closest to us first. Our family and close friends come before strangers. Our own country comes before other nations. This does not mean that we should neglect strangers or those outside our country. However, God has placed each of us in some particular place, and that is where our charity must begin. Our "mission field" does not end there, but it must begin there.

> So then, as we have opportunity, let us do good to all men, and especially to those who are of the household of faith (Galatians 6:10).

Fourth, we must act with charity toward our neighbor's *soul* (Jude 1:22-23). When a person's salvation is at stake, we must be willing to sacrifice our temporal goods to save him (1 John 3:16). Normally, we fulfill the obligation to care for our neighbor's soul by praying for him and giving him a good example. However, in some cases, we may be morally obligated to actually try to prevent him from sinning.

In rare occasions, we may even be called to make the supreme sacrifice, *our life*, for the sake of another's soul. If we regularly give of ourselves to others and remain in fellowship with Our Lord Jesus Christ, we will be better able to make this sacrifice if the situation should ever arise.

A few centuries before the coming of Christ, an old man named Eleazar was ordered, under pain of death, to eat swine's flesh (2 Maccabees 6:18), which was contrary to the Law of God at that time (the Old Law). When Eleazar refused, his acquaintances privately suggested that he should bring his own meat and *pretend* he was eating swine's flesh (2 Maccabees 6:21-22). However, for the sake of the souls of those who would be scandalized by such an example, Eleazar firmly rejected this suggestion:

> "Such pretense is not worthy of our time of life," he said, "lest many of the young should suppose that Eleazar in his ninetieth year has gone over to an alien religion, and through my pretense, for the sake of living a brief moment longer, they should be led astray because of me, while I defile and disgrace my old age. For even if for the present I should avoid the punishment of men, yet whether I live or die I shall not escape the hands of the Almighty. Therefore, by manfully giving up my life now, I will show myself worthy of my old age and leave to the young a noble example of how to die a good death willingly and nobly for the revered and holy laws." When he had said this, he went at once to the rack (2 Maccabees 6:24-28).

Fifth, the extent of the sacrifice we must make for our neighbor depends on his needs. We are generally obliged to give only from our abundance for the sake of our neighbor. However, if his very life is at stake, then we are obliged to share with him even what is necessary to suitably provide for our own needs. The *life* of our neighbor is more valuable than our comfort.

Vows

> A vow is an act of *devotion* in which the Christian dedicates himself to God or promises him some good work. By fulfilling his vows he renders to God what has been promised and consecrated to Him (*Catechism*, 2102).

A **vow** is a sacred act of devotion in which a person freely and deliberately dedicates himself to God or solemnly promises God to do some good work. Only someone who is mature enough to make suitable use of his reasoning powers is capable of making a vow.

A vow may be public or private. Examples of *public vows* include those made in the Sacraments of Baptism, Confirmation, Matrimony, and Holy Orders. A *private vow* is a sacred promise made to God to do some particular good work (Acts 18:18, 21:23-24). A vow made to the Blessed Virgin Mary or some other saint is actually a vow made to God in honor of Mary or that saint.

All vows to God are binding, under pain of sin. When a person fulfills his vows, he gives glory to God. If a person fails to fulfill a vow, he sins (Fr. Laux, p. 76).

If a vow was made for a certain period of time, the obligation of the vow ends when that time has elapsed. Otherwise, the obligation does not end unless one of the following conditions is met (Fr. Laux, pp. 76-77):

- it is impossible, unlawful, or useless to fulfill the vow;
- the person commanding the will of the one who made the vow intervenes (for example, a parent may intervene to free his or her child from a vow); or
- a lawful dispensation is given for just reasons.

The Marriage of the Virgin, by Philippe de Champaigne

A vow is a very serious act. **No one should make a vow unless** (1) he has spent sufficient time thinking about the consequences and implications of this vow; and (2) he has consulted with his confessor. At any time, we may decide to *increase* the scope of a vow we have made, but we should do so only after careful deliberation and consultation with our confessor. Whoever has the authority to dispense us from a vow may also lessen the scope of a vow (Fr. Laux, p. 77).

Oaths

> "An oath, that is the invocation of the divine name as a witness to truth, cannot be taken unless in truth, in judgment, and in justice" (*Catechism*, 2154).

An **oath** is a solemn act in which a person calls upon God as his witness that what he says is true and that he will do what he swears to do. Through this act, we acknowledge that we believe in God and that He is all-knowing, all-truthful, and all-just. God knows our deepest thoughts, and He neither deceives nor can be deceived.

As with making a vow, only someone who is mature enough to make suitable use of his reasoning powers is capable of taking an oath.

Oaths may be taken only for a serious reason, such as testimony in a court of law. Anything we swear to do must be in accord with the Divine Law, and whatever we say must be true. We have a sacred duty to keep all our oaths, as long as what we have sworn to do is not sinful.

If someone lies while under oath in a court of law, he commits the grave sin of **perjury**. Perjury shows great disrespect for God by invoking His Name as a witness to a falsehood. Perjury destroys faith and confidence among human beings, and it could cause serious injury to others.

Sins against Religion

> Little children, keep yourselves from idols (1 John 5:21).

There are several sins that are contrary to the virtue of religion and that violate the First Commandment. These sins fall into three main categories: superstition, irreligion, and atheism.

Superstition

> Superstition is a departure from the worship that we give to the true God. It is manifested in idolatry, as well as in various forms of divination and magic (*Catechism*, 2138).

Superstition is any practice that is contrary to the worship and devotion, in spirit and truth, that we are to give to the One True God. "Superstition in some sense represents a perverse excess of religion" (*Catechism*, 2110). The grave sins that fall under the category of superstition include idolatry, divination, and sorcery.

Idolatry. The First Commandment specifically forbids the grave sin of **idolatry** (adoring anything or anyone other than the One True God). This prohibition includes making **idols** (graven images worshiped as gods), which was a common practice among the nations surrounding Israel in Old Testament times.

> "Take heed to all that I have said to you; and make no mention of the names of other gods, nor let such be heard out of your mouth" (Exodus 23:13).

Idolatry is not restricted to the worship of graven images. Believing in or treating anything or anyone as a "god" other than the One True God is also idolatry. For example, Jesus warned not to put *money* (sometimes called "mammon") in place of God:

> "No one can serve two masters; for either he will hate the one and love the other, or he will be devoted to the one and despise the other. You cannot serve God and mammon" (Matthew 6:24).

Idolatry is a grave sin because it "rejects the unique Lordship of God," and hence is "incompatible with communion with God" (*Catechism*, 2113).

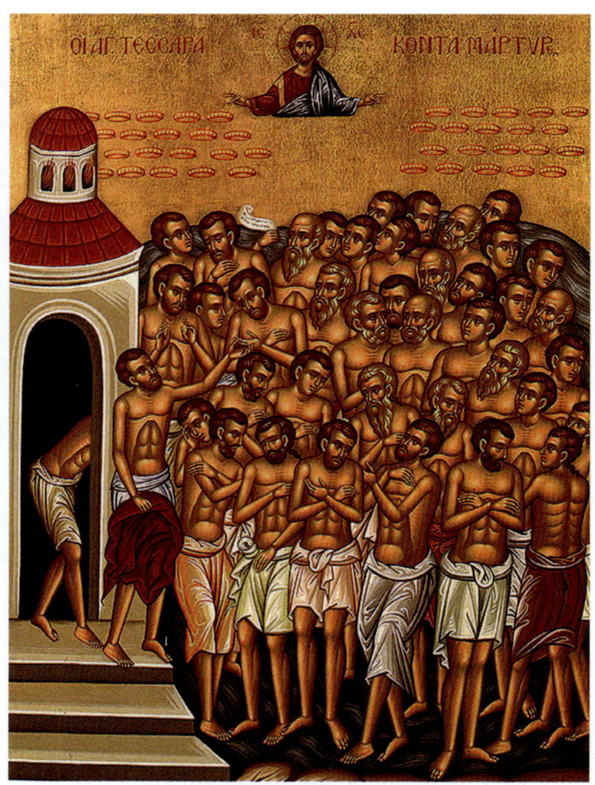

The Forty Martyrs of Sebaste

Divination. The sin of **divination** involves invoking evil spirits or the souls of the deceased to learn hidden things. Divination includes astrology, palm reading, tarot cards, fortune telling, consultation with so-called psychics, and other dark practices. All of these are evil, because they place faith and trust in something or someone other than God. They must be rejected. They are grave sins, and they are extremely dangerous.

> "When you come into the land which the Lord your God gives you, you shall not learn to follow the abominable practices of those nations. There shall not be found among you … anyone who practices divination, a soothsayer, or an augur, or a sorcerer, or a charmer, or a medium, or a wizard, or a necromancer. For whoever does these things is an abomination to the Lord; and because of these abominable practices the Lord your God is driving them out before you" (Deuteronomy 18:9-12).

The Forty Martyrs of Sebaste

In the winter of 320 A.D., the eastern parts of the Roman Empire were still ruled by anti-Christian pagans. Persecution was the penalty for those professing Christ. So it was that forty Christian soldiers belonging to Rome's 12th Legion, stationed in what is now modern Turkey, fell afoul of the authorities.

Their commander, Agricola, decided to force all his men to sacrifice to the Roman gods. When the forty Christians refused, Agricola threw them into prison, even though they formed an elite group in the bodyguard. The forty remained steadfast in their faith. So Agricola ordered them to be placed in the icy waters of a nearby lake until they were frozen to death. He also provided a warm bath for any who wished to save his life. Alas, one of the soldiers succumbed to this temptation, but he died just as he reached the warmth. The remaining thirty-nine soldiers stayed in the lake, singing psalms and praising God.

That night, one guard remained awake while his comrades rested. Suddenly, the guard, whose name was Aglaius, saw a brilliant light over the lake, with angels holding crowns above the heads of the martyrs. Aglaius was overcome by the sight. He woke the others and declared that he too was now a Christian. Knowing that the number forty was significant to Christians, he joined the others in the icy lake in order to complete the meaningful number.

The great light seen by Aglaius also served to warm the waters, so the forty soldiers did not freeze as planned. The next day, Agricola took them back to prison, where all of them, including Aglaius, were beaten to death. Their relics were preserved by pious Christians and distributed widely throughout the Eastern Empire.

The story of the Forty Martyrs of Sebaste is but one dramatic example of early Christians who died in obedience to the First Commandment. Temptations against this Commandment are always with us, of course. The idols of today may bear names such as pleasure, money, status, or power, but Christians are still called to refuse placing them before the Lord God.

Sacred Scripture also warns against placing one's trust in dreams.

> A man of no understanding has vain and false hopes, and dreams give wings to fools. As one who catches at a shadow and pursues the wind, so is he who gives heed to dreams (Sirach 34:1-2).

Sorcery. Magic and all other forms of **sorcery**, in which a person attempts to use supernatural powers to achieve some end (or goal), are also extremely dangerous. Even if the person's intentions are good, magic and all other forms of sorcery are *never* morally acceptable. They are grave sins against the First Commandment. **The end does not justify the means.**

Reading books, playing games, or watching entertainment that glorifies wizards, magicians, and so on can also be dangerous. It is sinful to approve (even implicitly) of practices that are evil in the sight of God. If the persons engaging in such evil practices appear to have good qualities or perform heroic acts, these forms of entertainment are even more dangerous, because they paint a false picture of good and evil. Good Christians will have nothing to do with them.

Irreligion

> Tempting God in words or deeds, sacrilege, and simony are sins of irreligion forbidden by the first commandment (*Catechism*, 2139).

Irreligion is any practice that directs a person away from rendering to God what He is owed in justice. Sins in this category include tempting God, sacrilege, and simony.

Tempting God. Testing, by words or deeds, the goodness or power of God is called **tempting God**. It is a grave sin against the First Commandment. "You shall not put the Lord your God to the test" (Deuteronomy 6:16). Behind this sin is often a lack of trust in God. It can also be related to the sin of *presumption*, in which a person acts in a reckless way and expects God to save him.

Sacrilege. The sin of **sacrilege** involves treating in an unworthy manner a person, place, action, or thing that is *holy*. It is a grave sin against the First Commandment. If the sacrilege is committed with contempt or malice, the sin is even greater.

Sometimes the word "holy" is used interchangeably with the word "righteous," but they do not mean the same thing. **Righteous** means morally upright and pleasing to God. **Holy** means sacred and set apart for God. Only *persons* can be *righteous*. However, any person, place, action, or thing consecrated to God is *holy*. For example, the altar, the chalice, the bells, the candles, and the vestments at Mass are all holy, as are the priest, the church building, Sacred Scripture, and the sacraments.

The opposite of righteous is *wicked*; the opposite of holy is *profane*. Something profane is not necessarily bad; it is just *common*, not set apart for God. The sidewalk is *profane*; anyone can walk on it. The tabernacle in the church is *holy*; it is set apart for God.

Those in a state of grace are *both* righteous and holy. They are righteous to the degree that they do what is right and do not sin. They are holy because the Blessed Trinity lives within them.

There are three *types of sacrilege*: personal, local, and real. A **personal sacrilege** is a sacrilege directed against a holy person. Abusing, striking, or killing a deacon, priest, bishop, or other person consecrated to God is a personal sacrilege.

In the Old Testament, an account of the patriarch David illustrates the importance of respecting a person who is *holy* because of his office (position), even if that person is not *righteous*. For a long time, David was being mercilessly pursued by King Saul, who out of jealousy was trying to kill him. One night, David and one of his men, Abishai, had an opportunity to sneak up on the king while he was sleeping (1 Samuel 26:3-7). Abishai encouraged David to kill Saul, and thus to finally put an end to the king's relentless attacks against him. However, David replied, "Do not destroy him; for who can put forth his hand against the Lord's anointed, and be guiltless?" (1 Samuel 26:9)

Saul was a wicked man, but his office as king, anointed by the prophet Samuel, was *holy*. Therefore, David still treated Saul with respect in virtue of this holy office, even though Saul was trying to kill him! No wonder David was called a man after God's own heart (1 Samuel 13:14).

A sacrilege directed against a holy place is called a **local sacrilege**. Stealing from or vandalizing a church or cemetery is a local sacrilege.

A sacrilege directed against a holy action or thing is called a **real sacrilege**. Administering or receiving the sacraments in an unworthy manner is a real sacrilege.

One of the most serious examples of a real sacrilege is **sacrilegious communion** (receiving Holy Communion while in a state of mortal sin). Sacrilegious communion is a grave sin against the Body, Blood, Soul, and Divinity of Our Lord Jesus Christ.

> Whoever, therefore, eats the bread or drinks the cup of the Lord in an unworthy manner will be guilty of profaning the body and blood of the Lord. Let a man examine himself, and so eat of the bread and drink of the cup. For anyone who eats and drinks without discerning the body eats and drinks judgment upon himself (1 Corinthians 11:27-29).

We should always examine our conscience before receiving Holy Communion. If we are aware of having committed any mortal sin since our last Confession, we must first confess this sin in the Sacrament of Penance before going to Holy Communion.

Simony. The sin of **simony** is an attempt to buy or sell spiritual goods. These spiritual goods may include indulgences, sacred offices, or spiritual gifts. Not only is simony a grave sin; it is also futile. It is impossible to buy or sell spiritual goods. They are from God, not man. God gives them freely; they are not for sale.

It is not sinful to make an offering in gratitude to the Church or a priest for baptizing a child or for offering a Mass. In doing so, we are not trying to buy spiritual goods. We are merely making an offering to help support the Church, and it is *voluntary*, not mandatory.

Atheism

> Since it rejects or denies the existence of God, atheism is a sin against the first commandment (*Catechism*, 2140).

One of the greatest evils that has become prevalent in recent decades is **atheism**, which is a denial of the existence of God. Atheism not only violates the First Commandment; it is also contrary to right reason. The existence of God can be known with certainty through reason alone, as St. Thomas Aquinas proved in several different ways (*Summa*, I, q. 2, a. 3). Without God, nothing else could ever possibly exist.

To deny that God exists requires denying all the revelations that He has given to man (both public and private), all the miracles that Jesus Christ performed in front of many witnesses, the many miracles that have occurred through the saints since then (including those in modern times, which science has been unable to explain or refute), the entire Word of God, the witness of all the martyrs who shed their blood for Christ, as well as the validity of the faith of billions of Christians throughout the world.

In practice, atheism is often closely related to idolatry. Those professing atheism tend to try to substitute something else in place of God as the source of their happiness, such as the State, money, sports, science, art, or the environment.

For example, **materialism** is a philosophy that accepts only physical matter as reality, and thus denies all spiritual realities. Because those who embrace materialism restrict their hopes and concerns to this life, they tend to seek their happiness in material possessions, which they try to substitute for God. As with all forms of atheism, materialism is a grave sin against the First Commandment.

Rationalism is the false teaching that all truth is based on reason alone, and hence not faith. Rationalism is the opposite of *fideism*. **Fideism** is the false teaching that all religious truth is based on faith alone, and hence not reason. The Catholic Church rejects both rationalism and fideism, as well as all forms of atheism. **The Catholic Church teaches that both faith and reason are gifts from God, which together can lead man to truth.**

Related to atheism is **agnosticism**, which is supposed uncertainty about whether God exists. As with atheism, agnosticism may come in many different forms. However, in practice, agnosticism is often equivalent to atheism.

> Agnosticism can sometimes include a certain search for God, but it can equally express indifferentism, a flight from the ultimate question of existence, and a sluggish moral conscience. Agnosticism is all too often equivalent to practical atheism (*Catechism*, 2128).

Some agnostics claim to be open to all possibilities, including the existence of God, but they typically live as if God did not exist. This is very foolish. For, if someone truly believes that God *might* exist, it would be far more prudent for him to act as if God *does* exist rather than to act as if He does not.

Veneration of Sacred Images and Relics

> Then Solomon began to build the house of the Lord in Jerusalem.... In the most holy place he made two cherubim of wood and overlaid them with gold.... He made an altar of bronze ... Then he made a molten sea ... Under it were figures of gourds ... It stood upon twelve oxen ... And he made ten golden lampstands.... Now when the priests came out of the holy place ... the house, the house of the Lord, was filled with a cloud ... for the glory of the Lord filled the house of God" (2 Chronicles 3:1–5:14).

In the First Commandment, God forbids making **idols** (graven images worshiped as gods). However, God does *not* forbid making *all* images. In fact, God *commanded* the Israelites to make the Ark of the Covenant (Exodus 25:10-16), images of cherubim (Exodus 25:18-20), and a bronze serpent (Numbers 21:8-9). Moreover, the Temple built by Solomon, which God clearly approved (as the quote above illustrates), included several carved images. Thus, it is morally acceptable to make images in order to honor God or adorn His House, as long as those images do not take the place of God.

In Old Testament times, God (Who is invisible) prohibited making any representation of Him, since He transcends all of creation and cannot be represented by any creature. However, because the Son of God became Man (and hence visible), it is now acceptable to make images of Jesus Christ, as well as of Our Blessed Mother, the angels, and the saints.

> By becoming incarnate, the Son of God introduced a new "economy" of images (*Catechism*, 2131).

Honoring these *sacred images* moves us to honor God, just as honoring the picture of a loved one moves us to honor that loved one. The Church condemns the grave error of **iconoclasm**, which is the rejection or destruction of sacred images because of the false teaching that such images are forbidden by God.

> The Christian veneration of images is not contrary to the first commandment which proscribes idols. Indeed, "the honor rendered to an image passes to its prototype," and "whoever venerates an image venerates the person portrayed in it." The honor paid to sacred images is a "respectful veneration," not the adoration due to God alone (*Catechism*, 2132).

The Church gives *inferior* and *relative* honor to sacred images of Jesus Christ, the Blessed Virgin Mary, and the angels and saints (Fr. Laux, p. 88). The Church does not *compel* anyone to kneel before such images, but the Church *allows* doing so, as long as the images themselves are not being worshiped. We must not pray *to* images. However, we may kneel or stand before them as we pray to God or ask for the assistance of His holy servants in Heaven.

In addition to sacred images, *relics* may be venerated. A **relic** is an object associated with a saint which the Church has confirmed as authentic and approved for veneration (for example, part of an article of clothing worn by the saint). Relics must be treated with honor and respect, and they must not be sold under any circumstances. They are sacred objects.

The veneration of relics was practiced from the very beginning of the Church, as evidenced by the veneration given to the bones of St. Ignatius of Antioch and St. Polycarp in the second century (Fr. Laux, p. 91). Even the shadow of St. Peter was an instrument of miracles in the early Church (Acts 5:15), and aprons and handkerchiefs that had touched St. Paul were used to bring about miraculous healings (Acts 19:11-12).

Finally, the words "adoration of the cross" are used in a *relative* sense only. We adore Our Savior Jesus Christ, Who died on the Cross, by *honoring* an image of the Cross in the church. A relic of the *True Cross*, however, receives actual adoration (*latria*), because it is stained with the very Blood of Christ. We do *not* adore the wood itself, but rather the Blood of Jesus *upon* the wood of the True Cross. **As Catholics, we adore God alone, and Jesus Christ is God.**

Saints Peter and John Healing the Lame Man, by Nicolas Poussin

Chapter 9 Review

Matching: For each statement, select the letter of the best term from the list below. There are more terms listed than there are statements, and no term can be used more than once.

A. almsgiving	E. vocal	I. penance	M. contemplative
B. mental	F. petition	J. contrition	N. acts of prayer
C. relic	G. religion	K. tolerance	O. works of mercy
D. *dulia*	H. *hyperdulia*	L. adoration	P. fraternal correction

1. The greatest of the moral virtues: ________.
2. An interior conversion of the heart to God, expressed through outward acts of charity, sacrifice, and mercy: ________.
3. ________ prayer is conversing with God.
4. The ________ are adoration, thanksgiving, contrition, and petition.
5. The highest form of veneration, which is reserved for the Blessed Virgin Mary: ________.
6. Act of charity in which we warn our neighbor to turn away from some particular sin ________.
7. Giving to the poor or others in need: ________.
8. ________ prayer is quietly resting in the presence of the Lord.
9. The veneration given to the angels and the saints: ________.
10. Act of prayer in which we express our sorrow to God for our sins, and we resolve not to sin again: ________.
11. ________ prayer is meditating on God, and on the truths He has revealed through His Holy Word and His Holy Church.
12. The corporal and spiritual ________ are the main ways in which we express our love for Jesus Christ by caring for the needs of our neighbor.
13. An object associated with a saint which the Church has confirmed as authentic and approved for veneration: ________.
14. The highest form of worship, in which we submit ourselves completely to God, giving our love and homage to the Supreme Being Who created us and upon Whom we depend entirely: ________.
15. Act of prayer in which we request favors from God: ________.

Matching II: For each statement, select the letter of the best term from the list below. There are more terms listed than there are statements, and no term can be used more than once.

A. holy	E. prayer	I. vow	M. righteous
B. rationalism	F. fideism	J. iconoclasm	N. tempting God
C. thanksgiving	G. irreligion	K. sorcery	O. superstition
D. divination	H. simony	L. idolatry	P. materialism

16. Any practice that directs a person away from rendering to God what He is owed in justice: ________.
17. Morally upright and pleasing to God: ________.
18. ________ is the grave sin of invoking evil spirits or the souls of the deceased to learn hidden things.
19. False teaching that all truth is based on reason alone: ________.
20. Grave sin in which a person attempts to use supernatural powers to achieve some end: ________.
21. Testing, by words or deeds, the goodness or power of God: ________.
22. Adoring anything or anyone other than the One True God: ________.
23. ________ is an attempt to buy or sell spiritual goods.
24. False teaching that all religious truth is based on faith alone: ________.
25. Any practice that is contrary to the worship and devotion, in spirit and truth, that we are to give to the One True God: ________.
26. Raising our mind and heart to God: ________.
27. Sacred and set apart for God: ________.
28. Rejection or destruction of sacred images because of the false teaching that such images are forbidden by God: ________.
29. Philosophy that accepts only physical matter as reality, and thus denies all spiritual realities: ________.
30. Sacred act of devotion in which a person freely and deliberately dedicates himself to God or solemnly promises God to do some good work: ________.

True or False: Write *True* or *False* for the following statements.

________ 31. Holiness is the same as righteousness.

________ 32. Atheism not only violates the First Commandment; it is also contrary to right reason.

________ 33. The Catholic Church teaches that both faith and reason are gifts from God, which together can lead man to truth.

________ 34. If a person fails to fulfill a vow, he has not committed a sin, but he has probably weakened his neighbor's trust in him.

_________ 35. We must never do anything, even in the name of charity, that would endanger the salvation of our soul.

Multiple Choice: Write the letter of the best answer in the space provided.

36. Which of the following statements about prayer is correct? _________
    A. Prayer is necessary for salvation.
    B. Prayer is useless because the outcome of everything in the universe is rigidly predetermined by fate.
    C. Prayer is useless because everything happens by chance, without any direction from a Supreme Being.
    D. All of the above
    E. None of the above

37. A sacrilege against a holy action or thing is called a _________.
    A. Personal sacrilege
    B. Real sacrilege
    C. Local sacrilege
    D. Material sacrilege
    E. None of the above

38. Which of the following is *not* correct? _________
    A. We must practice fraternal correction every time we become aware of some sin or fault of our neighbor.
    B. Just as God has been merciful to us, we must be merciful to others.
    C. Our charity must be informed by truth and right reason.
    D. We are required to provide for the Church, promote social justice, and give to the poor, according to our means.
    E. None of the above. They are all correct.

39. *Lex orandi, lex credendi* means: _________.
    A. "Laws must be organized and credible."
    B. "The king prays, and the king believes."
    C. "The law of prayer is the law of faith."
    D. "We pray with our soul, not our body."
    E. "We pray with our body, not our soul."

40. Which of the following is correct? _________
    A. The veneration of relics was practiced from the very beginning of the Church.
    B. In the First Commandment, God forbids making idols (graven images worshiped as gods). However, God does not forbid making all images.
    C. Because the Son of God became Man, it is now acceptable to make images of Jesus Christ, as well as of Our Blessed Mother, the angels, and the saints.
    D. The Church does not compel anyone to kneel before sacred images of Jesus, Mary, or the angels and saints, but the Church allows doing so, as long as the images themselves are not being worshiped.
    E. All of the above

Chapter 10. The Holiness of God: The Second and Third Commandments

"Holy, holy, holy is the Lord of hosts; the whole earth is full of his glory" (Isaiah 6:3).

THE LORD GOD IS HOLY, and He calls us to be holy as well (1 Peter 1:15-16). The Second and Third Commandments focus on the holiness of God and the reverence we must show Him. The Second Commandment requires us to revere God's Holy Name and all that is sacred. The Third Commandment requires us to show reverence for God's holy days.

Among all the words of Revelation, there is one which is unique: the revealed name of God. God confides his name to those who believe in him; he reveals himself to them in his personal mystery. The gift of a name belongs to the order of trust and intimacy (*Catechism*, 2143).

The Second Commandment

"You shall not take the name of the Lord your God in vain; for the Lord will not hold him guiltless who takes his name in vain" (Exodus 20:7).

The Name of God is holy, and we must always treat it with *reverence*. **Reverence** is an expression of deep respect and honor for someone or something that is holy or worthy of great esteem. In the Second Commandment, God commands us to revere His Holy Name, and He forbids us from taking His Name in vain.

A person takes God's Name in vain if he treats it as something less than sacred, something common. A person also takes the Name of God in vain if he does something evil while claiming to act in God's Name. It is also sinful to speak in an unworthy manner about any persons, places, actions, or things that are holy, because their holiness is a reflection of God's holiness. Thus, the Second Commandment governs our use of speech regarding all that is holy, but especially God's Holy Name.

The Holy Trinity in Heaven with the Blessed Mother
(from the Basilica of St. Michael, Innsbruck, Austria)

The reverence we must show for God's Name applies to the various ways we refer to God, such as "God," "the Lord," "Jesus Christ," and "the Holy Trinity." Whenever we speak of the All-Holy God, we must show reverence for His Holy Name.

Duties Related to the Second Commandment

> "The Lord's name is holy." For this reason man must not abuse it. He must keep it in mind in silent, loving adoration. He will not introduce it into his own speech except to bless, praise, and glorify it (*Catechism*, 2143).

St. Bernard, by El Greco

Our duty to revere the holiness of God is not restricted to what we say. In addition to guarding our speech, we must guard our actions, especially if we are speaking or acting in God's Name. We must show reverence for the holiness of all sacred persons, places, actions, and things. We must fulfill our sacred duty to keep our oaths.

In our modern culture, it is easy to lose the "sense of the sacred" (*Catechism*, 2144). We need to make an extra effort to restore this *sense of the sacred* in our heart and carefully guard it. We must make sure that all our speech and actions are fitting for a disciple and witness of the Lord Jesus Christ.

Guarding Our Speech. We must carefully govern our speech when speaking about God, Our Lord Jesus Christ, Our Blessed Mother, or the angels and saints. When we say the Name of Jesus, we should gently bow our head in reverence for "the name which is above every name" (Philippians 2:9). When we are in His presence, we should humble ourselves before Him, acknowledging Him as Our Lord and Savior, the Son of God.

> Therefore God has highly exalted him and bestowed on him the name which is above every name, that at the name of Jesus every knee should bow, in heaven and on earth and under the earth, and every tongue confess that Jesus Christ is Lord, to the glory of God the Father (Philippians 2:9-11).

Guarding Our Actions. Even if we do not sin with our words, we sin if our actions while using God's Name are unworthy of Him. We also sin if we fail to acknowledge God when we are acting in His Name, taking the credit ourselves rather than giving the glory to God.

When the Israelites complained to Moses in the desert because of their thirst, God instructed Moses to strike a rock with his rod

The Holy Name of God

Sometimes things happen that seem to elicit a forceful exclamation of some sort. Great care must be taken to leave God out of your comments when you accidentally hit your thumb with a hammer or meet with some other painful experience! After all, God did not cause your aching hand, and it is not His fault that you were careless. Perhaps it would be best to limit yourself to a quiet "Oh, that hurt!" and then find something else to do that does not involve the use of a thumb or a hammer.

As with all the Commandments, there is a positive side to the equation. Simply avoiding the disrespectful use of the Holy Name of God does not take full advantage of the opportunities for growth in virtue. A good point to remember is that virtually all the services and prayers of the Church begin with an invocation of God's Name: "In the Name of the Father, and of the Son, and of the Holy Spirit."

Many saints, including St. Anselm of Canterbury and St. Bernard of Clairvaux, have written extensively about the Holy Name. Feasts were established in the liturgical calendar specifically for the purpose of honoring the Name of God. The early English mystic Richard Rolle stated: "If you think on the Name of Jesus continually and hold it stably, it purges your sin and kindles your heart." He summed up his teaching by referring to the Holy Name as a "healing ointment" for the soul.

Any act of charity is a wonderful practice, but the value is much enhanced when the act is specifically connected to the Name of God. No public proclamation is necessary; you may simply say to yourself, "I will give this Christmas turkey to a poor family in the Name of Jesus!" Or "In the Name of the Holy Trinity, I will help my elderly neighbor with his yard work today."

In the ancient world, knowledge and use of a person's name was held to forge a powerful bond with that person. The same holds true for those who respectfully and prayerfully invoke the Holy Name of God.

and command it to yield water, so that water would miraculously flow from it (Exodus 17:6, Numbers 20:8). However, before he struck the rock, Moses said in anger to the people: "Hear now, you rebels; shall we bring forth water for you out of this rock?" (Numbers 20:10)

Moses was the servant of God, and he was acting in God's Name and through God's power. However, in his anger, he failed to revere God as holy. Moreover, he seems to have given the credit for this miracle to himself and his brother Aaron rather than to God ("shall *we* bring forth water?"). God punished Moses by not allowing him to enter the Promised Land (Deuteronomy 32:48-52), explaining that it was "because you broke faith with me" and "did not revere me as holy in the midst of the people of Israel" (Deuteronomy 32:51).

Sometimes we may be provoked to anger by the sins of others, and we could end up getting in heated debates with them about matters related to our Catholic Faith. We must be careful not to rashly act in anger while attempting to speak in God's Name. As Christians, we are witnesses of what it means to be a disciple of Jesus Christ. God will hold us accountable if we do not revere Him as holy before others. It was on account of the sins of the people, who kept grumbling against him, that Moses became angry and ended up sinning against the Lord's Holy Name (Deuteronomy 1:37). However, God still held Moses accountable. **We are responsible for our own actions, even if they are provoked by others.**

Showing Reverence for What is Holy. We must be mindful of the holiness of all sacred persons, places, actions, and things. All the sacraments are sacred, as is the Holy Sacrifice of the Mass, and they must be treated as such. Sacred Scripture is the Holy Word of God, and we must treat it with reverence at all times. Every Catholic church is a holy place consecrated to God. When we are in a Catholic church, we should keep a reverential silence, ever mindful that we are in the House of God. When we receive Holy Communion, we should approach the altar reverently, and walk back to our pew in the same way. We must also respect sacramentals and other sacred objects, such as rosaries, crucifixes, and holy cards.

Fulfilling Our Sacred Duty to Keep Oaths. An **oath** is a solemn act in which a person calls upon God as his witness that what he says is true and that he will do what he swears to do. Our Lord warned against taking oaths carelessly or too often:

> "Again you have heard that it was said to the men of old, 'You shall not swear falsely, but shall perform to the Lord what you have sworn.' But I say to you, Do not swear at all.... Let what you say be simply 'Yes' or 'No'; anything more than this comes from evil" (Matthew 5:33-37).

Our Lord is not forbidding taking any oaths whatsoever. We are not forbidden from taking a solemn oath before a court of law or a legitimate authority. However, we must not make *frequent* use of oaths through the course of our daily lives. A person's word must be true in *all* that he says, not only when he takes an oath. Jesus would not forbid taking all oaths, because God had already said that we *should* swear by His Name:

> "You shall fear the Lord your God; you shall serve him, and swear by his name" (Deuteronomy 6:13).

There are four moral requirements we must meet regarding taking oaths (Fr. Laux, pp. 75-76):

- **Judgment.** We may take an oath only for a grave reason.
- **Justice.** Anything we swear to do must be in accord with the Divine Law.
- **Truth.** Whatever we say under oath must be true.
- **Fidelity.** We have a sacred duty to keep all our oaths, as long as what we have sworn to do is not sinful. (If a person swears to do something sinful, he is *not* allowed to keep that oath, because it is never morally permissible to sin.)

Oaths should be made **only when they are absolutely necessary**, and only if they meet the above conditions. An oath is a sacred act of the virtue of *religion*, and an important part of a just society that fears and honors God. It must be treated with sacredness.

Sins against the Second Commandment

> The second commandment *forbids the abuse of God's name*, i.e., every improper use of the names of God, Jesus Christ, but also of the Virgin Mary and all the saints (*Catechism*, 2146).

The Name of God is holy, and it must never be used for an evil purpose or in an evil way, under any circumstances. The sins against the Second Commandment include infidelity to promises or oaths made in God's Name, blasphemy, profanity, and any other misuse of God's Holy Name. In the Our Father, we pray that God's Name will be **hallowed** (revered as holy). We must strive to always live by these words in everything we say and do.

Infidelity to Promises or Oaths. When we make a promise or oath in God's Name, we "engage the divine honor, fidelity, truthfulness, and authority" (*Catechism*, 2147). We must keep this promise or oath, as long as what we have promised or sworn is not sinful. If a person is not faithful to an oath or promise that he has made to God, he sins against the Second Commandment by misusing the Holy Name of God.

Blasphemy. The grave sin of **blasphemy** is any willful expression by word, thought, or deed directed against God with the intention of dishonoring, defying, harming, or offending Him. Since Jesus Christ is both God and Man, it is possible to harm Him in His *human* nature. For example, if someone intentionally desecrates the Holy Eucharist, it is an extremely grave sin of blasphemy against God.

It is also sinful to direct blasphemies against the Catholic Church, the Blessed Virgin Mary, the angels and saints, or any other person, place, thing, or action that is holy.

Profanity. Another sin against the Second Commandment is the use of **profanity**, which is speech concerning what is sacred without due reverence. Uttering profanities does not fall under the category of blasphemy, provided that such profanities are not uttered with intentional contempt for God or for anyone or anything sacred to Him. However, using profanity is still sinful. The gravity of this sin depends on the degree to which it shows disrespect toward what is sacred.

Profanity is contrary to the charity that we should have for God and our neighbor. The same can be said of crude, coarse, and vulgar language, which are degrading to culture and society.

> Do not accustom your mouth to lewd vulgarity, for it involves sinful speech. Remember your father and mother when you sit among great men; lest you be forgetful in their presence, and be deemed a fool on account of your habits.... A man accustomed to use insulting words will never become disciplined all his days" Sirach 23:13-15).

God calls us to be pure and edifying in our speech and actions, reverent toward His Holy Name, and sensitive to the delicacy of our soul and that of our neighbor. We must always strive to speak the truth with love, purity, and reverence.

> Let no evil talk come out of your mouths, but only such as is good for edifying, as fits the occasion, that it may impart grace to those who hear. And do not grieve the Holy Spirit of God, in whom you were sealed for the day of redemption (Ephesians 4:29-30).

If we hear someone else speaking profanity, we should make an act of reparation by quietly saying, "Blessed be the Name of God," or other suitable words. In fact, we can receive a partial indulgence for doing so. If we hear coarse language, we should quietly say a Hail Mary, "Jesus is Lord," or some other prayer to protect the purity of our soul and to make reparation to God.

The Third Commandment

> "Remember the Sabbath day, to keep it holy. Six days you shall labor, and do all your work; but the seventh day is a Sabbath to the Lord your God; in it you shall not do any work … for in six days the Lord made heaven and earth, the sea, and all that is in them, and rested the seventh day; therefore the Lord blessed the Sabbath day and hallowed it" (Exodus 20:8-11).

God requires trust and devotion from His people, whom He created in His image. A **covenant** is a sacred agreement and bond between God and one or more persons, or between two persons or groups under God. The **Old Covenant** was the sacred agreement and bond between God and the people of Israel. In this covenant, the people of Israel agreed to obey God's Law, as revealed in the *Old Law*. Under the Old Covenant, the people of Israel were required to keep holy the **Sabbath** (the seventh day of the week, Saturday). Just as God rested on the seventh day from His work in creating the universe (Genesis 2:2), His people were to refrain from work on the seventh day of the week.

When Our Lord Jesus Christ rose from the dead "on the first day of the week" (Mark 16:2), Sunday, He ushered in a *New Creation*. The day on which Jesus rose from the dead was the "eighth day" of the Old Creation, "when the

Adoration of the Magi, by Peter Paul Rubens

A Christmas Miracle

It was December 1914. World War I, "the war to end all wars," had already become the stalemate of the trenches. Millions of soldiers—French, English, Bavarian, German, Scot, and many others—suffered the danger, discomfort, mud, and cold of living in badly constructed holes in the frozen ground. The war that was supposed to end in a matter of weeks had become a war that would drag on for four more horrible years. Yet, in the midst of the misery, a miracle occurred with virtually no precedent: the Christmas Truce of 1914.

No one knows for certain just how it began, but many accounts speak of the strains of Stille Nacht ("Silent Night") coming from the German trenches early on Christmas Eve. A group of Scottish Highlanders responded by singing the carol in English. Soon, Adeste Fideles ("O Come, All Ye Faithful") rang out, with both sides joining in the Latin hymn. A German officer was heard pleading that there be no more shooting that night or the day after. Junior officers met in the devastation of no-man's land between the trenches and agreed on a truce—a truce sanctioned by no one in higher command, save God Himself. One estimate of the numbers involved gives a figure of no fewer than one hundred thousand soldiers!

In virtually no time at all, groups of soldiers from both sides began to congregate between the trenches, exchanging souvenirs and gifts, including some delicacies from the Christmas packages they had received from home. A soccer ball was found, triggering a match, which most agree was won by the Germans, 3-2.

More soberly, the chaplains from each army met and jointly provided decent burial for all the dead between the lines who could be recovered at no other time. Arrangements were made for proper Christmas services to be held, both Catholic and Protestant. Ruined barns were soon transformed into chapels; efforts were made to decorate and insulate them against the pervasive cold. Unbelievably, soldiers from several warring states peaceably celebrated the Savior's birth together in complete harmony!

Of course, generals were outraged, and some courts-martial were held on both sides of the conflict. At least one priest was severely reprimanded by his bishop and sent home to England. Nevertheless, for one brief moment on one of the holiest days of the year, Heaven miraculously reigned over a small corner of the Earth.

sabbath was past" (Mark 16:1), and the first day of this New Creation.

> The stone which the builders rejected has become the head of the corner. This is the Lord's doing; it is marvelous in our eyes. This is the day which the Lord has made; let us rejoice and be glad in it (Psalm 118:22-24).

Those born anew through Baptism are part of this New Creation. We are bound, not by the Old Covenant, but by the *New Covenant.* This **New Covenant** is the sacred agreement and bond between God and all baptized Christians. The signs and instruments of the New Covenant are the Mass and the seven sacraments. In the

New Covenant, the requirement of the Third Commandment to keep holy the Sabbath is fulfilled by our keeping holy the first day of the week (Sunday), the **Lord's Day**.

As members of this New Covenant, we are bound to show reverence for the Lord's Day, as well as all holy days of obligation. The Third Commandment prescribes two primary duties on Sundays and holy days of obligation: *worship* and *rest*. We must give God the worship He is owed in justice. We must refrain from any work or other activities that deprive us of the rest that God requires on His holy days, the joy befitting these days, or the ability to perform works of mercy.

> In the first place, therefore, Sunday is the day of rest because it is the day "blessed" by God and "made holy" by him, set apart from the other days to be, among all of them, "the Lord's Day" (Pope John Paul II, *Dies Domini* [Apostolic Letter on Keeping the Lord's Day Holy], May 31, 1998, no. 14).

We should also try to celebrate Sundays and all holy days in a way that is worthy of their sacredness. Celebrating God's holy days in a merely secular way, rather than truly honoring the Lord Jesus Christ, His Blessed Mother, and the saints, makes such celebrations empty and neglects to show God the reverence and gratitude He deserves. We are called to holiness and light (Ephesians 5:8-17), and we must treat all of God's holy days with reverence.

Sunday Worship

> The Sunday Eucharist is the foundation and confirmation of all Christian practice. For this reason the faithful are obliged to participate in the Eucharist on days of obligation, unless excused for a serious reason (for example, illness, the care of infants) or dispensed by their own pastor. Those who deliberately fail in this obligation commit a grave sin (*Catechism*, 2181).

The Catholic Church requires the faithful to attend Mass on Sundays and holy days of obligation. This is one of the **precepts of the Church**, which all Catholics are bound to obey:

1. Attend Mass and rest from servile labor on Sundays and holy days of obligation.
2. Confess your sins at least once a year.
3. Receive the Sacrament of the Holy Eucharist at least during the Easter season.
4. Observe the days of fasting and abstinence established by the Church.
5. Help provide for the needs of the Church.
6. Observe the laws of the Church concerning Holy Matrimony.

As Christians, we are all called to pray. Prayer includes both *private prayer* and *public prayer*. Private prayer naturally leads to collective prayer (where two or more are gathered in the Name of Jesus), and collective prayer naturally leads to public prayer (Fr. Laux, p. 72). In the Catholic Church, this public prayer is incorporated in her public worship, which is called the **Liturgy**.

The center of the Catholic Church's public worship is the Holy Sacrifice of the Mass. Sacred Scripture teaches, and the Catholic Church affirms, that the Holy Sacrifice of Jesus Christ on the Cross happened once, for all people and for all times (1 Peter 3:18). At every Mass, during the Consecration, this same Holy Sacrifice is made present again on the altar.

> At the altar all the barriers of time and space that separate the "three great provinces of the kingdom of God," the Church militant, suffering, and triumphant, are removed, each taking part, according to its needs and powers, in the blessings of the Eucharistic Sacrifice (Fr. Laux, p. 73).

On Sundays and holy days of obligation, Catholics throughout the world come together and join in public worship. In this public worship, we adore God, we hear His Word, we celebrate the Sacred Mysteries of our Faith, and we have the opportunity to receive the Holy Eucharist. Missing Mass on any of these days without a serious reason (sickness, natural disasters, etc.) or lawful dispensation is a grave sin.

Sunday Rest

> On Sundays and other holy days of obligation, the faithful are to refrain from engaging in work or activities that hinder the worship owed to God, the joy proper to the Lord's Day, the performance of the works of mercy, and the appropriate relaxation of mind and body (*Catechism*, 2185).

God is pleased when we have a good work ethic, in which we work hard, are diligent in performing our tasks, and devote ourselves to the occupation He has given us. However, He is not pleased if we disobey the Third Commandment by working on Sunday.

The Lord's Day is holy. It is the day of the glorious Resurrection of Jesus Christ from the dead. (It is also the day when the Holy Spirit descended upon the Apostles at Pentecost.) Therefore, we must keep **holy** (sacred and set apart for God) the Lord's Day, as well as every holy day of obligation. We do so chiefly by attending the Holy Sacrifice of the Mass, and by refraining from "those works and activities which could impede such a sanctification of these days" (*Catechism*, 2042). If we treat Sunday just like any other day, we *profane* the Lord's Day, and we sin.

We should also avoid doing anything that encourages others to work unnecessarily on Sunday. It is one thing to make a short trip to a grocery store to buy a few necessary items that unexpectedly run out, such as medicine, diapers, or bread. It is another thing to reserve Sunday as the day when we go to our favorite department store. Sunday is the *Lord's* Day, and we must treat it as such.

Pentecost, by El Greco

> Sanctifying Sundays and holy days requires a common effort. Every Christian should avoid making unnecessary demands on others that would hinder them from observing the Lord's Day (*Catechism*, 2187).

> In spite of economic constraints, public authorities should ensure citizens a time intended for rest and divine worship. Employers have a similar obligation toward their employees (*Catechism*, 2187).

Activities Not Forbidden on Sunday. Works of mercy, such as caring for the sick, the elderly, or the homeless, are acceptable and good at all times. Such works are particularly suitable on the Lord's Day. Sunday is also a good day to spend time relaxing with one's family.

> Christians will also sanctify Sunday by devoting time and care to their families and relatives, often difficult to do on other days of the week. Sunday is a time for reflection, silence, cultivation of the mind, and meditation which furthers the growth of the Christian interior life (*Catechism*, 2186).

A person may be legitimately excused from the obligation to observe the Sunday rest, for the sake of important social services or family needs, as long as doing so does not lead to habits that are contrary to the virtue of religion, or that harm family life or health (*Catechism*, 2185). Likewise, certain traditional activities such as sports and restaurants require some people to work on Sunday (*Catechism*, 2187). In order to provide social necessities to the community, many police officers, firemen, nurses, doctors, and others have to work on Sunday as well. However, they all must try to observe the Lord's Day as best as they can, including their obligation to attend Mass.

In countries where attending Mass on Sunday is not possible (for example, because of a hostile government), people must still try to observe the Lord's Day somehow, at least privately (*Catechism*, 2188). On their part, governments and employers have a moral obligation to ensure that people have sufficient time for rest and worship on Sunday.

The True Spirit of Our Sunday Rest. God's own "rest" on the Sabbath was not *inactivity*; He is always acting in His Love and Providence. This rest was God's loving gaze on the beauty of His creation, especially on the crown jewel of this creation, the human person (*Dies Domini*, no. 11).

Thus, it is fitting for us to contemplate the beauty of God's creation on the Lord's Day, *in addition to* fulfilling our obligation to worship God in the Holy Sacrifice of the Mass. It is also fitting to spend time relaxing and being with our family. Likewise, it is fitting to reach out to our neighbor in need.

Keeping the Lord's Day sacred does *not* mean keeping it *somber*. On the contrary, the Lord's Day should be *joyful*. Experiencing joy, fun, and laughter (provided that we do so in a way that is wholesome) is not contrary to holiness.

Recreational activities such as running, hiking, playing sports or games, attending social functions, watching wholesome movies, and so forth can also be beneficial to us in some way. God created us, and He knows we need some periods of rest and recreation to help us be more ready and fit to do the work we must do in our daily lives. However, we must make sure that these recreational activities are not near occasions of sin or harmful in any way, and that they are suitable for the Lord's Day.

Sundays and holy days of obligation are days to adore God in the Holy Sacrifice of the Mass. They are days to love God and love our neighbor with the joy of Christ. They are days to pray and rest and know the Lord. They are days when God calls us to contemplate His glory: "Be still, and know that I am God" (Psalm 46:10).

Chapter 10 Review

Matching: For each statement, select the letter of the best term from the list below. There are more terms listed than there are statements, and no term can be used more than once.

A. Liturgy	E. heresy	I. work	M. profanity
B. Sunday	F. Saturday	J. reverence	N. hallowed
C. covenant	G. rest	K. blasphemy	O. Judicial Law
D. contract	H. oath	L. anger	P. New Creation

1. The Third Commandment prescribes two primary duties on Sundays and holy days of obligation: worship and ________.
2. Any willful expression by word, thought, or deed directed against God with the intention of dishonoring, defying, harming, or offending Him: ________.
3. A sacred agreement and bond between God and one or more persons, or between two persons or groups under God: ________.
4. In the New Covenant, the requirement of the Third Commandment to keep holy the Sabbath is fulfilled by our keeping holy the Lord's Day, which is ________.
5. In the Our Father, we pray that God's Name will be ________ (revered as holy).
6. The public worship of the Catholic Church: ________.
7. A solemn act in which a person calls upon God as his witness that what he says is true and that he will do what he swears to do: ________.
8. An expression of deep respect and honor for someone or something that is holy or worthy of great esteem: ________.
9. When Our Lord Jesus Christ rose from the dead, He ushered in a ________.
10. Speech concerning what is sacred without due reverence: ________.

True or False: Write *True* or *False* for the following statements.

________ 11. The center of the Catholic Church's public worship is the Holy Sacrifice of the Mass.

________ 12. If our actions are provoked by others, God will not hold us accountable for those actions.

________ 13. Uttering profanities does not fall under the category of blasphemy, and hence is never sinful.

________ 14. Governments and employers have a moral obligation to ensure that people have sufficient time for rest and worship on Sunday.

________ 15. It is not a sin to work on Sunday, as long as we are diligent and honest in our work.

Multiple Choice: Write the letter of the best answer in the space provided.

16. According to the *precepts of the Church*, all Catholics must ________.
    A. Attend Mass and rest from servile labor on Sundays and holy days of obligation
    B. Confess their sins at least once a year
    C. Receive the Sacrament of the Holy Eucharist at least during the Easter season
    D. Observe the days of fasting and abstinence established by the Church
    E. Help provide for the needs of the Church
    F. Observe the laws of the Church concerning Holy Matrimony
    G. All of the above

17. The day on which Our Lord Jesus Christ rose from the dead was ________.
    A. Sunday
    B. Saturday
    C. The "eighth day" of the Old Creation
    D. The first day of the New Creation
    E. All except B

18. Our duty to show reverence for the holiness of God includes ________.
    A. Guarding our speech
    B. Guarding our actions, especially if we are speaking or acting in God's Name
    C. Showing reverence for the holiness of all sacred persons, places, actions, and things
    D. Fulfilling our sacred duty to keep our oaths
    E. All of the above

19. Which of the following statements regarding taking oaths is *not* correct? ________
    A. We may take an oath only for a grave reason, and anything we swear to do must be in accord with the Divine Law.
    B. All oaths are forbidden by God.
    C. Whatever we say under oath must be true.
    D. We have a sacred duty to keep all our oaths, as long as what we have sworn to do is not sinful.
    E. If a person is not faithful to an oath that he has made to God, he sins against the Second Commandment by misusing the Holy Name of God.

20. Which of the following is *never* permitted on Sunday? ________
    A. Treating it just like any other day
    B. Relaxing with one's family
    C. Performing works of mercy
    D. Contemplating the beauty of God's creation
    E. Laughing and having fun

Chapter 11. Honor and Duty: The Fourth Commandment

"Honor your father and your mother, that your days may be long in the land which the Lord your God gives you" (Exodus 20:12).

God has given man a participation in His authority, and this participation is manifested in four main areas: the *family*, the *Church*, the *State*, and the *workplace*. We have specific duties in each of these areas. The common thread that links all of these duties together is *honor*. **Honor** is distinction, respect, and esteem, in virtue of one's office, one's character, or one's accomplishments.

There are three main reasons why we should **honor** (treat with distinction, respect, and esteem) certain persons: their **office** (the position of authority or distinction that they hold), their **character** (their moral identity, which is the net effect of all their moral choices, good and bad), or their accomplishments.

The Holy Family with the Infant St. John, by Niccolo Frangipane

Honor and Duty in the Family

> Whoever honors his father atones for sins, and whoever glorifies his mother is like one who lays up treasure (Sirach 3:3).

A **family** is the lifelong union of one man and one woman under God, along with their children. Some different forms of family relationships are possible (for example, due to the death of a spouse). However, this is "the normal reference point by which the different forms of family relationship are to be evaluated" (*Catechism*, 2202).

The family is the domestic church, the foundation of society, and the heart of the nation. Our Lord sanctified the family by raising marriage to the dignity of a sacrament. In the family, God has given authority to both the father and the mother, and He commands that they be honored. The Fourth Commandment ("Honor your father and mother") is *unconditional*; children must honor their father and mother because of their *office* as parents. If a child is blessed with parents who are morally upright, then, in addition to the honor he owes them because they are his parents, he also owes them honor because of their morally upright *character*.

Children must also honor their grandparents and other family members, according to their respective positions in the family. However, the authority of the father and mother over the children takes precedence over the authority of all others in the family.

The Holy Family
(German, c. 18th century, artist unknown)

The Roles God Has Ordained for Husband and Wife

> The family is the *original cell of social life*. It is the natural society in which husband and wife are called to give themselves in love and in the gift of life. Authority, stability, and a life of relationships within the family constitute the foundations for freedom, security, and fraternity within society (*Catechism*, 2207).

When a man and a woman join together in marriage, God calls them to give themselves entirely to each other, and to cooperate with Him as His instruments in creating new life. **As husband and wife, they have equal dignity under God.** First, they each have the dignity that is proper to every human being: the dignity of being a person created in the image and likeness of God. Second, they have a special dignity in virtue of being chosen by God to be the father and mother of the children whom He has placed in their care, whether through natural means or through adoption.

Although a husband and wife have equal dignity, they have different roles, both in terms of how they relate to each other and regarding their primary contributions to the family. God established these different roles when He created the first man and woman, and He has consistently confirmed them, both in Sacred Scripture and through the Church.

The Role of a Husband and Father. In God's loving plan, **the head of the family is the father**. This authority refers not only to spiritual matters, but to all matters concerning the family. However, spiritual leadership is the most important, because it affects the sanctification of souls. God has ordained that the man is to gently and humbly lead his wife and children, just as Jesus Christ leads the Church.

A Husband's Responsibility toward His Wife. A man and a woman joined together in marriage are one. The man is the *head*, not the master, of his wife. **God commands every husband to love his wife as Jesus Christ loves the Church.** Just as Jesus Christ and His Bride, the Church, are one, so too are a man and a woman in marriage.

> Husbands, love your wives, as Christ loved the church and gave himself up for her.... He who loves his wife loves himself. For no man ever hates his own flesh, but nourishes and cherishes it, as Christ does the church, because we are members of his body (Ephesians 5:25-30).

How is a husband to love his wife? He is to follow the example of Our Lord Jesus Christ, and *serve her*. Our Lord washed the feet of His disciples as an example of what it means to lead, and He said that we must do the same (John 13:12-17). Jesus Christ is God Almighty, yet even He said, "I am among you as one who serves" (Luke 22:27). So too must a man serve his wife.

Jesus said, "Greater love has no man than this, that a man lay down his life for his friends" (John 15:13). That is how a man is called to love his wife. He must be willing to lay down his life in loving service for the sake of her happiness and salvation. A husband is called, not only to be the head of his wife, but also her protector, her defender, her advocate, her best friend, and her loving companion.

The Role of a Wife and Mother. Just as the head of the family is the father, **the heart of the family is the mother**. She is the one, primarily, who sets the mood of the home, and it is her warmth and sacrificial love that most clearly demonstrate that the family is more than just a society of persons living together.

A wife is the companion and helpmate of her husband (Genesis 2:18-24). At the same time, she is the mother of the family and has authority over her children. A good father will not allow his children to be disrespectful to their mother. He will confirm her authority over them, insisting that they honor her.

A mother's authority over her children is not delegated to her by her husband; it comes directly from God. No one, including her husband, can take away that authority. If a man neglects his duty as the head of the family, the woman must take his place in directing the family, while still striving to maintain the structure of the family ordained by God.

> For the Lord honored the father above the children, and he confirmed the right of the mother over her sons (Sirach 3:2).

The beauty of a woman adorned with "the imperishable jewel of a gentle and quiet spirit" (1 Peter 3:4) and the impact that she can have on the lives of her husband and their children are too great to express in words. The glory of a woman who fears the Lord is like a garden of flowers giving off a fragrant aroma throughout the entire family. She deserves to be praised, loved, and honored all the days of her life.

> Charm is deceitful, and beauty is vain, but a woman who fears the Lord is to be praised. Give her the fruit of her hands, and let her works praise her in the gates (Proverbs 31:30-31).

A Wife's Responsibility toward Her Husband. God has ordained that a woman is to humbly follow her husband, just as the Church humbly follows the Lord Jesus Christ. To understand how a wife should treat her husband, we need only look at how the Church treats Jesus Christ: She reveres His Word, honors Him, and respects Him. **That is how God calls a wife to treat her husband.** One of the ways a wife most perfectly honors Jesus is by honoring the authority of her husband. When a woman honors and respects her husband, she can inspire him to become greater than he ever would have become without her standing by his side.

> Wives, be subject to your husbands, as to the Lord. For the husband is the head of the wife as Christ is the head of the church, his body, and is himself its Savior. As the church is subject to Christ, so let wives also be subject in everything to their husbands (Ephesians 5:22-24).

In the Holy Family, we see the perfect model of what a family should be. St. Joseph was a just man, a holy man, and a good man. However, he could never be as great as the Blessed Virgin Mary, the most perfect human being ever created. Joseph is a saint, but Mary is the Mother of God! Yet, even *she* was submissive to her husband.

When the angel appeared to St. Joseph and told him to take the Child and his wife to Egypt, St. Joseph led, and Mother Mary humbly followed. When it was safe for them to return to the land of Israel, it was St. Joseph, not Mary, who received the message from the angel. Since even a woman as great as the Blessed Virgin Mary humbly submitted to the authority of her husband, every wife should do the same.

There are limits to a husband's authority over his wife, however. Their relationship is not that of a parent and a child, but rather of two loving companions joined together in a sacred bond. If a husband asks his wife to do something that is contrary to right reason, her dignity as a woman, or the teachings of the Catholic Church, she is not obligated to do what he asks. In fact, if he asks her to do something sinful, she *must* refuse.

The Authority and Responsibility of Parents

> Parents have the first responsibility for the education of their children. They bear witness to this responsibility first by *creating a home* where tenderness, forgiveness, respect, fidelity, and disinterested service are the rule. The home is well suited for *education in the virtues*. This requires an apprenticeship in self-denial, sound judgment, and self-mastery—the preconditions of all true freedom (*Catechism*, 2223).

Parents have the authority and duty to govern and care for every aspect of their children's lives. They are responsible for the entire welfare of their children, both temporal and spiritual. They must initiate their children into the Catholic Church and ensure their continued development in the Faith. They must make sure their children know the teachings of the Church, receive the sacraments, and attend Mass. They must teach them, by word and example, to be faithful disciples of Jesus Christ and to obey the Commandments. They are obligated to positively affirm good behavior in their children and to reasonably chastise bad behavior.

It is critical that parents stress the importance of moral uprightness, good character, and fidelity to Jesus Christ and His Holy Church more than they stress appearance, intellectual ability, talent at sports, financial success, and so forth. "Better is a poor man who walks in his integrity than a rich man who is perverse in his ways" (Proverbs 28:6).

There are three simple truths that all parents should make sure their children know: (1) their parents love them, (2) their parents are in charge and must be respected and obeyed by them, and (3) their parents want them to always do what is right and to be faithful to Jesus Christ and His Church, no matter what. Blessed are the children who know these three truths. Blessed are the parents whose children live by them.

Parents are the primary educators of their children. Education begins at home in the school of Christian charity. Parents must ensure that their children learn everything they need to succeed in this life and to be able to get to Heaven. They must teach their children good morals by word and example.

Parents also have the right and responsibility to determine how their children will receive their formal education—whether through homeschooling, private school, or some other means. Any law that denies this right, or that attempts to transfer to the State the parents' authority to determine how to educate their children, is unjust and injurious to the good of society.

Even if parents decide to send their children to a school for their formal education, they are still the primary educators of their children. Teachers and school administrators have a moral obligation to consult parents on all matters concerning their children, especially regarding morals, personal issues, and religion. Parents have a responsibility to be involved in their children's education and to be vigilant about the curriculum they allow for their children. Children have the responsibility to treat their teachers respectfully, and to obey them, as long as what their teachers ask is not sinful and does not contradict a higher authority—namely, their parents, the Church, or God.

The Duty of Children to Honor Their Parents

> The divine fatherhood is the source of human fatherhood; this is the foundation of the honor owed to parents. The respect of children, whether minors or adults, for their father and mother is nourished by the natural affection born of the bond uniting them. It is required by God's commandment (*Catechism*, 2214).

The honor that children owe their parents includes three duties: obedience, respect, and charity. Children owe **obedience** to their parents because of their authority. Children must obey their parents in all things, as long as what their parents ask them to do is not sinful. Children must obey their parents *promptly* (without delaying) and *cheerfully* (without complaining).

A child's duty to obey his parents remains until (1) he becomes an adult, and (2) he leaves the home and begins supporting himself (Fr. Laux, p. 149). If either of these conditions is not met, the duty of obedience remains. It is generally best for a child to remain at home until he is an adult. However, if, for some reason, a child lives with other guardians (such as grandparents or older brothers or sisters), he must be obedient both to his parents and those guardians—but the authority of his parents must come first, as long as what they ask is not sinful.

Once a child becomes an adult *and* leaves the home and begins supporting himself, he is no longer required to obey his parents. However, he should consult with them and seek their advice before making that decision (Fr. Laux, p. 149).

Unlike obedience, the duties of respect and charity never end. Children must show respect for their parents, simply because they

An Obedient Daughter

St. Rose of Lima, born Isabel de Flores y del Oliva, was the daughter of a Spanish soldier and colonist in Peru. She was born in 1586 and died in 1617, at the age of 31. She was canonized in 1671, the first saint born in the Western hemisphere.

Although she was born into a prosperous family, when she was still young her father fell on hard times. Young Isabel, already nicknamed Rose, helped the family with her needlework and gardening. She formally adopted the name Rose at her Confirmation. She came to realize early in life that she was reserved for the Lord. Her parents refused to allow her entrance into a convent, so Rose lived at the family home as a Third Order Dominican.

In all respects but one, she obeyed and helped support her parents her entire life. Only with regard to marriage did she not fulfill her father's wishes. Her parents wished her to marry into wealth, in the hopes of repairing the family fortunes. Of course, parental jurisdiction does not fully extend to the sacramental life, so Rose was entirely within her rights to insist upon her celibacy. Finally, her father was persuaded to allow her the use of a room as her own private convent.

Rose undertook a great many ascetic practices—for instance, eating no meat and sleeping only two hours each night. Whatever time she did not spend in prayer or needlework, she used in caring for the poor, the homeless, and the hungry of Lima. Often the sick were taken into her room so that she could nurse them back to health. Her charity and her sanctity became well-known to all in Lima. At her funeral, every public official in the city attended as a testimony to her valuable service to the people.

Devotion to the young saint of Lima spread rapidly, especially among the far-flung Spanish colonies. She was named the general patroness of the Americas and the Philippine Islands. Her name adorns cities, parks, missions, and lakes throughout South and North America.

are their parents. Children owe charity to their parents, in gratitude for all that their parents have done for them. This charity must be manifest in their entire conduct. They must always speak to their parents respectfully, be ready to help them, be patient with their faults and shortcomings, and pray for them.

> With all your heart honor your father, and do not forget the birth pangs of your mother. Remember that through your parents you were born; and what can you give back to them that equals their gift to you? (Sirach 7:27-28)

Children must also bear with the weaknesses and failings of their parents in their old age and be patient with them.

> O son, help your father in his old age, and do not grieve him as long as he lives; even if he is lacking in understanding, show forbearance; in all your strength do not despise him. For kindness to a father will not be forgotten, and against your sins it will be credited to you; in the day of your affliction it will be remembered in your favor; as frost in fair weather, your sins will melt away (Sirach 3:12-15).

Saint Rose of Lima, by Bartolome Esteban Murillo

Parents sacrifice an incredible amount of time, energy, material goods, and even their very selves for the sake of their children. We could never do enough to repay them.

Honor and Duty in the Church

> "All authority in heaven and on earth has been given to me. Go therefore and make disciples of all nations, baptizing them in the name of the Father and of the Son and of the Holy Spirit, teaching them to observe all that I have commanded you; and lo, I am with you always, to the close of the age" (Matthew 28:18-20).

The Catholic Church is the Body of Christ, the Bride of Christ, and the Family of Christ. The purpose of the Church is to secure the sanctification and spiritual welfare of all people. The *Church* is the "household of God" and "the pillar and bulwark of the truth" (1 Timothy 3:15).

The teaching authority of the Church is the **Magisterium**. The **threefold mission of the Magisterium** is to teach, govern, and sanctify. All Catholics have duties toward the Church in each of these three areas.

First, the Magisterium has the mission of *teaching* us everything God has revealed. This includes authentically interpreting the Word of God and explaining the truths of the Catholic Faith. We have a duty to accept these truths with humility and docility.

Second, the Magisterium has the mission of *governing* the Church. Jesus Christ has given the pope and the bishops in union with him, as the successors of St. Peter and the Apostles, the authority to loose and bind (Matthew 18:18). We have a duty to be faithful to all the teachings of the Catholic Church on faith and morals.

Third, the Magisterium has the mission of *sanctifying* us. The primary means of sanctification are the sacraments and the Mass. We have a duty to reverently receive the sacraments and to attend Mass on Sundays and holy days of obligation.

We have a duty to honor those in authority within the Church. We owe them this honor because of their *office*, which is from God. It is also fitting to honor those in the Church whose lives are a testimony to their good *character*. Thus, the Church venerates the Blessed Virgin Mary, the angels, and the saints. Failing to venerate those who have so faithfully followed Jesus would not be pleasing to God. We should also thank Catholic bishops, priests, nuns, and other religious for their faithful service and loving guidance. We should especially honor those who truly pour themselves out for others, and who courageously speak the truth and give glory to God.

Finally, the Catholic Church is our Mother in the Faith, and we owe her honor and gratitude. If we truly love and honor Jesus, we will also love and honor His Bride, the Catholic Church. We have a responsibility to fully participate in the life of the Church, and to live in solidarity with her. In addition to evangelizing others by spreading the Gospel, we should be prepared to practice **Catholic apologetics**: the art of explaining and defending the truths of the Catholic Faith.

> Always be prepared to make a defense to anyone who calls you to account for the hope that is in you, yet do it with gentleness and reverence (1 Peter 3:15).

Honor and Duty in the State

> Let every person be subject to the governing authorities. For there is no authority except from God, and those that exist have been instituted by God. Therefore he who resists the authorities resists what God has appointed, and those who resist will incur judgment (Romans 13:1-2).

God has ordained that man participate in His authority in order to ensure the rule of law for the common good. This authority is held by political regimes with influence over the affairs of the people. The **State** refers to an organized political community or territory governed by a political regime, and to the authorities in power within that regime.

The existence of the State is a reflection of the social nature of man. God did not create human beings to be isolated from one another, but rather to be in fellowship. It is natural for man to be *social*—to associate with other human beings. It is also natural for families to join together and form communities, and for communities to form nations. However, with the formation of nations comes additional duties that must be fulfilled.

The Duties of the State

> *Political authorities* are obliged to respect the fundamental rights of the human person. They will dispense justice humanely by respecting the rights of everyone, especially of families and the disadvantaged (*Catechism*, 2237).

Every human being has equal dignity as a person created in the image and likeness of God. Along with this dignity come certain **unalienable rights**: fundamental rights that belong to every human being and cannot be taken away. **These rights are not from man or the State, or even the Church; they are from God.** The United States Declaration of Independence aptly identifies some of these rights and describes the purpose of the State:

> We hold these truths to be self-evident, that all men are created equal, that they are endowed by their Creator with certain unalienable Rights, that among these are Life, Liberty and the pursuit of Happiness. — That to secure these rights, Governments are instituted among Men... (*United States Declaration of Independence*, July 4, 1776).

The **purpose of the State** is to promote the *temporal welfare* of the people within that State, in order to secure their unalienable rights and serve the *common good*. The **temporal welfare** refers to everything people reasonably need to secure their unalienable rights. The **common good** refers to both the good of the community as a whole and the good of every individual person within that community.

Ignoring the good of the community can lead to an exaggeration of individual autonomy which ignores the responsibilities that each person has toward the community. Ignoring the good of the individual person can lead to a *totalitarian* State, in which "the good of the community" devolves into "the good of the government."

Thomas Jefferson, by Rembrandt

A **totalitarian** State is one in which the government tries to control virtually every aspect of the lives of the people within that State. Embracing a totalitarian form of government inevitably leads to the systematic violation of one human right after another, until practically every human right has been violated. The result is neither the good of the community nor the good of the individual person, but *tyranny*.

Therefore, it is critical to maintain a proper understanding of the common good as encompassing *both* the good of the community *and* the good of every individual person within that community.

Furthermore, those in the State who are morally good should be honored and respected, not oppressed or condemned. Honoring the just, and not the wicked, is beneficial to the common good and the general welfare of the nation, as well as the entire human community. When those who are morally good are honored, all of society benefits.

> He who justifies the wicked and he who condemns the righteous are both alike an abomination to the Lord (Proverbs 17:15).

The primary focus of the State must be on the people *within that State*. A more complete understanding of the common good encompasses the entire human community. This fuller understanding can protect against an exaggerated sense of patriotism, which seeks national self-interests that are contrary to objective measures of right and wrong or that unjustly endanger people in other nations. No country may lawfully impose its will on other countries or promote policies that infringe on their rights.

At the same time, concern for the good of the entire human community must not be used to promote a totalitarian global power that ignores the sovereignty of nations, imposes burdensome taxes and laws on those nations, violates the human rights of their citizens, or disregards their constitutions. Striving for peace and unity among nations is good; violating human rights and the sovereignty of nations is not.

The Duties of Citizens

> Those subject to authority should regard those in authority as representatives of God, who has made them stewards of his gifts.... Their loyal collaboration includes the right, and at times the duty, to voice their just criticisms of that which seems harmful to the dignity of persons and to the good of the community (*Catechism*, 2238).

The State receives its authority from God. Therefore, its citizens are morally obligated to honor that authority. **Loving one's country is a duty under the Fourth Commandment.** We must do our share to contribute to the common good by making sacrifices for the sake of our country, abiding by its just laws, and paying our taxes.

In order for a law to be just and binding on our conscience, however, it must meet all four of the following criteria (Fr. Laux, p. 151):

- The law must be in accord with the Divine Law.
- It must be made by a lawful authority.
- The law must serve the common good.
- It must not infringe on the rights of anyone (individual persons, parents, families, local communities, etc.).

If a law fails to meet *any* of these criteria, it is unjust, and no one is obliged to follow it. If the State demands something contrary to the Divine Law, we have a duty to *disobey* the State. "We must obey God rather than men" (Acts 5:29).

Some States are extremely oppressive and continually violate the rights of their citizens. In such cases, is *armed resistance* legitimate? The answer is that **armed resistance is not morally acceptable unless several conditions are met**:

> Armed *resistance* to oppression by political authority is not legitimate, unless all the following conditions are met: 1) there is certain, grave, and prolonged violation of fundamental rights; 2) all other means of redress have been exhausted; 3) such resistance will not provoke worse disorders; 4) there is well-founded hope of success; and 5) it is impossible reasonably to foresee any better solution (*Catechism*, 2243).

All too often, people resort to armed resistance against authority when one or more of the above conditions are not met, and the result is disaster. Prudence and patience are needed to avoid rashly trying to solve problems through violence.

One of the most powerful ways to resist oppressive political authority in countries such as the United States is *voting*. Voting is a serious responsibility. Therefore, it is critical to spend adequate time investigating political candidates. There are many issues to consider, but they are not all equal. We must distinguish between issues that involve *moral absolutes* (the sanctity of life, the sanctity of marriage, etc.) and those that do not (the economy, immigration, taxes, trade, fiscal policy, etc.). **Issues involving moral absolutes must be given top priority in voting, because they involve a clear choice between good and evil.**

Finally, all people must be willing to defend the rights of their nation, and of every human being within that nation. We must be good citizens and do our part to help the common good. We should support our leaders when they do what is right, but hold them accountable when they do not. Our criticisms should be balanced and respectful, but we cannot tolerate evil. **The road to tyranny is paved with the tolerance of evil.**

The Link between Church and State: Morality

> "Render therefore to Caesar the things that are Caesar's, and to God the things that are God's" (Matthew 22:21).

Christians are citizens of both the nation in which they live and the Church. The purpose of the State is to promote the *temporal welfare* of the people within that State, in order to secure their unalienable rights and serve the common good. The purpose of the Church is to secure the *sanctification* and *spiritual welfare* of all people.

The Tribute Money, by Philippe de Champaigne

> The Almighty, therefore, has given the charge of the human race to two powers, the ecclesiastical and the civil, the one being set over divine, and the other over human, things. Each in its kind is supreme, each has fixed limits within which it is contained… (Pope Leo XIII, *Immortale Dei* [Encyclical on the Christian Constitution of States], November 1, 1885, no. 13).

The spheres of influence for the Church and the State are distinct: one spiritual, the other temporal. Both are important, and each can help and support the other, while still remaining within its respective boundaries. The area in which the Church and the State are most closely linked is *morality*.

The roles of the Church and the State regarding morality are different. The Catholic Church is the voice of Christ on Earth, with the authority to "loose and bind." The Holy Spirit leads the Church to all truth in matters of faith and morals (John 16:13). Therefore, the Catholic Church is a qualified *expert* on matters of morality. Her teachings on morality are right and just, because they are guided by the Holy Spirit.

The State is tasked with making and enforcing just laws, judging cases involving moral issues, and ensuring that no one is hindered from living morally good lives. The State must *practice* morality. However, the State is not an expert on morality. The State does not have the competence to discern on its own what is right or wrong in every case. To ensure that it consistently acts according to sound moral principles, the State needs the guidance and expertise of the Church.

Honor and Duty in the Workplace

> Whatever your task, work heartily, as serving the Lord and not men, knowing that from the Lord you will receive the inheritance as your reward; you are serving the Lord Christ (Colossians 3:23-24).

Honor and duty are required in the workplace as well. Employers have duties toward their employees, and employees have duties toward their employers. The key to a just workplace is the Golden Rule: "So whatever you wish that men would do to you, do so to them; for this is the law and the prophets" (Matthew 7:12). Neither employers nor employees can do without the other. Both must work together in a spirit of mutual respect, charity, and justice.

The Duties of Employers

> Those *responsible for business enterprises* are responsible to society for the economic and ecological effects of their operations. They have an obligation to consider the good of persons and not only the increase of *profits*. Profits are necessary, however. They make possible the investments that ensure the future of a business and they guarantee employment (*Catechism*, 2432).

Employers have several duties toward those who work for them (Fr. Laux, p. 150). First, **employers must respect their workers' dignity**. Their employees are not their slaves, and employers must not treat them as mere means to increase production, make money, or increase their power. Employers must treat their workers with the dignity and respect owed to all human persons.

Second, **employers must respect the conscience of their workers** and never ask them to act against it. Likewise, they must respect their workers' religious freedom and make allowances for their religious obligations.

Third, **working conditions must be suitable for human beings** and not degrading to their dignity. Employers must not ask workers to do more than should be reasonably expected, especially if the work is injurious to their health, is beyond their strength, is not appropriate for their age or sex, or interferes with their personal or religious duties. Employers must also ensure that the workplace is morally upright and not a source of temptation for their employees. Dishonesty, harassment, profanity, or impurity of any kind have no place in the workplace and should not be tolerated.

Fourth, **employers have a moral obligation to pay their workers a fair wage**. A **fair wage** is an amount of money that is generally sufficient for *one person* working full time to provide for the material needs of his family in reasonable, frugal comfort (Pope Leo XIII, *Rerum Novarum* [Encyclical on Capital and Labor], May 15, 1891, no. 45). When employers grow rich by overworking their employees at low wages, they sin against justice and charity. They also sin against the Seventh Commandment ("You shall not steal") by exploiting their workers for the sake of their own selfish gain, effectively robbing them of their health, dignity, and time. They are morally obligated to *make restitution* to those individuals.

This does not mean making profits is immoral. Profits are beneficial to the common good because they enable people to continue to have a means of employment (*Catechism*, 2432). **Businesses have a right to make profits.** However, businesses must acquire those profits justly, with respect for their employees and reasonable consideration for the community and the environment.

Finally, **those in the workplace who are morally upright should be honored and rewarded**, not those who climb to the top through dishonesty or at the expense of others. When someone who is known to have a bad moral character is rewarded, the entire workplace groans. When those of good moral character are honored, morale improves.

The Duties of Employees

> *Human work* proceeds directly from persons created in the image of God and called to prolong the work of creation by subduing the earth, both with and for one another. Hence work is a duty.... By enduring the hardship of work in union with Jesus, the carpenter of Nazareth and the one crucified on Calvary, man collaborates in a certain fashion with the Son of God in his redemptive work (*Catechism*, 2427).

Employees must honestly and diligently perform the work they have been hired to do, and strive to do good work at all times. They must truly give of themselves in doing their work. Honest labor, no matter how humble, is honorable and helps man to earn sustenance for his life and to provide for the material needs of his family in a morally upright way.

Employees must also show respect for their employers. They must not damage any property where they work, or harm the reputation of their employers. They must not be disrespectful, petty, or unpleasant, and they must not grumble.

At the same time, **employees need to observe their other duties**, including those toward God, the Church, and their family. They must not do anything that is against their conscience, nor should they be asked to do so.

Workers have a duty to uphold all just contracts to which they have freely agreed. It is not morally permissible for them to go on strike if doing so would violate such a contract. If there is no other way to secure their rights to work under suitable working conditions, including a fair wage, then it is morally permissible for workers to go on strike (Fr. Laux, pp. 150-151). However, it is never morally permissible to use threats or violence (for example, to punish other workers who decide not to go on strike).

Joseph Receives His Father and Brothers in Egypt, by Salomon de Bray

> Recourse to a *strike* is morally legitimate when it cannot be avoided, or at least when it is necessary to obtain a proportionate benefit. It becomes morally unacceptable when accompanied by violence, or when objectives are included that are not directly linked to working conditions or are contrary to the common good (*Catechism*, 2435).

In some cases, it may be necessary for the State to intervene to settle a labor dispute, especially if the common good is being harmed (Fr. Laux, p. 150). At the same time, the State should avoid undue or rash interference.

Chapter 11 Review

Matching: For each statement, select the letter of the best term from the list below. There are more terms listed than there are statements, and no term can be used more than once.

A. mainstream	E. Church	I. office	M. common good
B. exegesis	F. family	J. head	N. apologetics
C. dignity	G. roles	K. heart	O. totalitarian
D. political	H. honor	L. State	P. temporal welfare

1. Distinction, respect, and esteem, in virtue of one's office, one's character, or one's accomplishments: ________.
2. A husband and a wife have equal ________ under God.
3. The art of explaining and defending the truths of the Catholic Faith is called Catholic ________.
4. The ________ refers to both the good of the community as a whole and the good of every individual person within that community.
5. The normal reference point by which the different forms of ________ relationship are to be evaluated is the lifelong union of one man and one woman under God, along with their children.
6. A ________ State is one in which the government tries to control virtually every aspect of the lives of the people within that State.
7. The father is the ________ of the family.
8. The mother is the ________ of the family.
9. Everything people reasonably need to secure their unalienable rights: ________.
10. The position of authority or distinction that a person holds: ________.

True or False: Write *True* or *False* for the following statements.

________ 11. There are three main reasons why we should honor certain persons: their office, their character, or their accomplishments.

________ 12. God has appointed the husband as the head of his wife.

________ 13. A man must be willing to lay down his life in loving service for the sake of his wife's happiness and salvation.

________ 14. One of the ways a wife most perfectly honors Jesus Christ is by honoring the authority of her husband.

________ 15. A wife must always do what her husband asks.

________ 16. A mother's authority over her children is delegated to her by her husband; therefore, he can take away that authority.

________ 17. God commands every husband to love his wife as Jesus Christ loves the Church.

________ 18. Parents are responsible for the entire welfare of their children, both temporal and spiritual.

________ 19. A child's duty to obey his parents remains until (1) he becomes an adult and (2) he leaves the home and begins supporting himself.

________ 20. The duties of respect and charity that children owe their parents end when the children become adults and leave home.

________ 21. We have a duty to be faithful to all the teachings of the Catholic Church on faith and morals.

________ 22. Issues involving moral absolutes must be given top priority in voting, because they involve a clear choice between good and evil.

________ 23. The existence of the State is contrary to the nature of man.

________ 24. The purpose of the State is to control the possessions of the people and distribute them equitably.

________ 25. Loving one's country is a duty under the Fourth Commandment.

________ 26. Since the State receives its authority from God, we must do everything that the State demands.

________ 27. As Christians, we are citizens of both the nation in which we live and the Church.

________ 28. A fair wage is an amount of money that is generally sufficient for two persons working full time to provide for the material needs of their family.

________ 29. Businesses do not have a right to make profits. Out of Christian charity, they are morally obligated to devote all their surplus income to the salaries of their employees and to the community.

________ 30. Honest labor, no matter how humble, is honorable and helps man to earn sustenance for his life and to provide for the material needs of his family in a morally upright way.

Multiple Choice: Write the letter of the best answer in the space provided.

31. Which of the following statements is *not* correct? ________
    A. It is never morally permissible for workers to go on strike.
    B. It is not morally permissible for workers to go on strike if doing so would violate a just contract to which they have freely agreed.
    C. If there is no other way to secure their rights to work under suitable working conditions, including a fair wage, then it is morally permissible for workers to go on strike.
    D. It is always morally permissible for workers to go on strike.
    E. Both A and D

32. In order for a law to be just and binding on our conscience, it must ________.
    A. Be in accord with the Divine Law
    B. Be made by a lawful authority
    C. Serve the common good
    D. Not infringe on the rights of anyone
    E. All of the above

33. The right to determine how children receive their formal education rests with the ________.
    A. Parents
    B. Village
    C. State
    D. Local school board
    E. Children

34. The threefold mission of the Magisterium of the Catholic Church is to ________.
    A. Inspire, entertain, and encourage
    B. Teach, govern, and sanctify
    C. Strive for unity, resolve disputes, and serve the good of the State
    D. Raise money, promote tolerance, and make people feel comfortable
    E. Listen, learn, and change

35. The fundamental rights of every human person come from ________.
    A. The State
    B. The Church
    C. God
    D. The United Nations
    E. All of the above

Chapter 12. The Sanctity of Human Life: The Fifth Commandment

"You shall not kill" (Exodus 20:13).

The Fifth Commandment forbids the intentional killing of an innocent human being. Human life is sacred, and only God, the Author of life, has the right to determine when an innocent human being will die. Killing an innocent human being is an **intrinsically evil act** (an act that is evil always, everywhere, and in all cases, because of its very nature). It is always gravely sinful. Nothing could ever justify it, even if the State commanded it for the sake of public health, or for any other reason.

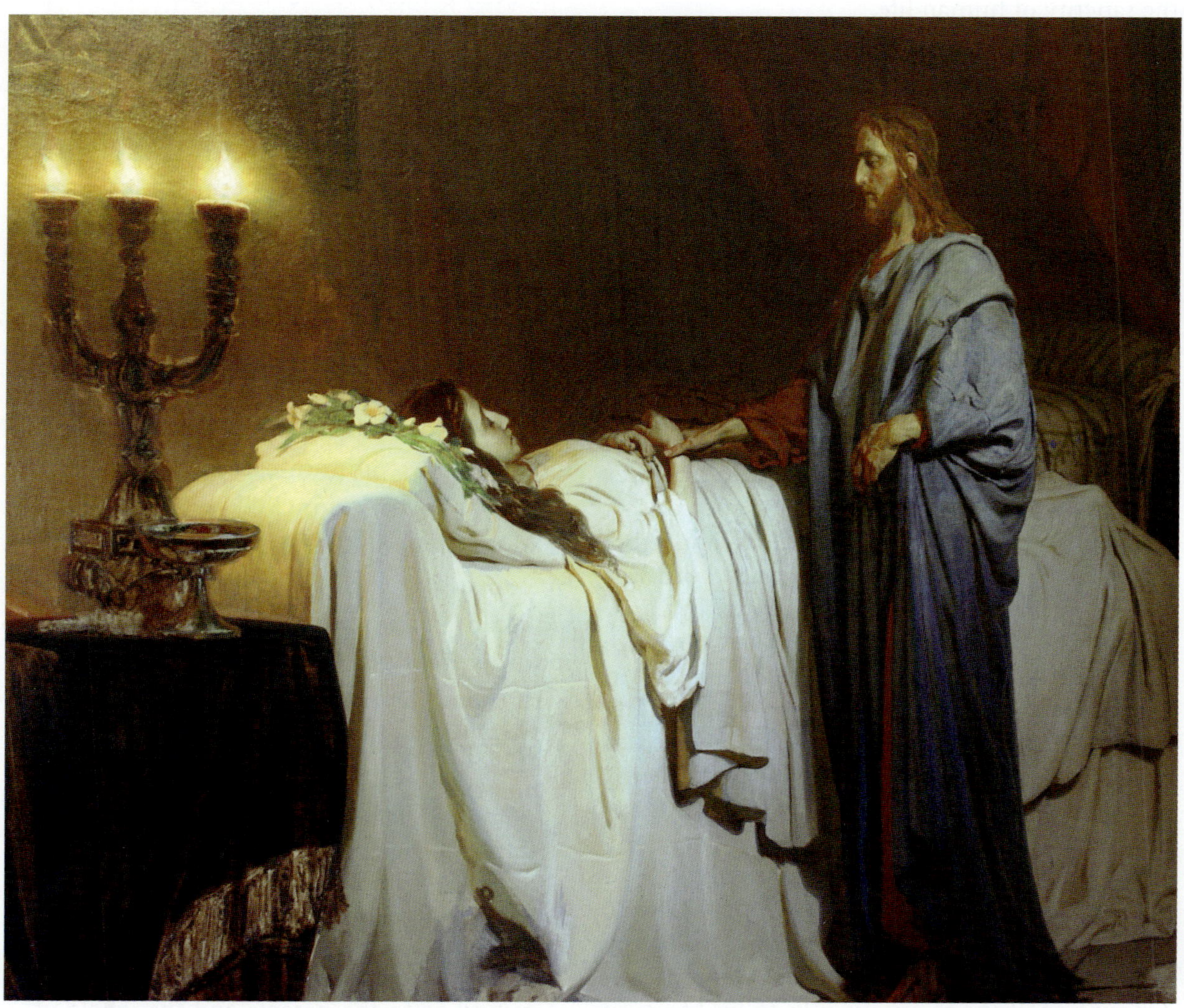

Raising of Jairus' Daughter, by Ilya Repin

Sins against the Fifth Commandment

And the Lord said, "What have you done? The voice of your brother's blood is crying to me from the ground" (Genesis 4:10).

Sins forbidden by the Fifth Commandment include murder, abortion, euthanasia, embryonic stem cell research and other illicit procedures, suicide, substance abuse and other harmful or degrading practices, the sin of anger (wrath), revenge, hatred, scandal, and all other sins against the sanctity of human life.

Murder

The fifth commandment forbids *direct and intentional killing* as gravely sinful. The murderer and those who cooperate voluntarily in murder commit a sin that cries out to heaven for vengeance (*Catechism*, 2268).

Anyone who murders an innocent human being "commits an outrage" against the rights of his neighbor, the Law of God, the safety of society, and his own soul (Fr. Laux, p. 134). The greatest temporal good a person possesses is his life.

The first murder in history was the murder of Abel by his brother Cain. At the root of this terrible sin was pride. When Cain and Abel presented their offerings to God, the Lord was pleased with Abel's offering, but not with Cain's. Perhaps this was because Abel, unlike Cain, gave God his best. Cain's bruised pride quickly led to anger and envy. God tried to help him by giving him good counsel. In his pride, Cain refused to listen to God's counsel, and instead murdered his own brother. This is one of the **sins that cry to Heaven** for justice.

If someone intentionally acts to directly or indirectly bring about an innocent person's death, he is guilty of murder. All who cooperate voluntarily with murder commit a grave sin. Unnecessarily exposing someone to serious risks to his life, even without intending to kill him, is also a grave sin.

Refusing to help a person in danger is a grave sin as well. This does not mean we must take imprudent risks. Nevertheless, when our neighbor is in grave danger, we must try to help him in some way, even if all we are able to do is call for help.

Abortion

Since the first century the Church has affirmed the moral evil of every procured abortion. **This teaching has not changed and remains unchangeable.** Direct abortion, that is to say, abortion willed either as an end or a means, is gravely contrary to the moral law (*Catechism*, 2271, emphasis added).

Abortion, which is the intentional killing of a preborn infant, is a grave sin against the Fifth Commandment. It is an intrinsically evil act, and thus never morally permissible. Anyone who formally cooperates in an abortion is automatically *excommunicated* from the Church. **Excommunication** is a very serious penalty for certain extremely grave sins, which prevents a person from being in full communion with the Church.

Anyone who has committed a sin incurring excommunication must repent and seek to be reconciled with the Church as soon as possible. This person should begin by consulting with a faithful Catholic priest, who can explain what he or she needs to do in order to be restored to full communion with the Church.

Formal cooperation in an abortion constitutes a grave offense. The Church attaches the canonical penalty of excommunication to this crime against human life.... The Church does not thereby intend to restrict the scope of mercy. Rather, she makes clear the gravity of the crime committed, the irreparable harm done to the innocent who is put to death, as well as to the parents and the whole of society (*Catechism*, 2272).

Anyone who pressures a woman to have an abortion is guilty of both murder and grave scandal. Politicians and judges who advocate legalized abortion commit a grave sin against the Fifth Commandment, and bring disgrace upon their office and the nation.

Helping to save the life of a preborn infant in danger of abortion is a corporal work of mercy toward the infant, and a spiritual work of mercy toward the infant's mother and father. Helping a woman who has had an abortion to reconcile with Our Lord Jesus Christ and the Catholic Church is a spiritual work of mercy as well.

Euthanasia

> Intentional euthanasia, whatever its forms or motives, is murder. It is gravely contrary to the dignity of the human person and to the respect due to the living God, his Creator (*Catechism*, 2324).

Respect for human life is all or nothing. Either the rights of *every* innocent human being are respected and protected by law, or the rights of *none* are secure. **Euthanasia** is the intentional killing of the handicapped, the sick, the old, the feeble, the dying, or anyone else deemed to have a poor "quality of life." It is an intrinsically evil act, never morally permissible under any circumstances. **Euthanasia is a grave sin against the Fifth Commandment, and it is extremely dangerous to society.**

Some governments have legalized so-called *assisted suicide*, which is essentially "voluntary" euthanasia. In *euthanasia*, someone performs an action, such as administering a lethal drug, that kills another person. In **assisted suicide**, the victim himself performs this action, usually with the "assistance" of a physician or some third party.

Assisted suicide is a grave sin against the Fifth Commandment for all involved, including the victim who voluntarily participates in this evil act. However, if the victim is influenced by intense emotions, suffering, pressure from the State or members of his family, or other factors inhibiting his freedom, his culpability might not be as great as those who cooperate in this act without being influenced by such factors.

It is very difficult to see someone we love suffering, but only God has the right to decide when a person should die. Even if death is imminent, normal care for the person must be continued.

It is morally permissible to administer pain killers, even if we know they will likely lead to the person dying sooner, **as long as death is not willed** as a means or an end, only tolerated as an unintended consequence of relieving the person's pain (*Catechism*, 2279). Also, it is not necessary to use extraordinary, burdensome medical procedures in order to keep a person alive. However, in refusing such extraordinary procedures, the death of the person must not be willed. Rather, "one's inability to impede it is merely accepted"

The Death of Saint Joseph, by Nicolas-Guy Brenet

(*Catechism*, 2278). If the patient is able to make such decisions, he or she must be allowed to do so.

A **feeding tube** is, in principle, an *ordinary* procedure, and hence **morally required as long as it accomplishes the goal of providing nutrition and hydration to the patient.** Eating and drinking are normal needs for every human being, *including those in a permanent vegetative state.*

> The administration of food and water even by artificial means is, in principle, an ordinary and proportionate means of preserving life. It is therefore obligatory to the extent to which, and for as long as, it is shown to accomplish its proper finality, which is the hydration and nourishment of the patient... (Congregation for the Doctrine of the Faith, *Responses to Certain Questions of the* [USCCB] *Concerning Artificial Nutrition and Hydration*, Aug. 1, 2007).

Under certain grave conditions, a feeding tube may be considered *extraordinary*, and thus not morally required: (1) if the patient cannot assimilate food or water at all; or (2) if the feeding tube would cause *significant* physical discomfort or other serious medical complications.

Embryonic Stem Cell Research and Other Illicit Procedures

> Since it must be treated from conception as a person, the embryo must be defended in its integrity, cared for, and healed, as far as possible, like any other human being (*Catechism*, 2274).

Embryonic stem cell research kills a human being in the earliest stage of development, purportedly to use this embryo's stem cells for medical purposes, such as helping people with certain diseases. However, there are alternatives to this research that do not kill an innocent human being. Moreover, even if there were no alternatives, **embryonic stem cell research could never be justified, because it destroys innocent human life**. It is an intrinsically evil act and a grave sin against the Fifth Commandment. Every human being, however small and regardless of his stage in human development, is sacred and has fundamental God-given rights that must be respected and protected by law.

Any medical procedure or scientific research on human embryos that respects his life and dignity, does not expose him to disproportionate risks or contravene the Moral Law in any way, and is performed in order to heal him, improve his health, or save his life is morally good. Any medical procedure or research that does not meet these conditions is gravely sinful.

"It is immoral to produce human embryos intended for exploitation as disposable biological material" (Joseph Cardinal Ratzinger, Congregation for the Doctrine of the Faith, *Donum Vitae*, no. I, 5, in *Catechism*, 2275). In vitro fertilization is also gravely sinful (*Catechism*, 2376-2378), as are attempts to produce human beings "selected according to sex or other predetermined qualities" (*Donum Vitae*, no. I, 6, in *Catechism*, 2275). Regardless of the motives, the manipulation of human embryos cannot be tolerated under any circumstances.

It is also gravely evil to solicit a diagnosis concerning a preborn infant (called a **prenatal diagnosis**) in order to decide whether to procure an abortion: "a diagnosis must not be the equivalent of a death sentence" (*Catechism*, 2274). However, if such a diagnosis is done, *not* to decide whether to procure an abortion, but to ensure a safe delivery for both the baby and the mother, then it is morally permissible.

Finally, **experimentation on human beings is sinful** if it is done without their consent. Moreover, even if they give their consent, any experimentation that exposes people to serious risks is gravely contrary to the dignity of the human person. In order for human experimentation to be morally permissible, three conditions must be met: those undergoing the experimentation must give their informed consent; the experimentation must not present serious risks to their lives, health, or dignity in any way; and the experimentation must have the potential to truly help them or other human beings (*Catechism*, 2294-2295). If *any* of these conditions is not met, the experimentation must not be performed.

Suicide

> Everyone is responsible for his life before God who has given it to him. It is God who remains the sovereign Master of life. We are obliged to accept life gratefully and preserve it for his honor and the salvation of our souls. We are stewards, not owners, of the life God has entrusted to us. It is not ours to dispose of (*Catechism*, 2280).

Suicide is a person's intentional and deliberate taking of his own life. It is an intrinsically evil act. It is never morally permissible. Suicide is a grave sin against (1) God, (2) oneself, and (3) one's neighbor (*Catechism*, 2281).

Suicide is a grave sin against God, because He alone gives life and has the right to determine how long our life will endure. Only God has ultimate ownership of our life. Suicide shows contempt for God by destroying this most precious gift.

Suicide is a grave sin against oneself, because every person has a moral obligation to take reasonable measures to preserve his life. Suicide is also a grave sin against one's own soul. Suicide abruptly separates the soul from the body before the time God intended to do so. **If someone commits suicide with full knowledge and complete consent, it is a mortal sin.** Suicide then separates the person's soul, not only from his body, but from God—and at the worst possible time: the hour of his death and eternal judgment. Suicide creates a permanent problem in order to try to solve a temporary problem.

Suicide is a grave sin against one's neighbor, because it robs the world of all the good this person could have done during the remaining time of his life. It also unjustly deprives the person's family, friends, and everyone else he knows (or would have known) of the opportunity to be in his company.

Even a person who is very sick and close to death could use his remaining moments to express contrition to God, pray for others, and offer up his suffering for the salvation of souls.

When a person takes his own life, he causes intense pain to all who care about him, and this pain will last for the rest of their lives. From that moment on, his loved ones must deal, not only with the pain of losing someone they love, but also with the tragedy that one of their loved ones might be lost for all eternity.

Those who are experiencing such pain over the tragic loss of a loved one should keep in mind that, in many cases, a person who commits suicide has grave psychological problems or fears, or is under such intense suffering (physical or emotional) that his freedom is seriously impaired. Also, certain medications intended to alleviate problems such as depression could actually *increase* the risk of suicidal tendencies. **We must be extremely careful about what medications we take or recommend to others**—especially those that could affect the mind or emotions in any way. **If the person's freedom was so impaired that he did not act with complete consent when he committed suicide, then one of the conditions for mortal sin was not met.**

There is also a possibility that the person repented after committing the act that led to his death, in the moments before he actually died. Those who have experienced the death of a loved one through suicide should not despair of his salvation. They should keep praying fervently for God's mercy.

The best safeguard against temptations related to suicide is our Catholic Faith, which can help us endure even the greatest and most intense trials of this life, while we keep our eyes fixed on our eternal reward in Heaven. We need to remember that if God has allowed us to remain in this world, it is for a reason. We must humbly accept His Will, even if we do not understand it. We must let God decide

The Death of St. Joseph, by Carlo Maratta

how long we will live and when we will die, for "whether we live or whether we die, we are the Lord's" (Romans 14:8). He loves us, and He knows what is best for us. We must trust Him.

Substance Abuse and Other Types of Self-Degradation

The virtue of temperance disposes us to *avoid every kind of excess*: the abuse of food, alcohol, tobacco, or medicine (*Catechism*, 2290).

God commands us to love our neighbor as ourselves. A just love of self is essential to our dignity as human beings created in the image and likeness of God. To be just, however, **our love of self must be subordinated to our love of God**. A person who puts himself before God displays a *false* self-love (Fr. Laux, p. 98).

A just self-love is a well-ordered love that seeks one's own eternal happiness, and that desires to protect one's soul from evil. We owe it to God and ourselves to earnestly seek our salvation, and to nourish and protect our soul. We also have the right and duty to respect and care for our natural life. It is morally just to fulfill our needs for food, drink, clothing, and shelter.

Gluttony. There is one primary rule we must follow regarding eating: **we must act according to right reason**. When we have had enough to eat, we should stop eating. When there is a limited amount of food available, we should share with those around us. When something clearly has an ill effect on our health, we should try to avoid it. When we find that we are too attached to some particular food or drink, we should abstain from it, at least periodically.

Gluttony is the sin in which a person indulges excessively in food or drink. It is one of the seven *capital sins*. Gluttony is typically a venial sin, but it can lead to other sins, such as greed and envy. A person who constantly gratifies inordinate desires for the pleasures of food or drink may weaken the mastery of his will over the flesh. This in turn could weaken his resolve when he is faced with more serious temptations of the flesh. Gluttony may also have natural consequences, such as the development of certain health disorders.

All types of food are available to us, and since the coming of Jesus Christ, none are forbidden, provided that we eat with moderation.

> The next day … Peter went up on the housetop to pray…. And he became hungry and desired something to eat; but while they were preparing it, he fell into a trance and saw the heaven opened, and something descending…. In it were all kinds of animals and reptiles and birds of the air. And there came a voice to him, "Rise, Peter; kill and eat" (Acts 10:9-13).

As the quotation above makes clear, both hunting for food and eating meat are morally acceptable. We may eat whatever food is set before us, as long as we do not injure the conscience of our neighbor (1 Corinthians 10:27-29), and provided that we observe the days of fasting and abstinence prescribed by the Church.

Alcohol Abuse. Adults are not morally forbidden from drinking alcohol. However, drinking can be dangerous if it is done at the wrong time, in the wrong place, or in the wrong way. **Caution is necessary.** There are many situations in which drinking alcohol is not prudent. Alcohol is dangerous for anyone driving an automobile, a boat, or an airplane, or working with dangerous tools or machinery. Alcohol can slow a person's reflexes and dull his awareness. Many people say or do things while drinking alcohol that they regret the next day. Some people compromise their dignity by acting very foolishly. Others become more prone to arguing or fighting.

The wise person will restrict his use of alcohol to the few occasions when it is safe and prudent for him to drink. Everyone is morally obligated to avoid the near occasions of sin associated with drinking alcohol. If a person is unable to do so, he should not drink alcohol at all.

Alcohol abuse is a sin against the Fifth Commandment, and it frequently leads to other sins as well, especially further sins against the Fifth Commandment and sins against purity. Alcohol abuse is very dangerous. It has often led to violence, and sometimes even murder.

It is a grave sin to willfully drink so much alcohol that one becomes intoxicated (drunk). One of the greatest dangers involved in excessive drinking is that it sabotages a person's ability to reason, which is needed to make sound moral decisions. The point at which drinking alcohol becomes gravely sinful is when it is *likely* that it will lead to the person doing something contrary to right reason—even if he does not end up doing so.

Drinking alcohol in the right place, at the right time, and in the right way (in moderation) can be enjoyable and wholesome. Drinking alcohol in the wrong place, at the wrong time, or in the wrong way can be disastrous.

> Who has woe? Who has sorrow? Who has strife? Who has complaining? Who has wounds without cause? Who has redness of eyes? Those who tarry long over wine, those who go to try mixed wine (Proverbs 23:29-30).

When people become addicted to alcohol, it is a bitter ordeal, which can seem insurmountable to overcome, but they must not despair. Through their Catholic Faith, the help of others, and God's grace, they can conquer this addiction. However, for the rest of their lives, those addicted to alcohol will need to be vigilant and obey one simple rule: **they must never drink alcohol again**.

Drug Abuse. Another very grievous sin is *drug abuse*, and its consequences can be catastrophic. Using drugs, or selling or giving them to others (except by legitimate authorities for medical reasons), is a grave sin against the Fifth Commandment.

> The *use of drugs* inflicts very grave damage on human health and life. Their use, except on strictly therapeutic grounds, is a grave offense. Clandestine production of and trafficking in drugs are scandalous practices. They constitute direct co-operation in evil, since they encourage people to practices gravely contrary to the moral law (*Catechism*, 2291).

Using drugs (other than medicine) is *never* morally permissible. Trying drugs even once can lead to a person becoming addicted for the rest of his life. Many people who end up addicted to drugs begin with the intention of trying a certain drug "just one time." However, this "one time" removes a sort of shield from their will. After a while, they try the same drug a second time, a third time, and so on. Then they try a more serious drug, and one day they "awake" to find themselves a *slave* to drugs.

Perhaps, by the grace of God, they will eventually free themselves from this addiction; others have done so. However, many others have not, and their lives have been ruined because of it. **The only wise approach to drugs is to stay away from them and never try them, no matter what.** There are some things in life that no one should ever try, even once; drugs are among them.

Other Harmful or Degrading Practices. Several other practices are contrary to a just love of self, and are sinful to one degree or another. Once again, we must use right reason in the way we treat our body. Endangering our life or health recklessly or for vain reasons such as fame, pride, or money is sinful (Fr. Laux, p. 105).

Submitting to any kind of mutilation or amputation of our body is also sinful, unless the good of the rest of the body *requires* it. Our body is a gift from God. We must preserve all the parts of our body, unless it is impossible to do so without jeopardizing the good of our whole body (Fr. Laux, p. 105).

No person is ever obligated to use *extraordinary measures* to preserve his life. However, one should consult with his confessor to determine whether the expense, pain, or inconvenience of any treatment would be considered extraordinary; many treatments that at one time would have been considered extraordinary are now routine.

We must also avoid idolizing the body. We must not sacrifice our moral or familial duties for the sake of perfecting the body. It is prudent to take reasonable measures to avoid eating unhealthy foods, but if a person is more concerned about avoiding unhealthy foods than about avoiding the near occasions of sin, his focus is off balance.

> If morality requires respect for the life of the body, it does not make it an absolute value. It rejects a neo-pagan notion that tends to promote the *cult of the body*, to sacrifice everything for its sake, to idolize physical perfection and success at sports (*Catechism*, 2289).

Risking our life or health is morally permissible if the act is good (or at least neutral), and it is just as likely to be safe as harmful (Fr. Laux, p. 105). Risking our life or health is also morally permissible if we honestly have a serious, legitimate reason for doing so. Some professions, such as law enforcement and firefighting, necessarily entail a risk to one's life. Risking one's life for the benefit of others and society is praiseworthy.

Anger, Revenge, and Hatred

> In the Sermon on the Mount, the Lord recalls the commandment, "You shall not kill," and adds to it the proscription of anger, hatred, and vengeance (*Catechism*, 2262).

The ***emotion*** of **anger** moves a person to fight against that which he sees as morally wrong or as an obstacle to his or someone else's happiness, peace, or security. Emotions are not sins. However, if we do not use our reason to keep our emotions in check, they can lead to sin. If the emotion of anger leads a person to think or act in a way that is contrary to justice or charity, he commits the ***capital sin*** of **anger** (or ***wrath***).

A person can sin through anger in three different ways. First, **he sins if his anger is unjust**

Nothing Is Impossible with God

In Egypt, during the early years of Christianity, there lived an intractable servant known as Moses the Ethiopian. Moses caused unending problems for his master—quarreling with his fellow servants, stealing from them, and shirking his share of the labor. Finally, when he was found guilty of theft and suspected of worse, his master sent him away. Because of his reputation, no one would hire Moses, and he turned to a life of robbery and violence. He had no regard for the lives of his victims, and he soon added murder to his list of terrible crimes.

The authorities pursued Moses vigorously, but when they were finally on the verge of seizing him, he took refuge in a monastery. Monasteries and churches in those days had a tradition of sheltering any criminals who came to them. The law respected the right of sanctuary, so even an awful fellow like Moses the Ethiopian found safety within the monastery walls.

Kindness and gentle treatment are capable of leading to great miracles, and so it proved in the case of Moses the Ethiopian. The monks impressed Moses so much that he repented of his crimes and eventually asked to join in their holy life!

Of course, there were occasional reminders of his former life. Once, four or five robbers, possibly members of his own former gang, came to pillage the monastery. Moses, being immensely strong, was able to overcome them and tie them together. He dragged them before a meeting of his fellow monks and asked what to do with them. The monks acted with their usual wisdom and kindness, and the robbers were converted. They even joined the community, and it was decided that Moses would act as their spiritual father, since he was familiar with their character and thus could guide them in their spiritual growth.

Incredibly, Moses the Ethiopian, once a thief and a murderer, became the head of his own monastic community, later adding some twelve more of his former fellow criminals to the fold! Eventually, he was even ordained a priest, and he gained a mighty reputation among the desert monks for his holiness and wisdom. Truly, nothing is impossible with God!

(that is, if he deliberately responds in anger about something for which he has no right to be angry). Second, **he sins if he allows his anger to be too intense** in proportion to the offense, even if his anger is just; in other words, he overreacts.

Third, **he sins if he acts on his anger in the wrong way**. The other two ways of sinning through anger are often closely related to the way a person acts on his anger. If one's anger is unjust in the first place, then any action he takes against the object of his anger will also be unjust. If one's anger is excessively intense, then he will likely act on his anger in a sinful way.

When a person acts on his anger by willfully seeking to inflict harm on his neighbor, he is guilty of desiring *revenge*, which is always sinful. **Revenge** is a deliberate act or intention to harm someone because of a real or perceived wrong. Besides being a sin against one's neighbor, **revenge is a sin against God**.

> Beloved, never avenge yourselves, but leave it to the wrath of God; for it is written, "Vengeance is mine, I will repay, says the Lord." ... Do not be overcome by evil, but overcome evil with good (Romans 12:19-21).

Closely related to anger and revenge is the sin of *hatred*. Unlike anger, which can spring up quickly in the heat of a moment, hatred has deeper roots. It is not a sin to dislike someone; emotions are not sins. However, if a person moves beyond such feelings and willfully desires that harm come to his neighbor, he commits the sin of **hatred**.

Hating another person, even one's enemy, is a sin against the Fifth Commandment. If left unchecked, hatred could easily turn from sins of the mind (evil thoughts) to sins of the tongue (hateful words), to sins of violence; ultimately, it could even lead to murder.

It is *good* to *hate evil*. "The fear of the Lord is hatred of evil" (Proverbs 8:13). **We should hate all evil acts, evil laws, and evil policies.** We should hate everything that is contrary to the Natural Law. **We should hate all sin.** However, hatred of a *person* is sinful.

The most serious form of hatred toward one's neighbor is desiring that he go to Hell. When a person willfully has this desire, he effectively tries to stand in the place of God, Who alone has the right to make such judgments. "Judge not, that you be not judged" (Matthew 7:1).

Scandal

> Scandal is an attitude or behavior which leads another to do evil. The person who gives scandal becomes his neighbor's tempter. He damages virtue and integrity; he may even draw his brother into spiritual death. Scandal is a grave offense if by deed or omission another is deliberately led into a grave offense (*Catechism*, 2284).

Leading others to sin by word or example is called **scandal**. Because scandal can lead to the *spiritual death* of one's neighbor, it falls under the Fifth Commandment. The gravity of scandal varies according to the seriousness of the sins that it leads others to commit, the authority of those giving the scandal, and the moral weakness of those scandalized. If a person deliberately leads his neighbor to commit a mortal sin, he is guilty of a grave sin of scandal. There are two *types of scandal*: direct and indirect.

Direct Scandal. A person is guilty of **direct scandal** if he intentionally leads another person to sin. **Direct scandal is always sinful.** This sin offends Our Lord very much, especially when it is committed against children or other innocent persons:

> "Whoever receives one such child in my name receives me; but whoever causes one of these little ones who believe in me to sin, it would be better for him to have a great millstone fastened round his neck and to be drowned in the depth of the sea!" (Matthew 18:5-6)

Indirect Scandal. When scandal occurs without being intended, it is called **indirect scandal**. A person commits a *sin* of indirect scandal if (1) he foresees that his actions will lead his neighbor to sin, and (2) he can reasonably avoid those actions, but he performs them anyway. If either of these conditions is not present, indirect scandal may still occur, but it is *not* sinful.

If performing our *duties* has the unintended effect of leading others to sin, we cannot neglect those duties. At the same time, however, we should try to be sensitive to the weaknesses and faults of others. We should also be careful not to discuss certain topics with others at the wrong time, in the wrong place, or at too early of an age. If we can reasonably perform our duties in a way that does not lead others to sin, then we should try to do so.

Other Sins against the Sanctity of Human Life

> Life and physical health are precious gifts entrusted to us by God. We must take reasonable care of them, taking into account the needs of others and the common good (*Catechism*, 2288).

We must love our neighbor as ourselves. We must safeguard his life, respect his dignity, and avoid endangering or injuring his physical, mental, emotional, or spiritual health. Willfully inflicting bodily injuries or severe pain on our neighbor is sinful. We must also avoid injuring his interior peace by quarreling with him, exciting him to anger or worry, or robbing him of his tranquility.

It is sinful to play dangerous practical jokes on someone or to harm him through hazing (Fr. Laux, p. 133). We must not make fun of our neighbor, especially in front of others. We are to love our neighbor as ourselves, not exploit him for the sake of our own amusement.

Any culpable negligence toward our neighbor is sinful, in proportion to the degree to which it endangers his life or health (Fr. Laux, pp. 133-134). Drunk or reckless driving is very dangerous and gravely sinful. Landlords must not expose their tenants to unhealthy living conditions. Restaurants must not endanger their customers through unsanitary practices.

Likewise, disregard for the environment by polluting the air or waterways with toxic waste, littering, or engaging in any other practice that recklessly endangers the lives or health of human beings is sinful, in proportion to the harm done. The State has a responsibility to protect the health of its citizens, while also respecting their individual rights, as well as the rights of families. However, it is gravely sinful for the State to exert pressure on anyone to restrict child births for the sake of public health, or for any other reason.

Intimidation, threats, and indiscriminate violence are gravely sinful, as are **kidnapping**, **hostage taking**, and **terrorism**. **Torture**, even of those guilty of serious crimes, is *never* justifiable (*Catechism*, 2297). It is contrary to the Natural Law, which requires respect for the dignity of the human person.

Racism is also sinful and must be rejected in all its forms. Racism is contrary to the dignity of the human person, and it can cause grave harm to one's neighbor. **Every human being, regardless of his or her race, must be loved and respected** as a person created in the image and likeness of God for whom Jesus Christ died on the Cross.

Any other act that harms, degrades, or kills innocent human life is morally evil as well. Forced sterilization, contraception, and abortion are gravely sinful and contrary to the love of neighbor. Mutilations and amputations are also gravely sinful, except for strict medical reasons, and, even then, only if the person consents.

Finally, we must show respect for the dead. Burying the dead is a corporal work of mercy. **We are obligated to ensure that our family members receive a Christian burial.** Autopsies for legal inquiry or scientific research are permissible, provided that they show proper respect for the human body. Donating organs after death is also allowed.

To safeguard faith in the resurrection of the body, for many centuries the Church did not allow cremation. Today, cremation is allowed, **as long as it does not constitute a denial of the resurrection of the body** (*Catechism*, 2301). However, the solemn Christian funeral rites must still be included.

Every human being is a person created in the image and likeness of God; his body and soul must be respected at all times, including after his death.

Acts Not Forbidden by the Fifth Commandment

> "Every moving thing that lives shall be food for you; and as I gave you the green plants, I give you everything.... Whoever sheds the blood of man, by man shall his blood be shed; for God made man in his own image" (Genesis 9:3-6).

In the Fifth Commandment ("You shall not kill"), the Hebrew word translated as "kill" is *ratsach*, which more precisely refers to the **unjust killing of a human being**. This word does not refer to the killing of animals or trees, acts defending ourselves or others, the death penalty, or the use of military force in a just war. If all killing were meant, the word used would have been *nakah*, which means "to kill." In fact, some translations of the Bible render the Fifth Commandment as "You shall not murder."

Treatment of Animals and Other Living Things

> God entrusted animals to the stewardship of those whom he created in his own image. Hence it is legitimate to use animals for food and clothing (*Catechism*, 2417).

The Fifth Commandment does not forbid the killing of animals, trees, or any other living creature that is not human. When God created the Heavens and the Earth, He gave dominion over the entire creation to man for him to "subdue" and "have dominion over" (Genesis 1:28). Therefore, it is lawful for us to use and own all living and nonliving things in the visible creation, except human beings. However, we must do so responsibly and temperately, with charity and consideration for our neighbor.

Animals. There is a vast difference between human beings and all the other beings in the visible universe, including animals. **Human beings are persons whom we must love and respect; animals are living things that we may own or use.** Human beings are created in the image and likeness of God, and they have a rational soul. Animals are *not* created in the image and likeness of God, and they do *not* have a rational soul. We should act responsibly in the way we treat animals. However, we have the right to own and use animals for ourselves, our neighbor, or the good of humanity.

God explicitly gave man permission to kill animals for food (Genesis 9:3), and He clothed Adam and Eve with animal skins (Genesis 3:21). Thus, it is morally permissible to hunt animals for food or clothing. Conducting medical or scientific experiments on animals is also morally acceptable, as long as such experiments remain within reasonable limits and are for the purpose of helping human beings (*Catechism*, 2417).

At the same time, we should not needlessly cause animals to suffer or die. **Cruelty to animals is sinful**, and it is contrary to our human dignity. God created the animals, and He has given them to us as gifts. They are part of the wonder of creation, and they can be a great help to us. As persons created in the image and likeness of God, we should model our behavior after His. God does not treat His creatures with cruelty, but with compassion (Jonah 4:11), and He expects us to do the same. **We honor God when we treat animals with compassion.**

> A righteous man has regard for the life of his beast, but the mercy of the wicked is cruel (Proverbs 12:10).

It is also contrary to our human dignity to spend an inordinate amount of money on animals, since this money could instead be used to help some of the many people in the world who are suffering (*Catechism*, 2418). We must act according to right reason in our treatment of animals, neither treating them cruelly nor elevating them to the same status as human beings.

Other Living Things. God has given the entire visible creation, including trees and other living things, to mankind. We need to use all such things in a reasonable way that is worthy of our human dignity and that respects the rights of other human beings. We need to be prudent in our use of natural resources, and we must avoid engaging in any practices that could be harmful to our neighbor.

Self-Defense

> The legitimate defense of persons and societies is not an exception to the prohibition against the murder of the innocent that constitutes intentional killing. "The act of self-defense can have a double effect: the preservation of one's own life; and the killing of the aggressor.... The one is intended, the other is not" (*Catechism*, 2263).

Every human being has certain fundamental rights. These include, among others, the right to life, purity, property, and a good name. We have a right to defend these fundamental rights from an aggressor. However, our actions must be in proportion to the nature and importance of the rights being threatened, as well as the level of aggression against them.

Defending Our Life. The first fundamental right is the right to life. No one has the right to take the life of an innocent human being. We have a right to defend ourselves from any threats to our life. If the *only* way to defend our life is to take the life of the aggressor, then we are morally permitted to do so, **provided that certain conditions are met** (Fr. Laux, p. 135):

- We must not use any greater physical force than is necessary to protect ourselves from the aggressor. **If we can protect ourselves without killing the aggressor, we must avoid taking his life.**
- We may use force against the aggressor only *during* the act of aggression. We must not use force *after* the act of aggression, nor may we use force *before*.
- If there is any other way to avoid the danger, without sinning or surrendering our rights, then we must *not* use physical force.
- Our intention must be primarily to defend ourselves, *not* to kill the aggressor. We must not directly intend to kill the aggressor.

If all four of these conditions are met, and we are forced to take the life of the aggressor who is threatening our life, we have not sinned against the Fifth Commandment. If any of these conditions is not met, then we do not have the right to take the life of the aggressor.

> Love toward oneself remains a fundamental principle of morality. Therefore it is legitimate to insist on respect for one's own right to life. Someone who defends his life is not guilty of murder even if he is forced to deal his aggressor a lethal blow (*Catechism*, 2264).

Defending Our Purity. No one has the right to violate a person's purity or personal intimacy. We have a duty to never consent to such attacks, and we have the right to defend ourselves from them. If someone threatens our purity, we may use whatever force is necessary to stop the aggressor, as long as all four of the conditions above are met.

> A woman has the right to defend her virtue by taking the life, if need be, of the aggressor. One who threatens a woman's honor not only violates her right to personal integrity, but also her right of natural independence (Fr. Laux, p. 135).

Defending Our Property. We have a right to defend ourselves from anyone threatening to steal or destroy our property or other material goods. If the property is of great worth, and we have no other way of stopping the aggressor, then we have the right to use force to do so, provided that all the other conditions above are met (Fr. Laux, p. 135). However, if the property is not of great worth, then **we do not have the right to take the life of the aggressor**.

Defending Our Good Name. We also have a right to defend our *good name and reputation*. In this case, however, **we do not have the right to use force**. We must use some other means instead.

Defending Others

> Legitimate defense can be not only a right but a grave duty for one who is responsible for the lives of others (*Catechism*, 2265).

We have the duty to defend the rights of those under our care. A man must protect and defend the rights of his wife and children. A woman must protect the good name of her husband and the rights of her children. The State must protect and defend the rights of its citizens. Employers must defend the rights of their employees.

Our actions must be in proportion to the nature and importance of the rights being threatened. The same four conditions regarding defending our own life, purity, and property apply when we are defending these rights for someone else. In defending someone's property, the worth of that property must be taken into account. We may *not* use force to defend someone's good name.

Landscape, with the Good Samaritan, by Heinrich Reinhold

The Death Penalty

> Assuming that the guilty party's identity and responsibility have been fully determined, the traditional teaching of the Church does not exclude recourse to the death penalty, if this is the only possible way of effectively defending human lives against the unjust aggressor (*Catechism*, 2267).

The *death penalty* (capital punishment) is *not* forbidden by the Fifth Commandment. In fact, in the Old Law, God *commanded* capital punishment for certain offenses (Leviticus 20:1-10), and God could never command anything sinful. The State has the right to punish its citizens for behavior that seriously harms others, infringes on their rights, or is injurious to the common good (*Catechism*, 2266). This punishment may include, under certain grave circumstances, the death penalty.

The **purpose of civil punishmen**t is not to execute vengeance, but to protect people from harm and to defend public order, which would suffer greatly if criminals were allowed to act in contempt of the law. However, the State has a grave duty to prove that a person is guilty before inflicting punishment on him. **No punishment must ever be inflicted on the innocent.** This is even more critical in the case of the death penalty. Before someone is sentenced to death, the utmost care must be taken to make sure there is positive, *incontrovertible proof* that, without any doubt whatsoever, the person is guilty. When it is possible to protect society from an aggressor without having recourse to the death penalty, the Church urges the State to use other means at its disposal instead (*Catechism*, 2267).

Just War

> The defense of the common good requires that an unjust aggressor be rendered unable to cause harm. For this reason, those who legitimately hold authority also have the right to use arms to repel aggressors against the civil community entrusted to their responsibility (*Catechism*, 2265).

A soldier does not break the Fifth Commandment when he kills an enemy combatant in a just war, as long as his intention is primarily to stop the enemy from doing further harm. Such deaths are *permitted* for the sake of defeating the enemy, but they must not be desired for their own sake.

If a soldier kills anyone either outside of battle or without legitimate military orders to do so, he is guilty of murder, just like anyone else. Every soldier has a solemn duty to honor his country by acting nobly, both on and off the battlefield.

The use of military force is *not* an intrinsically evil act. There are some cases when it is morally just, but only if certain conditions are met. The Catholic Church's **just war doctrine** defines these conditions as follows (*Catechism*, 2309):

- First, "the damage inflicted by the aggressor on the nation or community of nations must be lasting, grave, and certain."
- Second, "all other means of putting an end to it must have been shown to be impractical or ineffective."
- Third, "there must be serious prospects of success."
- Fourth, "the use of arms must not produce evils and disorders graver than the evil to be eliminated. The power of modern means of destruction weighs very heavily in evaluating this condition."

The decision regarding when to go to war rests with the lawful authorities in the State. In assessing whether the use of military force would be just, these authorities may have information not known to the public which could affect their decision. However, some of the conditions above can be difficult to assess. Therefore, those in authority have a moral responsibility to exercise the utmost caution when making such decisions.

War is extremely serious, and it can have devastating consequences. All nations and citizens have a moral obligation to strive for peace and, if possible, to avoid war. "Blessed are the peacemakers, for they shall be called sons of God" (Matthew 5:9).

Chapter 12 Review

Matching: For each statement, select the letter of the best term from the list below. There are more terms listed than there are statements, and no term can be used more than once.

A. pride	E. euthanasia	I. embryonic	M. direct scandal
B. abortion	F. pluripotent	J. revenge	N. capital punishment
C. sloth	G. gluttony	K. life	O. indirect scandal
D. anger	H. hatred	L. liberty	P. excommunication

1. Sin in which a person indulges excessively in food or drink: ________.
2. The first fundamental right is the right to ________.
3. A very serious penalty for certain extremely grave sins, which prevents a person from being in full communion with the Church: ________.
4. The intentional killing of the handicapped, the sick, the old, the feeble, the dying, or anyone else deemed to have a poor "quality of life": ________.
5. A person is guilty of ________ if he intentionally leads another person to sin.
6. When a person acts on his anger by willfully seeking to inflict harm on his neighbor, he is guilty of desiring ________, which is always sinful.
7 The intentional killing of a preborn infant, which is a grave sin: ________.
8. Closely related to anger and revenge is the sin of ________, in which a person willfully desires that harm come to his neighbor.
9. A person commits a sin of ________ if (1) he foresees that his actions will lead his neighbor to sin, and (2) he can reasonably avoid those actions, but he performs them anyway.
10. ________ stem cell research, which kills a human being in the earliest stage of development, is a grave sin against the Fifth Commandment.

True or False: Write *True* or *False* for the following statements.

________ 11. Killing an innocent human being is permissible only if the State commands it for a serious reason, such as concerns about overpopulation.

________ 12. If someone intentionally acts to indirectly bring about an innocent person's death, he is not guilty of murder, but he has committed a serious venial sin.

________ 13. Torture is sometimes justifiable, but only against those who are believed to be guilty of very serious crimes.

________ 14. Anyone who formally cooperates in an abortion is automatically excommunicated from the Church.

________ 15. Euthanasia is a grave sin that is never morally permissible under any circumstances, and it is extremely dangerous to society.

_________ 16. It is gravely sinful for the State to exert pressure on anyone to restrict child births for the sake of public health, or for any other reason.

_________ 17. A feeding tube is an extraordinary medical procedure. Therefore, it is always morally permissible to remove it.

_________ 18. Every human being, regardless of his or her race, must be loved and respected as a person created in the image and likeness of God for whom Jesus Christ died on the Cross.

_________ 19. We are obligated to ensure that our family members receive a Christian burial.

_________ 20. Risking one's own life or health is never morally permissible.

_________ 21. A just self-love is a well-ordered love that seeks one's own eternal happiness, and that desires to protect one's soul from evil.

_________ 22. There is one primary rule we must follow regarding eating: we must act according to right reason.

_________ 23. Getting drunk is not a grave sin, unless one is driving or is operating dangerous tools or machinery.

_________ 24. Hunting animals for food is immoral.

_________ 25. In all cases, if someone is threatening to steal or destroy our property, we have the right to use whatever force is necessary to stop him.

_________ 26. We have the duty to defend the rights of those under our care.

_________ 27. The death penalty is forbidden by the Fifth Commandment.

_________ 28. A soldier does not break the Fifth Commandment when he kills an enemy combatant in a just war, as long as his intention is primarily to stop the enemy from doing further harm.

_________ 29. Any culpable negligence toward our neighbor is sinful, in proportion to the degree to which it endangers his life or health.

_________ 30. The use of military force is an intrinsically evil act.

Multiple Choice: Write the letter of the best answer in the space provided.

31. Which of the following statements about anger is *not* correct? _________
    - A. A person sins if his anger is unjust (that is, if he deliberately responds in anger about something for which he has no right to be angry).
    - B. The emotion of anger is always sinful.
    - C. A person sins if he allows his anger to be too intense in proportion to the offense (in other words, he overreacts).
    - D. A person sins if he acts on his anger in the wrong way.
    - E. If the emotion of anger leads a person to think or act in a way that is contrary to justice or charity, he commits the capital sin of anger.

32. Suicide is a grave sin against ________.
    A. God
    B. Oneself
    C. One's neighbor
    D. All of the above
    E. None of the above

33. Which of the following is correct? ________
    A. Animals are persons; therefore, their lives must be protected at all costs.
    B. God created the animals, and He has given them to us as gifts. We honor God when we treat animals with compassion.
    C. Since animals are *not* persons, cruelty to animals is *not* sinful.
    D. Both A and B
    E. Both B and C

34. We have the right to defend ourselves from any threat to our life, even if we must take the life of the aggressor to do so, as long as which of the following conditions are met? ________
    A. We must not use any greater physical force than is necessary to protect ourselves from the aggressor. If we can protect ourselves without killing the aggressor, we must avoid taking his life.
    B. We may use force against the aggressor only during the act of aggression. We must not use force after the act of aggression, nor may we use force before.
    C. If there is any other way to avoid the danger, without sinning or surrendering our rights, then we must *not* use physical force.
    D. Our intention must be primarily to defend ourselves, *not* to kill the aggressor. We must not directly intend to kill the aggressor.
    E. All of the above

35. According to the Church's *just war doctrine*, in order for the use of military force to be just, all of the following conditions must be met, *except* ________.
    A. The use of military force must be approved by the international community.
    B. The damage inflicted by the aggressor on the nation or community of nations must be lasting, grave, and certain.
    C. All other means of putting an end to the aggression must have been shown to be impractical or ineffective.
    D. There must be serious prospects of success.
    E. The use of arms must not produce evils and disorders graver than the evil to be eliminated.

Chapter 13. The Sanctity of Marriage: The Sixth and Ninth Commandments

"Have you not read that he who made them from the beginning made them male and female, and said, 'For this reason a man shall leave his father and mother and be joined to his wife, and the two shall become one'? So they are no longer two but one. What therefore God has joined together, let no man put asunder" (Matthew 19:4-6).

When God created man and woman in His image and likeness (Genesis 1:27), He intended something very special, profound, and sacred. In His Providence, God willed that a man and a woman would enjoy mutual friendship, companionship, and love in the security of a lifelong union called *marriage*.

Marriage of the Virgin, by Vittore Carpaccio

The famous poet William Shakespeare once wrote:

> What's in a name? That which we call a rose
> By any other name would smell as sweet.

Nothing could ever change the *reality* of what a rose is, even if someone were to call it by some other name. There is a corollary to this statement that also holds true:

> Nothing else *called* a rose could ever *be* a rose,
> Except that which truly *is* a rose.

Calling *something else* a rose could never change the *reality* that it is *not* actually a rose. The same is true of marriage. **Marriage** is the union of one man and one woman under God for life. Nothing else *called* a marriage could ever *be* a marriage, except that which truly *is* a marriage. The union of one man and one woman under God for life is the *reality* of what marriage is.

The **Natural Law** is the Divine Law inscribed in the soul of man, so that man may know right from wrong. Like the Divine Law, the Natural Law is absolute, universal, and unchangeable. It applies to all people, in all circumstances, in all places, and at all times. The institution of marriage, as the union of one man and one woman under God for life, is ordained by the Divine Law, and thus is part of the Natural Law. Therefore, **the institution of marriage is absolute, universal, and unchangeable**.

> Civil authority should consider it a grave duty "to acknowledge the true nature of marriage and the family, to protect and foster them, to safeguard public morality, and promote domestic prosperity" (*Catechism*, 2210).

Any laws attempting to redefine marriage are intrinsically evil, and null and void. Neither the State, nor the media, nor the workplace, nor anyone else has the right—or the ability—to change the *reality* of what marriage is. Not even the Church may do so.

Marriage is not merely a private matter. Marriage is a *public* institution, with implications for all of society. It is an error to claim that the State should treat marriage as only a private religious matter and have no laws regarding it, including those protecting marriage as the union of one man and one woman. Marriage is not merely a function of the Church. Marriage is part of the Natural Law. Both the Church and the State have a duty to protect and foster the true meaning and nature of marriage, and to reject any attempts to redefine it.

The Sixth Commandment

> "You shall not commit adultery" (Exodus 20:14).

Marriage is a holy institution. A man and a woman united in marriage are set apart for God in a special way, and their marriage is sacred and honorable to Him. When a man and a woman marry, they make a vow to be faithful to each other for the rest of their lives. Their love for each other is special and unique. No one else could ever take the place of one's husband or wife, as long as they both shall live.

Marriage is a covenant. Marriage is a sacred agreement and bond between one man and one woman under God for life. Our Lord Jesus Christ elevated marriage between two baptized Christians even further, making it a *sacrament*. The Sacrament of Holy Matrimony is a living sign of the covenant between Jesus Christ and His Church.

The very first public miracle that Our Lord Jesus Christ performed was at a wedding, for the sake of the dignity and joy of the bride and groom (John 2:1-11). Sacred Scripture also paints a vivid picture of the joyous wedding of Jesus Christ, the Lamb of God, with His Bride, the Church:

> "Let us rejoice and exult and give him the glory, for the marriage of the Lamb has come, and his Bride has made herself ready; it was granted her to be clothed with fine linen, bright and pure"—for the fine linen is the righteous deeds of the saints" (Revelation 19:7-8).

The Purposes of Marriage

> The spouses' union achieves the twofold end of marriage: the good of the spouses themselves and the transmission of life. These two meanings or values of marriage cannot be separated without altering the couple's spiritual life and compromising the goods of marriage and the future of the family (*Catechism*, 2363).

Through the holy institution of marriage, God joins a man and a woman together in a sacred bond. At the same time, He gives them the privilege of sharing in His creative power to bring forth new human life; this special privilege is called **procreation**.

The **two main purposes of marriage** are the procreation and upbringing of children and the good of the husband and wife. These two purposes are inseparably connected, and they are both essential to marriage.

> "The matrimonial covenant, by which a man and a woman establish between themselves a partnership of the whole of life, is by its nature ordered toward the good of the spouses and the procreation and education of offspring..." (*Catechism*, 1601).

The Procreation and Upbringing of Children. In His Providence, God created man and woman, and He ordained marriage between them, so that every human being would belong to a family of persons united in love. In God's plan, marriage and children go together. A married couple must be open to the gift of human life, as an expression of their openness to the Will of God and their love for each other. This is the **procreative purpose** of the unique expression of the love between a husband and wife in marriage.

> By its very nature the institution of marriage and married love is ordered to the procreation and education of the offspring and it is in them that it finds its crowning glory (*Gaudium et Spes*, no. 48).

Adoption is a loving way to help children in need and to act as God's instruments in providing them a home and family, especially for married couples who are unable to have their own biological children.

> Sacred Scripture and the Church's traditional practice see in *large families* a sign of God's blessing and the parents' generosity (*Catechism*, 2373).

Raising a family is not easy. It is difficult, and it requires many sacrifices, several of which are unique to the vocation of marriage. However, it is also a *blessing*. Children are a gift from God, and the ability of a husband and wife to share in God's creative power to bring forth new human life is a sacred privilege.

> Children are the supreme gift of marriage.... Hence, true married love and the whole structure of family life which results from it, without diminishment of the other ends of marriage, are directed to disposing the spouses to cooperate valiantly with the love of the Creator and Savior, who through them will increase and enrich his family from day to day (*Gaudium et Spes*, no. 50).

The best gift that parents can give their children is a holy, happy marriage. The love between a husband and a wife can transform the world, one child at a time.

The Good of the Husband and Wife. God designed man and woman to physically, emotionally, and spiritually complement each other for their mutual good and sanctification, and for the good of the children whom He wills to be the fruit of their love. When God created the first woman, He "brought her to the man" (Genesis 2:22), and the man (Adam) uttered the first poetry in history:

> "This at last is bone of my bones and flesh of my flesh; she shall be called Woman, because she was taken out of Man" (Genesis 2:23).

The Marriage of the Virgin, by Bartolome Esteban Murillo

A man and a woman joined together in marriage form an intimate union, a holy bond, and a sacred friendship. Those who are married in the Church are consecrated to one another, in Christ.

> My soul takes pleasure in three things, and they are beautiful in the sight of the Lord and of men: agreement between brothers, friendship between neighbors, and a wife and husband who live in harmony (Sirach 25:1).

God calls a man and a woman in marriage to give themselves to each other *completely*, so that they may be totally united as husband and wife: physically, emotionally, mentally, and spiritually. This is the **unitive purpose** of the unique expression of the love between a husband and wife in marriage. They are no longer merely two individuals; they are *one* married couple, united in their love for each other. This unitive purpose cannot be separated from the procreative purpose of marriage. Both of these purposes, the procreative and the unitive, are inherent to the unique expression of the love between a husband and wife in marriage (Pope Paul VI, *Humanae Vitae* [Encyclical on the Regulation of Birth], July 25, 1968, no. 12).

The love between a man and a woman is an exclusive love, which only a husband and wife united in marriage can experience in its fullness. The husband *belongs* to his wife, and the wife *belongs* to her husband. The relationship of a man and a woman in marriage requires trust, and **the cornerstone of this trust is faithfulness**.

Faithful Christian marriage is a blessing. Through it, God brings about the mutual sanctification of the husband and wife for their good and the good of their children, as well as the good of society itself.

The Goods of Marriage

> The "intimate union of marriage, as a mutual giving of two persons, and the good of the children, demand total fidelity from the spouses and require an unbreakable union between them" (*Catechism*, 1646).

The three main **goods of marriage** are children, fidelity, and permanence (or indissolubility). These *goods* are blessings that God brings about through the institution of marriage.

Children are a blessing from God. When God created mankind, He said, "be fruitful and multiply" (Genesis 1:28, 9:1). This is both a command and a blessing. Marriage is the sacred institution through which God calls a man and a woman united in love to fulfill this command and receive His blessing.

> Blessed is everyone who fears the Lord, who walks in his ways! You shall eat the fruit of the labor of your hands; you shall be happy, and it shall be well with you.

Parents from Heaven

"God gave me a mother and father more worthy of Heaven than of Earth," said Saint Therese of Lisieux about her parents, Saints Louis and Zelie Martin.

Louis Martin was a quiet, resourceful man who earned his trade as a watch maker. When he was in his 20s, he sought to join the Monastery of Great Saint Bernard in the Swiss Alps. The charity and contemplative life of the monks appealed to Louis, but before he could be admitted he had to learn Latin. So, he returned to Alencon, where he lived, and began studying Latin. At some point during this time, he came to the conclusion that he did not have a vocation to the priesthood.

Zelie Guerin was a brilliant young woman, who also sought to enter the religious life. She decided to enter the religious order of the sisters of the Hotel-Dieu, but she was not accepted. Later, she realized that she was called to be married. Eventually, she became an expert in the fine art of lacemaking. She started her own business and was quite successful.

Louis, who was eight years older than Zelie, met his bride-to-be, thanks to some match-making by his mother. Mrs. Martin had met Zelie while taking a lacemaking class, and she was determined to have Louis meet her as well. Her plan worked! Louis and Zelie were married in July of 1858.

They had nine children: seven girls and two boys. However, both of the boys and two of the girls died at a young age. The grief of losing one child is a great trial for any parent. Yet, Zelie's strength and deep faith in God saw her through this grief four times.

In 1873, Louis and Zelie had their last child, a young fragile girl whom they feared would be their fifth little one to die at a tender age. However, this time, God granted them the favor for which they begged in their prayers. Their child would live. Her name was Marie-Francoise-Therese. She is known today as Saint Therese.

Zelie herself died just four years later, and Louis was left to raise his five daughters alone. With calm determination and resourcefulness, he held the family together and raised his girls to love the Lord. All five of them ended up entering the religious life.

Throughout their lives, Mr. and Mrs. Louis and Zelie Martin showed their children what it means to have deep faith in God and trust in His Providence. Their willingness to make great sacrifices for each other and their children can serve as a model of Christian charity. They are now saints in Heaven.

Your wife will be like a fruitful vine within your house; your children will be like olive shoots around your table. (Psalm 128:1-3).

Another blessing of marriage is the fidelity of the husband and wife. This fidelity is a blessing, not only to the couple themselves, but also to their children and to society. By its very nature, **true love requires faithfulness**. It also requires commitment. The covenant of marriage is the sacred bond through which God unites a man and a woman in a lifelong commitment of faithfulness and love.

The sacred bond between a man and a woman united in marriage is permanent, for as long as they both shall live. This permanence provides the stable soil in which their love can grow and their children can flourish. Children are blessed when their mother and father are committed to each other in an unbreakable bond of friendship, love, and fidelity. Society as a whole inherently benefits from, and depends on, this stability.

Sins against the Sixth Commandment

> The sixth commandment and the New Testament forbid adultery absolutely. The prophets denounce the gravity of adultery; they see it as an image of the sin of idolatry (*Catechism*, 2380).

God has given human beings natural procreative instincts, abilities, and passions that are meant only for marriage. It is healthy and normal for a man to be attracted to a woman, and for a woman to be attracted to a man. Such attractions draw men and women together in marriage, so that God can bring more people into the world. It is also normal for young people to have questions about such things. They should direct those questions privately to their parents.

When a man and a woman are joined together in marriage, they agree to turn aside from any attractions they may feel regarding any other person. They make a solemn vow that they will be faithful to each other for as long as they both shall live. In the special love between a man and a woman, and in all the intimate expressions of that love, they will reserve themselves exclusively for each other as husband and wife.

True love between a man and a woman is possible only when their relationship is built on a foundation of friendship, faithfulness, and mutual respect. This foundation must begin *before* the couple is married. In order to build this foundation, both the man and the woman must be **committed to remaining pure**. Attractions between a man and a woman are normal, but they can also be very powerful. **It is critical that both the man and the woman are firmly committed to avoiding all the near occasions of sin in this area.** Other than innocent gestures such as holding hands, they should avoid all intimate expressions of affection until they are married.

If either person is not committed to remaining pure, their relationship will not be pleasing to God, and they will end up hurting each other. So many couples ruin their chance at happiness by pretending to be married when they are not. A "jewel of great price" is worth the wait.

It is also important to remember that dating is meant to be a preparation for marriage. The purpose of dating is to discern whether someone is the right person to marry. If someone is too young to be married, he or she should not be going out on dates. When either person is not prepared to be married, dating can lead to sins of impurity and to deep heartache.

Sins of Impurity. When a person willfully uses or takes pleasure in his procreative instincts, abilities, or passions outside of marriage, he commits a *sin of impurity*. Sins of impurity may be *internal* (willful thoughts or desires) or *external*. At the root of these sins is the capital sin of *lust*. **Lust** is the sin in which a person has a disordered desire for, or inordinate enjoyment of, the pleasure associated with his procreative instincts, abilities, and passions. This pleasure "is morally disordered when sought for itself, isolated from its procreative and unitive purposes" (*Catechism*, 2351).

The Sixth Commandment forbids all *external sins of impurity*. The Ninth Commandment forbids all *internal sins of impurity* (willful thoughts or desires that are impure). These sins are closely related. When a person commits an internal sin of impurity, it is more likely that he will also commit an external sin of impurity, unless he repents and earnestly strives to avoid all the near occasions of sin in this area.

By their very nature, **all sins of impurity are grave sins, and they are intrinsically evil acts**. However, some sins of impurity are more grave than others, depending on the persons involved and the nature of the sin.

The Sixth Commandment explicitly forbids the sin of *adultery*. **Adultery** is the grave sin in which a man is not faithful to his wife, or a woman is not faithful to her husband, thus violating their marriage vows. Adultery includes all sins of impurity and inappropriate affection between a married person and anyone other than that person's spouse.

The sin of adultery is extremely grave, and is considerably worse than sins of impurity voluntarily committed by unmarried persons or by a person alone (but those sins are also grave). Moreover, when people married in the Church commit adultery, they break their marriage vows, thereby sinning against the First Commandment as well.

Adultery is a grave sin of injustice against one's spouse, as well as a grievous sin against one's children. It is an intrinsically evil act, **never justifiable under any circumstances**. It causes intense pain to the injured spouse, serious spiritual and emotional harm to the children, and numerous disorders in society. It is a reprehensible act.

> Adultery is an injustice. He who commits adultery fails in his commitment. He does injury to the sign of the covenant which the marriage bond is, transgresses the rights of the other spouse, and undermines the institution of marriage by breaking the contract on which it is based. He compromises the good of human generation and the welfare of children who need their parents' stable union (*Catechism*, 2381).

Marriage is the cornerstone of the family, and the family is the foundation of society. Healthy marriages lead to healthy families, and healthy families lead to a healthy society. The sin of adultery destroys the lifeblood of a healthy marriage and family, which is *trust*. The result is pain, chaos, and disorder, both in the family and in society itself.

Sins in which someone uses violence to violate a person's right to purity and modesty are extremely grave as well. Besides being grave sins of impurity, they are also grievous sins against justice and charity, as well as against human decency and respect.

Also extremely grave are sins of impurity that are contrary even to the natural procreative instincts, abilities, and passions that draw a man and a woman together. Besides violating the Sixth Commandment, such sins are contrary to the natural order established by the Creator. **When a nation institutionalizes such grave evils, that nation destroys itself from within.**

It is extremely dangerous and sinful to tamper with the natural order established by our Creator. God creates every human being in the way He intends for that person to be: *either male or female* (Genesis 1:27). This is the *reality* of the way every human being is created; it is stamped on every cell in the person's body.

Contraception. The use of *contraception* is also a grave sin against the Sixth Commandment. **It is an intrinsically evil act, never morally permissible** under any circumstances. **Contraception** refers to any method or procedure that attempts to prevent a child from being conceived when a man and a woman exercise their procreative abilities. The use of contraception shows contempt for God's blessing and command that human beings are to "be fruitful and multiply" (Genesis 1:28, 9:1). The same is true of any procedure that is intended to cause *sterilization*. **Such procedures are gravely sinful, as are every other form of birth control**.

Some forms of contraception also act as *abortifacients*. An **abortifacient** is a type of contraception that kills a human being through a chemical abortion if it is unable to prevent that human being from being conceived. **The use of abortifacients is a grave sin against both the Fifth and Sixth Commandments.**

Divorce and Remarriage. Marriage is the union of one man and one woman under God for life. A **civil divorce** is a decree issued by civil authorities of the State that affects the legal status of a married couple, whom the State subsequently treats as being no longer married. However, the notion of "divorce," which claims that a married man and woman who are both still living can become unmarried, is contrary to God's Law. A civil divorce is an attempt by human beings to do something that God has made *impossible*. **In reality, no married couple can ever truly be "divorced."**

A man and a woman united in marriage are joined together by God Himself. Jesus said, "they are no longer two but one flesh" (Mark 10:8). Attempting to become "divorced" is like trying to rip a person in half and expecting each half to go on living independently of the other. No wonder divorce is so painful! "What therefore God has joined together, let no man put asunder" (Matthew 19:6).

> *Divorce* is a grave offense against the natural law.... Contracting a new union, even if it is recognized by civil law, adds to the gravity of the rupture: the remarried spouse is then in a situation of public and permanent adultery (*Catechism*, 2384).

Whoever procures a civil divorce and marries someone else while their true husband or wife is still alive, commits the grave sin of adultery, because in the eyes of God they are still married. Even the Church cannot change this teaching, because **it is the teaching of the Lord Jesus Christ Himself.**

> And he said to them: "Whoever divorces his wife and marries another, commits adultery against her; and if she divorces her husband and marries another, she commits adultery" (Mark 10:11-12).

In certain cases, such as those affecting someone's safety, the Church may allow a legal separation between a husband and wife. However, even then, the couple must not attempt to marry someone else, because in reality they are still married to each other.

An **annulment** is a declaration by the Catholic Church that what was thought to be a valid marriage is actually null and void. Only the Church has the authority to make the determination regarding whether there are sufficient grounds to issue an annulment. Because an annulment is *not* a divorce, but rather a declaration that a true marriage never existed, those who receive an annulment are free to marry another person if they choose.

Finally, sometimes one spouse wants to get divorced, and the other doesn't, but the civil-divorce laws where they live do not require the consent of both spouses. If a person is divorced against his or her will, that person has not sinned, as long as he or she remains faithful to his or her wedding vows.

The Ninth Commandment

> "You shall not covet your neighbor's wife" (Exodus 20:17).

If we are ever to see God, we must be *pure*. It is impossible for a person to see God if he is focused on what is forbidden by Him. **"Purity of heart is the precondition of the vision of God"** (*Catechism*, 2519, emphasis added).

Purity of Heart

> Purity of heart will enable us to see God: it enables us even now to see things according to God (*Catechism*, 2531).

The two pillars of purity are *chastity* and *modesty*. **Chastity** is the virtue by which a person regulates his procreative instincts and abilities according to his state in life and moderates his related passions according to right reason. **Modesty** is the virtue by which a person maintains a proper amount of reserve in his conduct and manner of dressing.

Certain virtues strengthen the will in the totality of the human person. Chastity is one of those virtues. When a person is completely chaste, he grows in courage and fortitude, has a deep peace in his soul, and becomes like the angels in Heaven, who constantly behold the face of God (Fr. Laux, p. 108). Chastity helps us to avoid both external and internal sins of impurity. **Perseverance in chastity is essential to maintaining purity of heart.**

Also essential to maintaining purity of heart is the virtue of modesty. It is impossible to be completely chaste without also being modest. **Modesty is the guardian of chastity.**

> Modesty is decency. It inspires one's choice of clothing. It keeps silence or reserve where there is evident risk of unhealthy curiosity. It is discreet (*Catechism*, 2522).

The purpose of clothing is to cover and respectfully adorn the body, not to entice others to sin. We must be modest in our manner of dress and our behavior. We must treat everyone with respect, even those who do not show respect for themselves. We cannot control what others do, but we can and must control ourselves.

Marriage of the Virgin, by Raphael

Cultivating chastity and modesty, and hence purity of heart, requires purity of intention, purity of vision, and prayer (*Catechism*, 2520). **Purity of intention** means desiring the Will of God above all else. Purity of intention is an integral part of the *fear of the Lord*.

Purity of vision means refusing to focus on anything impure, either externally or internally. The person who has purity of vision becomes more like God, "who art of purer eyes than to behold evil and canst not look on wrong" (Habakkuk 1:13). **It is impossible to develop purity of vision if we watch movies, television shows, or other things that are tainted with impurity.** We must be very guarded regarding what we allow ourselves to take into our heart.

One of the best ways to strengthen our purity of vision is to spend time gazing on the Holy Face of Jesus from the *Shroud of Turin* (widely venerated as the burial cloth that covered Our Lord after His death on the Cross). When we focus on the Holy Face of Jesus, the image of Our Lady of Guadalupe, or other holy images, we elevate our heart and mind toward Heaven. The soul whose gaze is focused on Heaven is not easily lured into temptation.

Prayer helps us keep our focus on Heaven by cultivating our relationships with God, the Blessed Virgin Mary, and the angels and saints. If we are in the habit of regularly conversing with God and His servants, we are more likely to do so when we experience temptation.

Sins against the Ninth Commandment

> The heart is the seat of moral personality: "Out of the heart come evil thoughts, murder, adultery, fornication…" The struggle against carnal covetousness entails purifying the heart and practicing temperance (*Catechism*, 2517).

The Ninth Commandment forbids all internal sins of impurity. Such sins can easily lead to external sins of impurity.

> "You have heard that it was said, 'You shall not commit adultery.' But I say to you that everyone who looks at a woman lustfully has already committed adultery with her in his heart" (Matthew 5:27-28).

To **covet** means to have an unjust or inordinate willful desire for someone or something that rightfully belongs to one's neighbor. **Coveting another person's spouse is a grave sin against the Ninth Commandment.** It is also a sin against the Ninth Commandment to deliberately consent to an impure thought or to willfully desire something impure. Even when a person is merely aware of impure thoughts or desires, if he freely and deliberately allows them to remain, he commits a sin. However, if an impure thought or desire flashes through a person's mind, and he experiences a feeling of pleasure *without willing it*, he is merely being tempted. He has not sinned unless he *freely* and *deliberately* **wills** to focus on impurity or to take pleasure in it.

Those who commit sins of impurity sin against the dignity of the human person. They degrade themselves and sin against their own bodies, which are meant to be holy. **They treat themselves and others like objects to use rather than persons to love and respect.**

> Shun immorality. Every other sin which a man commits is outside the body; but the immoral man sins against his own body. Do you not know that your body is a temple of the Holy Spirit within you, which you have from God? You are not your own; you were bought with a price. So glorify God in your body (1 Corinthians 6:18-20).

Temptations of impurity come in an endless chain. If a person grasps at the first temptation, he unwittingly takes hold of the entire chain. Very quickly, he may pass from one sin to another, and the chain will go on and on, with each temptation growing stronger and more serious than the next. Therefore, **it is critical to reject all impure thoughts, feelings, and desires as soon as one first becomes aware of them**.

The more a person gives into lust and other sins of impurity, the more he will be enslaved by them. He may even develop a serious addiction, one that is even more powerful and degrading than alcohol or drug abuse. As long as he continues on this path, nothing will ever fill the emptiness and insatiable hunger in his soul, unless he repents and turns to the only one Who can save him: Jesus Christ.

The very foundations of society depend on "the propagation of the human race in moral purity and strength, on marriage and the family" (Fr. Laux, p. 110). Impurity destroys civil society. Chastity builds up civil society. Impurity poisons human relationships. Chastity purifies human relationships. Impurity breeds selfishness, shame, and violence. Chastity cultivates selfless love, peace, and harmony. Impurity engenders weakness and self-degradation. Chastity fosters strength and self-respect. Impurity leads to corruption and spiritual blindness. Chastity leads to purity of heart and the vision of God. "Blessed are the pure in heart, for they shall see God" (Matthew 5:8).

Marriage of the Virgin, by Jacques Stella

Chapter 13 Review

Matching: For each statement, select the letter of the best term from the list below. There are more terms listed than there are statements, and no term can be used more than once.

A. unitive	E. only	I. procreation	M. marriage
B. covet	F. civil contract	J. annulment	N. contraception
C. attract	G. adultery	K. celibacy	O. abortifacient
D. divorce	H. lust	L. infatuation	P. purity of heart

1. The union of one man and one woman under God for life: ________.
2. A grave sin in which a man is not faithful to his wife, or a woman is not faithful to her husband: ________.
3. God calls a man and a woman in marriage to give themselves to each other completely. This is the ________ purpose of the unique expression of the love between a husband and wife in marriage.
4. Sin in which a person has a disordered desire for, or inordinate enjoyment of, the pleasure associated with his procreative instincts, abilities, and passions: ________.
5. Any method or procedure that attempts to prevent a child from being conceived when a man and a woman exercise their procreative abilities: ________.
6. To ________ means to have an unjust or inordinate willful desire for someone or something that rightfully belongs to one's neighbor.
7. The privilege that God gives to a man and a woman of sharing in His creative power to bring forth new human life: ________.
8. The precondition of the vision of God: ________.
9 A declaration by the Catholic Church that what was thought to be a valid marriage is actually null and void: ________.
10. A type of contraception that kills a human being through a chemical abortion: ________.

True or False: Write *True* or *False* for the following statements.

________ 11. The institution of marriage, as the union of one man and one woman under God for life, is ordained by the Divine Law, and thus is part of the Natural Law.

________ 12. The two main purposes of marriage are the procreation and upbringing of children and the good of the husband and wife.

________ 13. Any laws attempting to redefine marriage are intrinsically evil, and null and void.

________ 14. Marriage is the cornerstone of the family, and the family is the foundation of society.

_________ 15. Marriage is a private religious matter, not a public institution.

_________ 16. The Sacrament of Holy Matrimony is a living sign of the covenant between Jesus Christ and His Church.

_________ 17. Adultery is a grave sin of injustice against one's spouse, as well as a grievous sin against one's children. It is an intrinsically evil act.

_________ 18. The three main goods of marriage are children, fidelity, and permanence (or indissolubility).

_________ 19. The use of contraception is permissible under certain circumstances.

_________ 20. Coveting another person's spouse is a grave sin against the Ninth Commandment.

Multiple Choice: Write the letter of the best answer in the space provided.

21. Cultivating chastity and modesty, and hence purity of heart, *requires* _________.
    A. Prayer
    B. Purity of intention and purity of vision
    C. A vocation to the religious life
    D. Both A and B
    E. All of the above

22. Which of the following is correct? _________
    A. The relationship of a man and a woman united in marriage requires trust, and the cornerstone of this trust is faithfulness.
    B. A married couple must be open to the gift of human life, as an expression of their openness to the Will of God and their love for each other.
    C. Through faithful Christian marriage, God brings about the mutual sanctification of the husband and wife for their good and the good of their children, as well as the good of society itself.
    D. Adoption is a loving way for married couples to help children in need and to act as God's instruments in providing them a home and family.
    E. All of the above

23. Which of the following statements is *not* correct? _________
    A. A civil divorce is a decree issued by civil authorities of the State that affects the legal status of a married couple.
    B. The Church's current teachings may be changed to allow divorce and remarriage under certain circumstances.
    C. Divorce is against God's Law.
    D. Whoever procures a civil divorce and then marries someone else while their true husband or wife is still alive commits the grave sin of adultery.
    E. If a person is divorced against his or her will, that person has not sinned, as long as he or she remains faithful to his or her wedding vows.

24. Those who commit sins of impurity: ________.
    A. Sin against the dignity of the human person
    B. Degrade themselves and sin against their own bodies, which are meant to be holy
    C. Treat themselves and others like objects to use rather than persons to love and respect
    D. All of the above
    E. None of the above

25. Marriage is ________.
    A. A public institution, with implications for all of society
    B. A holy institution that is absolute, universal, and unchangeable
    C. Whatever the State or the Church defines it to be
    D. Both A and B
    E. Both A and C

Marriage of the Virgin, by Johann Friedrich Overbeck

Chapter 14. Truth and Freedom: The Seventh, Eighth, and Tenth Commandments

Jesus then said ..., "If you continue in my word, you are truly my disciples, and you will know the truth, and the truth will make you free" (John 8:31-32).

GOD CREATED MAN to be free. Every human being has a right to *personal liberty*, within just limits. The **right to personal liberty** is the right to do good, and to choose between two or more courses of action that are good. It includes the right to follow our conscience, to worship God freely, to establish and raise a family, to choose a means of employment and education, to make our own decisions regarding buying and selling goods, and to enjoy other reasonable freedoms that are in accordance with the common good.

Our right to personal liberty is not to be confused with our **free will**, which is our *ability*

Joshua Passing the River Jordan with the Ark of the Covenant, by Benjamin West

to decide what we will believe and what we will do. Because we have free will, we are *capable* of choosing between good and evil. However, we only have the *right* to choose *good*, because no one has the right to do evil. Everyone is morally obligated to do what is good and to avoid what is evil. **The right to personal liberty is not the right to choose between good and evil, but rather the right to choose between good and good.**

Intrinsic to our personal liberty is our right to own *private property*. Without this right, we would need to depend on the State for our sustenance and advancement, and we would ultimately become slaves of the State. Also intrinsic to our liberty is our right to live in *truth*. Truth is the foundation of all human relationships and all knowledge. Without the truth, we could never truly be free. **We have a duty to always seek the truth, speak the truth, and live according to the truth.**

The Seventh Commandment

"You shall not steal" (Exodus 20:15).

In order to live and survive, man needs food, clothing, shelter, and other material goods. He also needs material goods for his family. Because he is meant to be free, he has the right to *own* these material goods, rather than depending on the State or others for them.

The Right and Benefits of Private Property

> The goods of creation are destined for the whole human race. However, the earth is divided up among men to assure the security of their lives, endangered by poverty and threatened by violence. The appropriation of property is legitimate for guaranteeing the freedom and dignity of persons and for helping each of them to meet his basic needs and the needs of those in his charge (*Catechism*, 2402).

Man has a right to own private property. God has consistently confirmed this right, and He has given us Commandments that protect it. The right to own private property is an incentive for man to work. By earning a living, he can afford to purchase material goods for himself and his family. **The Seventh Commandment implicitly confirms the right to own private property, since it forbids stealing what rightfully *belongs* to others** (Fr. Laux, p. 115).

Some have claimed that, according to the following passage from Sacred Scripture, owning private property is contrary to Christianity:

> Now the company of those who believed were of one heart and soul, and no one said that any of the things which he possessed was his own, but they had everything in common.... There was not a needy person among them, for as many as were possessors of lands or houses sold them, and brought the proceeds of what was sold and laid it at the apostles' feet: and distribution was made to each as any had need (Acts 4:32-35).

This passage, however, does *not* deny the right to own private property. Those who decided to hold their possessions in common did so *voluntarily*. They were not forced to do so by the State or the Church. This is clear from the following incident.

A married couple named Ananias and Sapphira sold their property and deceitfully held back part of the proceeds, placing the remainder at the Apostles' feet as if it were the entire amount received (Acts 5:1-2). St. Peter rebuked them for lying to the Holy Spirit by trying to deceive the Church. However, he also made it clear that they had been free to keep the land for themselves or to keep the money they had received for selling the land. It was *their* property:

> But Peter said, "Ananias, why has Satan filled your heart to lie to the Holy Spirit and to keep back part of the proceeds of the land? *While it remained unsold, did it not remain your own?*

And after it was sold, was it not at your disposal? How is it that you have contrived this deed in your heart? You have not lied to men but to God" (Acts 5:3-4, emphasis added).

Far from denying the right to own private property, this account in Sacred Scripture actually *confirms* this right, while highlighting the importance of being truthful and morally upright.

Furthermore, those who decided to hold their possessions in common did not give their money or land to the *State*. They gave it to the *Magisterium of the Catholic Church*: St. Peter and the Apostles in union with him. **This passage does not advocate giving control of our property or wages to the State.**

In fact, this passage does not even require us to give control of our property or wages to the Church. Deciding to hold everything in common under the jurisdiction of the Apostles was not a moral law, but rather a *voluntary* outpouring of Christian charity and fellowship. **This passage does not prescribe what must be done; it reports what was done** in this instance, as evidence of the love the disciples had for one another. It also shows the trust that the people had for those in authority in the Church.

We are all called to love one another and to make sacrifices for the sake of following Jesus Christ. Some are even called to a form of religious life in which they voluntarily decide to give up their possessions. However, others are called to be married, and they will need material possessions to provide for their families.

Return of the Prodigal Son, by Bartolome Esteban Murillo

Sins against the Seventh Commandment

The seventh commandment forbids unjustly taking or keeping the goods of one's neighbor and wronging him in any way with respect to his goods (*Catechism*, 2401).

Since man has the right to own private property, this right must be respected by others. The Seventh Commandment forbids all acts that violate this right in any way. These include all forms of stealing, fraud, intentional violations of contracts, usury and speculation, vandalism, slavery and exploitation, and any other act that harms our neighbor with respect to his material goods.

Stealing. The Seventh Commandment forbids all forms of stealing. **Stealing** is the sin in which a person takes someone's goods unjustly. **Theft** is stealing someone's goods secretly. **Robbery** is stealing someone's goods openly or violently. Refusing to pay a worker his wages is another form of stealing, and it is one of the **sins that cry to Heaven** for justice.

Stealing is an intrinsically evil act. The gravity of the sin depends on the value of what is stolen and the harm done. Stealing is a grave sin if the amount taken is significant, and generally a venial sin if the amount taken is small. However, if serious harm is done (because the victim is very poor, for example), then stealing is gravely sinful, even if the amount stolen is small.

Borrowing money from one's neighbor without making any effort to repay it is another form of stealing. When a person borrows money, he must sincerely try his best to pay back the lender in a reasonable amount of time, including selling some of his possessions to raise the money, if necessary. He must not take advantage of the lender's kindness. However, the love of neighbor places demands on the lender as well. He must be merciful and patient with the borrower, even if the latter takes a long time to pay him back (Matthew 18:23-35).

A person also steals if he knowingly purchases or hides stolen goods. A person who *unknowingly* purchases stolen goods and later discovers that they were stolen has an obligation to restore them to the original owner, if possible.

Taking another's goods is *not* stealing if the owner's consent could reasonably be presumed. For example, one Sabbath, Jesus was going through the grain fields, and his disciples began to pluck ears of grain. The disciples did not ask permission from the grain field owners to do this, but consent could reasonably be presumed, because such actions were expressly permitted by the Law (Deuteronomy 23:25). The Pharisees still complained, but not because they saw it as stealing. Rather, they considered this action to be work, in violation of the Sabbath, but Jesus rebuked them (Mark 2:25-28).

In cases of extreme and obvious necessity, someone may appropriate for himself or his family the essential material goods that are needed to live, when he has no way of earning an income to pay for these goods. If a person's family is literally starving to death, he has the right to acquire the bread he needs for his family (*Catechism*, 2408). The *lives* of human persons are more valuable than bread or any other material good.

The principle behind this teaching is what the Church calls the **universal destination of goods** (*Catechism*, 2403-2408): God has given all of creation to the entire human race, and He intends everyone to have the essential material goods that are needed to live (food, clothing, shelter, etc.). When someone is deprived of even these most basic needs and truly has no way to pay for them, he has effectively been robbed of what is rightfully his. When he appropriates for himself or his family these goods, he is not stealing; he is exercising his right to share in the goods of creation. Even in such cases, however, he must have the intention of restoring what he has taken to the rightful owner, if he ever becomes able to do so.

This principle must not be misused to advocate actions that are contrary to the Seventh Commandment. If someone is poor and hungry because he refuses to work, he does *not* have the right to appropriate for himself or his family the goods of others. "For even when we were with you, we gave you this command: If anyone will not work, let him not eat" (2 Thessalonians 3:10).

Fraud. Another sin against the Seventh Commandment is **fraud**, in which a person cheats or deceives others regarding material goods or services. Fraud includes falsifying documents through forgery or other means, trying to pass counterfeit money, deliberately concealing defects in an item one is selling, using false weights and measures, declaring bankruptcy fraudulently, accepting or offering bribes, and evading just taxes (Fr. Laux, p. 136).

Violations of Contracts. Intentionally violating a just contract or agreement into which one has freely entered is also sinful. Honoring contracts and agreements is an integral part of a just society (*Catechism*, 2410). If a person or business agrees to perform some service, this service must be performed in its entirety, or the customer must be reimbursed for the difference. It is sinful to charge customers for more work than was actually done, or to provide goods or services inferior to what one has agreed to provide.

Usury and Speculation. It is sinful to charge excessive interest on loans (called **usury**). The Old Law did not allow charging any interest, and for centuries the Church did not allow it either. Because interest is an intrinsic part of the modern economic system, the Church now allows charging some interest. However, it is still sinful to charge *excessive* interest, because doing so takes unfair advantage of those in need (Fr. Laux, p. 137). Another form of usury is the sin of **speculation**, in which someone artificially manipulates the price of material goods in order to gain some advantage while harming others.

Vandalism. Intentionally damaging another's property (**vandalism**) is also a sin. Vandalism is a serious sin if the damage is significant or if it is done with malice. Painting graffiti on someone else's property is a form of vandalism. Justifying graffiti on the grounds of its artistic merit is contrary to truth and justice. Those who possess such talent should use it to give glory to God, not to deface the property of others.

Slavery and Exploitation. Man's most fundamental possession is *himself*. No one has the right to "own" another human being or to force him into servitude. **Slavery and all other forms of forced servitude of innocent human beings are gravely contrary to the dignity of the human person**, as are all practices that exploit human beings for the sake of profit or for any other reason.

If someone commits a serious crime deserving punishment, forced servitude is morally acceptable, within just limits, as long as it is not conducted in a way that is contrary to human dignity. The State has the right to punish criminals, provided that this punishment is just and commensurate with the crime committed.

The obedience that children owe their parents, including doing whatever chores their parents command them, is *not* to be construed as forced servitude. It is part of the obligation that God has placed on children in the Fourth Commandment to honor their father and mother.

Restitution for Sins of Injustice

> Those who, directly or indirectly, have taken possession of the goods of another, are obliged to make restitution of them, or to return the equivalent in kind or in money, if the goods have disappeared, as well as the profit or advantages their owner would have legitimately obtained from them (*Catechism*, 2412).

The Slave of the Slaves

It was the early 1600s. The slave trade had been flourishing for 100 years. Every year, tens of thousands of Africans were violently taken from their homes and shipped across the Atlantic to South America. One-third of them would die on the way. Conditions on the slave ships were so foul, so brutal, and so cruel that even the most hardened criminals would be astonished. The slaves were chained together in the belly of the ship night and day. The stench of human waste and disease filled the air. These poor people were broken, neglected, and terrified.

When the ship finally reached the port of Cartagena (now Colombia), the slaves would encounter kindness for the first time. A humble servant of God would come into the ship and minister to their needs. He would bring food, medical supplies, and whatever else he could provide to comfort them. He would lend his cloak to anyone who asked for it. He would even kiss their wounds. He was, in his own words, "the slave of the slaves." His name was Father Peter Claver.

St. Peter Claver was a Jesuit priest from Spain who devoted his life to serving the African slaves. In addition to caring for their physical needs, he instructed them in the Catholic Faith and administered the sacraments to them. In his forty years of service in Cartagena, St. Peter Claver personally baptized more than 300,000 slaves, and he heard thousands of confessions.

After the slaves were taken from the ships and sold, St. Peter Claver did not forget them. He would go from village to village, across mountains and through forests, so that he could meet with his flock. He would also speak with their "owners" and insist that the slaves be treated with kindness and be given their Christian and civil rights. If he could have taken their place, he would have done so.

In all of history, there have been relatively few people who have had the courage, charity, and moral conviction to rise above the culture of their day and pour themselves out for their fellow man. St. Peter Claver was one of them. He knew that every human being is precious and must be respected. He understood that human life is not property. Human life is a gift from God, and it must be cherished.

Restitution means restoring to its rightful owner a material good that has been stolen or damaged, or its equivalent value, along with just compensation for any profit or advantage that the owner would have legitimately derived from that material good.

The moral obligation to make restitution falls on whoever committed the act, those who cooperated with the act, and anyone who was morally obligated to prevent the act from occurring but failed to do so. Only the person who has been wronged may cancel this obligation (Fr. Laux, p. 137).

If the owner is no longer living or cannot be located, the person who committed the sin must still make restitution by giving an equivalent

Saint Peter Claver

good or amount of money to the person's family, the poor, the Church, or wherever his confessor directs him to give it.

A person who *unintentionally* ends up with someone else's property must try to restore that property to its rightful owner. Any expenses incurred because of the property may be deducted, within reason (Fr. Laux, p. 137).

If a person unintentionally and unknowingly damages his neighbor's property, he is not guilty of sin. However, if a court of law demands that restitution be made, he is morally obligated to comply (Fr. Laux, p. 138) Moreover, even if a court does not make such a demand, his actions should be guided by the Golden Rule: "So whatever you wish that men would do to you, do so to them" (Matthew 7:12).

Totalitarian Forms of Government

> Moral judgment must condemn the plague of totalitarian states which systematically falsify the truth, exercise political control of opinion through the media, manipulate defendants and witnesses at public trials, and imagine that they secure their tyranny by strangling and repressing everything they consider "thought crimes" (*Catechism*, 2499).

God confirms the rights of States to exist for the sake of the common good. However, He does not give the State the right to treat its citizens like slaves. A **totalitarian** State is one in which the government tries to control virtually every aspect of the lives of the people within that State. Examples of totalitarian forms of government include communism, socialism, and fascism.

The Church condemns all totalitarian forms of government. Such regimes are contrary to the dignity of the human person and his natural right to personal liberty.

The Eighth Commandment

> "You shall not bear false witness against your neighbor" (Exodus 20:16).

We are called to be holy and to bear witness to the Lord Jesus Christ, "who is the truth and wills the truth" (*Catechism*, 2464). Like Jesus, we must always speak the truth and live according to the truth. We must also try to show respect for our neighbor and honor his good name, just as we would want our good name to be honored.

The Necessity to Live in Truth

> The Old Testament attests that *God is the source of all truth*. His Word is truth. His Law is truth. His "faithfulness endures to all generations." Since God is "true," the members of his people are called to live in the truth (*Catechism*, 2465).

The **intellect** is the faculty of our rational soul through which we think, reason, understand, and know. We perfect our intellect through our knowledge of the truth. Without this knowledge, we could easily be led astray in matters concerning our salvation, our vocation, our occupation, and various other areas (Fr. Laux, pp. 98-99).

First, and most important, there are certain truths we must know that concern our *salvation*. We must earnestly seek to know God and to learn what He requires of us. We need to know the truth regarding faith and morals, and thus we need to know the teachings of the Catholic Church. If we are led astray, our salvation could be placed in jeopardy.

Second, we must have sufficient knowledge to fulfill our *vocation*. If we are misled in this area, souls that would have been saved through us might not be saved, and we will not experience as much joy in this life as we would if we had followed our true vocation.

Third, we need a certain set of knowledge regarding our *occupation* (doctor, nurse, plumber, teacher, lawyer, carpenter, farmer, homemaker, and so forth). If we acquire erroneous information pertaining to our occupation, we will be less likely to succeed in our work, and there could be serious consequences.

We also need to have sufficient knowledge in various other areas as well, including history, political and legal issues, and practical knowledge such as how to drive a car and use a computer.

The Virtue of Truthfulness. Knowing the truth is critical to our happiness and the happiness of others. However, *knowing* the truth is not enough; we must also *act* on the truth. Along with educating the intellect, we must train our will and our conscience by always doing what is right and never compromising with the truth in our actions (Fr. Laux, pp. 98-99). Little by little, we can strengthen our will and purify our conscience. With God's help, we will be committed to *truthfulness* and grow in goodness.

Truthfulness is the virtue by which a person is morally upright, true, and sincere in all his words and deeds. Being truthful requires that our words coincide with our understanding of what is true. Speaking only the truth is the duty of all. **Telling a lie is never morally permissible under any circumstances.**

Truthfulness includes both *honesty* and *discretion*. **Honesty** is saying only what one believes is true, and doing only what one believes is right and just. **Discretion** is the use of caution and reserve in one's speech and actions, for the sake of prudence and charity.

Truthfulness does not mean saying everything that is on our mind. We have the right, and sometimes the duty, to keep certain things private. Charity often demands that we *not* let others know how we are feeling. Being truthful does not mean being blunt. However, we must always be honest and never intentionally say something that we know is false.

Love of the Truth. God's Word is truth. God's Law is truth. God *is* Truth. If we truly love God, then we will also love the truth. **The love of the truth and the fear of the Lord always go together.** It is impossible to maintain the fear of the Lord without remaining steadfast in our love of the truth. It is impossible to maintain a sincere love of the truth without cultivating the fear of the Lord by seeking to know and love God, Who is Truth. A person who loves the truth will cultivate other virtues as well, including **fidelity** (faithfulness to one's given word and promises) and **righteousness** (conduct that is morally upright and pleasing to God).

Truth, fidelity, and righteousness are essential elements of every society. A nation that is grounded in the truth can withstand any storm or adversity. A nation that leaves the sure foundation of the truth cannot endure for long.

> Strive even to death for the truth and the Lord God will fight for you (Sirach 4:28).

We must strive for the truth "even to death"—that is, even at the risk of being a martyr for the truth—and God will fight for us. God loves the truth, and if we truly are His disciples, we will love the truth as well.

Sins against the Eighth Commandment

> Christ's disciples have "put on the new man, created after the likeness of God in true righteousness and holiness." By "putting away falsehood," they are to "put away all malice and all guile and insincerity and envy and all slander" (*Catechism*, 2475).

Anything that is contrary to the truth or that harms the honor, good name, or reputation of our neighbor is a sin against the Eighth Commandment. Every sin against truth and justice requires reparation. When someone wrongfully harms his neighbor's good name, he has a duty to try to repair the damage done. Depending on the extent and nature of this damage, material compensation (money or goods) may also be required.

Lying. The most direct sin against the truth is **lying** (saying something that one believes is false, with the intention to deceive). Our words must coincide with what we believe to be true. If a person *mistakenly* says something that is false, it is not a sin, but rather an *error*. However, if a person *intentionally* says something that he knows is not true, he lies.

Every deliberate lie is sinful, for several reasons (Fr. Laux, p. 138). First, lying is contrary to the moral order that God has established. Second, lying is, by its nature, a sin against God, Who is Truth itself. Third, the very reason that God gave us the ability to speak intelligently is so that we can *communicate truth*. Fourth, lying often harms one's neighbor, and it always harms the person who is guilty of lying. When a person becomes accustomed to lying, it does serious harm to his character: he becomes a *liar*.

> A lie is an ugly blot on a man; it is continually on the lips of the ignorant. A thief is preferable to a habitual liar, but the lot of both is ruin. The disposition of a liar brings disgrace, and his shame is ever with him (Sirach 20:24-26).

All lying is sinful. The *gravity* of the sin depends on the nature of the truth that it is against, the harm done, the intentions of the person telling the lie, and the circumstances.

There are three *types of lies*: malicious lies, officious lies, and jocose lies (Fr. Laux, p. 138). When a person tells a lie with the intention of harming his neighbor, he tells a **malicious lie**. Malicious lies are the most serious form of lying, because they are also sins against charity. When a person tells a lie in order to gain an advantage for himself or his neighbor, or to avoid some disadvantage to himself or his neighbor, he tells an **officious lie**. Officious lies are not as grave as malicious lies, but they are still sinful. Lying for the sake of our neighbor is usually not as sinful as lying for ourselves.

Finally, when a person says something *believable* that is not true, in an attempt to be funny, he tells a **jocose lie**. He is intentionally deceiving his neighbor for the sake of a laugh. Such lying is typically a venial sin, unless it is told with malicious intent, is harmful to justice or charity, or causes scandal. Jokingly saying something that is *obviously* not true (and hence not believable) is not lying and is not sinful.

Saint John Nepomucene Confessing the Queen of Bohemia, by Giuseppe Maria Crespi

Mental Reservation. Making use of discreet speech to conceal a truth that someone does not have the right to know or that we do not have the right to divulge is not lying, but rather **mental reservation**. However, mental reservation should be used only *rarely*, for a serious reason. Mental reservation is morally permissible only if all of the following conditions are met: (1) there is a just reason for using it; (2) the person to whom we are speaking does not have the right to know the truth, or we do not have the right to divulge it; and (3) it is not impossible to discern its true meaning. **If a person uses mental reservation when any of these conditions is not met, then it is sinful.**

Mental reservation is always sinful when a person uses it while freely taking an oath; entering into a contract or agreement; or making a vow, such as a marriage vow (Fr. Laux, p. 139).

We must try to be straightforward and honest at all times. A person of good moral character will hate every kind of lying and deceitfulness. When we are not at liberty to reveal something, the wisest and safest course is often *silence*. "Abhorrence of lies in every shape and form is the test of character" (Fr. Laux, pp. 139-140).

False Witness and Perjury. A lie told in public is more grievous than a lie told in private. When a lie is told in a *court of law*, which is called **false witness**, it is even more serious. If a person lies *while under oath* in a court of law, he also commits the sin of **perjury**. An **oath** is a solemn act in which a person calls upon God as his witness that what he says is true and that he will do what he swears to do. Because perjury breaks an oath, it is a sin against the Second Commandment as well.

Sins of false witness and perjury can lead to excessive punishment of the guilty or, even worse, punishment of the innocent or exoneration of the guilty, **both of which are grave evils**. These sins harm society by undermining justice.

Giving Glory to God through Silence

In the late 1300s, a holy and pious priest named Father John Nepomucene was assigned to the court of King Wenceslaus IV, as counselor and advocate for the poor. One of the persons for whom Father Nepomucene was confessor was the king's wife, Queen Joanna of Bavaria. King Wenceslaus was ill-tempered and unjustly jealous of the queen, who was a holy, virtuous woman.

Father John Nepomucene counseled the queen to joyfully take up her cross and follow the Lord Jesus Christ, and she grew in holiness. Yet, the king, ever suspicious, became even more irate. He summoned Father Nepomucene and demanded that he reveal what the queen told him in the Sacrament of Confession.

Father Nepomucene, bound by the seal of the confessional, naturally refused. However, the king wouldn't take no for an answer. He had Father Nepomucene thrown into a dungeon, but the holy priest remained silent. So, the king ordered that Father Nepomucene be tortured until he "confessed." The good priest was put on the rack and burned with torches. Still, he refused to reveal the queen's confession.

Furious at the resolve and strength of this humble priest, King Wenceslaus had him put to death. Father John Nepomucene was tied to a wheel and thrown into the Moldau River. It is said that seven stars were seen shining over the place where he drowned.

More than three hundred years later, his body was exhumed, and his tongue was found to be incorrupt. St. John Nepomucene, martyr for the secrecy of the confessional, gave glory to God through his silence. He is the patron saint of Bohemia.

Dissimulation and Hypocrisy. The sin of **dissimulation** involves acting in a way that conceals one's true character or motives. When a person commits this sin, he lies through his actions in order to conceal what is truly in his heart. A young man who pretends to be virtuous so that he can take advantage of unsuspecting young women is guilty of a grave sin of dissimulation. A building contractor who pretends to be honest but in reality cheats his customers is guilty of dissimulation as well.

Hypocrisy is a form of dissimulation. A person commits the sin of **hypocrisy** when he intentionally pretends to be someone he is not, or pretends to believe something that he does not truly believe. If a person pretends to be virtuous but in reality lives a life of vice, he is a hypocrite.

Rash Judgment. A person's honor and good name are more important than his material goods (Fr. Laux, p. 140). *Rash judgment*, *detraction*, and *calumny* do unjust harm to a person's honor and good name. **Rash judgment** is the sin in which a person assumes, without sufficient grounds, that his neighbor is guilty of some moral fault or failure. Even if the person does not openly express this judgment, he is still guilty of sin if he rashly judges the person in his heart.

It is not a sin to judge that a person is guilty of a sin when there are sufficient grounds to do so. Our Lord's words, "Judge not, that you be not judged" (Matthew 7:1), are often misapplied to claim that people must not make any moral judgments whatsoever, but this is not what Jesus was saying. Rather, we must not judge whether a person is going to Heaven or Hell, and we must not make *rash* judgments.

The reason both of these are forbidden is the same: **we have no right to judge someone on the basis of what we do not know**. Only God knows whether or not a person repented of his sins the moment before he died and, like the thief on the Cross beside Jesus during the Crucifixion (Luke 23:39-43), was granted salvation. Only God knows what is truly in a person's heart.

To the extent that it is possible and prudent, we should always try to interpret our neighbor's thoughts, words, and deeds favorably. However, this does *not* mean that we must *trust* everyone, which would be very foolish. "One who trusts others too quickly is lightminded" (Sirach 19:4). On the contrary, God warns us to be on our guard, because not everyone is as he seems.

> Let those that are at peace with you be many, but let your advisers be one in a thousand. When you gain a friend, gain him through testing, and do not trust him hastily (Sirach 6:6-7).

Being on our guard does not mean that we should assume the worst until our neighbor proves otherwise. If we are suspicious of everyone, we might end up hurting ourselves and others. However, if we trust others too quickly, we could expose ourselves and others to grave danger. The wisest course is to delay making any judgment, one way or the other, until we have sufficient knowledge.

Detraction and Calumny. More serious than rash judgment is the sin of **detraction**, in which a person makes known, without good reason, some fault or sin of his neighbor. Detraction can cause serious damage to someone's good name. If there is no good reason to reveal someone's sins or faults, we should not do so, just as we would not want our sins or faults to be made known.

If it is *necessary* to reveal another's sins or faults for the moral or physical safety of others, then it is *not* detraction. In fact, we may even have a moral obligation to do so in some cases. Typically, however, it is not necessary, and we should keep silent.

Before we say something negative about someone, we should ask ourselves three questions: (1) Are we certain that it is true? (2) Is it necessary to say it? (3) Are we willing to say it in a charitable manner, if possible? If we cannot answer *yes* to all three questions, then we should keep silent until, if ever, we can.

Even worse than detraction is the sin of **calumny** (or *slander*), in which a person intentionally says something negative that is *false* about his neighbor. Both detraction and calumny are sins against justice. Calumny is a sin against truthfulness as well.

It is also sinful to take pleasure in *hearing* detraction or calumny. How would we feel if others were taking pleasure in hearing something negative about us?

The gravity of detraction and calumny depends primarily on the intention and the damage done to the person's good name. If the harm is serious, the sin is grave. Even if the harm is not serious, the sin is grave if the person *intends* to do grave harm. Detraction and calumny can destroy reputations, increase strife, and lead to many other sins. Reparation must be made for such sins, insofar as it is possible.

We must be very careful not to unnecessarily injure someone's good name. The desire to protect one's good name can serve as motivation for a person to stay on the right path. When a person's good name is seriously damaged, he could give in to despair and lose this motivation, and end up committing many sins that he otherwise never would have committed—especially if he is not morally strong (lacking in the virtue of fortitude).

Detraction and calumny can also cause scandal to others who are influenced by the person whose good name has been damaged. For this and other reasons, we have a duty to safeguard our own good name as well. This does not mean we should be excessively sensitive and not accept any criticism. However, if our good name is attacked, we have the right to defend it. In fact, if the honor of our vocation, our family, the Church, our country, or our place of employment is at stake, we are *morally obligated* to do so (Fr. Laux, p. 99). We are also morally obligated to defend our good name and character if others will be scandalized by the charges against us.

The best defense against rash judgment, detraction, and calumny is a *clear conscience* before God and men (Acts 24:16, 2 Corinthians 1:12).

Gossip and Talebearing. Closely related to detraction and calumny are the sins of gossip and talebearing. **Gossip** is spreading personal information or rumors about someone. **Talebearing** is spreading a negative report about someone, or going back and revealing such a report to him, from a warped sense of pleasure in causing strife. Sometimes called "whispering" in Sacred Scripture, talebearing "is a detestable sin" (Fr. Laux, p. 141). Talebearing "has destroyed many who were at peace" (Sirach 28:13).

> Never repeat a conversation, and you will lose nothing at all. With friend or foe do not report it, and unless it would be a sin for you, do not disclose it (Sirach 19:7-8).

Deliberately encouraging or taking pleasure in listening to gossip or talebearing about one's neighbor is also sinful. We must love our neighbor as ourselves, not take pleasure in rumors or negative reports about him.

Contumely, Ridicule, and Boasting. In the sin of **contumely**, a person speaks against his neighbor's good name directly to his face. Rather than treating his neighbor with kindness and respect, he treats him with contempt. Rather than treating his neighbor with charity, he calls him names, speaks harshly against him, mocks him, or scorns him. Contumely is a sin against justice and charity, and it is contrary to the dignity of the human person.

Likewise, it is sinful to treat one's neighbor with **ridicule** (the sin in which a person maliciously makes fun of his neighbor). It is also sinful for a person to *boast* or *brag* about himself, exaggerating his talents or accomplishments. Humility does not require us to deny the skills, talents, and good qualities that God has given us. However, when we try to make ourselves seem better than we are, especially when we put down our neighbor to do so, we sin.

Flattery and Adulation. It is sinful to use **duplicitous speech** (speech that is insincere, with an ulterior motive), such as flattery or adulation. **Flattery** means giving insincere praise to someone. **Adulation** means showing excessive admiration for someone, for the sake of some ulterior motive. If a person expresses approval, either implicitly or explicitly, of behavior that is gravely sinful, he commits a serious sin.

> Every word or attitude is forbidden which by flattery, adulation, or complaisance encourages and confirms another in malicious acts and perverse conduct. Adulation is a grave fault if it makes one an accomplice in another's vices or grave sins. Neither the desire to be of service nor friendship justifies duplicitous speech. Adulation is a venial sin when it only seeks to be agreeable, to avoid evil, to meet a need, or to obtain legitimate advantages (*Catechism*, 2480).

The Tenth Commandment

> "You shall not covet … anything that is your neighbor's" (Exodus 20:17).

The ownership of private property is one of the fundamental rights of the human person. The Tenth Commandment forbids all *internal sins* of covetousness regarding our neighbor's property. *Coveting* our neighbor's property means having an unjust or inordinate willful desire for something that rightfully belongs to him. The gravity of the sin of coveting another person's goods depends on the value of what is coveted and the harm that would be caused if this good were taken from its rightful owner.

Sins against the Tenth Commandment

> The sensitive appetite leads us to desire pleasant things we do not have, e.g., the desire to eat when we are hungry or to warm ourselves when we are cold. These desires are good in themselves; but often they exceed the limits of reason and drive us to covet unjustly what is not ours and belongs to another or is owed to him (*Catechism*, 2535).

When a person is too attached to material possessions, he tends to place more importance on those possessions than on justice and charity. This can lead to various other sins, including the capital sins of greed and envy.

Greed. When a person has an inordinate desire or immoderate passion for material goods, he commits the capital sin of **greed**. The greedy person is never satisfied. If he has little, he wants more. If he has much, he is afraid of losing what he has. As with all capital sins, greed can lead to many other sins, such as dishonesty, sins against charity, and even murder.

Envy. One of the most dangerous capital sins is the sin of *envy*, which is also a sin against the Tenth Commandment. **Envy** is the sin in which a person resents that his neighbor possesses something that he would like to have instead for himself. That which the person envies may be a material good or something else, such as talents, skills, success, fame, or power. "The tenth commandment requires that *envy* be banished from the human heart" (*Catechism*, 2538).

Envy is typically accompanied by a feeling of sadness or displeasure at the other person's good fortune, as well as a sense of deprivation and injustice. The envious person believes he has been unjustly deprived of what he thinks ought to be his, and he wants it. If he cannot have what he wants, he might even try to punish his neighbor for this alleged injustice. Thus, envy can lead to many other sins.

The sin of envy is even more serious when a person envies his neighbor's virtue, holiness, or other spiritual goods. The most grave form of envy is when someone envies God Himself. This was one of the sins that led the devil to rebel against God.

Jealousy. Sometimes *jealousy* is confused with envy. However, they are not the same. *Envy* concerns what belongs to *another*. **Jealousy** is a person's vigilant zeal and determination not to lose or share someone or something that he sees as belonging to *himself*. Unlike envy, which is always sinful, jealousy may or may not be sinful.

Jealousy is a sin when it is contrary to right reason, and in such cases it often takes the form of irrational fear. This can lead to many other sins, such as unfounded suspicions, rash judgment, false accusations, and contumely.

Jealousy is not a sin when it is in accordance with right reason. When God gave the First Commandment ("You shall have no other gods before me"), He Himself said, "I the Lord your God am a jealous God" (Exodus 20:3-5). God will not share His people with other "gods." It is God's right to demand complete fidelity.

Likewise, a husband and wife have the right to expect each other to be faithful and to avoid all the near occasions of sin regarding the grave sin of adultery. This type of jealousy is *not* sinful; it is prudent and just. A woman belongs to her husband, and a man belongs to his wife. Each one has the right to demand complete fidelity from the other.

When a person has a *godly jealousy* (2 Corinthians 11:2) for someone, such as a spouse, he cherishes that person as a precious treasure given to him by God to love and honor as his own. When a person has a *sinful jealousy* for someone, he treats that person like an object to own, use, or control, rather than a person to love and respect. This kind of jealousy can be very destructive and dangerous.

If someone truly loves another person, he will not seek to harm that person in any way, even if he thinks he has lawful grounds to be jealous. Lawful jealousy does not justify

Christ and the Rich Young Ruler, by Heinrich Hofmann

Freedom from Worldly Attachments

Jerome Emiliani was a rich young man born in 1486 to noble parents in Venice, Italy. When his father died, Jerome left home and joined the military. While guarding a fortress for the Venetian army, he was captured in battle and chained in a dungeon.

Until that time, Jerome did not have much of a relationship with God. But in his great suffering and solitude, he began to think about his life. He realized that without his weapons and fellow soldiers, he was helpless. All his worldly possessions were useless to him. Only God could save him.

Jerome decided to commit his life to God and to let go of his attachments to worldly possessions and ambitions. He prayed and asked the Blessed Virgin Mary to help him. Miraculously, he escaped from prison. He was freed, not only from his physical chains, but also from the chains of his worldly attachments.

As a reminder of his freedom in Christ, he hung up his old chains in the church of Treviso, where he began studying for the priesthood. He decided to use his fortune to help others. During the plague, he was seen going through the streets at night, caring for the sick.

Because of the war, as well as the famine and plague that followed, there were increasing numbers of orphans needing help. Using his own money, St. Jerome Emiliani rented a house for orphans, where he provided for their needs. Eventually, he built six orphanages and a hospital. In 1532, he founded a religious order, the Order of Somascan Fathers, dedicated to caring for orphans. The order continues to perform this charitable work to this day.

St. Jerome Emiliani served Our Lord Jesus Christ by serving those in need, especially orphans. He had an earnest desire to help the Church return to the level of holiness that the early Christians had shown. May we imitate his kindness and charity, and respond to his call for holiness.

committing acts that *are* sinful. **Violence against one's spouse is always gravely sinful, regardless of the reason.**

Detachment from Riches

> Jesus enjoins his disciples to prefer him to everything and everyone.... The precept of detachment from riches is obligatory for entrance into the Kingdom of heaven (*Catechism*, 2544).

Material goods must not be our primary focus, nor should we have anxiety about them. We must put God first and trust in Him, and He will provide for us: "But seek first his kingdom and his righteousness, and all these things shall be yours as well" (Matthew 6:33).

Although man has a fundamental right to own private property, he does not have the right to selfishly hoard material goods at the expense of others. Material goods are finite and limited. The more we use them, the less there are remaining. We have a moral obligation to practice charity toward our neighbor and to exercise temperance in our use of material goods.

Accumulating wealth or material possessions is not sinful in every instance (Fr. Laux, p. 115). Whether it is sinful depends on the circumstances and one's intentions. However, it can be a dangerous near occasion of sin. If someone becomes so enthralled with his wealth that he is deaf to the voice of the Church or the cries of the poor, then he is treating wealth like an idol, and his soul is in grave danger.

Consider the parable of Lazarus and the rich man (Luke 16:19-31). The rich man's sin was one of *omission*: he neglected to show any concern for his neighbor's needs, and God condemned him for it.

It is important to develop a spirit of **detachment**: the willingness to let go of our material goods for the sake of our love of God. Being detached from material goods is possible only if we trust in God, and love Him more than anything else. He is the one Who ultimately owns all our property, and His Providence is unlimited and eternal. "Blessed are the poor in spirit, for theirs is the kingdom of heaven" (Matthew 5:3).

The Rich Man and the Poor Lazarus, by Hendrick ter Brugghen

Chapter 14 Review

Matching: For each statement, select the letter of the best term from the list below. There are more terms listed than there are statements, and no term can be used more than once.

A. fidelity	E. adulation	I. discretion	M. perjury
B. lying	F. fraud	J. restitution	N. speculation
C. usury	G. greed	K. stealing	O. slander
D. hypocrisy	H. honesty	L. vandalism	P. talebearing

1. Faithfulness to one's given word and promises: _________.
2. Sin in which a person cheats or deceives others regarding material goods or services: _________.
3. Charging excessive interest on loans: _________.
4. An inordinate desire or immoderate passion for material goods: _________.
5. Sin in which a person artificially manipulates the price of material goods in order to gain some advantage while harming others: _________.
6. Sin in which a person takes someone's goods unjustly: _________.
7. Saying only what one believes is true, and doing only what one believes is right and just: _________.
8. Sin in which a person intentionally damages another's property: _________.
9. Sin in which a person intentionally pretends to be someone he is not, or pretends to believe something that he does not truly believe: _________.
10. Spreading a negative report about someone, or going back and revealing such a report to him, from a warped sense of pleasure in causing strife: _________.
11. Saying something that one believes is false, with the intention to deceive: _________.
12. Sin in which a person lies while under oath in a court of law: _________.
13. The use of caution and reserve in one's speech and actions, for the sake of prudence and charity: _________.
14. Restoring to its rightful owner a material good that has been stolen or damaged, or its equivalent value: ________.
15. Showing excessive admiration for someone, for the sake of some ulterior motive: ________.

Matching II: For each statement, select the letter of the best term from the list below. There are more terms listed than there are statements, and no term can be used more than once.

A. envy	E. gossip	I. acedia	M. truthfulness
B. detraction	F. detachment	J. ridicule	N. rash judgment
C. contumely	G. jealousy	K. robbery	O. false witness
D. dissimulation	H. calumny	L. theft	P. flattery

16. Virtue by which a person is morally upright, true, and sincere in all his words and deeds: _________.
17. The willingness to let go of our material goods for the sake of our love of God: _________.
18. Sin in which a person resents that his neighbor possesses something that he would like to have instead for himself: _________.
19. Sin in which a person assumes, without sufficient grounds, that his neighbor is guilty of some moral fault or failure: _________.
20. Giving insincere praise to someone, a type of duplicitous speech: _________.
21. Acting in a way that conceals one's true character or motives: _________.
22. A person's vigilant zeal and determination not to lose or share someone or something that he sees as belonging to himself: _________.
23. Sin in which a person makes known, without good reason, some fault or sin of his neighbor: _________.
24. When someone speaks against his neighbor's good name directly to his face, he is guilty of the sin of _________.
25. Stealing someone's goods secretly: _________.
26. Sin in which a person tells a lie in a court of law: ________.
27. Stealing someone's goods openly or violently: ________.
28. Sin in which a person intentionally says something negative that is false about his neighbor: ________.
29. Sin in which a person maliciously makes fun of his neighbor: _________.
30. Spreading personal information or rumors about someone: ________.

True or False: Write *True* or *False* for the following statements.

_________ 31. Perjury is a sin against both the Second and Eighth Commandments.

_________ 32. The right to personal liberty is the right to choose between good and evil.

_________ 33. Slavery and all other forms of forced servitude of innocent human beings are gravely contrary to the dignity of the human person.

_________ 34. Jealousy is always sinful.

_________ 35. Envy is always sinful.

_________ 36. Lying is not always sinful.

_________ 37. Out of Christian charity, we have a moral obligation to trust everyone.

_________ 38. It is impossible to maintain the fear of the Lord without remaining steadfast in our love of the truth.

_________ 39. We have a duty to safeguard our own good name if the honor of our vocation, our family, the Church, our country, or our place of employment is at stake.

_________ 40. Intrinsic to our personal liberty is our right to own private property.

Multiple Choice: Write the letter of the best answer in the space provided.

41. Which of the following is *not* sinful? _________
    A. Knowingly purchasing or hiding stolen goods
    B. Intentionally violating a just contract or agreement into which one has freely entered
    C. A person appropriating for himself, in cases of extreme and obvious necessity, the essential material goods needed to live, when he has no way of earning an income to pay for these goods
    D. A person appropriating for himself the essential material goods needed to live, when he has no way to pay for them because he does not want to work
    E. Both C and D

42. Which of the following is morally permissible only if (1) there is a just reason for using it; (2) the person to whom we are speaking does not have the right to know the truth, or we do not have the right to divulge it; and (3) it is not impossible to discern its true meaning?

    ____

    A. Malicious lie
    B. Officious lie
    C. Jocose lie
    D. Mental reservation
    E. All of the above

43. The worst type of lie: _________.
    A. Malicious lie
    B. Officious lie
    C. Jocose lie
    D. Mental reservation
    E. Boasting

44. When a person tells a lie in order to gain an advantage for himself or his neighbor, he is guilty of which of the following? _________
    A. Malicious lie
    B. Officious lie
    C. Jocose lie
    D. Mental reservation
    E. None of the above

45. When a person says something believable that is not true, in an attempt to be funny, he is guilty of which of the following? _________.
    A. Malicious lie
    B. Officious lie
    C. Jocose lie
    D. Mental reservation
    E. None of the above

Ave Maria, by Adrian Ludwig Richter

Christ Carrying the Cross, by El Greco

Section III: Christian Perfection

Introduction

> But the wisdom from above is first pure, then peaceable, gentle, open to reason, full of mercy and good fruits, without uncertainty or insincerity. And the harvest of righteousness is sown in peace by those who make peace (James 3:17-18).

God has given every human being a rational soul, with an intellect and a will and other natural gifts, so that he can know, love, and serve Him, and be happy with Him in Heaven. He has given us the Natural Law, so that we can discern His Divine Law and know what is right and wrong. He has given us the Word of God in Sacred Scripture and Sacred Tradition to teach us. He has given us the Magisterium of the Catholic Church to guide us. He sustains us by His Providence, and He blesses us in His mercy.

He has given Catholic Christians even more. He has given us supernatural gifts through the sacraments. He has given us the Gift of the Holy Spirit living within us, transforming us to be more like Jesus Christ, the Son of God. He has given us a taste of Heaven itself through Holy Communion, in which we become one with the Body, Blood, Soul, and Divinity of Jesus Christ.

Christ Washing the Disciples' Feet, by Bernhard Strigel

A Christian in a state of grace will not be content with meeting only the minimum requirements of the Moral Law. He will want to do even more for his Lord and Savior Jesus Christ. He will want to be holy, as God is holy. He will want to strive for Christian perfection. The love of God will move him to do great things for the glory of God and the salvation of souls. With all his strength, he will strive to be a living witness of Jesus Christ and an instrument of His goodness, truth, and love. In Christ, through Christ, and for Christ, he will be "the salt of the earth" (Matthew 5:13) and "the light of the world" (Matthew 5:14).

This third section focuses on Christian perfection. Through His life and teachings, Our Lord Jesus Christ has shown us how to perfectly follow God's Law, and He calls us to be His disciples, and to love even as He has loved us. This section is organized as follows:

- Chapter 15 presents an effective strategy to resist temptation.
- Chapter 16 emphasizes Christian charity and the Beatitudes—the ideal of the Christian moral life, as modeled by Our Lord Jesus Christ.

Chapter 15. A Strategy to Resist Temptation

> Finally, be strong in the Lord and in the strength of his might. Put on the whole armor of God, that you may be able to stand against the wiles of the devil (Ephesians 6:10-11).

Our life on Earth is a journey with many ups and downs. There are moments of joy and moments of sadness, moments of hope and moments of fear, moments of love and moments of loneliness. In the midst of it all, whether we realize it or not, we are in a battle for our salvation.

For those who have left this world in a state of grace, the battle is over; the war has been won. Like St. Paul, they can proclaim: "I have fought the good fight, I have finished the race, I have kept the faith" (2 Timothy 4:7). For those of us who are still on Earth, the race continues, the war goes on, our work remains.

> "The life of man upon earth is a warfare, and his days are like the days of a hireling" (Job 7:1).

Christ in the Desert, by Ivan Kramskoi

In order to be successful in this battle, we must have an effective strategy to resist temptation. This chapter lists some of the key elements of this strategy.

The Fear of the Lord

> If a man is not steadfast and zealous in the fear of the Lord, his house will be quickly overthrown (Sirach 27:3).

The first essential element in our strategy to resist temptation is the *fear of the Lord*, which is the beginning of wisdom and knowledge, and hence is necessary for salvation. One of the seven gifts of the Holy Spirit, the **fear of the Lord** instills in us a fervent zeal to put God before all else, attentively listen to Him, and obey His commands.

> The fear of the Lord is the beginning of wisdom, and the knowledge of the Holy One is insight (Proverbs 9:10).

Ideally, we will cultivate the fear of the Lord through our love of God and our desire to never offend Him. However, it is acceptable, and can even be *beneficial*, if we are also motivated by fear of being punished for our sins. In fact, Our Lord Himself told us to have this fear:

> "And do not fear those who kill the body but cannot kill the soul; rather fear him who can destroy both soul and body in hell" (Matthew 10:28).

A healthy fear of God and of the eternal punishment for mortal sin, coupled with a sincere love of God, can help protect us from becoming lukewarm in the spiritual life, and can motivate us to be morally good. The more faithful and steadfast we are in living a morally upright life, truly striving "to sin no more and to avoid the near occasions of sin," the more we will love goodness and truth, and hate evil.

The Armor of God

> Therefore take the whole armor of God, that you may be able to withstand in the evil day, and having done all, to stand. Stand therefore, having girded your loins with truth, and having put on the breastplate of righteousness, and having shod your feet with the equipment of the gospel of peace; above all taking the shield of faith, with which you can quench all the flaming darts of the evil one. And take the helmet of salvation, and the sword of the Spirit, which is the word of God. Pray at all times in the Spirit, with all prayer and supplication. To that end keep alert with all perseverance, making supplication for all the saints... (Ephesians 6:13-18).

Before a soldier goes into battle, he must be equipped with the proper "armor." The battle to resist temptation is no different. In order to be ready for this battle, we must take up the **Armor of God**: the spiritual equipment we need to win the battle against temptation. The quotation above paints a picture of a knight in a suit of armor. As this quotation illustrates, the Armor of God includes several key parts:

- the girding of truth,
- the breastplate of righteousness,
- the footwear of the gospel of peace,
- the shield of faith,
- the helmet of salvation,
- the sword of the Spirit, and
- perseverance in prayer and supplication.

The fear of the Lord is critical to cultivating the wisdom, zeal, and steadfastness we need to take up and stand firm in the Armor of God.

The Girding of Truth

> The mission of the Magisterium is linked to the definitive nature of the covenant established by God with his people in Christ. It is this Magisterium's task to preserve God's people from deviations and defections and to guarantee them the objective possibility of professing the true faith without error (*Catechism*, 890).

To succeed in the battle against temptation, we must stand on the sure foundation of the *truth*. "Stand therefore, having girded your loins with truth" (Ephesians 6:14). When we are committed to the truth, we are strong, and God protects us from the lies of the devil. When we are not committed to the truth, we are weak, and we are vulnerable to a crushing attack from the devil, who "is a liar and the father of lies" (John 8:44). In fact, some believe that this verse (Ephesians 6:14) alludes to the wide belt that a Roman soldier would wear, upon which hung his sword and other equipment for battle. It is the *truth* that holds our equipment for spiritual battle in place. We must always seek the truth, speak the truth, live with integrity according to the truth, and accept the truth when we find it.

Sometimes it is difficult to know the truth, even when we are sincerely seeking it. We need a sure guide to help us distinguish truth from falsehood. God has given us this sure guide: the **Magisterium of the Catholic Church**. If we refuse to obey the teachings of the Magisterium, we will not be "girded with truth," and we will suffer one spiritual defeat after another. However, if we strive with all our heart to hold fast to the truth and remain faithful to all the teachings of the Magisterium of the Catholic Church on faith and morals, God Himself will fight for us.

The Breastplate of Righteousness

> By his obedience unto death, Jesus accomplished the substitution of the suffering Servant, who "makes an *offering for sin*," when "he bore the sin of many," and who "shall make many to be accounted righteous," for "he shall bear their iniquities." Jesus atoned for our faults and made satisfaction for our sins to the Father (*Catechism*, 615).

The breastplate in a suit of armor protects the heart from a lethal blow. In the Armor of God, *justice* and *righteousness* are the fabric of this breastplate. **Justice** is the cardinal virtue that disposes our will to always give God and our neighbor their due. **Righteousness** refers to conduct that is morally upright and pleasing to God. Like St. Joseph (Matthew 1:19), we must always strive to do what is right and just. Then, "having put on the breastplate of righteousness" (Ephesians 6:14), we will be better equipped to protect our soul from sin.

However, we cannot rely on only *our* righteousness. We need the righteousness of Our Lord Jesus Christ. By His Passion and Resurrection, Jesus set us free from the slavery of sin, and through the sacraments He gives us the grace to be like Him. When we cooperate with this grace by living a morally good life in Jesus Christ, we are sanctified and transformed by the Holy Spirit to become more like Jesus.

> Do not be conformed to this world but be transformed by the renewal of your mind, that you may prove what is the will of God, what is good and acceptable and perfect (Romans 12:2).

If we live as faithful disciples of Jesus Christ, always doing what is right and treating everyone justly, God will clothe us with an inviolable breastplate: the breastplate of Jesus Christ Himself; and the righteousness of God will shine through us. To wear this breastplate, we must be obedient to *all* of God's Commandments, fervently striving to live a morally good life and to be virtuous in every way. Three virtues, in particular, are especially important to this breastplate: charity, humility, and purity.

Charity. Our breastplate of righteousness must include the virtue of *charity*, "which binds everything together in perfect harmony" (Colossians 3:14). We must love God with all our mind, all our heart, all our soul, and all our strength, and we must love our neighbor as ourselves. If we love God above all else, we will not want to allow anything to hurt our relationship with Him. This will strengthen our resolve to avoid the near occasions of sin and to overcome every obstacle to living a morally good life. Through our love for God, we must also love our neighbor and treat him the way we would want to be treated.

> A real personal love of Christ is the best armor against all the assaults of temptation, whether they come from within or from without, from the world, the devil, or the flesh (Fr. Laux, p. 46).

Charity is a critical part of our strategy to resist temptation. Without it, our breastplate of righteousness will not hold together, and we will fail. With it, we will be more like Jesus Christ, Who has already won the victory over sin and death.

Humility. Pride is *not* one of the spiritual weapons in the Armor of God. We are called to be bold *in Christ*, not in ourselves. Succumbing to pride is like allowing a spy from the enemy to infiltrate our camp. Practicing the virtue of *humility* is like building an impregnable fortress around our camp.

Humility is the virtue by which a person moderates his estimation of his own importance, and acknowledges his limitations and imperfections. We must humble ourselves before the Lord Jesus Christ and confess that He is the Son of God. We must admit that God is perfect, and we are not; and that God is always right, and we are not. We must acknowledge that we need Our Lord and Savior Jesus Christ, and that any good we do comes from Him.

Purity. Finally, we must live in *purity* by steadfastly protecting the two pillars of purity: chastity and modesty. The chaste person practices purity at all times, including with regard to what he or she wears, looks at, listens to, thinks about, and willfully desires.

It is impossible to be completely chaste without also being modest. When people dress immodestly, they sin against their own dignity as persons created in the image and likeness of God—persons to be loved and respected, not objects to be owned or used. They also commit the sin of **scandal** (leading others to sin by word or example), because their immodest dress can easily tempt others to think or act impurely. "Scandal can be provoked by laws or institutions, by fashion or opinion" (*Catechism*, 2286). A truly humble person will not wear loud, flashy clothes, let alone dress immodestly.

A woman who fears the Lord will dress modestly at all times, protecting her chastity and glorifying God through her humility. A man who fears the Lord will do likewise.

> Let not yours be the outward adorning with braiding of hair, decoration of gold, and wearing of robes, but let it be the hidden person of the heart with the imperishable jewel of a gentle and quiet spirit, which in God's sight is very precious. So once the holy women who hoped in God used to adorn themselves (1 Peter 3:3-5).

In addition to *modesty of dress*, we must also maintain *modesty of the eyes*. A person who intentionally stares at someone dressed immodestly can easily be tempted to sin. If he continues along this path, it is only a matter of time before he will sin against the virtue of chastity.

We must vigilantly guard our chastity by always practicing modesty of dress and modesty of the eyes. We must also guard our chastity by being careful about what we read, watch, and hear, including the jokes we allow ourselves to listen to. God detests impure jokes (Ephesians 5:3-6), and we should detest them as well. If someone begins telling such a joke, we should gently withdraw from the conversation and walk away, then quietly say a prayer such as a Hail Mary or "Jesus is Lord."

The best way to cultivate the virtue of modesty is to model ourselves after the saints, especially Our Blessed Mother and St. Joseph. As with charity and humility, chastity and modesty—the two pillars of purity—are essential to our breastplate of righteousness and our strategy to resist temptation.

The Footwear of the Gospel of Peace

> The Church is catholic: she proclaims the fullness of the faith. She bears in herself and administers the totality of the means of salvation. She is sent out to all peoples. She speaks to all men. She encompasses all times (*Catechism*, 868).

As a Christian soldier, "having shod your feet with the equipment of the gospel of peace" (Ephesians 6:15), you must be willing to go wherever God sends you. All of us are called to share in the Church's mission to evangelize and spread the Gospel of Jesus Christ. "For I am not ashamed of the gospel; it is the power of God for salvation to everyone who has faith" (Romans 1:16). The manner in which we do so may vary, depending on our state in life. However, we must all spread the Gospel in some way.

Our Blessed Mother, by Joos van Cleve

The **Gospel** is the "Good News" of the love and mercy of God, revealed and imparted to man through the Life, Passion (suffering and death), and Resurrection of Jesus Christ. Our Lord and Savior Jesus Christ has freed us from the slavery of sin and won for us the gift of eternal life. To *receive* this gift, we must enter His Kingdom, the Church, through faith and Baptism. To *keep* this gift, we must remain in fellowship with the Holy Trinity by cooperating with the grace that God gives us through the Mass and the sacraments, and by practicing the virtues and obeying the Commandments.

> For I delivered to you as of first importance what I also received, that Christ died for our sins in accordance with the scriptures, that he was buried, that he was raised on the third day… (1 Corinthians 15:3-4).

Before we can effectively spread the Gospel, we must *know* the Gospel. We must learn and practice our Faith by studying the teachings of the Catholic Church; attending Mass and receiving the sacraments; carefully reading Sacred Scripture; remaining constant in prayer; making acts of faith, hope, and charity; and loving God and our neighbor.

It is impossible to stand still in the spiritual battle we are fighting. We are either advancing or drifting backward. We must continue to advance by living and spreading the Gospel in truth and charity.

The Shield of Faith

> Faith is first of all a personal adherence of man to God. At the same time, and inseparably, it is a *free assent to the whole truth that God has revealed* (*Catechism*, 150).

You are a child of God, a person with intrinsic value and dignity, for whom the Lord Jesus Christ, the Son of God, died on the Cross. Stand firm, then, and be not afraid (Joshua 1:9), "above all taking the shield of faith, with which you can quench all the flaming darts of the evil one" (Ephesians 6:16). An unwavering faith in Jesus Christ will cause the "flaming darts" of the enemy to bounce off us like arrows bouncing off a knight's shield. In order for our faith to be such a powerful shield, it must be a *living faith*, an *authentic faith*, and an *obedient faith*.

Living Faith. We must put our faith into action through acts of charity (1 Corinthians 13:2), abounding in good works. Otherwise, our faith will be dead (James 2:17), and a dead faith cannot be an effective shield.

God does not want us only *part* of the time; He wants us *all* the time. He does not want us to just go through the motions; He wants us to have a fervent love for Him through the Holy Spirit living within us. He does not want us to pay Him lip service; He wants us to serve Him by living our life in goodness and truth.

To truly have a living faith, we need to *have a personal relationship with Jesus Christ* and, at the same time, *remain in fellowship with the Catholic Church* by being obedient to the Magisterium and by attending Mass and receiving the sacraments.

Having a personal relationship with Jesus Christ and remaining in fellowship with the Catholic Church go hand in hand. If a person does not have a personal relationship with Jesus Christ, his membership in the Catholic Church will be empty. If a person is not in fellowship with the Catholic Church, his personal relationship with Jesus Christ will be incomplete. The Church is the Body of Christ, and Our Lord wants each of us to be members of this Body (Ephesians 4:4-6, 1 Corinthians 12:27).

Authentic Faith. The Catholic Church is the one true Church established by Jesus Christ. In order for our faith to be completely authentic, it must be grounded in this One, Holy, Catholic, and Apostolic Church.

> "This is the sole Church of Christ, which in the Creed we profess to be one, holy, catholic and apostolic." These four characteristics, inseparably linked with each other, indicate essential features of the Church and her mission (*Catechism*, 811).

The Magisterium of the Catholic Church has the mind of Christ. If a person's beliefs are not grounded in the teachings of the Magisterium, his faith is not grounded in Jesus Christ. To have an authentic faith, we must accept all the teachings of the Magisterium of the Catholic Church on faith and morals, and strive to always remain faithful to those teachings.

Obedient Faith. If we have a living faith and an authentic faith, we will express this faith by being *obedient* to Jesus Christ and His Church. The **obedience of faith** is man's free submission of himself, through faith, to the Authority of God, leading him to accept God's Word, obey His Commandments, and remain faithful to His Church.

> "He who hears you hears me, and he who rejects you rejects me, and he who rejects me rejects him who sent me" (Luke 10:16).

The perfect embodiment of the *obedience of faith* is Our Blessed Mother (*Catechism*, 144). If we truly are in fellowship with Jesus Christ, we will also be in fellowship with His Mother,

Mary, who is our Mother as well (John 19:26-27). Just as the Father of Jesus declares from Heaven, "This is my beloved Son; listen to Him" (Mark 9:7), the Mother of Jesus declares, "Do whatever he tells you" (John 2:5).

The Helmet of Salvation

> In every circumstance, each one of us should hope, with the grace of God, to persevere "to the end" and to obtain the joy of heaven, as God's eternal reward for the good works accomplished with the grace of Christ (*Catechism*, 1821).

To protect against a fatal blow to the head, a soldier wears a helmet. In our battle to resist temptation, we must do the same: "And take the helmet of salvation" (Ephesians 6:17). **In the Armor of God, the helmet is our hope of salvation through Jesus Christ**. We must keep our eyes fixed on the prize: life on high with Christ Jesus (Philippians 3:14). If we keep our trust in Him, God will help us to be firm and steadfast, amid all the disappointments, suffering, and attacks from the enemy that we endure in this life.

> For I am sure that neither death, nor life, nor angels, nor principalities, nor things present, nor things to come, nor powers, nor height, nor depth, nor anything else in all creation, will be able to separate us from the love of God in Christ Jesus our Lord (Romans 8:38-39).

Our hope is not in our own ability, not in the world, not in the government, not even in our family or friends. Our hope is in our Holy, Mighty God—Father, Son, and Holy Spirit. With Him, all things are possible (Mark 10:27).

The Sword of the Spirit

> "In many and various ways God spoke of old to our fathers by the prophets, but in these last days he has spoken to us by a Son." Christ, the Son of God made man, is the Father's one, perfect, and unsurpassable Word. In him he has said everything; there will be no other word than this one (*Catechism*, 65).

In the spiritual battle, as in a military battle, we need both *defense* and *offense*. In the Armor of God, our principal weapon against moral evil is "the sword of the Spirit, which is the word of God" (Ephesians 6:17).

The **Word of God** is God's revelation of Himself to man, which He has accomplished definitively through Jesus Christ, the Word Incarnate (John 1:1-18). The Word of God is revealed to us in two ways: orally through *Sacred Tradition*, and in writing through *Sacred Scripture*.

Public versus Private Revelation. The Word of God is **public revelation**: the revelation given by God to man for the sake of his salvation, which all Christians are bound to believe. Public revelation ended with the death of the last Apostle, St. John, and the completion of the last book of the Bible. Since then, there has been no new public revelation, nor will there be until the end of time. **We are morally obligated to believe all public revelation.**

A **private revelation** is a revelation given during some period in history after the end of public revelation, to draw people closer to Jesus Christ or to help them better live out their Catholic Faith. Private revelations are not necessary for salvation. No one is obligated to believe a private revelation, except the one who actually receives it. The person who *receives* a private revelation is obligated to believe it if he is *certain* that it is from God, but **he must be very careful**. As soon as possible, he should seek counsel with a confessor who is completely faithful to the Magisterium of the Catholic Church. **Any supposed "revelation" that is contrary to one or more of the teachings of the Magisterium on faith or morals is definitely *not* from God, and therefore must be rejected.**

When someone claims to have received a private revelation, there are three possibilities:

(1) the person is mistaken or lying; (2) it is a trick of the devil, who often "disguises himself as an angel of light" (2 Corinthians 11:14); or (3) it truly is a revelation from Heaven. Only the Church has the authority and capacity to discern which of these possibilities is actually the case.

We must be very cautious about giving credence too quickly to reported visions or apparitions. We need to wait for the judgment of the Church and act accordingly:

- We are *permitted* to believe all private revelations that the Church has judged to be "worthy of belief" (such as the apparitions by the Blessed Virgin Mary at Guadalupe, Lourdes, and Fatima).
- We are *forbidden* from believing any purported private revelations that the Church has deemed "unworthy of belief."
- If the Church has suspended her judgment about the credibility of a particular reported private revelation, we should suspend our judgment as well.

Even those private revelations that the Church has deemed "worthy of belief" do not add anything new to the *public revelation* given in the Word of God. However, they can lead many souls to Jesus Christ and His Holy Catholic Church, and they can help us grow closer to God and Our Blessed Mother. For example, millions of people in Mexico converted to the Catholic Faith after the appearance of **Our Lady of Guadalupe** to **St. Juan Diego** in 1531.

Sacred Tradition. The Apostles preached and taught the Word of God to spread the Gospel and to instruct believers in matters of faith and morals. **Sacred Tradition** is the transmission of the Apostles' preaching and teaching, along with the institutions and practices they established, in a continuous line down to the pope and bishops of today. This passing down of authority from St. Peter and the Apostles to the pope and bishops is called **Apostolic Succession**.

Jesus Returning the Keys to St. Peter,
by Jean-Auguste-Dominique Ingres

Much of the oral teaching of the Apostles preceded the completion of the New Testament. Moreover, an important part of Sacred Tradition was the discernment of which writings were part of Sacred Scripture. Without the Catholic Church and Sacred Tradition, no one would even know which writings belonged in the Bible and which did not. Sacred Tradition and Sacred Scripture are intrinsically related.

> Both Scripture and Tradition must be accepted and honored with equal sentiments of devotion and reverence (*Catechism*, 82).

In fact, Sacred Scripture itself clearly exhorts the Christian faithful to "stand firm and hold to the traditions which you were taught by us, either by word of mouth or by letter" (2 Thessalonians 2:15).

Sacred Scripture. If we are to succeed in our battle against temptation, we need to know the Word of God. **Sacred Scripture** is "the speech of God as it is put down in writing under the breath of the Holy Spirit" (*Dei Verbum*, no. 9, in *Catechism*, 83).

The principal Author of Sacred Scripture is the Holy Spirit. The *instruments* He used to write the Scriptures are the human authors. While still maintaining their own distinct personalities, natural talents, and free will, these human authors were inspired by the Holy Spirit to write exactly what He wanted them to write and nothing else.

Because the Author of Sacred Scripture is the Holy Spirit, **Sacred Scripture is free from all error**. In the Armor of God, the "sword of the Spirit, which is the word of God," is pure, holy, and without any blemishes whatsoever. As the great Doctor of the Church St. Augustine once explained, if someone thinks he has found an error in Sacred Scripture, then either there is an error in the translation he is using, an error in the particular manuscript upon which this translation is based, or an error in his own understanding; there can be no errors in Sacred Scripture itself (St. Augustine, *Letter of Augustine to Jerome*, [82, 1, 3], 405 A.D., Jurgens, vol. 3, no. 1421, p. 4).

Many different styles of writing and expression are present in the Bible, so it is important to understand the Scriptures correctly. However, it is not possible for any of the Scriptures to contain errors. The Holy Spirit is God, all-perfect and all-knowing. He does not make mistakes.

> For all the books which the Church receives as sacred and canonical, are written wholly and entirely, with all their parts, at the dictation of the Holy Ghost; and so far is it from being possible that any error can co-exist with inspiration, that inspiration not only is essentially incompatible with error, but excludes and rejects it as absolutely and necessarily as it is impossible that God Himself, the supreme Truth, can utter that which is not true. **This is the ancient and unchanging faith of the Church**... (Pope Leo XIII, *Providentissimus Deus* [Encyclical on the Study of Sacred Scripture], Nov. 18, 1893, no. 20, emphasis added).

The complete list of all the books of Sacred Scripture is called the **Canon of Scripture**. It includes all the writings of both the Old Testament (**46 books**) and the New Testament (**27 books**), **73 books in all**. The Canon of Scripture is closed; no other books will ever be part of Sacred Scripture besides these 73 books.

There are two principal ways to learn Sacred Scripture: by attentively listening to the readings at Mass and by prayerfully reading the Bible. At every Mass, the Scriptures are proclaimed during the Liturgy of the Word. In fact, the entire Mass is immersed in Sacred Scripture. By carefully listening to the words of the Mass, we can grow in our knowledge of Sacred Scripture. In addition, we should try to spend some time every day reading the Bible in the quiet of our own home.

We must listen attentively to what the Holy Spirit is saying, both in His Word and through the sure guide He has given us to interpret His Word: the Magisterium of the Catholic Church. **The Magisterium is the final authority on the interpretation of Sacred Scripture.**

It is *not* the Church's teaching that we should avoid reading the Bible, as some have been incorrectly told. The Catholic Church not only *allows* us to read the Bible; she *exhorts* us to do so:

> The Church "forcefully and specifically exhorts all the Christian faithful ... to learn 'the surpassing knowledge of Jesus Christ,' by frequent reading of the divine Scriptures. 'Ignorance of the Scriptures is ignorance of Christ'" (*Catechism*, 133).

The final words in the quotation above are from St. Jerome, who translated the Latin Vulgate of Sacred Scripture in the 4th century. Look carefully at those words again: "Ignorance of the Scriptures is ignorance of Christ." If we do not know the Scriptures, then we do not truly know Jesus Christ, and we are in danger of taking on the mindset of whatever we immerse ourselves in, instead of the Word of God.

An example of using the Word of God as the sword of the Spirit is when Jesus rejected the temptations of the devil in the desert. Every time the devil tried to tempt Our Lord, Jesus refuted him by quoting Sacred Scripture (Matthew 4:1-10). The devil then tried to quote Scripture to suit his own purposes. However, Jesus rebuked him, and, once again quoting Sacred Scripture, He sent the devil away (Matthew 4:10-11).

Another example can be seen from the life of **St. Anthony of the Desert**, a holy monk from Egypt who is considered to be the Father of Monasticism in the East. St. Anthony used Sacred Scripture and prayer to fight against the demons who attacked him. Singing the Psalms and reciting other verses of Sacred Scripture, St. Anthony repeatedly drove the demons away. In the end, he vanquished them completely (St. Athanasius, *Life of St. Anthony*, circa 360 A.D. [online ed. by Kevin Knight, New Advent, 2009]; www.newadvent.org/fathers/2811.htm).

To really know the Word of God, we need to read Sacred Scripture *regularly*, *reverently*, and *carefully*. One suggestion is to make a commitment to read at least one page of the Bible every day. (You will probably find it easier to start with the New Testament.) The benefit of making such a small commitment is that we can be certain that we will always be able to meet our goal, no matter what.

If you are new to reading the Bible, at first there may be many passages in the Bible that you do not understand, and some that may even bother you. Be humble in such situations, admitting to God your difficulty and then moving on to the next verse, **always prepared to submit your judgment to that of the Catholic Church**.

Each time you read Sacred Scripture will be like a drop of water penetrating a new sponge. At first, no change will be noticed. However, over time, like the sponge, your mind will expand, as you grow in the wisdom and knowledge of the Lord. Your heart will become more steadfast, yet more pliable in the Hand of God. Your soul will be filled with the Holy Word of God. One day, you will look back and realize that the Holy Spirit has transformed your life.

> All scripture is inspired by God and profitable for teaching, for reproof, for correction, and for training in righteousness, that the man of God may be complete, equipped for every good work (2 Timothy 3:16-17).

Applying the Word of God in Our Lives.

We need the Word of God, "the sword of the Spirit," in order to win the battle against temptation and to grow in our walk with God. We need to know the *entire* Word of God, both Sacred Scripture and Sacred Tradition, while always following the sure guidance of the Magisterium of the Catholic Church. Right alongside our Bible, we should keep a copy of the *Baltimore Catechism* and the *Catechism of the Catholic Church*, and read them frequently as well.

Perseverance in Prayer and Supplication

> In his teaching, Jesus teaches his disciples to pray with a purified heart, with lively and persevering faith, with filial boldness. He calls them to vigilance and invites them to present their petitions to God in his name. Jesus Christ himself answers prayers addressed to him (*Catechism*, 2621).

A soldier cannot fight a war by himself; he needs help from his fellow soldiers and an effective way to communicate with them. In the spiritual life, prayer is our communications system. "Pray at all times in the Spirit, with all prayer and supplication. To that end keep alert with all perseverance, making supplication for all the saints" (Ephesians 6:18). Prayer is the sacred bond that unites the three main parts of the Church:

- the **Church Militant,** which includes all the faithful on Earth;
- the **Church Suffering,** which includes all the souls in Purgatory; and
- the **Church Triumphant**, which includes all the angels and saints in Heaven.

Saint Christopher, by Orazio Gentileschi

Three Crowns of Glory

During the late 3rd century, a young Egyptian Christian named Menas served as a soldier in the Roman army. When Menas heard about the edict of the Emperor Diocletian against Christians, and other pagan atrocities, he decided to leave the military. He began living in the wilderness, where he devoted himself to prayer, penance, and self-denial.

One day, Menas saw a vision of angels crowning Christian martyrs in glory. He longed to join those holy martyrs. Suddenly, he heard a voice from Heaven: "Blessed are you, Menas, because you have been called to the pious life from your childhood. You shall be granted three immortal crowns: one for your celibacy, another for your asceticism, and a third for your martyrdom."

Upon hearing these words, St. Menas was moved to action. He hastened to Rome, where a great festival was being held in the Circus. There he stood amid the crowd and boldly proclaimed his Christian faith. He was arrested, and subsequently tortured. But, through it all, St. Menas stood firm. Finally, he was beheaded, and his body was thrown into a fire. Miraculously, his body would not burn. His sister paid a large sum of money to retrieve the body. Then she and other Christians buried his body in the desert between Alexandria, Egypt, and the valley of Natron.

For centuries, the site of his tomb was venerated as a holy place. Miraculous healings occurred through a holy well there, and a basilica was built on the site. A great city emerged as well. In the 7th century, the Arabs destroyed this city, and the site was hidden. However, in 1905, excavations uncovered the ancient city, the holy well, and the tomb of St. Menas.

Some historians believe that St. Menas is none other than the saint known in the West as St. Christopher. The name Christopher is actually a Christian title meaning "Christ Bearer." There are several parallels between the story of St. Christopher and the life of St. Menas. So, some believe they are one and the same. In any case, St. Menas truly was a Christ Bearer, and he was granted three crowns of glory.

Through prayer, we can help one another here on Earth, as well as the holy souls in Purgatory. We can also communicate with the angels and saints in Heaven and ask for their help and intercession. All three parts of the Church belong to the Family of God and are joined together in prayer.

Prayer even enables us to talk with God Himself, Who desires us to be with Him always. We must *persevere* in our prayer, trusting that God will answer us according to His perfect timing and Providence.

Along with prayer, we should practice *self-denial* (or *asceticism*), tailored to the situations that confront us. This self-denial can help us during times of temptation. As Father Laux puts it: "In times of peace we must prepare for war, training our will by deliberate acts of self-denial and self-conquest" (Fr. Laux, p. 45).

Fasting and other forms of self-denial are not ends in themselves, but means to an end. It is best to use them to target the areas where we need the most help. For example, a person who is struggling with temptations against gluttony (overeating) might fast from eating certain foods or at certain times. However, this same tactic would not be beneficial for someone suffering from anorexia (obsessive fear about gaining weight). You should discuss with your parents and your confessor which types of self-denial would be best for you. Your parents and your confessor can also protect you from practices that might be harmful to you.

Our prayer should also be accompanied by **almsgiving** (giving to the poor or others in need). If possible, we should increase our almsgiving in conjunction with our self-denial. For example, we could use the money saved from fasting to purchase a gift card for someone in need, or we could use the time saved from denying ourselves some form of entertainment to volunteer at the Church.

Most important, our prayer should always be accompanied by *righteousness*. God sees into the depths of our heart (Psalm 139), and He knows that we are weak. He is merciful to sinners, and He loves us. However, He also expects us to strive with all our strength to obey His Commandments. The prayer of a *humble* person who is truly trying to live a morally good life is always pleasing to God.

> "Prayer is good when accompanied by fasting, almsgiving, and righteousness. A little with righteousness is better than much with wrongdoing. It is better to give alms than to treasure up gold" (Tobit 12:8).

Prayer is a critical part of the Armor of God. We should focus on our relationship with God throughout our life and spend time with Him in prayer *every day*.

Our Armor Must Be Complete

> To live, grow, and persevere in the faith until the end we must nourish it with the word of God; we must beg the Lord to increase our faith; it must be "working through charity," abounding in hope, and rooted in the faith of the Church (*Catechism*, 162).

Examine Ephesians 6:13-18 again. It is critical that our spiritual armor be *complete*. If there is one area where we are lacking, the enemy will attack that weakness. With God's help, **we must stand firm in the entire Armor of God**: the girding of truth, the breastplate of righteousness, the footwear of the gospel of peace, the shield of faith, the helmet of salvation, the sword of the Spirit, and perseverance in prayer and supplication.

The Mass and the Sacraments

> "Truly, truly, I say to you, he who believes has eternal life. I am the bread of life.... I am the living bread which came down from heaven; if anyone eats of this bread, he will live forever; and the bread which I shall give for the life of the world is my flesh" (John 6:47-51).

A major part of our strategy to resist temptation is our participation in the Holy Sacrifice of the Mass and the sacraments. The Mass and the sacraments give us the grace we need to cultivate the fear of the Lord, and they can help perfect the Armor of God in us, especially if we attend Mass daily.

Two important points bear mentioning. First, it is essential that we receive *all* the sacraments that we are eligible to receive, **including the Sacrament of Confirmation**. The Sacrament of Confirmation makes us soldiers for Christ. Through it, we receive "the seal of the Holy Spirit" and an outpouring of His gifts (*Catechism*, 1294-1296). This sacrament is very important for our strategy to resist temptation. The Sacrament of Confirmation gives us the grace and wisdom to take up the Armor of God with courage and the fear of the Lord.

Second, we should receive Holy Communion and the Sacrament of Penance *frequently*. We should try to attend Mass daily, and go to Confession at least once a month. The Holy Eucharist nourishes our soul, strengthens our charity, and removes venial sins. It also helps

The Last Supper, by Jean-Baptiste de Champaigne

preserve us from committing mortal sins, especially if we are going to daily Mass. When we receive the Holy Eucharist every day in a state of grace, it becomes increasingly less likely that we will fall into mortal sin.

> By the same charity that it enkindles in us, the Eucharist *preserves us from future mortal sins*. The more we share the life of Christ and progress in his friendship, the more difficult it is to break away from him by mortal sin (*Catechism*, 1395).

Through faith, we believe in Jesus Christ, and we put our trust in Him. Through Sacred Scripture and Sacred Tradition, we learn Who God is, and we hear Him speak to us. Through prayer, we raise our mind and heart to God. **Through Holy Communion, we become one with Him.** When we are one with the Son of God, we are also one with the Father and the Holy Spirit. Every time we receive Holy Communion, we enjoy a profound intimacy with the Blessed Trinity.

It is also important to receive the Sacrament of Penance frequently. **Each sacrament has *particular* graces associated with it.** Among the many benefits of the Sacrament of Penance are "peace and serenity of conscience, and spiritual consolation" (*Catechism*, 1496). Moreover, frequent Confession can benefit us when we receive Holy Communion. When the windshield of our car has been washed, the rays of the sun can shine more brilliantly into our car. When we have been purified through the Sacrament of Penance, the graces available from Holy Communion can shine more brilliantly into our soul.

Finally, Eucharistic Adoration can strengthen the Armor of God in us. Spending at least one hour each week in front of the Blessed Sacrament can help us to grow in intimacy with Our Lord

Supper at Emmaus, by Carl Bloch

and to cultivate an interior peace and calm in our life. Eucharistic Adoration is an important part of our personal relationship with Jesus Christ, our best and closest friend.

Devotion to Mary and the Saints

> And Mary said, "My soul magnifies the Lord, and my spirit rejoices in God my Savior, for he has regarded the low estate of his handmaiden. For behold, henceforth all generations will call me blessed; for he who is mighty has done great things for me, and holy is his name" (Luke 1:46-49).

Devotion to the Blessed Virgin Mary is like a "secret weapon" in our strategy to resist temptation. The enemy cannot withstand this secret weapon; he is overwhelmed by Mary's purity, humility, and perfect obedience to God. When we unite ourselves to Our Lord Jesus Christ by uniting ourselves to His Mother, the devil and all his legions are helpless.

Mary is "the woman" who, through "her seed" (Jesus Christ), has crushed the head of the ancient serpent (the devil). God foretold this victory after the original sin of Adam and Eve when He rebuked the devil:

> "I will put enmities between thee and *the woman*, and thy seed and *her seed*: she shall crush thy head, and thou shalt lie in wait for her heel" (Genesis 3:15, emphasis added).

Within this rebuke is a merciful promise of hope for mankind. It is the first promise of the coming of the Redeemer, Jesus Christ.

One of the best ways to express our devotion to Mary is through the Holy Rosary. Praying a daily Rosary, whether individually, as a family, or as a parish community, can be a powerful weapon in our strategy to resist temptation. It takes humility to be devoted to Mary, and her Son will not refuse a humble and contrite heart (Psalm 51:17).

The Rosary is an example of a *sacramental.* **Sacramentals** are "sacred signs instituted by the Church" that "prepare men to receive the fruit of the sacraments and sanctify different circumstances of life" (*Catechism*, 1677). Other sacramentals that can help in our strategy to resist temptation include the Chaplet of Divine Mercy, the scapular, holy water, and the Sign of the Cross.

Praying a daily **Chaplet of Divine Mercy** is an excellent practice that can help us trust in the mercy of God. The **scapular** is a gift from the Blessed Virgin Mary herself, lovingly given to her children. **Holy water** is a simple, yet powerful weapon against the enemies of God. In fact, **St. Teresa of Avila** (a Doctor of the Church from the 15th century who was devoted to *mental prayer*) noticed that the demons greatly feared holy water.

The **Sign of the Cross** is both the sign of the Holy Trinity and the sign of the Redemption that Jesus Christ won for us on the Cross. The Sign of the Cross is sacred, and it can help protect us (*Catechism*, 2157).

A way to strengthen our spiritual armor is through **consecration to the Sacred Heart of Jesus and the Immaculate Heart of Mary**, by which we commit our life to Our Lord Jesus Christ and Our Blessed Mother. We should devote ourselves to the **Holy Face of Jesus**, as it appears in the Shroud of Turin.

Devotion to the saints can help us greatly as well. Their example can inspire us, and their prayers can assist us. In addition, we should cultivate a relationship with our **guardian angel**, who protects us and can help us in many ways.

Besides the Blessed Virgin Mary, there is no greater saint than **St. Joseph**, her most chaste spouse. Guardian of the Holy Family, Patron of the Church, Protector of Families, and Patron of a Happy Death, St. Joseph is a powerful friend in Heaven who can help us stay on God's holy path.

Finally, our strategy to resist temptation would not be complete without the **Prayer to St. Michael the Archangel**:

> St. Michael the Archangel, defend us in battle; be our protection against the wickedness and snares of the devil. May God rebuke him, we humbly pray: and do thou, O Prince of the Heavenly Host, by the Power of God, cast into hell Satan and all the evil spirits who prowl throughout the world seeking the ruin of souls. Amen.

This prayer, which was given to the Church by Pope Leo XIII, was at one time said after every Mass. We should say this prayer often, and St. Michael will fight for us, just as he fought against the devil and his followers when they rebelled against God, and he cast them out of Heaven forever (Revelation 12:7-9).

Determination to Avoid the Near Occasions of Sin

> Flee from sin as from a snake; for if you approach sin, it will bite you. Its teeth are lion's teeth, and destroy the souls of men (Sirach 21:2).

Even if we follow all the steps described above, we will fail miserably in our strategy to resist temptation if we do not avoid the near occasions of sin. A **near occasion of sin** is any person, place, or thing that will likely lead us to fall into sin. **If we are to succeed in our strategy to resist temptation, we must have a firm determination to avoid all the near occasions of sin.**

Some things tend to be near occasions of sin for everyone—for example, watching an impure movie or keeping company with someone who does not have reverence for God. Other things might not tempt others, but *will* tempt *us*. Therefore, we need to know ourselves sufficiently so that we will be aware of our weaknesses and what tempts us. This **self-knowledge** can help us avoid the near occasions of sin.

When it is impossible to completely avoid a near occasion of sin, we must use every virtuous means to minimize our susceptibility to the temptation. We must be on our guard at all times. This does not mean that we should be scrupulous, worrying that we are sinning when we are not. However, we need to "test everything; hold fast to what is good, abstain from every form of evil" (1 Thessalonians 5:21-22).

The devil has been compared to a ferocious dog on a chain. If we stay away from him, he may try to scare us and threaten us, but he cannot touch our soul. However, if, like a fool, we go near him, he will tear us to shreds. Therefore, we must stay away from the enemy by avoiding all the near occasions of sin in our lives.

> Be watchful. Your adversary the devil prowls around like a roaring lion, seeking someone to devour. Resist him, firm in your faith, knowing that the same experience of suffering is required of your brotherhood throughout the world. And after you have suffered a little while, the God of all grace, who has called you to his eternal glory in Christ, will himself restore, establish, and strengthen you (1 Peter 5:8-10).

We must always firmly resist temptations as soon as we become aware of them. If we initially allow ourselves to go along with a temptation, it can become stronger and more difficult to resist. As soon as we experience a temptation, we must reject it (Fr. Laux, p. 46).

> Above all, we must be especially alert against the beginnings of temptation, for the enemy is more easily conquered if he is refused admittance to the mind and is met beyond the threshold when he knocks (Thomas à Kempis, *The Imitation of Christ*, [online ed. by Leadership Univ., Cyber Library, 1995], I, 13; www.leaderu.com/cyber/books/imitation/imitation.html).

Avert your eyes, turn off the television or radio, change the conversation, walk away, think about something else. Avoiding the near occasions of sin is an essential part of a successful strategy to resist temptation.

Conclusion

> God is faithful, and he will not let you be tempted beyond your strength, but with the temptation will also provide the way of escape, that you may be able to endure it (1 Corinthians 10:13).

In our battle against temptation, we are not alone. God is with us, and as long we remain in fellowship with Him, He will not allow us to be tempted beyond our strength. As members of the Mystical Body of Christ (1 Corinthians 12:27), we are all part of His Family, and He wants us to help one another.

Our entire strategy to resist temptation can be summed up in a simple exhortation: **Stay close to Jesus**. He is the Savior of the World, the Son of the Living God, the King of Kings, Our Holy Redeemer. Stay close to Jesus, invoke His Name, and be not afraid!

> Since then we have a great high priest who has passed through the heavens, Jesus, the Son of God, let us hold fast our confession.... Let us then with confidence draw near to the throne of grace, that we may receive mercy and find grace to help in time of need (Hebrews 4:14-15).

Our Lord Jesus Christ is present in the Church He established, and in the sacraments He instituted. He is in the Holy Eucharist with which He nourishes us, and in the Holy Word He has given us. He is wherever two or three are gathered in His Name (Matthew 18:20), and He is with us in the loving service we give to others (Matthew 25:31-40). He is with the priest who hears our confession, and He is in every tabernacle of every Catholic Church throughout the world. He is in Heaven, and He is in every soul that is in a state of grace.

Stay close to Jesus, then, striving with all your might to remain in fellowship with Him. Always remember that, **as long as you are in a state of grace, the Holy Trinity is in your soul!** "He who is in you is greater than he who is in the world" (1 John 4:4).

Chapter 15 Review

Matching: For each statement, select the letter of the best term from the list below. There are more terms listed than there are statements, and no term can be used more than once.

A. self-knowledge	E. *Summa Theologica*	I. Sacred Scripture	M. Church Militant
B. public revelation	F. righteousness	J. Sacred Tradition	N. Church Suffering
C. private revelation	G. Canon of Scripture	K. Armor of God	O. Church Triumphant
D. Confirmation	H. Gospel	L. fear of the Lord	P. obedience of faith

1. Gift of the Holy Spirit that instills in us a fervent zeal to put God before all else, attentively listen to Him, and obey His commands: ________.
2. Conduct that is morally upright and pleasing to God: ________.
3. The complete list of all the books of Sacred Scripture: ________.
4. Includes all the angels and saints in Heaven: ________.
5. Man's free submission of himself, through faith, to the Authority of God, leading him to accept His Word, obey His Commandments, and remain faithful to His Church: ________.
6. The secrets revealed by Our Lady of Fatima in 1917 are examples of ________.
7. The Sacrament of ________ makes us soldiers for Christ.
8. The speech of God as it is put down in writing under the breath of the Holy Spirit: ________.
9. Includes all the faithful on Earth: ________.
10. The revelation given by God to man for the sake of his salvation, which all Christians are bound to believe: ________.
11. The spiritual equipment needed to win the battle against temptation: ________.
12. The transmission of the Apostles' preaching and teaching, along with the institutions and practices they established: ________.
13. Includes all the souls in Purgatory: ________.
14. Helps us to be aware of our weaknesses and what tempts us, so that we can avoid the near occasions of sin: ________.
15. The "Good News" of the love and mercy of God, revealed and imparted to man through the Life, Passion, and Resurrection of Jesus Christ: ________.

True or False: Write *True* or *False* for the following statements.

________ 16. Having a personal relationship with Jesus Christ and remaining in fellowship with the Catholic Church go hand in hand.

________ 17. We are not expected to wear the *entire* Armor of God, only those aspects of it that are relevant to our particular vocation.

________ 18. Mary is "the woman" who, through "her seed" (Jesus Christ), has crushed the head of the ancient serpent, as God foretold after the original sin of Adam and Eve.

_________ 19. At some point in the future, the Magisterium of the Catholic Church may decide to designate additional writings as belonging to Sacred Scripture.

_________ 20. An authentic faith is one that consistently coincides with whatever we choose to believe.

_________ 21. The Holy Rosary, the Sign of the Cross, the Chaplet of Divine Mercy, and holy water are examples of sacramentals.

_________ 22. Each sacrament has particular graces associated with it.

_________ 23. Sacred Scripture is free from all error.

_________ 24. When we experience temptation, we should not resist it too quickly, lest we repress our true feelings and deny our deepest inner self.

_________ 25. The principal Author of Sacred Scripture is the Holy Spirit.

Multiple Choice: Write the letter of the best answer in the space provided.

26. God's revelation of Himself to man, accomplished definitively through Jesus Christ: _________.
    A. Magisterium of the Catholic Church
    B. Word of God
    C. Writings of the saints
    D. Catholic apologetics
    E. All of the above

27. A holy monk from Egypt who is considered the Father of Monasticism in the East: _________.
    A. St. Anthony of the Desert
    B. St. Benedict
    C. St. Augustine
    D. St. Juan Diego
    E. None of the above

28. Sacred Scripture includes a total of _________.
    A. 66 Books: 39 in the Old Testament and 27 in the New Testament
    B. 63 Books: 38 in the Old Testament and 25 in the New Testament
    C. 73 Books: 46 in the Old Testament and 27 in the New Testament
    D. 84 Books: 50 in the Old Testament and 34 in the New Testament
    E. The actual number of Books in Sacred Scripture cannot be known with certainty until the Church has considered all the archaeological evidence, such as the Dead Sea Scrolls.

29. Which of the following is *not* part of the Armor of God? _________
    A. The helmet of salvation and the breastplate of righteousness
    B. Pride
    C. The girding of truth and the footwear of the gospel of peace
    D. The sword of the Spirit and the shield of faith
    E. Perseverance in prayer and supplication

30. A sure guide to help us distinguish truth from falsehood: ________.
    A. The majority opinion of Christians throughout the world
    B. The predominant teaching at Catholic universities
    C. The Magisterium of the Catholic Church
    D. The consensus of Biblical scholars
    E. The media

31. Essential to the breastplate of righteousness: ________.
    A. Chastity and modesty
    B. Charity
    C. Humility
    D Righteousness and justice
    E. All of the above

32. The Word of God includes ________.
    A. Sacred Scripture
    B. Sacred Tradition
    C. All reported private revelations
    D. Both A and B
    E. All of the above

33. Which of the following accurately reflects the Catholic Church's teachings regarding reading Sacred Scripture? ________
    A. We should not read the Bible, because it can be dangerous to our faith.
    B. As long as we read the Bible every day, there is no need to go to Church.
    C. The Church forcefully and specifically exhorts all the Christian faithful to learn the surpassing knowledge of Jesus Christ by frequent reading of the divine Scriptures. Ignorance of the Scriptures is ignorance of Christ.
    D. We must listen attentively to what the Holy Spirit is saying, both in His Word and through the Magisterium of the Catholic Church, which is the final authority on the interpretation of Sacred Scripture.
    E. Both C and D

34. Which of the following can be a near occasion of sin? ________
    A. A person
    B. A place
    C. A thing
    D. All of the above
    E. None of the above

35. The sword of the Spirit: ________.
    A. The Word of God
    B. Faith
    C. Reason
    D. Our talents and skills
    E. All of the above

36. In order for our faith to be an effective shield in our spiritual armor, it must be ________.
   A. A living faith
   B. An authentic faith
   C. An obedient faith
   D. All of the above
   E. None of the above

37. In the Armor of God, the "helmet" is our ________.
   A. Intelligence
   B. Hope of salvation through Jesus Christ
   C. Self-esteem
   D. Pride
   E. All except D

38. Our prayer should be accompanied by ________.
   A. Fasting
   B. Almsgiving
   C. Righteousness
   D. Humility
   E. All of the above

39. Our entire strategy to resist temptation can be summed up in the following exhortation: ________.
   A. Charge!
   B. Don't take life too seriously.
   C. Stay close to Jesus!
   D. We must fight alone, but we shall prevail!
   E. Relax, breathe deeply, and think happy thoughts.

40. Jesus Christ is present ________.
   A. In the Church He established
   B. In the sacraments He instituted
   C. In the Holy Eucharist with which He nourishes us
   D. In the Holy Word He has given us
   E. Wherever two or three are gathered in His Name
   F. In the loving service we give to others
   G. With the priest who hears our confession
   H. In every tabernacle of every Catholic Church throughout the world
   I. In Heaven
   J. In every soul that is in a state of grace
   K. All of the above

The Sermon on the Mount, by James Tissot

Chapter 16. The Christian Ideal: Christian Charity and the Beatitudes

> That which was from the beginning, which we have heard, which we have seen with our eyes, which we have looked upon and touched with our hands, concerning the word of life—the life was made manifest, and we saw it, and testify to it, and proclaim to you the eternal life which was with the Father and was made manifest to us—that which we have seen and heard we proclaim also to you, so that you may have fellowship with us; and our fellowship is with the Father and with his Son Jesus Christ. And we are writing this that our joy may be complete (1 John 1:1-4).

Christianity is not based on unfounded speculation, clever myths, or the unverified claims of one person. Christianity is based on *eye-witness accounts* of what God has revealed, in glory and power, through His saving work among His people. These eye-witness accounts

The Transfiguration, by Carl Bloch

confirm that God sent His Only-Begotten Son, Jesus Christ, to become Man and live among us, and "to bear witness to the truth" (John 18:37).

> For we did not follow cleverly devised myths when we made known to you the power and coming of our Lord Jesus Christ, but we were eyewitnesses of his majesty (2 Peter 1:16).

The Apostles spent three years with Jesus Christ. They spoke with Him, they heard His words, and they saw Him. They touched Him, they walked with Him, and they ate and drank with Him. They *knew* He was truly a man, living among them.

At the same time, they began to realize that He was more than a man. They were there when He made the blind see, the deaf hear, the mute speak, and the lame walk. They were there when He walked on the water, multiplied the loaves and fish to feed thousands, and healed the lepers. With their own eyes, they saw Him bring Lazarus back to life after he had been dead for four days (John 11:17-44).

At the Transfiguration, Peter, James, and John saw the clothes of Jesus become dazzling white, and they heard the majestic voice of God the Father speaking to His Son from the bright cloud of the Holy Spirit. They were overcome with amazement, and they fell on their faces in fear and awe (Matthew 17:1-6).

After He was publicly crucified on the Cross, confirmed dead by a soldier thrusting a lance into His side, and buried in a tomb, Jesus rose from the dead and appeared to them! They saw the Risen Lord. They ate and drank with Him, they touched Him, and they spoke with Him.

Of all the Apostles, it was the one who had doubted the most, the one who had insisted on empirical proof of the Resurrection, St. Thomas, to whom Jesus *proved* that He truly had risen, Body and Soul, from the dead (John 20:24-27). St. Thomas then made the proclamation regarding the identity of Jesus that expressed what all the other Apostles had finally come to realize as well: "My Lord and my God!" (John 20:28). **Jesus Christ truly was God**—and the world would never be the same.

> Therefore God has highly exalted him and bestowed on him the name which is above every name, that at the name of Jesus every knee should bow, in heaven and on earth and under the earth, and every tongue confess that Jesus Christ is Lord, to the glory of God the Father (Philippians 2:9-10).

So certain was their knowledge of this truth that every one of the Apostles except St. John was martyred for his faith, and St. John was exiled. Had the Apostles been following "cleverly devised myths," they never would have been willing to suffer and give up their lives for Jesus Christ. It was because they *knew* Him and were *eye-witnesses* of His glory that they were willing to make this supreme sacrifice to defend the truth of the Gospel.

Moreover, they were not alone. Just as He had promised, Jesus sent them the Holy Spirit, the Counselor and Spirit of Truth, to lead them to all truth (John 14:16-17, 20:19-23; Acts 2:1-4). Now, through the ministry of the Church, we who have been baptized have also received the Holy Spirit in our souls, and He gives us grace and power so that we may abide in Jesus Christ, and He may abide in us (John 15:1-11).

Jesus is the beloved Son, Who is pleasing to the Father in every way. Through His life and teachings, Jesus has shown us how to perfectly follow God's Law, and He gives us the grace to be His disciples, so that we may be perfect, just as He is perfect (Matthew 5:48).

The Perfect Example of Christ

> Put on then, as God's chosen ones, holy and beloved, compassion, kindness, lowliness, meekness, and patience, forbearing one another and, if one has a complaint against another, forgiving each other; as the Lord has forgiven you, so you also must forgive. And above all these put on love, which binds everything together in perfect harmony. And let the peace of Christ rule in your hearts, to which indeed you were called in the one body. And be thankful (Colossians 3:12-15).

All people must live in accordance with the Divine Law. However, as Christians, we are called to go even further. God asks us to strive for **Christian perfection**, the ideal of the Christian life, whereby we truly become like Our Lord and Savior Jesus Christ. Christian perfection should be the aim of every disciple of Jesus. We must strive to practice every virtue, at all times, for the love of God and in gratitude to Him.

We will never completely attain Christian perfection in this life. However, it is an ideal that each of us should strive to reach—not trusting in our own abilities, but trusting in the Lord Jesus Christ. With God's help, we must strive with all our heart to live a morally good life and to love God above all else by remaining in fellowship with Jesus.

> Indeed I count everything as loss because of the surpassing worth of knowing Christ Jesus my Lord. For his sake I have suffered the loss of all things, and count them as refuse, in order that I may gain Christ… (Philippians 3:8).

Our Lord Jesus Christ has given us the ultimate example of what it means to attain Christian perfection. Jesus practiced all the virtues perfectly. With perfect devotion and love, He was obedient to the Father in all things, even suffering death on the Cross (Philippians 2:5-8). Jesus loved His neighbor with a love that was perfect in every way. He loved both His friends and His enemies. He even prayed from the Cross for those who were crucifying Him!

As the obedient Son of the Father, Jesus modeled perfect obedience, patience, humility, magnanimity, sincerity, simplicity, kindness, truthfulness, chastity, purity, modesty, fidelity, loyalty, clemency, mildness, meekness, and gentleness. Throughout His life, He demonstrated perfect faith, hope, and charity, as well as prudence, justice, fortitude, and temperance. Jesus is "the way, and the truth, and the life" (John 14:6), and He commands that we, His disciples, imitate Him. "If any man would come after me, let him deny himself and take up his cross daily and follow me" (Luke 9:23).

The only way to reach the Christian ideal is to become like Jesus Christ, because Jesus Christ *is* the Christian Ideal. If we are to be perfect, we must follow Jesus, be united to Jesus, and become like Jesus. "I am the vine, you are the branches. He who abides in me, and I in him, he it is that bears much fruit, for apart from me you can do nothing" (John 15:5). It is Jesus Who is the Holy One of God; it is Jesus Who has the words of everlasting life (John 6:68-69). To obtain Christian perfection, we must imitate Him.

Christian Charity

> "A new commandment I give to you, that you love one another; even as I have loved you, that you also love one another. By this all men will know that you are my disciples, if you have love for one another" (John 13:34-35).

Our Lord calls us to an interior holiness that manifests itself in Christian charity. **Christian charity** is the love of Jesus Christ within us,

Suffer the Little Children to Come unto Me, by Fritz von Uhde

whereby we love God as Jesus loves His Father, and we love our neighbor as Jesus loves us. True Christian charity is possible only when we are in fellowship with God, so that *He* may love others *through us*. Christian charity is the heart of Christian perfection, because Christian charity is the heart of Jesus.

> Jesus makes charity the *new commandment*. By loving his own "to the end," he makes manifest the Father's love which he receives. By loving one another, the disciples imitate the love of Jesus which they themselves receive (*Catechism*, 1823).

Christian charity is essential to Christianity. Through Christian charity, we recognize, not only what we see in our neighbor, but also what we do not see: his rational soul. Christian charity requires us to embrace the truth that **every human being is a person created in the image and likeness of God whom we must love and respect**. If we do not put this truth into practice in our life, then our religion will be empty, and our faith will miss the mark. "But be doers of the word, and not hearers only, deceiving yourselves" (James 1:22).

In addition to our own families and those close to us (for whom it is natural to have feelings of friendship and compassion), Christian charity requires us to love everyone who is in the *household of God*, for they are our brothers and sisters in Christ. "So then, as we have opportunity, let us do good to all men, and especially to those who are of the household of faith" (Galatians 6:10).

We must also love the poor, the sick, the homeless, the downtrodden, and the imprisoned. We must love our neighbor, regardless of his race or ethnicity, his class or status, and his talents or appearance. We must love both the beggar and the rich man. We must love those who cannot repay us.

We must even love our enemies. We must not seek revenge against those who hurt us. Rather than focusing only on the offenses they have committed against us, we must try to see their good qualities (Fr. Laux, p. 131). We must even wish them well and pray for them.

> "You have heard that it was said, 'You shall love your neighbor and hate your enemy.' But I say to you, Love your enemies and pray for those who persecute you, so that you may be sons of your Father who is in heaven..." (Matthew 5:43-45).

Christian charity does not require us to give up our rights (Fr. Laux, p. 131). We still have the right to defend ourselves and to demand justice. Moreover, Christian charity does not require us to trust everyone or to put ourselves in grave danger. However, it does require us to forgive all those who harm or offend us, and not just one time or seven times, but *every* time (Matthew 18:21-22). We must not return evil for evil. We must be willing to do good to those who hate us. Our Lord Jesus Christ showed us how to love our enemies, by dying on the Cross for us poor sinners.

> While we were yet helpless, at the right time Christ died for the ungodly. Why, one will hardly die for a righteous man—though perhaps for a good man one will dare even to die. But God shows his love for us in that while we were yet sinners Christ died for us (Romans 5:6-8).

Christian charity has several distinct qualities (Fr. Laux, p. 123). First, it is an *act of the will*, not an emotion. We do not need to *feel* love for our enemies; we need to *practice* it. The simplest way to begin loving someone is to pray for him. This is an act of the will that we can easily perform, even if our emotions do not initially dispose us to do so. Perhaps we can make a commitment to pray each day for someone we do not like, or for someone who has injured or offended us. This simple practice can help us develop true Christian charity, even to the point of loving our enemies.

Second, Christian charity is *selfless*. If we are kind to others only so that they will be kind to us and do what we want, we are not truly loving them. "Love does not insist on its own way" (1 Corinthians 13:5).

Third, Christian charity is *universal*: we cannot make exceptions on the basis of race, ethnicity, age, financial status, whether the person is born or preborn, or any other consideration. We must love and respect every human being as a person created in the image and likeness of God.

Fourth, Christian charity is *alive and active*. We must express our concern for our neighbor's welfare in concrete acts. We must help those in need, be kind to everyone, and always be ready to forgive an injury or offense. God has brought about many conversions through the Christian charity of His saints.

Fifth, Christian charity is *always faithful to God's Commandments*. Helping the poor is not a substitute for living a morally good life. It is *part* of living a morally good life, but it is not the only part. Christian charity demands that we obey *all* of God's Commandments, and therefore remain faithful to all the teachings of the Magisterium of the Catholic Church on faith and morals. "For whoever keeps the whole law but fails in one point has become guilty of all of it" (James 2:10).

The General Means for Cultivating Christian Charity

> Fruit of the Spirit and fullness of the Law, charity keeps the *commandments* of God and his Christ: "Abide in my love. If you keep my commandments, you will abide in my love" (*Catechism*, 1824).

God has created us to know, love, and serve Him, so that we may be happy with Him in Heaven. **The ultimate goal of morality is happiness through union with God in Heaven.** Achieving this goal *depends on both God and us*. God has taken the first step by sending us His Son, Jesus Christ, to die on the Cross for us, and by giving us the grace to have faith in Him and to receive forgiveness for our sins (*Catechism*, 2017-2023). We must cooperate with this grace by taking advantage of **the means that God has given us to attain our salvation**: "faith, Baptism and the observance of the Commandments" (*Catechism*, 2068).

We must have faith in Jesus Christ, the Son of God. We must receive the Sacrament of Baptism to be freed from Original Sin, restored to a state of sanctifying grace, and united to Jesus Christ and His Church. We must do the Will of God, as manifested in the Divine Law, by obeying God's Commandments.

We need to avail ourselves of the general means that God has given all of us to grow in sanctity and Christian charity in order to attain Christian perfection. Many of these means are identical to the elements of an effective strategy to resist temptation, which we discussed in the previous chapter. The first essential element for achieving Christian perfection is the fear of the Lord. **It is impossible to cultivate true Christian charity or reach Christian perfection without the fear of the Lord.**

Second, we must equip ourselves with the entire *Armor of God*: the girding of truth (and hence obedience to all the teachings of the Magisterium of the Catholic Church); the breastplate of righteousness; the footwear of the gospel of peace; the shield of faith; the helmet of salvation (hope); the sword of the Spirit, which is the Word of God; and perseverance in prayer and supplication, joined with almsgiving, self-denial, righteousness, and humility.

Third, we should frequently receive the *sacraments* and participate in the *Holy Sacrifice of the Mass*, through which we encounter the Lord Jesus Christ and receive the grace to live in fellowship with Him. We should also participate in *Eucharistic Adoration*, adoring and cherishing Jesus in the Blessed Sacrament.

Fourth, in order to truly be close to Jesus, we also need to be close to His Mother, as well as His friends and servants. *Devotion to Mary and the angels and saints* is an excellent way to grow toward Christian perfection. In particular, we should practice *devotion to St. Joseph*, and we should cultivate a relationship with our *guardian angel*, who protects us and can help us to become more like Jesus. We will also be blessed if we regularly pray the *Holy Rosary* and the *Chaplet of Divine Mercy*, and we should frequently avail ourselves of other *sacramentals*, such as holy water, the scapular, and the *Sign of the Cross*.

Consecration to the *Sacred Heart of Jesus* and the *Immaculate Heart of Mary* can also be a great blessing to us. Devotion to the *Holy Face of Jesus* can help us as well.

Fifth, **we must have a firm determination to avoid all the near occasions of sin**. If a person claims to be "spiritual," yet he does not follow the Commandments, he is fooling himself. Christian perfection is impossible without obedience to the Commandments.

We need to stay close to Jesus and become more like Him. When we imitate Jesus Christ, we imitate Christian perfection, and we grow in sanctity and Christian charity. It is critical that we have a personal relationship with Jesus and remain in fellowship with His Church. If we have a personal relationship with Jesus Christ that is centered on His Holy Word and the Holy Eucharist, we will love Him so much that we will never want to offend Him. At the same time, to truly abide in Jesus Christ and know Him more fully, we must remain in fellowship with His Church by remaining faithful to the teachings of the Magisterium that He established and by participating in the Mass and the sacraments that He instituted.

The Specific Means for Cultivating Christian Charity

> Both the sacrament of Matrimony and virginity for the Kingdom of God come from the Lord himself. It is he who gives them meaning and grants them the grace which is indispensable for living them out in conformity with his will (*Catechism*, 1620).

In addition to the general means for cultivating Christian charity and attaining Christian perfection, God has given each of us a specific way to achieve this goal: our *vocation* (or *state in life*). A **vocation** is an invitation by God to serve Him in a particular way, so that we may grow in sanctity and Christian charity. There are **three main vocations**: single, married, and religious. Saints have come, and will continue to come, from all three vocations. Those who follow the vocation God has for them are more likely to have peace and joy in this life, and receive the sanctification they need to attain eternal life.

Discerning Your Vocation. Saying yes to the vocation God has for you, whatever it may be, is one of the best decisions you will make in your life. You should not close your mind or heart to any vocation until you have honestly discerned which one God is calling you to accept. God will bless you for your generosity.

Each vocation is a means of happiness and sanctification for those called to that vocation. Therefore, it is prudent, in fact, imperative, that everyone spend time discerning his or her vocation. What does God want *you* to do? In order to learn the answer to this question, you must open your heart to His Will for your life, whatever it may be. "Ask, and it will be given to you; seek, and you will find; knock, and it will be opened to you. For everyone who asks receives, and he who seeks finds, and to him who knocks it will be opened" (Matthew 7:7-8).

Is it possible for someone to be *morally obligated* to follow a particular vocation? If a person were somehow *certain* that the only way he could get to Heaven was to follow a particular vocation, then he would be bound to accept that vocation (Fr. Laux, p. 35). However, a vocation is generally a *calling*, an invitation by God, not a moral obligation. Nevertheless, when God calls, we should listen. Therefore, each person should try to discern his or her vocation. The best way to begin is to pray about it, and then discuss it with your parents and your confessor.

Vocation to Single Life. The vocation to be single does *not* refer to those who are single by circumstance because they haven't yet found the right person to be their husband or wife. It refers to those who make a *commitment* to remain single while remaining in the world, because they believe they are called by God to do so—for example, to fulfill some important, even if humble, mission.

An example of someone who clearly had a vocation to be single is St. Joan of Arc. God gave this young woman the incredible mission of saving France. Amazingly, she led the armies of France in the 1400s, when any woman serving in battle (let alone a 19-year-old peasant girl) was unheard of. Despite her age and other personal limitations, her lack of money and resources, and the weakness and treachery of the king of France, St. Joan of Arc, a single handmaid of the Lord, fulfilled her amazing mission, culminating with her martyrdom and eventual canonization.

Vocation to Married Life. Marriage is a holy and noble vocation. The married state is the cornerstone of the family, which is the domestic church and the foundation of society. The married state and the religious state are mutually beneficial. Today's bishops, priests, and religious brothers and sisters can help Catholic families to grow in holiness. Many of tomorrow's bishops, priests, and religious brothers and sisters are being raised in today's Catholic families.

Vocation to Religious Life. Each vocation is holy and is used by God for our sanctification. However, not all vocations are equal. **The highest vocation is the religious life.** The **religious life** is a state in life in which a person devotes himself or herself to the service of God and publicly professes to practice what are called the *Evangelical Counsels*.

The **Evangelical Counsels** are special means for achieving Christian perfection, recommended by Our Lord Jesus Christ. They are called *Evangelical* (from the Latin *Evangelium*, meaning "Gospel"), since they are recommended in the Gospels. The **three Evangelical Counsels** are voluntary poverty, perpetual chastity in **celibacy** (a commitment to never marry), and complete obedience to a religious superior.

Not all Christians are called to practice *all* the Evangelical Counsels. This is evident from the account of the rich young man in the Gospel of St. Matthew. When this man asked Jesus, "What good deed must I do, to have eternal life?" Jesus made it clear that he must obey the Commandments. It was only when the young man persisted, stating that he had kept the Commandments but wanted to know what he still lacked, that Our Lord said, "If you would be perfect, go, sell what you possess and give to the poor, and you will have treasure in heaven; and come, follow me" (Matthew 19:21).

Clearly, Jesus was *not* saying that no one can go to Heaven unless he sells all his possessions and gives the money to the poor; He had already stated that to attain eternal life, one must keep the Commandments. Jesus was giving this rich young man counsel about what *he* personally needed to do in order "to be perfect." This man had a *vocation* to give up his possessions and follow Jesus. Unfortunately, he could not bring himself to do so, and "he went away sorrowful; for he had great possessions" (Matthew 19:22).

In another case, there was a man who *wanted* to go with Jesus, but Our Lord actually told him to go home to his family instead:

> And as he was getting into the boat, the man ... begged him that he might be with him. But he refused, and said to him, "Go home to your friends, and tell them how much the Lord has done for you, and how he has had mercy on you" (Mark 5:18-19).

Thus, we must distinguish between the Commandments and the Evangelical Counsels (Fr. Laux, pp. 34-35). The Commandments *require* all people to act in accordance with the Divine Law, and hence the Natural Law, by obeying God's precepts. **The Commandments are binding on all persons, in all places, and at all times.** Those who obey the Commandments do their duty. Those who do not obey them act contrary to the Will of God, and thus commit sin.

The Evangelical Counsels are *recommended* for certain persons, who are called to act in a way that is better and more difficult than what is required of all. **The Evangelical Counsels are binding only on those who voluntarily promise or vow to live according to them.** Those who practice the Evangelical Counsels receive a greater reward from God in this life and in Heaven. Those who do not practice them are not sinning, unless they have made a promise or vow to practice them.

The Evangelical Counsels are **Counsels of Perfection**, high ideals for the Christian life, proposed by Our Lord Jesus Christ. They are intended to purify those in the religious life, like refined gold, from whatever could hinder the development of Christian charity in their souls—even those things that are not in themselves sinful.

The Evangelical Counsels directly combat the **three aspects of temptation**: the lust of the flesh, the lust of the eyes, and the pride of life (Fr. Laux, p. 34). Voluntary *poverty*, in which those in a religious community hold all material goods in common, combats the *lust of the eyes*. Perpetual *chastity* in celibacy combats the *lust of the flesh*. Complete *obedience* to a religious superior, which helps those in the religious life to more perfectly practice humility and obedience to the Will of God, combats the *pride of life*.

> The perfection of the New Law consists essentially in the precept of love of God and neighbor. The counsels point out the more direct ways, the readier means, and are to be practiced in keeping with the vocation of each (*Catechism*, 1974).

One of the main ends of the religious life is to achieve Christian perfection through Christian charity. The Evangelical Counsels are the primary means for those in the religious life to achieve this end (Fr. Laux, p. 35). Those who accept this calling receive special graces that help them to have peace and joy in this life, and to attain their salvation in the next (Matthew 19:29).

Those in the religious life help the Church and society in many ways:

> The religious state ... has also proved most beneficial to the Church by supplying her with excellent workers in every field of Christian endeavor—in spreading the Gospel, in educating the young, in combating error, in reclaiming the fallen, in caring for the orphan, the sick, and the aged. At every epoch of the history of the Church religious orders have contributed largely to the material, intellectual, and artistic progress of society (Fr. Laux, p. 36).

The religious life is referred to as the *consecrated life*, because those who enter it are **consecrated** (set apart by God for a holy purpose) to His service.

There are two main forms of organized consecrated life: *religious institutes* and *secular institutes*. A **religious institute** refers to a religious order or congregation approved by the Church, whose members publicly profess the Evangelical Counsels while living in community, such as in a convent. A **secular institute** refers to a religious society approved by the Church, whose members profess the Evangelical Counsels while continuing to live in the world.

The **clergy** are those who are ordained as deacons, priests, or bishops through the Sacrament of Holy Orders. The **laity** refers to all Catholics who are not ordained or in a religious state of life approved by the Church.

Diocesan priests are members of the clergy who profess celibate chastity and obedience to their bishop and his successors, but do not take a vow of poverty (since they do not all live in common). The consecrated life also includes **nuns**, **sisters**, **hermits**, and **consecrated virgins**, in accordance with Canon Law.

The Beatitudes

> "You are the light of the world.... Let your light so shine before men, that they may see your good works and give glory to your Father who is in heaven" (Matthew 5:14-16).

The **New Law** (or the *Law of the Gospel*) is the final stage of Revealed Law, given by God to all mankind through His Son, Jesus Christ. In the New Law, Our Lord confirmed all the moral precepts of the Moral Law, including the Ten Commandments. He also further perfected the Moral Law, insisting on a righteousness that is sincere and comes from the heart (Matthew 5:17-7:27).

The core of the New Law, and of Our Lord's call for His disciples to strive for Christian perfection, is found in the *Beatitudes* (Matthew 5:1-12), which Jesus proclaimed during His Sermon on the Mount. The **Beatitudes** are promises by the Lord Jesus Christ of eternal happiness for those who remain faithful to the Divine Law, and hence the Moral Law, by cultivating the interior dispositions of the heart necessary to practice Christian charity.

> In the Beatitudes, the New Law *fulfills the divine promises* by elevating and orienting them toward the "kingdom of heaven." It is addressed to those open to accepting this new hope with faith—the poor, the humble, the afflicted, the pure of heart, those persecuted on account of Christ—and so marks out the surprising ways of the Kingdom (*Catechism*, 1967).

The Beatitudes are concerned with reforming the *heart*, "the root of human acts, where man chooses between the pure and the impure, where faith, hope, and charity are formed and with them the other virtues" (*Catechism*, 1968). It is common today to equate the "heart" with the emotions. However, in Sacred Scripture, the **heart** is a metaphor, not for the emotions, but for the depths of our soul, where we decide what we truly value and want with our *will*, on the basis of what we know and understand with our *intellect*.

The Sermon on the Mount, by Carl Bloch

Jesus said, "For where your treasure is, there will your heart be also" (Luke 12:34). Whatever we cherish the most (our "treasure") is what our heart will value and seek the most, and this will be the primary motivation for what we do. In the Beatitudes, Jesus instructs us to direct our heart toward that which is pleasing to Him, and He promises that if we do, we will be happy with Him in Heaven. **Living a morally upright life in fellowship with God, through a genuine righteousness that comes from the heart, is the only way to achieve lasting happiness.**

Blessed Are the Poor in Spirit

> "Blessed are the poor in spirit, for theirs is the kingdom of heaven" (Matthew 5:3).

There is only One God, and He has a right to demand our singular devotion and fidelity. He will not share our heart with an idol, whether it be a graven image, money, or some other disordered attachment. "For the love of money is the root of all evils; it is through this craving that some have wandered away from the faith and pierced their hearts with many pangs" (1 Timothy 6:10).

The **poor in spirit** are those whose treasures are not the riches of this life, but rather the riches of Heaven. We must have a spirit of *detachment* regarding material possessions. This does not mean that we all must take a vow of poverty or that material possessions are bad. It does not even mean that a person may not have earthly wealth. However, we must not be so attached to material possessions that we make them our "treasure." Jesus wants us to devote ourselves to *gaining treasures in Heaven* through the obedience of faith lived out in charitable works, rather than devoting ourselves to gaining material riches in this world.

St. Francis of Assisi Adoring the Crucifix, by Bernardo Strozzi

> "Do not lay up for yourselves treasures on earth, where moth and rust consume and where thieves break in and steal, but lay up for yourselves treasures in heaven, where neither moth nor rust consumes and where thieves do not break in and steal" (Matthew 6:19-20).

Being poor in spirit is not the same as having little money or possessions. There are some poor persons who are not poor in spirit, and there are some rich persons who are. However, in general, the poor may be able to cultivate a spirit of detachment more easily than the rich if, in their poverty, they learn to depend on God rather than on material possessions for their happiness.

The poor in spirit are those who love God more than money, possessions, or anything else. They recognize that the Kingdom of Heaven is the "one pearl of great value" (Matthew 13:45), and they are willing to let go of everything they have in order to obtain it. Therefore, "theirs is the kingdom of heaven" (Matthew 5:3).

Blessed Are Those Who Mourn

> "Blessed are those who mourn, for they shall be comforted" (Matthew 5:4).

Jesus has compassion for those who mourn the death of a loved one, and He will comfort them. However, this Beatitude has a deeper meaning than the natural mourning that a person has when someone he cares for leaves this life, as real and painful as that mourning is. Our Lord is primarily speaking of the torturous mourning

St. Francis and the Beatitudes

The Beatitudes show us how to perfectly follow the Commandments by becoming more like Our Lord Jesus Christ. Every saint has embraced the Beatitudes, but some have been more explicit in living "in the world but not of the world."

St. Francis of Assisi is one of the most beloved saints of all time, admired not only by Catholics but also by the Orthodox and even non-Christians. Many see St. Francis as one of the holiest of God's saints. He truly was a "fool for Christ."

St. Francis and his followers strictly followed the Beatitudes in their religious order, the Franciscans. For example, they embraced poverty as a positive value, in contrast to the worldly ambition of always trying to acquire more money and material possessions. Poverty was a special love of St. Francis, and he went to great lengths to embrace it fully for the sake of following Jesus more perfectly. St. Francis also exemplified the virtues of humility, charity, and love of the truth.

Near the end of his life, St. Francis received the stigmata, the wounds of Jesus Christ on his hands, his feet, and his side. St. Francis was canonized as a saint in 1228, just two years after his death. The life of St. Francis stands as a shining example of how to walk with Jesus in the true spirit of the Beatitudes.

that His disciples experience because of the oppression of evil in the world and because of the sins of those they hold dear (2 Peter 2:7-8).

A person may experience this mourning when a loved one turns away from the Catholic Faith or embraces a way of life that is sinful. St. Monica mourned for many years while her son Augustine drifted from God and lived a sinful life. She prayed for him constantly, and she never gave up. In the end, she saw her son, not only turn back to God, but also become a Catholic priest, a bishop, and even a Doctor of the Church. **St. Monica was comforted.**

A person may also experience this mourning when he sees the Catholic Church treated with disrespect and contempt. In recent decades, Catholics have witnessed the stripping of holy statues and adornments from their churches; distracting innovations in certain parishes; terrible scandals among some Church leaders; and the removal of the tabernacle from its position of honor in the front of the church. **Those who mourn for our Holy Church will be comforted.**

A person may likewise experience this mourning when he sees his nation corrupted by unjust laws, wicked officials, and evil agendas. There have been many grave sins throughout the history of this country, such as the terrible practice of slavery. Somehow, through the grace of God and the good will of the people, many flaws have been overcome. However, now this nation is rapidly turning away from God's Law. Those who love this country mourn with much anguish and tears because of this. We do not know whether our nation will one day turn back from the path it is on. However, even if we are not comforted in this life, **God will comfort us when we reach our true and permanent homeland in Heaven.**

Finally, Our Lord Himself experienced this mourning when many of His own people, whom He came to save, rejected Him. As He stood outside the gates of Jerusalem, the "city of peace," He proclaimed these heart-wrenching words:

> "O Jerusalem, Jerusalem, killing the prophets and stoning those who are sent to you! How often would I have gathered your children together as a hen gathers her brood under her wings, and you would not! Behold, your house is forsaken. And I tell you, you will not see me until you say, 'Blessed is he who comes in the name of the Lord!'" (Luke 13:34-35)

Our Heavenly Father loves those who mourn, because He sees His Beloved Son, Jesus Christ, mourning *in them*. In the end, He will bless them, and "they shall be comforted" (Matthew 5:4).

Blessed Are the Meek

> "Blessed are the meek, for they shall inherit the earth" (Matthew 5:5).

When Jesus Christ comes again in His glory and judges all the people and nations of this world, a new Earth will be established, where truth, justice, peace, and love will reign (2 Peter 3:13, Revelation 21:1). Those who are meek will inherit this new Earth at the end of the age, when God raises our bodies from the dust, and we dwell with Him for all eternity.

> And I saw the holy city, New Jerusalem, coming down out of heaven from God, prepared as a bride adorned for her husband; and I heard a great voice from the throne saying, "Behold the dwelling of God is with men..." (Revelation 21:2-3).

Meekness is the virtue by which a person restrains his anger. The ***emotion*** of **anger** moves a person to fight against that which he sees as morally wrong or as an obstacle to his or someone else's happiness, peace, or security. When this emotion leads a person to think or act in a way that is contrary to justice or charity, he commits the ***capital sin*** of **anger** (or ***wrath***).

God exhorts His children to "overcome evil with good" (Romans 12:21). The battle we are in is a spiritual battle; therefore, our weapons must be of the Spirit, not of the flesh. To win this battle, we need to humble ourselves before the righteousness of God, so that He will fight for us. We must act in charity and meekness, not anger, "for the anger of man does not work the righteousness of God" (James 1:20).

> "You have heard that it was said to the men of old, 'You shall not kill; and whoever kills shall be liable to judgment.' But I say to you that everyone who is angry with his brother shall be liable to judgment; whoever insults his brother shall be liable to the council, and whoever says, 'You fool!' shall be liable to the hell of fire" (Matthew 5:21-22).

Experiencing the emotion of anger is not a sin. However, when a person fails to control his anger, he is on a path of sin, which is contrary to the love that God requires us to have for our neighbor. The stronger and more serious the anger is, the more serious are the consequences. If, in his anger, a person begins to desire to inflict harm on someone—calling him derogatory names, threatening him, or plotting to hurt him—then this person risks losing his salvation.

We must learn to restrain our anger and be meek like Jesus. "Let every man be quick to hear, slow to speak, slow to anger" (James 1:19). The person who can rule over his own anger can rule over a city (Proverbs 16:32). Thus, it is fitting that when the Lord comes again in His glory, it is the meek who "shall inherit the earth" (Matthew 5:5).

Blessed Are Those Who Hunger and Thirst for Righteousness

> "Blessed are those who hunger and thirst for righteousness, for they shall be satisfied" (Matthew 5:6).

While Jesus was on the Cross, He said, "I thirst" (John 19:28). Anyone whose blood was drained from his body would certainly have an intense natural thirst. However, Our Lord's "thirst" was deeper than that. **He thirsted for the souls of lost sinners to return to Him. He thirsted for goodness, truth, and love to triumph over evil. He thirsted for justice and righteousness to reign.**

> "But let justice roll down like waters, and righteousness like an ever-flowing stream" (Amos 5:24).

God is not pleased with external religious practices that are devoid of any internal meaning. **God hates when people make a show of religion but do not live a morally good life.** "Beware of practicing your piety before men in order to be seen by them; for then you will have no reward from your Father who is in heaven" (Matthew 6:1).

True spirituality cannot be separated from morality. Trying to do so would be like a thief piously abstaining from meat on Friday and then going out and stealing from his neighbor. Obviously, God is pleased when faithful Catholics obey all the laws of the Church, including the precept of not eating meat on Fridays during Lent. However, God is not pleased if someone only goes through the motions. **God wants our heart.**

> My son, give me your heart, and let your eyes observe my ways (Proverbs 23:26).

Christ Crucified, by Philippe de Champaigne

Those who give their heart to God will love goodness and truth, because God *is* Goodness and Truth. When a person truly loves goodness and truth, he thirsts for them like a man thirsting for water in the desert. As he looks around, he sees many *mirages* of goodness and truth. However, the Holy Spirit helps him to recognize them for what they really are.

Those who hunger and thirst for righteousness are pleasing to God, and He will bless them abundantly. Our Heavenly Father will lead them to the water that never runs out: the grace of the Holy Spirit.

"Ho, everyone who thirsts, come to the waters; and he who has no money, come, buy and eat! Come, buy wine and milk without money and without price.... Incline your ear, and come to me; hear, that your soul may live; and I will make with you an everlasting covenant, my steadfast, sure love for David" (Isaiah 55:1-3).

The food that God gives us is *Himself*; the drink that He gives us is *Himself*. He satisfies our hunger and quenches our thirst with His Word. "Man shall not live by bread alone, but by every word that proceeds from the mouth of God" (Matthew 4:4). He nourishes us with His Precious Body, Blood, Soul, and Divinity in the Holy Eucharist. "For my flesh is food indeed, and my blood is drink indeed. He who eats my flesh and drinks my blood abides in me, and I in him" (John 6:55-56). He gives us the wisdom and grace to do His Will (John 4:34). The Lord God will bless those who hunger and thirst for righteousness, and "they shall be satisfied" (Matthew 5:6).

Blessed Are the Merciful

"Blessed are the merciful, for they shall obtain mercy" (Matthew 5:7).

The **Golden Rule** teaches us that we are to treat others the way we want others to treat us. "And as you wish that men would do to you, do so to them" (Luke 6:31). If we read the Scriptures carefully, we will also see a corollary to this rule: **We must treat others the way we want God to treat us.** Although these exact words are not explicitly written in Sacred Scripture, they are often implied. "For with the judgment you pronounce you will be judged, and the measure you give will be the measure you get" (Matthew 7:2).

If we want God to be merciful to us, we must be merciful to others. This does not mean that we should condone sin. If we *condone* sin, we act as if sinning were okay, or we deny that there is any sin at all. When we *forgive* someone for sinning, we acknowledge that the person has done something wrong, but we decide that we will not hold it against him.

As Christians, we must be ready to forgive at all times. We must let go of all resentment, anger, and hatred against those who have injured or offended us in any way—physically, mentally, emotionally, or spiritually. This is not easy, especially if these injuries are still painful to us. We should begin by asking God for the grace to be able to forgive all of these persons. Then, we should pray for them, regardless of how we feel. **God will not judge us on the basis of our emotions; He will judge us on the basis of how we freely decide to act.**

"For if you forgive men their trespasses, your heavenly Father also will forgive you; but if you do not forgive men their trespasses, neither will your Father forgive your trespasses" (Matthew 6:14-15).

When a person forgives a great wrong, he demonstrates the mercy of Jesus Christ, and he too will receive mercy. God will give him special graces, so that he will sincerely seek God's forgiveness for his own sins, and Jesus Christ will call him to Himself in the sacraments.

In addition to forgiving wrongs, being merciful means showing compassion for the weak, the poor, the small, the oppressed, and the neglected, all of whom are very special to God. "Religion that is pure and undefiled before God and the Father is this: to visit orphans and widows in their affliction, and to keep oneself unstained from the world" (James 1:27).

Among the poorest and most defenseless in our midst are the preborn babies whose lives are threatened by abortion. **We must not forget them.** We must show mercy toward them through our prayers, our voice, our vote, and our actions.

Just as truth and love go together, so do righteousness and mercy. God is not pleased with those who are merciful in some ways, yet do not obey the Commandments. When someone does not live a morally upright life, he is not being merciful to those he hurts through his sins, nor to his own soul, nor to the Church, nor to society itself. Likewise, God is not pleased with those who are righteous in some ways, yet are not merciful. When someone fails to be merciful, he commits a **sin of omission** by neglecting to do something that God has commanded, and thus he is not truly acting righteously.

Righteousness and mercy always go together. They are *both* from God, and they are both His Will. Those who are truly righteous are also merciful, and vice versa. God will bless them, and "they shall obtain mercy" (Matthew 5:7).

Blessed Are the Pure in Heart

> "Blessed are the pure in heart, for they shall see God" (Matthew 5:8).

We must be pure if we wish to see God. The pure in heart *treasure* purity, and that is where their *heart* is. They practice chastity and modesty at all times. They **avoid all the near occasions of sin** against purity and in every other area. If they are married, they are faithful to their husband or wife. If they are single, they practice abstinence. If they are religious sisters, nuns, priests, or brothers, they are faithful to their vow of chastity.

> "You have heard that it was said, 'You shall not commit adultery.' But I say to you that everyone who looks at a woman lustfully has already committed adultery with her in his heart. If your right eye causes you to sin, pluck it out and throw it away; it is better that you lose one of your members than that your whole body be thrown into hell" (Matthew 5:27-29).

Obviously, Our Lord does not want us to literally pluck out our eyes. However, He does want us to turn our eyes away from impurity and to remove from our life whatever is an obstacle to us seeing God and loving God.

The Immaculate Conception, by Giovanni Battista Tiepolo

Those who are pure in heart grow in their understanding of true *beauty*, because they begin to see as God sees. They are not fooled by flashy or degrading attempts at beauty, because their true focus is on God, Who *is* Beauty. They also grow in *single-mindedness*, because they are determined, above all else, to do the Will of God at all times.

After Our Lord Jesus Christ, the Blessed Virgin Mary is the one person who most fully embodies purity of heart. Her beauty lies principally in her humility, her obedience, and her purity. God saw these virtues when He first created Mary, and now *she sees God*. Those who imitate Mary will be pure in heart, and, like her, "they shall see God" (Matthew 5:8).

Blessed Are the Peacemakers

> "Blessed are the peacemakers, for they shall be called sons of God" (Matthew 5:9).

God did not create people to argue and fight. He created us to know, love, and serve Him, so that we may be happy with Him in Heaven. God wants His people to live in *peace*, and He desires that we have peace in every area of our lives, to the highest degree possible. **Peace** is tranquility through order, harmony, stability, and security. It is one of the fruits of the Holy Spirit, and at the same time it is "the work of justice and the effect of charity" (*Catechism*, 2304).

Peace with God. God wants His people to be at peace with Him. When a person is in a state of mortal sin, he is separated from God, and he is effectively *at war* with Him. Jesus said, "He who is not with me is against me, and he who does not gather with me scatters" (Matthew 12:30). When a person receives forgiveness for his sins in the Sacrament of Penance, he returns to a state of grace. Only a person in a state of grace can truly be at peace with God. In fact, Confession is also called the Sacrament of Reconciliation. Through this sacrament, we are reconciled with God and His Church.

Peace with the Church. God wants all people to be at peace with His Bride, the Catholic Church. There are many Christians who are not yet Catholic but who sincerely love Jesus. If they truly are open to the Will of God, Jesus will lead them to the Catholic Church, and gently tell them: "Come and see" (John 1:39).

Peace with Ourselves. If we are not at peace with God, it is impossible to be at peace with ourselves. How can a fish be comfortable if it is not in water? Likewise, how can a human being be comfortable if he is not where he is meant to be: in fellowship with God? When we are in fellowship with God, He gives us His peace, which surpasses all understanding, and this peace will keep our heart and mind in Christ Jesus (Philippians 4:7). Only then, can we truly be at peace with ourselves.

Peace in Our Home. The family is the domestic church and the cornerstone of society. If our home is filled with strife, our family will suffer, and society will suffer with it. Sometimes, it is difficult to avoid conflict when people live in close quarters; it is easy to disagree and annoy one another about many things. We must try to minimize these disagreements and be more patient with the faults and shortcomings of others. We must strive to be charitable toward every member of our family. We must try to treat them the way Jesus, Mary, and Joseph treated one another in the Holy Family.

> "So if you are offering your gift at the altar, and there remember that your brother has something against you, leave your gift there before the altar and go; first be reconciled to your brother, and then come and offer your gift" (Matthew 5:23-24).

We should firmly resolve not to argue with those in our family unless it would be a sin not to do so (for example, if it were necessary to gently rebuke someone regarding some moral issue). In this way, we can be an instrument for peace, rather than strife, in our home. A family at peace is a family that is blessed, and society itself will be blessed through such a family.

Peace with Our Neighbor. To the extent that it is possible, we must try to be at peace with our neighbor—in other words, with all people. How can we fulfill the Commandment to love our neighbor as ourselves if we are constantly bickering with him, maligning his name, or coveting what belongs to him?

> Live in harmony with one another; do not be haughty, but associate with the lowly; never be conceited. Repay no one evil for evil, but take thought for what is noble in the sight of all. If possible, so far as it depends upon you, live peaceably with all (Romans 12:16-18).

Peace among Nations. We should all pray for peace on Earth. Every nation has the right to defend itself, and a strong military is necessary to protect its citizens. However, at the same time, nations must strive for peace with one another and resist the temptation to solve their problems through the use of force. When the threat of violence is through a *civil war*, the obligation for peace is even greater; a civil war can be utterly devastating to a nation.

There are strict criteria for what constitutes a *just war*. If a nation ignores these criteria and attacks other nations, it transgresses the Divine Law and endangers its own citizens. Violence begets violence, and war begets war. There are times when a nation must use its military to defend itself or its allies. However, such cases should be the exception, not the rule. The rule ought to be **peace among men**.

Peace with the Truth. Finally, we must be at peace with the *truth*. Peace does not mean going along with the "mainstream" ideas of the world in order to avoid being divisive. It is impossible for a good Christian to remain silent when the very foundations of civilized society, the sanctity of life and the sanctity of marriage, are being trampled upon. Peace cannot endure without truth and justice.

To the extent that it depends on us, we must try to be at peace with everyone. However, when it is impossible to maintain both, **we must always choose truth over peace**. If we devote ourselves to the truth and do not swerve from it, there will be many who will not want to be at peace with us. However, we will be at peace with Jesus Christ, Who *rejects* a shallow "peace," which places the avoidance of conflict before all else:

> "I have a baptism to be baptized with; and how I am constrained until it is accomplished! Do you think that I have come to give peace on earth? No, I tell you, but rather division" (Luke 12:49-51).

Jesus came to bring upon the Earth the fire of the Holy Spirit, the Spirit of Truth (John 14:16-17). The "baptism" that He came to be baptized with was His saving death on the Cross. Jesus Christ came to bear witness to the truth, so that everyone who surrenders to the truth can be saved. In order to fulfill this mission, Jesus divides the faithful from the unfaithful, the good from the evil, the hot from the cold, the sheep from the goats (Matthew 25:31-32).

> "For this I was born, and for this I have come into the world, to bear witness to the truth. Everyone who is of the truth hears my voice" (John 18:37).

True peace cannot coexist with evil. Truth is like a fortress, with peace and goodness on the inside, and evil and falsehood on the outside. Those who follow the evil agendas of the world may be in agreement with one another for a time, but they will never truly be at peace. It is only *inside* the fortress of truth that we can find the lasting peace and joy that come from God.

Jesus calls us to invite those who are outside the "fortress of truth" to lay down their arms and surrender to Him. When we heed His call and, by our words and example, help our neighbor to make peace with God, we truly are "the peacemakers," and we "shall be called sons of God" (Matthew 5:9).

Blessed Are Those Who Are Persecuted for Righteousness' Sake

> "Blessed are those who are persecuted for righteousness' sake, for theirs is the kingdom of heaven. Blessed are you when men revile you and persecute you and utter all kinds of evil against you falsely on my account. Rejoice and be glad, for your reward is great in heaven, for so men persecuted the prophets who were before you" (Matthew 5:10-12).

The world would not accept Jesus when He came, and it does not accept Him now. Jesus is "the light of the world" (John 8:12). A world accustomed to darkness does not want to be near the light. Just as the world will not accept Jesus, so it will not accept those who follow in His footsteps.

> "If the world hates you, know that it has hated me before it hated you.... If they persecuted me, they will persecute you; if they kept my word, they will keep yours also. But all this they will do to you on my account, because they do not know him who sent me" (John 15:18-21).

Suffering is a part of life for all people. Not everyone suffers in the same way or to the same degree; some experience far more suffering than others. However, everyone experiences at least some suffering in this life. If a person remains in a state of mortal sin, he will surely suffer for it, and, along with this suffering, he will experience shame and disgrace. If a person lives a morally good life as a disciple of Jesus Christ, he will suffer as well. However, along with his suffering, he will enjoy peace and honor, and will receive a crown of glory in Heaven.

When we experience persecution for doing what is right, we should not be surprised or dismayed. We should ask Jesus to help us to be worthy to suffer for Him. Jesus blesses those who sincerely follow Him, and He will not forget those who are persecuted for His sake.

> Beloved, do not be surprised at the fiery ordeal which comes upon you to prove you, as though something strange were happening to you. But rejoice in so far as you share Christ's sufferings, that you may also rejoice and be glad when his glory is revealed (1 Peter 4:12-13).

It is not easy to be a faithful Christian in this world. However, when we *are* faithful to Our Lord Jesus Christ, He remains with us and strengthens us so that we can endure whatever comes. Our Lord expects us to stand up for what is right, even when it is not popular, and even if we will be persecuted for it.

> "Enter by the narrow gate; for the gate is wide and the way is easy, that leads to destruction, and those who enter by it are many. For the gate is narrow and the way is hard, that leads to life, and those who find it are few" (Matthew 7:13-14).

It is not enough to *say* that we believe in Jesus Christ or to profess that He is Our Lord and Savior. We must put His teachings into practice in our life. If we do, He will help us to withstand whatever suffering or persecution we face.

> "Everyone then who hears these words of mine and does them will be like a wise man who built his house upon the rock; and the rain fell, and the floods came, and the winds blew and beat upon that house, but it did not fall, because it had been founded on the rock" (Matthew 7:24-25).

The Christian martyrs suffered persecution and death because of their commitment to Jesus Christ and the truths of the Catholic Faith. Only God knows whether we will be asked to suffer such persecution, but we must be ready. We must *not* depend on our own strength, but on the strength that comes from Christ. We must be willing to suffer persecution, and even martyrdom, if God asks this of us, for the sake of remaining faithful to Our Lord Jesus Christ and His Holy Church.

The Christian martyrs teach us how to endure persecution and suffering. **We must have faith in Jesus Christ and remain in fellowship with Him.** We must heed His warning that we can do nothing apart from Him (John 15:5), and we must entrust ourselves entirely to Him. If we do, He will give us the grace to endure whatever may come. Those who suffer persecution because they are in fellowship with Jesus Christ and are living a morally good life are truly *blessed*, "for theirs is the kingdom of heaven" (Matthew 5:10).

Conclusion

> "O righteous Father, the world has not known thee, but I have known thee; and these know that thou hast sent me. I made known to them thy name, and I will make it known, that the love with which thou has loved me may be in them, and I in them" (John 17:25-26).

Jesus Christ is the perfect Son, and the perfect model of obedience to the Father. Through His life and teachings, and His saving Passion and Resurrection, Jesus has shown us the way of Christian perfection through Christian charity.

True Christian charity always leads to obedience to the Moral Law. Through the Beatitudes, Jesus teaches us how to follow the Moral Law, not only externally, but also from our heart. In the Beatitudes, Our Lord imparts the promise of eternal life to those who faithfully follow Him to the end. The Beatitudes teach us how to embrace the Will of God in our life, with a morally upright heart devoted to Christian charity.

Our Lord Jesus Christ walked on this Earth, died on the Cross, rose from the dead, and ascended into Heaven. However, that is not the end of the story. He will come again in glory, and will judge all people according to their works. "Behold, I am coming soon, bringing my recompense, to repay everyone for what he has done" (Revelation 22:12).

For those who refuse to do the Will of God, "who are factious and do not obey the truth, but obey wickedness, there will be wrath and fury" (Romans 2:8). For those who are obedient to the Will of God, "who by patience in well-doing seek for glory and honor and immortality, he will give eternal life" (Romans 2:7). "There will be tribulation and distress for every human being who does evil" (Romans 2:9), and there will be "glory and honor and peace for everyone who does good" (Romans 2:10).

"The Lord is faithful in all his words, and gracious in all his deeds" (Psalm 145:13). Therefore, "let us not grow weary in well-doing, for in due season we shall reap, if we do not lose heart" (Galatians 6:9). Let us hold fast to the One, Holy, Catholic, and Apostolic Church—built on the rock, St. Peter, the first pope—against which the gates of Hell shall not prevail (Matthew 16:18). Let us be faithful to all the teachings of the Magisterium of the Catholic Church on faith and morals. Let us abide in God, and praise Him for loving us so much that He abides in us.

> By this we know that we abide in him and he in us, because he has given us of his own Spirit. And we have seen and testify that the Father has sent his Son as the Savior of the world. Whoever confesses that Jesus is the Son of God, God abides in him, and he in God (1 John 4:13-15).

Let us sincerely try to be more like Jesus Christ, and to always stay close to Him. Let us do the Will of God above all things. Let us love God with all our mind, all our heart, all our soul, and all our strength, and love our neighbor as ourselves for His sake. Let us love the truth and strive to live by it with all our might. Let us praise and glorify the Holy Trinity through all that we think, say, and do. Let us be thankful to God for all the blessings He has given us. Let us love, adore, and praise Him always! "Blessed be the Name of the Lord from this time forth and forevermore!" (Psalm 113:2)

Chapter 16 Review

Matching: For each statement, select the letter of the best term from the list below. There are more terms listed than there are statements, and no term can be used more than once.

A. merciful	E. meek	I. poor in spirit	M. New Law
B. pure in heart	F. weak	J. peacemakers	N. vengeance
C. persecuted	G. mourn	K. powerful	O. righteousness
D. praised	H. suffer	L. riches	P. Golden Rule

1. The final stage of Revealed Law, given by God to all mankind through His Son, Jesus Christ: _________.
2. "Blessed are the _________, for theirs in the kingdom of heaven."
3. "Blessed are those who _________, for they shall be comforted."
4. "Blessed are the _________, for they shall inherit the earth."
5. "Blessed are those who hunger and thirst for _________, for they shall be satisfied."
6. "Blessed are the _________, for they shall obtain mercy."
7. "Blessed are the _________, for they shall see God."
8. "Blessed are the _________, for they shall be called sons of God."
9. "Blessed are those who are _________ for righteousness' sake, for theirs is the kingdom of heaven."
10. The _________ teaches us that we are to treat others the way we want others to treat us.

Matching II: For each statement, select the letter of the best term from the list below. There are more terms listed than there are statements, and no term can be used more than once.

A. fear of the Lord	E. clergy	I. Beatitudes	M. Christian charity
B. secular institute	F. peace	J. heart	N. religious institute
C. consecrated	G. timidity	K. vocation	O. Evangelical Counsels
D. religious life	H. meekness	L laity	P. Christian perfection

11. The love of Jesus Christ within us, whereby we love God as Jesus loves His Father, and we love our neighbor as Jesus loves us: _________.
12. An invitation by God to serve Him in a particular way, so that we may grow in sanctity and Christian charity: _________.
13. Special means for achieving Christian perfection, recommended by Our Lord Jesus Christ: _________.

14. A religious society approved by the Church, whose members profess the Evangelical Counsels while continuing to live in the world: ________.

15. Set apart by God for a holy purpose: ________.

16. A religious order or congregation approved by the Church, whose members profess the Evangelical Counsels while living in community, such as in a convent: ________.

17. The ideal of the Christian life, whereby we truly become like Our Lord and Savior Jesus Christ: ________.

18. Those ordained as deacons, priests, or bishops: ________.

19. Promises by the Lord Jesus Christ of eternal happiness for those who remain faithful to the Divine Law, and hence the Moral Law, by cultivating the interior dispositions of the heart necessary to practice Christian charity: ________.

20. The first essential element for achieving Christian perfection, and without which it is impossible to cultivate true Christian charity: ________.

21. The ________ includes all Catholics who are not ordained or in a religious state of life approved by the Church.

22. A metaphor for the depths of our soul, where we decide what we truly value and want with our will, on the basis of what we know and understand with our intellect: ________.

23. Virtue by which a person restrains his anger: ________.

24. State in life in which a person devotes himself or herself to the service of God and publicly professes to practice the Evangelical Counsels: ________.

25. Tranquility through order, harmony, stability, and security: _______.

True or False: Write *True* or *False* for the following statements.

________ 26. Christianity is based on eye-witness accounts of what God has revealed, in glory and power, through His saving work among His people.

________ 27. We must treat others the way we want God to treat us.

________ 28. Only a person in a state of grace can truly be at peace with God.

________ 29. Each vocation is a means of happiness and sanctification for those called to that vocation.

________ 30. True Christian charity always leads to obedience to the Moral Law.

________ 31. It is possible to achieve Christian perfection without obeying the Commandments, as long as we feel good about ourselves.

_________ 32. The vocation to be single refers to all those who, because of the circumstances of their lives, have not yet found the right person to be their husband or wife.

_________ 33. Living a morally upright life in fellowship with God, through a genuine righteousness that comes from the heart, is the only way to achieve lasting happiness.

_________ 34. Diocesan priests profess celibate chastity and obedience to their bishop and his successors.

_________ 35. The only way to reach the Christian ideal is to become like Jesus.

_________ 36. As long as we are merciful, we do not need to be righteous.

_________ 37. The Evangelical Counsels directly combat the three aspects of temptation: the lust of the flesh, the lust of the eyes, and the pride of life.

_________ 38. Christian mercy demands that we condone the sins of others.

_________ 39. We will be judged by God on the basis of our emotions, because they are an outward manifestation of the inward disposition of our heart.

_________ 40. Those who are truly righteous are also merciful.

_________ 41. True peace cannot coexist with evil.

_________ 42. When it is impossible to maintain both truth and peace, we must sometimes choose peace over truth.

_________ 43. Happiness has nothing to do with morality.

_________ 44. We must be pure if we wish to see God.

_________ 45. Every human being is a person created in the image and likeness of God whom we must love and respect.

Multiple Choice: Write the letter of the best answer in the space provided.

46. Which of the following is *not* correct? _________
    A. The poor in spirit are those whose treasures are not the riches of this life, but rather the riches of Heaven.
    B. The poor in spirit are all those who have little money or possessions.
    C. The poor may be able to cultivate a spirit of detachment more easily than the rich if, in their poverty, they learn to depend on God rather than on material possessions for their happiness.
    D. The poor in spirit are those who love God more than money, possessions, or anything else.
    E. The poor in spirit recognize that the Kingdom of Heaven is the "one pearl of great value," and they are willing to let go of everything they have in order to obtain it.

47. To the extent that it is possible, we must try to be at peace with ________.
  A. God
  B. The Church, our family, and ourselves
  C. All people
  D. Both A and B
  E. All of the above

48. All of the following are Evangelical Counsels, *except* ________.
  A. Voluntary poverty
  B. Perpetual chastity in celibacy
  C. Power to influence others and bring about change in the Church
  D. Complete obedience to a religious superior
  E. Both A and D

49. Which of the following is correct? ________
  A. The Commandments are binding only on those who voluntarily promise or vow to live according to them.
  B. Those who do not obey the Commandments are not sinning, unless they have made a promise or vow to obey them.
  C. The Evangelical Counsels are binding on all persons, in all places, and at all times.
  D. Those who do not practice the Evangelical Counsels act contrary to the Will of God, and thus commit sin.
  E. None of the above

50. Christian charity: ________.
  A. Is an act of the will, not an emotion
  B. Is selfless, alive and active, and universal
  C. Is always faithful to God's Commandments
  D. Requires us to trust everyone
  E. Is essential to Christianity
  F. Requires us to forgive all those who harm or offend us
  G. Requires us to give up our rights for the sake of our neighbor
  H. Is the heart of Christian perfection, because it is the heart of Jesus
  I. All except A and C
  J. All except D and G
  K. All of the above
  L. None of the above

The Last Judgment, by Fra Angelico

Glossary

abortifacient – a type of contraception that kills a human being through a chemical abortion if it is unable to prevent that human being from being conceived. The use of abortifacients is a grave sin against both the Fifth and Sixth Commandments. See **abortion** and **contraception**.

abortion – the intentional killing of a preborn infant. Abortion is a grave sin against the Fifth Commandment and an intrinsically evil act. It is never morally permissible. Anyone who formally cooperates in an abortion is automatically excommunicated from the Church.

absolute – unchanging and universal. The standard for what is morally good versus morally evil is absolute, not relative. See **standard of morality**.

acedia – carelessness of heart, spiritual laxness, and insufficient vigilance in the spiritual life, leading to a type of spiritual depression. Acedia is closely related to the capital sin of sloth (laziness). It is a grievous sin against charity.

acts of prayer – adoration, thanksgiving, contrition, and petition. See **prayer**.

acts of religion – the ways we practice the virtue of religion. Acts of religion include adoration, penance, fasting, prayer, almsgiving, vows, and oaths. See **religion**.

actual sin – any sinful act of the will. There are two categories of actual sin: mortal sin and venial sin. See **mortal sin** and **venial sin**.

Adam – the first man in all of creation. God created the body of Adam from the dust of the Earth. God created Adam's soul (and likewise creates the soul of every other human being) directly, out of nothing. See **Eve** and **Original Sin**.

adoration – the highest form of worship, in which we submit ourselves completely to God, giving our love and homage to the Supreme Being Who created us and upon Whom we depend entirely. Only God may be the object of adoration. Adoration is the first act of religion. It is also an act of prayer, in which we give worship, honor, and praise to God. Our worship of God is *direct* when we adore and honor God Himself. Our worship of God is *indirect* when we honor God by honoring the Blessed Virgin Mary, the angels, or the saints. See **veneration**.

adulation – showing excessive admiration for someone, for the sake of some ulterior motive. Adulation is a form of duplicitous speech, and it is a sin against the Eighth Commandment. If a person expresses approval, either implicitly or explicitly, of behavior that is gravely sinful, he commits a serious sin. See **duplicitous speech**.

adultery – grave sin in which a man is not faithful to his wife, or a woman is not faithful to her husband, thus violating their marriage vows.

agape – Greek word for the highest form of love: the self-giving love that truly seeks the good of another. This is the selfless love that Jesus Christ has for His Church, and it is the love that God calls us to have for our neighbor. This love is called *charity*. See **charity**.

agnostic – someone who claims not to know whether God exists.

agnosticism – supposed uncertainty about whether God exists. Agnosticism may come in many different forms. However, in practice, agnosticism is often equivalent to atheism.

almsgiving – giving to the poor or others in need. We have a duty to express our love for Jesus Christ by caring for the bodily and spiritual needs of our neighbor. The main ways in which we fulfill this duty are the seven corporal works of mercy and the seven spiritual works of mercy. Also, we are required to provide for the Church, promote social justice, and give to the poor, according to our means. See **corporal works of mercy**, **spiritual works of mercy**, and **tithe**.

angels – spirits who are servants and messengers of God. See **spirit**.

anger – may refer to the emotion of anger or the capital sin of anger. The ***emotion of anger*** moves a person to fight against that which he sees as morally wrong or as an obstacle to his or someone else's happiness, peace, or security. If the emotion of anger leads a person to think or act in a way that is contrary to justice or charity, he commits the ***capital sin of anger*** (or ***wrath***). A person can sin through anger in three different ways: (1) if his anger is unjust, (2) if he allows his anger to be too intense in proportion to the offense, or (3) if he acts on his anger in the wrong way. See **revenge**.

annulment – a declaration by the Catholic Church that what was thought to be a valid marriage is actually null and void. Only the Church has the authority to make the determination regarding whether there are sufficient grounds to issue an annulment.

Anthony of the Desert, St. – a holy monk from Egypt who is considered to be the Father of Monasticism in the East.

apostasy – the total rejection of Christianity by a person who has been baptized. Apostasy is the worst evil that a person can inflict upon himself, because he is rejecting the only Way there is to Heaven: Jesus Christ. See **incredulity**.

Apostolic Succession – the passing down of authority from St. Peter and the Apostles to the pope and the bishops.

Armor of God – the spiritual equipment we need to win the battle against temptation. The Armor of God includes the girding of truth, the breastplate of righteousness, the footwear of the gospel of peace, the shield of faith, the helmet of salvation, the sword of the Spirit, and perseverance in prayer and supplication (Ephesians 6:13-18).

art – intellectual virtue that perfects the intellect in its knowledge of how to make things. See **intellectual virtues**.

assisted suicide – a form of euthanasia in which the victim himself, usually with the "assistance" of a physician or some third party, performs an action, such as administering a lethal drug, that ends his life. Assisted suicide is a grave sin against the Fifth Commandment. See **euthanasia**.

atheism – denial of the existence of God. Atheism not only violates the First Commandment; it is also contrary to right reason. In practice, atheism is often closely related to idolatry.

atheist – someone who denies the existence of God.

basis of morality – that which makes morality possible for human beings. The basis of morality is freedom—or, more precisely, *free will*. See **free will** and **morality**.

Beatitudes – promises by the Lord Jesus Christ of eternal happiness for those who remain faithful to the Divine Law, and hence the Moral Law, by cultivating the interior dispositions of the heart necessary to practice Christian charity. The core of the New Law, and of Our Lord's call for His disciples to strive for Christian perfection, is found in the Beatitudes (see Matthew 5:1-12). See **Christian charity**, **Christian perfection**, and **heart**.

being – anyone or anything that exists.

Bible – see **Sacred Scripture**.

Blackstone, Sir William – widely recognized and respected 18th-century English legal scholar who authored the famous four-volume treatise on law called *Commentaries on the Laws of England*.

blasphemy – any willful expression by word, thought, or deed directed against God with the intention of dishonoring, defying, harming, or offending Him. Blasphemy is a grave sin against the Second Commandment.

calumny – sin in which a person intentionally says something negative that is false about his neighbor. Calumny (or *slander*) is a sin against the Eighth Commandment, a sin against justice, and a sin against truthfulness. It is also sinful to take pleasure in *hearing* calumny.

Canon of Scripture – the complete list of all the books of Sacred Scripture. The Canon of Scripture includes all the writings of both the Old Testament (46 books) and the New Testament (27 books): 73 books in all. The Canon of Scripture is closed; no other books will ever be part of Sacred Scripture besides these 73 books.

capital sins – sins that are the chief sources of other sins, which they engender. The seven capital sins are pride, greed (or avarice), envy, anger (or wrath), lust, gluttony, and sloth.

cardinal virtues – the four principal moral virtues, around which all the other moral virtues are grouped. The four cardinal virtues are prudence, justice, fortitude, and temperance. See **moral virtues**.

Catholic apologetics – the art of explaining and defending the truths of the Catholic Faith.

Catholic Church – see **Church**.

celibacy – a commitment to never marry. See **Evangelical Counsels**.

Ceremonial Law – the part of the Law of Moses that prescribed the system of worship that Israel was to follow. See **Law of Moses**.

certain conscience – a conscience that judges with assurance and conviction, and without any doubt or suspicion of error. If we have a certain conscience, we are morally obliged to follow it.

chance – false notion claiming that prayer is useless because everything happens without any direction from a Supreme Being. Chance is the opposite of *fate*. Neither extreme is correct. See **fate** and **prayer**.

character – our moral identity, which is the net effect of all our moral choices, good and bad. A person of *good character* habitually does what is right. A person of *bad character* habitually does what is evil. See **honor**, **virtue**, and **vice**.

charity – theological virtue by which we love God above all else for His own sake, and we love our neighbor as ourselves for the sake of God. Charity is the greatest of all the virtues, and it is necessary for salvation. There are different types of love. The highest form of love (*agape*, in Greek) is the self-giving love that truly seeks the good of another. This is the selfless love that Jesus Christ has for His Church, and it is the love that God calls us to have for our neighbor. This love is called charity. Our charity may be *perfect* or *imperfect*. See **Christian charity**, **fruits of charity**, **imperfect charity**, and **perfect charity**.

chastity – virtue by which a person regulates his procreative instincts and abilities according to his state in life, and moderates his related passions according to right reason. Perseverance in chastity is essential to maintaining *purity of heart*. Chastity is closely related to the virtue of modesty and the cardinal virtue of temperance. It is also one of the twelve *fruits of the Holy Spirit*. See **marriage**, **modesty**, **purity of vision**, and **temperance**.

Christian charity – the love of Jesus Christ within us, whereby we love God as Jesus loves His Father, and we love our neighbor as Jesus loves us. Christian charity is the heart of Christian perfection, because Christian charity is the heart of Jesus. True Christian charity is possible only when we are in fellowship with God, so that He may love others through us. See **charity** and **Christian perfection**.

Christian perfection – the ideal of the Christian life, whereby we truly become like Our Lord and Savior Jesus Christ. Christian perfection should be the aim of every disciple of Jesus. We must strive to practice every virtue, at all times, for the love of God and in gratitude to Him. The only way to reach the Christian ideal is to become like Jesus Christ, because Jesus Christ *is* the Christian Ideal. See **Christian charity**.

Church – the household of God and "the seed and beginning" of the Kingdom of Heaven on Earth (*Catechism*, 541). The Catholic Church is the one true Church founded by Jesus Christ. It is the Body of Christ, the Bride of Christ, and the Family of Christ. The purpose of the Church is to secure the sanctification and spiritual welfare of all people. The Church is "the pillar and bulwark of the truth" (1 Timothy 3:15). There are three main parts of the Church: the Church Militant, the Church Suffering, and the Church Triumphant.

Church Militant – the part of the Church that includes all the faithful on Earth.

Church Suffering – the part of the Church that includes all the souls in Purgatory.

Church Triumphant – the part of the Church that includes all the angels and saints in Heaven.

circumcision – see **Law of Circumcision**.

circumstances – all the conditions surrounding an act, including its consequences: *who*, *what kind*, *when*, *where*, *how*, *how much*, etc. Along with the object and the intention, the circumstances constitute one of the three elements that determine the morality of every human act. See **elements of morality**.

civil divorce – a decree issued by civil authorities of the State that affects the legal status of a married couple, whom the State subsequently treats as being no longer married. However, the notion of "divorce," which claims that a married man and woman who are both still living can become unmarried, is contrary to God's Law. A civil divorce is an attempt by human beings to do something that God has made *impossible*. In reality, no married couple can ever truly be "divorced." See **adultery** and **marriage**.

clemency – virtue by which a person seeks to moderate the punishment of others so that this punishment remains within the limits of right reason. The virtue of clemency is related to the cardinal virtues of fortitude and temperance. See **fortitude** and **temperance**.

clergy – those who are ordained as deacons, priests, or bishops through the Sacrament of Holy Orders. See **religious life**.

common good – both the good of the community as a whole and the good of every individual person within that community. See **State**.

complete consent – consent that is deliberate enough to be a personal choice, meaning the person has freely and deliberately decided to perform the act. Complete consent is one of the three conditions for a sin to be mortal. See **mortal sin**.

concupiscence – an inclination to sin due to disordered physical appetites and desires. Concupiscence is a direct consequence of Original Sin. Although Baptism removes the state of Original Sin from our soul, our *inclination* to sin (concupiscence) remains. See **Original Sin**.

concupiscible passions – passions of the sense appetite that pertain to what is perceived as good (that is, whatever attracts us). The concupiscible passions include desire, aversion, like, dislike, joy, and sadness. The virtue of temperance moderates these passions and related desires so that we keep them within the bounds of right reason. See **sense appetite** and **temperance**.

confessor – a priest to whom one regularly goes to receive the Sacrament of Penance (Confession).

conflict of temptation – the internal struggle we experience when we recognize that we cannot fulfill the desire with which we are being tempted, without compromising our morals. This is the second stage of temptation. See **temptation** and **three stages of temptation**.

conscience – a judgment of reason by which we apply the Divine Law to our acts (thoughts, words, and deeds) and recognize whether those acts are morally good or evil. Conscience evaluates three types of acts: those we are thinking of doing, those we are in the process of doing, and those we have already done. There are four main kinds of conscience: a true conscience, an erroneous conscience, a certain conscience, and a doubtful conscience. We have a moral obligation to form our conscience.

consecrated – set apart by God for a holy purpose. See **holy** and **religious life**.

consecrated life – see **religious life**.

contemplative prayer – quietly resting in the presence of the Lord. See **prayer**.

contraception – any method or procedure that attempts to prevent a child from being conceived when a man and a woman exercise their procreative abilities. The use of contraception is a grave sin against the Sixth Commandment, and it is an intrinsically evil act. See **procreation**.

contrition – act of prayer in which we express our sorrow to God for our sins, and we resolve not to sin again. See **prayer**.

contumely – sin in which a person speaks against his neighbor's good name directly to his face. Contumely is a sin against the Eighth Commandment. It is also a sin against justice and charity, and it is contrary to the dignity of the human person.

corporal works of mercy – seven ways in which we express our love for Jesus Christ by caring for the bodily needs of our neighbor. The seven corporal works of mercy are feeding the hungry, giving drink to the thirsty, clothing the naked, sheltering the homeless, visiting the sick, visiting the imprisoned, and burying the dead.

Counsels of Perfection – high ideals for the Christian life, proposed by Our Lord Jesus Christ. The Evangelical Counsels are Counsels of Perfection. See **Evangelical Counsels**.

covenant – a sacred agreement and bond between God and one or more persons, or between two persons or groups under God. See **New Covenant** and **Old Covenant**.

covet – to have an unjust or inordinate willful desire for someone or something that rightfully belongs to one's neighbor. Coveting another person's spouse is a grave sin against the Ninth Commandment. Coveting another person's goods is a sin against the Tenth Commandment, the gravity of which depends on the value of what is coveted and the harm that would be caused if this good were taken from its rightful owner. See **envy** and **greed**.

culpable – morally responsible.

culpably erroneous conscience – a conscience that judges falsely because of the person's own fault.

Decalogue – see **Ten Commandments**.

Deist – someone who believes in God, but rejects His Providence in creation.

demons – spirits who are enemies of God. See **spirit**.

despair – sin in which a person no longer trusts in God for his salvation or for the forgiveness of his sins. Despair is a grave sin against the virtue of hope. Sometimes, people give up hope regarding some aspect of their earthly life. This type of despair is not as serious as despairing of one's salvation. However, failing to trust in God's

Providence is still sinful and can lead to other sins and disorders.

detachment – the willingness to let go of our material goods for the sake of our love of God. Being detached from material goods is possible only if we trust in God, and love Him more than anything else.

detraction – sin in which a person makes known, without good reason, some fault or sin of his neighbor. Detraction is a sin against the Eighth Commandment and a sin against justice. It is also sinful to take pleasure in *hearing* detraction.

dictates of conscience – the firm conclusions of our conscience about what we may and may not do. If we do not follow the dictates of our conscience, we sin. See **certain conscience**.

difficulty – the inability to understand, or reconcile with other information we have, a truth that we accept in faith. Voluntary doubts are sinful; difficulties are not sinful. See **involuntary doubt** and **voluntary doubt**.

diocesan priests – members of the clergy who profess celibate chastity and obedience to their bishop and his successors, but do not take a vow of poverty (since they don't all live in common). See **clergy** and **religious life**.

direct scandal – sin in which a person intentionally leads another person to sin. Direct scandal is always sinful. See **indirect scandal**.

discretion – the use of caution and reserve in one's speech and actions, for the sake of prudence and charity. See **honesty** and **truthfulness**.

dissimulation – acting in a way that conceals one's true character or motives. Dissimulation is a sin against the Eighth Commandment. When a person commits this sin, he lies through his actions in order to conceal what is truly in his heart. See **hypocrisy**.

divination – invoking evil spirits or the souls of the deceased to learn hidden things. All forms of divination are evil, because they place faith and trust in something or someone other than God. They are grave sins, and they are extremely dangerous. See **superstition**.

Divine Law – God's eternal, objective, and universal plan through which He orders, directs, and governs the entire universe in love and wisdom. The Divine Law (also called the Eternal Law or God's Law) is the highest *norm* (rule of conduct) for human behavior; it applies to all people, in all circumstances, in all places, and at all times. It is absolute and universal. God manifests His Divine Law to us in two ways: Natural Law and Revealed Law.

divorce – see **civil divorce**.

doubt – see **involuntary doubt** and **voluntary doubt**.

doubtful conscience – a conscience that is not certain about what is right or wrong, and therefore about what the person ought to do. As long as this uncertainty continues, the person's conscience is unable to function. He must try to clear up this doubt before taking any action.

dulia – the veneration given to the angels and saints. See **veneration**.

duplicitous speech – speech that is insincere, with an ulterior motive. Duplicitous speech is a sin against the Eighth Commandment. Examples of duplicitous speech include flattery and adulation.

elements of morality – that which determine the morality of human acts. The three elements of morality are the object, the intention (or end), and the circumstances. These three elements of morality are also called sources of morality, since together they determine the morality of every human act. For an act to be morally good, all three elements of morality must be good. See **circumstances**, **intention**, and **object**.

embryo – see **human embryo**.

embryonic stem cell research – research that kills a human being in the earliest stage of development, purportedly to use this embryo's stem cells for medical purposes, such as helping people with certain diseases. Embryonic stem cell research is an intrinsically evil act and a grave sin against the Fifth Commandment. See **human embryo**.

end – goal; intention. The end does not justify the means. See **means** and **intention**.

envy – sin in which a person resents that his neighbor possesses something that he would like to have instead for himself. That which the person envies may be a material good or something else, such as talents, skills, success, fame, or power. Envy is one of the seven capital sins, and it is a sin against the Tenth Commandment. See **covet**.

erroneous conscience – a conscience that judges as right something that is actually wrong, or judges as wrong something that is actually right. A conscience may be *culpably* or *inculpably* erroneous.

Eternal Law – see **Divine Law**.

eternal punishment – punishment that lasts for all eternity. Anyone who dies in a state of mortal sin will experience eternal punishment in Hell. See **state of mortal sin**.

euthanasia – the intentional killing of the handicapped, the sick, the old, the feeble, the dying, or anyone else deemed to have a poor "quality of life." Euthanasia is a grave sin against the Fifth Commandment, and it is extremely dangerous to society. It is an intrinsically evil act.

Evangelical Counsels – special means for achieving Christian perfection, recommended by Our Lord Jesus Christ. The three Evangelical Counsels are voluntary poverty, perpetual chastity in celibacy (a commitment to never marry), and complete obedience to a spiritual superior. The Evangelical Counsels are Counsels of Perfection, which those in the religious life publicly profess to practice. See **Christian perfection**, **Counsels of Perfection**, and **religious life**.

Eve – the first woman in all of creation. God created the body of Eve from the side of Adam. God created Eve's soul (and likewise creates the soul of every other human being) directly, out of nothing. See **Adam** and **Original Sin**.

excommunication – a very serious penalty for certain extremely grave sins, which prevents a person from being in full communion with the Church.

expressions of prayer – ways of praying. The three main expressions of prayer are vocal prayer, mental prayer, and contemplative prayer. See **prayer**.

fair wage – an amount of money that is generally sufficient for *one* person working full time to provide for the material needs of his family in reasonable, frugal comfort. Employers have a moral obligation to pay their workers a fair wage.

faith – theological virtue by which we believe in God, and we accept everything He has revealed to us, as well as everything His Church teaches that we are to believe. Faith is necessary for salvation. See **obedience of faith** and **theological virtues**.

false witness – sin in which a person tells a lie in a court of law. False witness is a sin against the Eighth Commandment. See **perjury**.

family – the lifelong union of one man and one woman under God, along with their children. Some different forms of family relationships are possible (for example, due to the death of a spouse). However, this is "the normal reference point by which the different forms of family relationship are to be evaluated" (*Catechism*, 2202). The family is the domestic church, the foundation of society, and the heart of the nation. See **marriage**.

fate – false notion claiming that prayer is useless because the outcome of everything in the universe is rigidly predetermined. Fate is the opposite of *chance*. Neither extreme is correct. See **chance** and **prayer**.

fear of the Lord – gift of the Holy Spirit that instills in us a fervent zeal to put God before all else, attentively listen to Him, and obey His commands. The fear of the Lord is the beginning of wisdom and knowledge, and hence is necessary for salvation. See **gifts of the Holy Spirit**.

feigned ignorance – pretending not to know something, especially regarding some moral issue. Feigned ignorance increases one's guilt for sin.

fideism – the false teaching that all religious truth is based on faith alone, and hence not reason. The Catholic Church teaches that both faith and reason are gifts from God, which together can lead man to truth. See **rationalism**.

fidelity – faithfulness to one's given word and promises. See **truthfulness**.

first principles – the fundamental self-evident truths that are at the root of human knowledge. See **understanding**.

flattery – giving insincere praise to someone. Flattery is a form of duplicitous speech, and is a sin against the Eighth Commandment. See **duplicitous speech**.

formal heresy – heresy in which a person knows that his position on some issue is contrary to the Catholic Faith, but he embraces that position anyway. Formal heresy is a grave sin. See **heresy**.

fortitude – cardinal virtue that regulates the irascible passions of our sense appetite so that we remain firm and constant in doing what is right, despite difficulties, hardships, or dangers. Fortitude helps us to persist in doing what is right, no matter how difficult or dangerous it is. Moral virtues related to the virtue of fortitude include patience, perseverance, magnanimity, clemency, and meekness. See **cardinal virtues** and **irascible passions**.

fraternal correction – act of charity in which we warn our neighbor to turn away from some particular sin. One of the spiritual works of mercy, admonishing the sinner, must sometimes be expressed through fraternal correction. Those in authority must practice fraternal correction toward those under their care. In all other cases, we are to practice fraternal correction only when it is likely to profit our neighbor's soul. See **spiritual works of mercy**.

fraud – sin in which a person cheats or deceives others regarding material goods or services. Fraud includes falsifying documents through forgery or other means, trying to pass counterfeit money, deliberately concealing defects in an item one is selling, using false weights and measures, declaring bankruptcy fraudulently, accepting or offering bribes, and evading just taxes. Fraud is a sin against the Seventh Commandment.

free will – our ability to decide what we will believe and what we will do. It is free will that makes morality possible for human beings. Because we have free will, we are able to make our own free choices about our actions. Since God has given us the freedom to make our own choices, He holds us accountable for those choices. See **morality**.

free-will offering – a voluntary offering above and beyond a tithe. Under the Old Law, the Israelites were expected to make free-will offerings to God, in addition to their tithes. See **tithe**.

freedom – see **free will** and **right to personal liberty**.

freemasonry – an anti-Christian system of morality and religion, upheld by a secret society organized into a federation of fraternal lodges. Knowingly supporting or participating in freemasonry, or belonging to any of the lodges or organizations affiliated with it, is a sin against the First Commandment.

fruits of charity – peace, joy, and mercy. See **charity**.

fruits of the Holy Spirit – "perfections that the Holy Spirit forms in us as the first fruits of eternal glory" (*Catechism*, 2832). The twelve fruits of the Holy Spirit are charity, joy, peace, patience, kindness, goodness, generosity, gentleness, faithfulness, modesty, self-control, and chastity.

full knowledge – sufficient knowledge about the moral quality (moral good or evil) and gravity of an act. Full knowledge is one of the three conditions for a sin to be mortal. See **mortal sin**.

gifts of the Holy Spirit – permanent dispositions in our soul that perfect and complete the virtues. The seven gifts of the Holy Spirit are wisdom, understanding, counsel, fortitude, knowledge, piety, and fear of the Lord. The Holy Spirit infuses these gifts in our soul when we receive the Sacrament of Baptism, and He further showers them upon us in the Sacrament of Confirmation.

gluttony – sin in which a person indulges excessively in food or drink. Gluttony is one of the seven capital sins. See **temperance**.

Golden Rule – Our Lord's teaching that we are to treat others the way we want others to treat us. "And as you wish that men would do to you, do so to them" (Luke 6:31).

goods of marriage – blessings that God brings about through the institution of marriage. The three main goods of marriage are children, fidelity, and permanence (or indissolubility). See **marriage**.

Gospel – the "Good News" of the love and mercy of God, revealed and imparted to man through the Life, Passion (suffering and death), and Resurrection of Jesus Christ. Our Lord and Savior Jesus Christ has freed us from the slavery of sin and won for us the gift of eternal life. To *receive* this gift, we must enter His Kingdom, the Church, through faith and Baptism. To *keep* this gift, we must remain in fellowship with the Holy Trinity by cooperating with the grace that God gives us through the Mass and the sacraments, and by practicing the virtues and obeying the Commandments.

gossip – spreading personal information or rumors about someone. Gossip is a sin against the Eighth Commandment. It is closely related to the sins of detraction and calumny. Deliberately encouraging or taking pleasure in listening to gossip or talebearing about one's neighbor is also sinful. See **calumny**, **detraction**, and **talebearing**.

grave matter – refers to any morally evil act that is serious in nature. Grave matter is one of the three conditions for a sin to be mortal. See **mortal sin**.

greed – sin in which a person has an inordinate desire or immoderate passion for material goods. Greed is a sin against the Tenth Commandment. It is one of the seven capital sins.

hallowed – revered as holy. See **holy**.

hardened conscience – a conscience that is closed to the Word of God, and therefore to good counsel. A hardened conscience is an extreme form of an erroneous conscience, and it is the opposite of a tender conscience. See **erroneous conscience** and **tender conscience**.

hardness of heart – an obstinate refusal to obey the Word of God or to accept good counsel. Hardness of heart increases one's guilt for sin.

hatred – sin in which a person willfully desires that harm come to his neighbor. Hating another person, even one's enemy, is a sin against the Fifth Commandment. See **anger** and **revenge**.

hatred of God – extremely grave sin in which a person wishes harm to God Himself. The root of this sin is pride. See **pride**.

heart – a metaphor for the depths of our soul, where we decide what we truly value and want with our will, on the basis of what we know and understand with our intellect. See **Beatitudes**.

heresy – "the obstinate post-baptismal denial of some truth which must be believed with divine and catholic faith" or "an obstinate doubt concerning the same" (*Catechism*, 2089). The Church distinguishes between two kinds of heresy: material and formal. See **formal heresy**, **incredulity**, and **material heresy**.

holy – sacred and set apart for God.

Holy Sacrifice of the Mass – the center of the Catholic Church's public worship. Sacred Scripture teaches, and the Catholic Church affirms, that the Holy Sacrifice of Jesus Christ on the Cross happened once, for all people and for all times. At every Mass, during the Consecration, this same Holy Sacrifice is made present again on the altar. The Catholic Church requires the faithful to attend Mass on Sundays and holy days of obligation. See **Liturgy** and **Lord's Day**.

honesty – saying only what one believes is true, and doing only what one believes is right and just. See **truthfulness**.

honor – distinction, respect, and esteem, in virtue of one's office, one's character, or one's accomplishments; to treat with distinction, respect, and esteem. See **character** and **office**.

hope – theological virtue by which we desire the happiness of eternal life with God in Heaven, and we trust in His promises and rely on His grace to lead us there. Hope is necessary for salvation. See **theological virtues**.

human being – an individual person who is the union of a body and a soul. God created man (male and female) in His image and likeness. Every human being is a unique person with immeasurable intrinsic value, whom God knows personally by name, and for whom Jesus Christ died on the Cross. Human life is sacred, and each and every human being possesses a dignity that nothing else in the entire visible creation could ever possess. See **person** and **rational soul**.

human embryo – a human being in the earliest stage of development. See **embryonic stem cell research**.

humility – virtue by which a person moderates his estimation of his own importance, and acknowledges his limitations and imperfections.

hyperdulia – the highest form of veneration, which is reserved only for the Blessed Virgin Mary. See **veneration**.

hypocrisy – sin in which a person intentionally pretends to be someone he is not, or pretends to believe something that he does not truly believe. Hypocrisy is a form of dissimulation. It is a sin against the Eighth Commandment. See **dissimulation**.

iconoclasm – the rejection or destruction of sacred images because of the false teaching that such images are forbidden by God. Iconoclasm is a grave sin.

idol – a graven image worshiped as a god. Making idols is forbidden by the First Commandment.

idolater – someone who worships a false god.

idolatry – adoring anything or anyone other than the One True God. Idolatry is a grave sin against the First Commandment.

imperfect charity – loving God because of what He has done for us or what we hope He will do for us. See **charity** and **perfect charity**.

impurity – see **lust**.

incredulity – "the neglect of revealed truth or the willful refusal to assent to it" (*Catechism*, 2089). Incredulity manifests itself in three different ways: heresy, schism, and apostasy.

inculpably erroneous conscience – a conscience that judges falsely through no fault of the person.

indifference – insufficient concern or conviction about one's faith or religion. See **practical indifference** and **theoretical indifference**.

indirect scandal – scandal that occurs without being intended. A person commits a *sin* of indirect scandal if (1) he foresees that his actions will lead his neighbor to sin, and (2) he can reasonably avoid those actions, but he performs them anyway. If either of these conditions is not present, indirect scandal may still occur, but it is not sinful. See **direct scandal**.

infidelity – the state of an unbaptized person who does not believe in the Gospel of Jesus Christ. Those who do not believe in the Gospel because they have never heard it are in a state of *negative infidelity*, and are not guilty of mortal sin. Those who hear and understand the Gospel but *refuse* to accept it are in a state of *positive infidelity*, and are guilty of mortal sin. See **Gospel**.

ingratitude – sin in which a person is not sufficiently grateful to God for all the gifts and blessings that he has received from Him. The sin of ingratitude is closely related to the sins of indifference and lukewarmness.

intellect – the faculty of our rational soul through which we think, reason, understand, and know.

intellectual virtues – virtues that perfect the intellect in its grasp of the truth. The intellectual virtues include wisdom, understanding, science, art, and prudence. Prudence is also a moral virtue.

intention – the reason, or motive, for performing an act. The intention (or *end*) is *why* the act is done. Any given act may have just one intention, or there may be several intentions. Along with the object and the circumstances, the intention constitutes one of the three elements that determine the morality of every human act. See **elements of morality**.

intrinsically evil act – an act that is evil always, everywhere, and in all cases, because of its very nature. Intrinsically evil acts include all the acts forbidden by the Ten Commandments, as well as various other acts that are forbidden elsewhere in Sacred Scripture or by the Church.

involuntary doubt – hesitation or difficulty in believing a truth that God has revealed or that the Catholic Church teaches. Involuntary doubt is generally not sinful or is a venial sin, depending on whether we have consented to it and the degree to which we are responsible for it. See **difficulty** and **voluntary doubt**.

irascible passions – passions of the sense appetite that pertain to what is perceived as a difficult good or a threatening difficulty or danger. The irascible passions include daring, fear, and anger. The virtue of fortitude regulates the irascible passions so that we remain firm and constant in doing what is right, despite difficulties, hardships, or dangers. See **fortitude** and **sense appetite**.

irreligion – any practice that directs a person away from rendering to God what He is owed in justice. Sins in this category include tempting God, sacrilege, and simony.

jealousy – a person's vigilant zeal and determination not to lose or share someone or something that he sees as belonging to himself. Jealousy is a sin when it is contrary to right reason, and in such cases it often takes the form of irrational fear. Jealousy is not a sin when it is in accordance with right reason.

jocose lie – a lie in which a person says something *believable* that is not true, in an attempt to be funny. Lying is a sin against the Eighth Commandment. Jokingly saying something that is *obviously* not true (and hence not believable) is not lying and is not sinful. See **lying**.

Joseph, St. – the most chaste spouse of the Blessed Virgin Mary. Besides Our Blessed Mother, there is no greater saint than St. Joseph.

Juan Diego, St. – saint to whom Our Lady of Guadalupe, the Blessed Mother, appeared in Mexico, in1531. See **Our Lady of Guadalupe**.

Judicial Law – the part of the Law of Moses that included various precepts and ordinances to regulate the civil government of Israel. See **Law of Moses**.

just war doctrine – the Catholic Church's teaching regarding the legitimate use of military force. In order for the use of military force to be just, all of the following conditions must be met (*Catechism*, 2309): (1) "the damage inflicted by the aggressor on the nation or community of nations must be lasting, grave, and certain"; (2) "all other means of putting an end to it must have been shown to be impractical or ineffective"; (3) "there must be serious prospects of success"; and (4) "the use of arms must not produce evils and disorders graver than the evil to be eliminated."

justice – cardinal virtue that disposes our will to always give God and our neighbor their due. Justice regulates our will and helps us to do what is right and in the right way. See **cardinal virtues** and **will**.

laity – all Catholics who are not ordained or in a religious state of life approved by the Church.

latria – adoration, the highest form of worship. Only God may be the object of adoration. See **adoration** and **veneration**.

Law of Circumcision – Patriarchal Law in which God commanded that Abraham, as well as every male among him and his descendants, be circumcised, as the sign of the covenant between God and His People. See **Old Covenant** and **Patriarchal Laws**.

Law of Moses – the vast majority of the Old Law revealed by God to His Chosen People through His servant Moses. The Law of Moses (also called the Mosaic Law) had three main parts: Judicial, Ceremonial, and Moral. See **Old Law**.

lex orandi, lex credendi – an ancient Latin saying, meaning "the law of prayer is the law of faith." The way we pray and adore God is not only an expression of our faith; it also *affects* our faith.

liberty – see **right to personal liberty**.

Liturgy – the public worship of the Catholic Church. The center of the Catholic Church's public worship is the Holy Sacrifice of the Mass.

local sacrilege – a sacrilege directed against a holy place. See **sacrilege**.

Lord's Day – Sunday, the first day of the week. In the New Covenant, the requirement of the Third Commandment to keep holy the Sabbath is fulfilled by our keeping holy the Lord's Day. The Third Commandment prescribes two primary duties on Sundays and holy days of obligation: worship and rest. See **New Covenant**.

love – see **charity**.

lukewarmness – lack of zeal regarding serving God or obeying His Commandments. Lukewarmness is closely related to practical indifference. It is the *opposite* of the zeal that accompanies the fear of the Lord. See **fear of the Lord** and **practical indifference**.

lust – sin in which a person has a disordered desire for, or inordinate enjoyment of, the pleasure associated with his procreative instincts, abilities, and passions. Lust is one of the seven capital sins. See **chastity**.

lying – saying something that one believes is false, with the intention to deceive. Lying is a sin against the Eighth Commandment. There are three types of lies: malicious lies, officious lies, and jocose lies. See **truthfulness**.

magic – a form of sorcery, which is a grave sin against the First Commandment and is extremely dangerous.

Magisterium – the teaching authority of the Catholic Church. This authority is vested in either the pope acting alone or all the bishops acting in union with the pope, when teaching, sanctifying, or governing the faithful on issues concerning faith or morals. The faithful are morally obligated to accept and obey all the teachings of the Magisterium on faith and morals. See **Church**.

magnanimity – virtue that enables a person to perform heroic acts of virtue. Magnanimity, or *greatness of soul*, is related to the cardinal virtue of fortitude. See **fortitude**.

malicious lie – a lie that a person tells with the intention of harming his neighbor. Lying is a sin against the Eighth Commandment. Malicious lies are the most serious form of lying, because they are also sins against charity. See **lying**.

marriage – the union of one man and one woman under God for life. The Sacrament of Holy Matrimony is a living sign of the covenant between Jesus Christ and His Church. There are ***two main purposes of marriage***: the procreation and upbringing of children and the good of the husband and wife. A married couple must be open to the gift of human life, as an expression of their openness to the Will of God and their love for each other. This is the ***procreative purpose*** of the unique expression of the love between a husband and wife in marriage. God calls a man and a woman in marriage to give themselves to each other completely, so that they may be totally united as husband and wife: physically, emotionally, mentally, and spiritually. This is the ***unitive purpose*** of the unique expression of the love between a husband and wife in marriage. See **goods of marriage** and **procreation**.

Mass – see **Holy Sacrifice of the Mass**.

material heresy – heresy in which a person is unaware that his position on some issue is contrary to the Catholic Faith. A person who holds such a position is still in a state of heresy, but he is not necessarily guilty of sin. See **heresy**.

materialism – philosophy that accepts only physical matter as reality, and thus denies all spiritual realities. Materialism is a form of atheism. It is a grave sin against the First Commandment.

meaning and purpose of life – to know, love, and serve God, so that we may be happy with Him in Heaven.

means – the way someone attains an end. A good intention (or end) cannot justify using evil means to attain that end. See **end** and **object**.

meekness – virtue by which a person restrains his anger. The virtue of meekness is related to the cardinal virtues of fortitude and temperance. See **anger**, **fortitude**, and **temperance**.

mental prayer – meditating on God, and on the truths He has revealed through His Holy Word and His Holy Church. See **prayer**.

mental reservation – making use of discreet speech to conceal a truth that someone does not have the right to know or that we do not have the right to divulge. Mental reservation should be used only rarely, for a serious reason. Mental reservation is morally permissible only if all of the following conditions are met: (1) there is a just reason for using it; (2) the person to whom we are speaking does not have the right to know the truth, or we do not have the right to divulge it; and (3) it is not impossible to discern its true meaning. Mental reservation is always sinful when a person uses it while freely taking an oath; entering into a contract or agreement; or making a vow, such as a marriage vow.

Michael the Archangel, St. – an angel known as the Prince of the Heavenly Host. When one of the spirits God had created, Lucifer, rebelled against God, St. Michael and the other angels who remained loyal to God battled against Lucifer and his followers, and cast them out of Heaven forever. The *Prayer to St. Michael the Archangel*, given to the Church by Pope Leo XIII, should be said often, as part of our strategy to resist temptation.

modesty – virtue by which a person maintains a proper amount of reserve in his conduct and manner of dressing. In addition to *modesty of dress*, we must also maintain *modesty of the eyes*. Modesty is closely related to chastity and humility, as well as the cardinal virtue of temperance.

moral absolute – a moral precept that applies always, everywhere, and in all cases, with no exceptions. Moral absolutes include all the precepts stated in the Ten Commandments, as well as several other moral precepts given in Sacred Scripture or taught by the Church. See **intrinsically evil act**.

moral evil – any freely chosen act that is contrary to the Will of God. Every time we deliberately decide to do something that is morally evil, we sin. Moral evil exists because (1) God created spirits and human beings to be free; (2) some of the spirits used their freedom to rebel against God, thereby introducing moral evil into creation; and (3) Adam and Eve, tempted by the devil, used their freedom to rebel against God, thereby introducing moral evil into the *visible* creation. See **sin**.

moral good – any freely chosen act that is in accordance with the Will of God.

Moral Law – all the moral principles of the Divine Law governing human behavior. The Moral Law includes both those moral principles known through the Natural Law and those that God has communicated through Revealed Law. The foundation of the Moral Law is the Ten Commandments. See **Divine Law**, **Natural Law**, **Revealed Law**, and **Ten Commandments**.

moral life – the path by which we walk toward God or walk away from God. If we sin, we walk away from God. If we repent and follow His commands, we walk toward God.

moral quality – the moral good or evil of a human act.

moral virtues – virtues that regulate our moral life. See **cardinal virtues**.

morality – the measure of the good or evil of concrete human acts: thoughts, words, and deeds. Morality concerns what is right versus what is wrong, what is good versus what is evil.

mortal sin – any morally evil act that is grave (serious) in nature, undertaken with full knowledge, and committed with complete consent. There is nothing more evil in the world than mortal sin. The effects of mortal sin include total separation from God, the complete loss of sanctifying grace in the soul, spiritual death to the soul, the complete loss of charity in the soul, dramatically increased vulnerability to attacks from the devil, an increased likelihood to commit other mortal sins, and eternal punishment in Hell if the person does not repent and return to God. See **sin** and **venial sin**.

Mosaic Law – see **Law of Moses**.

motives of religion – our complete dependence on God, our debt of gratitude to Him, and our recognition of His glory and perfection as God. See **religion**.

Natural Law – the Divine Law inscribed in the soul of man, so that man may know right from wrong. The Natural Law is binding on all people, in all circumstances, in all places, and at all times. The precepts of the Natural Law are absolute and universal. The Divine Law is manifested through the Natural Law in three distinct grades: the primary precepts of morality, the proximate conclusions of morality, and the remote conclusions of morality. See **Divine Law**.

natural virtues – virtues that are acquired through repeated good actions. Everyone is capable of acquiring natural virtues. See **supernatural virtues**.

near occasion of sin – any person, place, or thing that will likely lead us to fall into sin. We must have a firm determination to avoid all the near occasions of sin. See **Armor of God**, **self-knowledge**, **sin**, and **temptation**.

New Adam – Jesus Christ. Unlike the first Adam, Jesus remained obedient to the Father in all things. See **New Eve**.

New Age – religious movement that purports to combine elements from different religions with Christianity. This religious movement effectively denies that there is one God, one Lord, and one Church. It is not compatible with Christianity, and it is very dangerous to the virtue of faith.

New Covenant – sacred agreement and bond between God and all baptized Christians. The signs and instruments of the New Covenant are the Mass and the seven sacraments.

New Eve – the Blessed Virgin Mary. Just as the first Eve cooperated in the sin of the first Adam, Mary has cooperated in the work of Redemption of her Son, Jesus Christ, the New Adam. See **New Adam**.

New Law – the final stage of Revealed Law, given by God to all mankind through His Son, Jesus Christ. This New Law is also called the *Law of the Gospel*. See **Revealed Law**.

norm – rule of conduct. The Divine Law is the highest norm for human behavior.

oath – a solemn act in which a person calls upon God as his witness that what he says is true and that he will do what he swears to do. There are four moral requirements we must meet regarding taking oaths: (1) *judgment* (we may take an oath only for a grave reason); (2) *justice* (anything we swear to do must be in accord with the Divine Law); (3) *truth* (whatever we say under oath must be true), and (4) *fidelity* (we have a sacred duty to keep all our oaths, as long as what we have sworn to do is not sinful). See **perjury**.

obedience to authority – see **principle regarding obedience to authority**.

obedience of faith – man's free submission of himself, through faith, to the Authority of God, leading him to accept God's Word, obey His Commandments, and remain faithful to His Church. See **faith**.

object – what a person deliberately decides to do in performing an act. The object is the act itself, apart from any intentions or circumstances surrounding the act. Along with the intention and the circumstances, the object constitutes one of the three elements that determine the morality of every human act. The object is the *primary element* for determining whether a human act is morally good or evil. See **elements of morality**.

objective – universally the same for all persons, times, places, and cultures. Moral good and evil are objective, not subjective. See **moral evil**, **moral good**, and **standard of morality**.

occasion of sin – see **near occasion of sin**.

occasion of temptation – the person, place, or thing that arouses a desire in us to commit sin. This is the first stage of temptation. See **temptation** and **three stages of temptation**.

office – the position of authority or distinction that a person holds. See **honor**.

officious lie – a lie that a person tells in order to gain an advantage for himself or his neighbor, or to avoid some disadvantage to himself or his neighbor. Lying is a sin against the Eighth Commandment. See **lying**.

Old Covenant – sacred agreement and bond between God and the people of Israel. In this covenant, the people of Israel agreed to obey God's Law, as revealed in the Old Law.

Old Law – the first stage of Revealed Law, as recorded in the Old Testament. The Old Law included both the Patriarchal Laws and the Law of Moses. See **Revealed Law**.

Original Sin – refers to (1) the first sin of Adam, in cooperation with Eve, at the beginning of the history of man, and (2) the resulting state of separation from God that mankind inherited because of this sin. This inherited state, called the *state of Original Sin*, is the absence of God's sanctifying grace in the soul. See **Adam**, **Eve**, and **sanctifying grace**.

Our Lady of Guadalupe – title of Our Blessed Mother, who appeared to St. Juan Diego in Mexico, in 1531. This private revelation led to the conversion of millions of people to the Catholic Faith. See **private revelation**.

passions – emotions and physical impulses. See **concupiscible passions** and **irascible passions**.

patience – virtue by which a person, out of love for God, endures suffering or hardship without being unreasonably saddened or agitated. Patience is related to the cardinal virtue of fortitude. See **fortitude**.

Patriarchal Laws – those commands that God gave to (1) Adam and Eve; (2) Noah; and (3) Abraham, Isaac, and Jacob. The Patriarchal Laws recorded in Sacred Scripture represent the beginning of God's revelation to man about His Divine Law. See **Old Law** and **Revealed Law**.

peace – tranquility through order, harmony, stability, and security. Peace is one of the fruits of the Holy Spirit, and at the same time it is "the work of justice and the effect of charity" (*Catechism*, 2304).

penance – an interior conversion of the heart to God, expressed through acts of charity, sacrifice, and mercy. Penance is an act of religion.

perfect charity – loving God for His own sake because of Who He is. Either perfect charity or imperfect charity is sufficient to fulfill the First Commandment. However, perfect charity is a strong indication that a person is in union with God. See **charity** and **imperfect charity**.

perjury – sin in which a person lies while under oath in a court of law. Perjury is a form of false witness, and it is a sin against both the Second and Eighth Commandments. See **oath**.

perseverance – virtue by which a person firmly strives for the good, regardless of the obstacles involved or the time required. Perseverance is related to the cardinal virtue of fortitude.

person – an individual being, existing in and of himself, who has a rational nature, and thus can know and love God. All of creation can be divided into two types of beings: persons and things. Persons are to be loved and respected; things may be owned or used. Spirits and human beings are *persons*. All other beings in creation (animals, trees, plants, rocks, and so on) are *things*. See **human being** and **rational soul**.

personal sacrilege – a sacrilege directed against a holy person. See **sacrilege**.

Peter, St. – Apostle upon whom Jesus promised to build His Church, and to whom Jesus gave "the keys of the kingdom of heaven" (Matthew 16:19). St. Peter was the first pope. The office given to St. Peter has been passed down from one pope to another, right down to the pope today. See **Apostolic Succession**.

petition – act of prayer in which we request favors from God. See **prayer**.

polytheism – belief in many gods, which is a grave sin against the First Commandment.

poor in spirit – those whose treasures are not the riches of this life, but rather the riches of Heaven.

practical indifference – sin in which a person acts as if his faith or religion doesn't matter, or he neglects to put them into practice in his life. See **indifference**.

prayer – raising our mind and heart to God. Prayer is an act of religion, and it is necessary for salvation. There are two main reasons why we must pray: (1) because God wills that we pray; and (2) so that we may remain in fellowship with Him, upon Whom we depend for our salvation. Prayer includes both private prayer and public prayer. The four main acts of prayer are adoration, thanksgiving, contrition, and petition. The three main expressions of prayer are vocal prayer, mental prayer, and contemplative prayer.

precepts of the Church – laws of the Church which all Catholics are bound to obey: (1) Attend Mass and rest from servile labor on Sundays and holy days of obligation. (2) Confess your sins at least once a year. (3) Receive the Sacrament of the Holy Eucharist at least during the Easter season. (4) Observe the days of fasting and abstinence established by the Church. (5) Help provide for the needs of the Church. (6) Observe the laws of the Church concerning Holy Matrimony.

prenatal diagnosis – a diagnosis concerning a preborn infant. It is gravely evil to solicit a prenatal diagnosis in order to decide whether to procure an abortion. See **abortion**.

presumption – sin in which a person is overconfident about his salvation. Presumption is a grave sin against the virtue of hope. The sin of presumption may take different forms, including having excessive confidence in oneself, presuming on God's mercy, presuming on God's power, and intentionally deferring repentance.

pride – capital sin in which a person has an inflated self-image and an inordinate desire to be honored above everyone else. A person given over to pride is capable of committing any sin, even hatred of God, because pride distorts his view of reality. See **hardness of heart** and **hatred of God**.

primary precepts of morality – the first grade of moral precepts in the Natural Law. These are the most fundamental moral principles of the Natural Law. See **Natural Law**.

principle of double effect – If an act, which is neither forbidden nor required by a moral absolute, has two consequences (or effects), one of them good and one of them bad, the act is morally permissible *only if* all of the following conditions are met: (1) The object of the act (apart from the effects, or consequences) must be good, or at least morally neutral. (2) The bad effect must *not* be the *means* of attaining the good effect. The good effect must be caused by the act itself, *not* the bad effect. (3) The intentions of the act must be good. The bad effect must *not* be *intended*, only allowed. (4) There must be a grave reason for allowing the bad effect. The good effect must be at least as important as the bad effect. This principle does not apply to intrinsically evil acts or moral absolutes, nor can it be used to justify an evil moral object or an evil intention.

principle regarding obedience to authority – We must obey the lawful authority above us unless the directives of that authority contradict those of a higher lawful authority. God is the highest Authority, and His Divine Law is higher than any other law. Obedience to lawful authority is never an excuse for sin. See **Divine Law**.

private revelation – a revelation given during some period in history after the end of public revelation, to draw people closer to Jesus Christ or to help them better live out their Catholic Faith. See **public revelation**.

procreation – the privilege that God gives to a man and a woman of sharing in His creative power to bring forth new human life. See **marriage**.

procreative – see **marriage** and **procreation**.

profanity – speech concerning what is sacred without due reverence. Profanity is a sin against the Second Commandment. The gravity of this sin depends on the degree to which it shows disrespect toward what is sacred.

proximate conclusions of morality – the second grade of moral precepts in the Natural Law. These precepts can easily be known with a minimal amount of thought, because they immediately follow from the primary precepts of morality. Included in this category are all of the Ten Commandments except the Third Commandment. See **Natural Law**.

prudence – virtue that perfects our intellect in its use of reason, so that we discern the true good in every circumstance and the right means to achieve it. Prudence is both a cardinal virtue and an intellectual virtue. Prudence helps us to know what is right and how to attain it, and what is wrong and how to avoid it. See **reason**.

public revelation – the revelation given by God to man for the sake of his salvation, which all Christians are bound to believe. Public revelation ended with the death of the last Apostle, St. John, and the completion of the last book of the Bible. See **Word of God**.

purity of intention – desiring the Will of God above all else. See **standard of morality**.

purity of vision – refusing to focus on anything impure, either externally or internally. See **chastity** and **modesty**.

purposes of marriage – See **marriage**.

rash judgment – sin in which a person assumes, without sufficient grounds, that his neighbor is guilty of some moral fault or failure. Rash judgment is a sin against the Eighth Commandment.

rational soul – the spiritual principle that animates the body of a human being, and that enables him to think and reason, to understand and know, and to decide what he will believe and what he will do. See **human being**, **intellect**, **person**, and **will**.

rationalism – the false teaching that all truth is based on reason alone, and hence not faith. The Catholic Church teaches that both faith and reason are gifts from God, which together can lead man to truth. See **fideism**.

real sacrilege – a sacrilege directed against a holy action or thing. Administering or receiving the sacraments in an unworthy manner is a real sacrilege. See **sacrilege**.

reason – the ability to think logically, make judgments, and draw conclusions.

relative – changing according to the situation. The standard for what is morally good versus morally evil is absolute, not relative.

relic – an object associated with a saint which the Church has confirmed as authentic and approved for veneration.

religion – moral virtue by which we practice justice toward God. Religion is the greatest of all the moral virtues. Through this virtue, we recognize God as the Supreme Being, Who has dominion over our life and eternal destiny, and we freely subject ourselves to Him through frequent acts of worship. The *acts of religion* include adoration, penance, fasting, prayer, almsgiving, vows, and oaths. See **justice**.

religious institute – a religious order or congregation approved by the Church, whose members profess the Evangelical Counsels while living in community, such as in a convent.

religious life – state in life in which a person devotes himself or herself to the service of God and publicly professes to practice the Evangelical Counsels. The religious life is the highest vocation. The main goal of the religious life is Christian perfection with Christian charity. See **Evangelical Counsels**.

remote conclusions of morality – the third grade of moral precepts in the Natural Law. Many of the remote conclusions of morality are not easy to discern by the average person. Without the aid of God's revelation, these remote conclusions can be determined only by those who have perfected the virtue of prudence. See **Natural Law** and **prudence**.

resolution of temptation – the point at which we make a decision for or against committing the sin that we are being tempted to commit. This is the third stage of temptation. See **temptation** and **three stages of temptation**.

restitution – restoring to its rightful owner a material good that has been stolen or damaged, or its equivalent value, along with just compensation for any profit or advantage that the owner would have legitimately derived from that material good.

Revealed Law – God's supernatural revelation of His Divine Law. God gave this Revealed Law to man in stages, as recorded in Sacred Scripture. Revealed Law is also called Positive Divine Law. See **Divine Law**, **New Law**, **Old Law**, and **supernatural revelation**.

revelation – see **supernatural revelation**.

revenge – a deliberate act or intention to harm someone because of a real or perceived wrong. Revenge is a sin against the Fifth Commandment. See **anger** and **hatred**.

reverence – an expression of deep respect and honor for someone or something that is holy or worthy of great esteem. The Second Commandment requires us to revere God's Holy Name and all that is sacred. The Third Commandment requires us to show reverence for God's holy days. See **holy** and **Lord's Day**.

ridicule – sin in which a person maliciously makes fun of his neighbor. Ridicule is a sin against the Eighth Commandment.

right to personal liberty – the right to do good, and to choose between two or more courses of action that are good. The right to personal liberty includes the right to follow our conscience, to worship God freely, to establish and raise a family, to choose a means of employment and education, to make our own decisions regarding buying and selling goods, and to enjoy other reasonable freedoms that are in accordance with the common good. See **common good**.

right reason – clear, rational thinking that leads to sound judgment.

righteous – morally upright and pleasing to God.

righteousness – conduct that is morally upright and pleasing to God.

robbery – stealing someone's goods openly or violently. Robbery is a sin against the Seventh Commandment. See **stealing** and **theft**.

Sabbath – the seventh day of the week, Saturday. Under the Old Covenant, the people of Israel were required to keep holy the Sabbath. In the New Covenant, this requirement is fulfilled by our keeping holy the Lord's Day. See **Lord's Day**, **New Covenant**, and **Old Covenant**.

sacramentals – "sacred signs instituted by the Church" that "prepare men to receive the fruit of the sacraments and sanctify different circumstances of life" (*Catechism*, 1677).

Sacred Scripture – "the speech of God as it is put down in writing under the breath of the Holy Spirit" (*Catechism*, 83). The principal Author of Sacred Scripture is the Holy Spirit. The instruments He used to write the Scriptures are the human authors. Because the Author of Sacred Scripture is the Holy Spirit, Sacred Scripture is *free from all error*. See **Canon of Scripture** and **Word of God**.

Sacred Tradition – the transmission of the Apostles' preaching and teaching, along with the institutions and practices they established, in a continuous line down to the pope and bishops of today. See **Word of God**.

sacrilege – treating in an unworthy manner a person, place, action, or thing that is holy. There are three types of sacrilege: personal, local and real. Sacrilege is a grave sin against the First Commandment. See **irreligion**.

sacrilegious communion – receiving Holy Communion while in a state of mortal sin. Sacrilegious communion is a grave sin against the Body, Blood, Soul, and Divinity of Our Lord Jesus Christ. See **real sacrilege**.

sanctifying grace – the supernatural gift of God's presence in a person's soul, by which that person shares in the Divine Life of the Holy Trinity. A person who has sanctifying grace in his soul is in a *state of grace*. See **state of grace**.

scandal – leading others to sin by word or example. The gravity of scandal varies according to the seriousness of the sins that it leads others to commit, the authority of those giving the scandal, and the moral weakness of those scandalized. If a person deliberately leads his neighbor to commit a mortal sin, he is guilty of a grave sin of scandal. There are two types of scandal: direct and indirect.

schism – refusal to submit to the pope or to be in communion with the members of the Church who are subject to him. See **incredulity**.

science – intellectual virtue that perfects the intellect in its grasp of scientific matters. See **intellectual virtues**.

scrupulosity – a disorder of the soul characterized by excessive worry that some act is a sin which truly isn't, or that some act is a mortal sin when it is actually only a venial sin or an imperfection.

scrupulous conscience – a conscience that is affected by a disorder known as scrupulosity.

secular institute – a religious society approved by the Church, whose members profess the Evangelical Counsels while continuing to live in the world. See **Evangelical Counsels**.

self-knowledge – sufficient knowledge of ourselves so that we will be aware of our weaknesses and what tempts us. Self-knowledge can help us avoid the near occasions of sin.

sense appetite – the physical drives and tendencies within us that draw us toward what is perceived as desirable, and away from what is perceived as undesirable. The sense appetite includes both the irascible passions and the concupiscible passions. See **concupiscible passions**, **fortitude**, **irascible passions**, and **temperance**.

Sign of the Cross – sacramental that is both the sign of the Holy Trinity and the sign of the Redemption that Jesus Christ won for us on the Cross. The Sign of the Cross is sacred, and it can help protect us. See **sacramentals**.

simony – an attempt to buy or sell spiritual goods. Simony is a grave sin against the First Commandment. See **irreligion**.

sin – any thought, word, deed, or omission that is contrary to God's Law. We must have a firm determination to avoid all the near occasions of sin. See **moral evil**, **mortal sin**, and **venial sin**.

sin of commission – a sin in which we do something that God has forbidden.

sin of omission – a sin in which we neglect to do something that God has commanded.

sins that cry to Heaven – sins that are so offensive to God that they cry to Heaven for justice. These sins include "the blood of Abel"; "the sin of the Sodomites"; "the cry of the people oppressed in Egypt"; "the cry of the foreigner, the widow, and the orphan"; and "injustice to the wage earner" (*Catechism*, 1867).

slander – see **calumny**.

sloth – laziness. Sloth is one of the seven capital sins. See **acedia**.

sorcery – sin in which a person attempts to use supernatural powers to achieve some end (or goal). Magic and all other forms of sorcery are extremely dangerous. They are grave sins against the First Commandment. See **superstition**.

soul – see **rational soul**.

sources of morality – see **elements of morality**.

speculation – sin in which someone artificially manipulates the price of material goods in order to gain some advantage while harming others. Speculation is a form of usury. It is a sin against the Seventh Commandment. See **usury**.

spirit – a rational being that is not physical, and thus is invisible. See **angels** and **demons**.

spiritual works of mercy – seven ways in which we express our love for Jesus Christ by caring for the spiritual needs of our neighbor. The seven spiritual works of mercy are admonishing the sinner, instructing the ignorant, counseling the doubtful, comforting the sorrowful, bearing wrongs patiently, forgiving injuries, and praying for the living and the dead.

standard of morality – that by which moral good and evil are measured. The standard of morality is the Will of God, and ultimately God Himself. Every action in which we are obedient to the Will of God is a good action; every action in which we are not obedient to the Will of God is a bad action. See **purity of intention**.

State – an organized political community or territory governed by a political regime, and the authorities in power within that regime. The purpose of the State is to promote the temporal welfare of the people within that State, in order to secure their unalienable rights and serve the common good. See **common good**, **temporal welfare**, and **unalienable rights**.

state in life – see **vocation**.

state of grace – the state of a person who has sanctifying grace in his soul. Every person who is in a state of grace is in fellowship with God. See **sanctifying grace**.

state of mortal sin – the state of a person who lacks sanctifying grace in his soul because of one or more mortal sins he has committed for which he has not repented. See **mortal sin**.

state of Original Sin – see **Original Sin**.

stealing – sin in which a person takes someone's goods unjustly. Stealing is an intrinsically evil act. The gravity of the sin depends on the value of what is stolen and the harm done. A person also steals if he knowingly purchases or hides stolen goods. Refusing to pay a worker his wages is another form of stealing, and it is one of the sins that cry to Heaven for justice. See **restitution, robbery**, and **theft**.

subjective – relative to one's own personal preferences or philosophy, the historical period in which one lives, the part of the world where one lives, one's culture, and so on. Moral good and evil are objective, not subjective.

suicide – a person's intentional and deliberate taking of his own life. Suicide is an intrinsically evil act. It is never morally permissible. Suicide is a grave sin against (1) God, (2) oneself, and (3) one's neighbor.

supernatural revelation – God's communication to man about Who He is and what He requires. See **public revelation** and **Word of God**.

supernatural virtues – those virtues resulting from God acting on our soul in some way. See **natural virtues**.

superstition – any practice that is contrary to the worship and devotion, in spirit and truth, that we are to give to the One True God. The grave sins that fall under the category of superstition include idolatry, divination, and sorcery.

talebearing – spreading a negative report about someone, or going back and revealing such a report to him, from a warped sense of pleasure in causing strife. Talebearing is a sin against the Eighth Commandment. It is closely related to the sins of detraction and calumny. Deliberately encouraging or taking pleasure in listening to gossip or talebearing about one's neighbor is also sinful. See **calumny**, **detraction**, and **gossip**.

temperance – cardinal virtue that regulates the concupiscible passions of our sense appetite so that we keep our emotions, desires, and attractions within reasonable limits, and we maintain balance in our treatment of created goods. The virtue of temperance helps us to *use things* according to right reason, and to *love persons* rather than use them. See **concupiscible passions**, **person**, and **thing**.

temporal punishment – punishment that does not last forever. All sins, mortal and venial, incur some temporal punishment. This punishment may take place on Earth or in Purgatory. Temporal punishment helps purify us so that we may one day stand in the presence of God.

temporal welfare – everything people reasonably need to secure their unalienable rights. See **unalienable rights**.

temptation – an incitement to act contrary to God's Law, and thus to commit sin. There are *three sources of temptation*: the world, the flesh, and the devil. All three sources of temptation are tied in some way to *three aspects of temptation*: the lust of the flesh, the lust of the eyes, and the pride of life. Every temptation typically has *three stages*: the occasion, the conflict, and the resolution. See **sin**.

tempting God – testing, by words or deeds, the goodness or power of God. Tempting God is a grave sin against the First Commandment. See **irreligion**.

Ten Commandments – the foundation of the Moral Law, which God Himself inscribed on tablets of stone for His servant Moses. The Ten Commandments (also called the *Decalogue*) are the foundation of equal rights for all mankind, the weak and the strong alike. See **Moral Law**.

tender conscience – a conscience that has a heightened sense of awareness of even the slightest offense against God. The person who acquires a tender conscience will grow in his determination to never offend God.

Teresa of Avila, St. – a Doctor of the Church from the 15th century who was devoted to mental prayer. See **mental prayer**.

thanksgiving – act of prayer in which we express our gratitude to God. See **prayer**.

theft – stealing someone's goods secretly. Theft is a sin against the Seventh Commandment. See **robbery** and **stealing**.

theological virtues – those virtues that relate directly to God and dispose us to have a personal relationship with Him. God infuses these virtues in our soul at Baptism so that we can live as His children and merit eternal life. The three theological virtues are faith, hope, and charity. It is primarily through the theological virtues that we surrender ourselves completely to God.

theoretical indifference – sin in which a person believes that it doesn't matter which religion one chooses. If the person includes non-Christian religions in his indifference, he effectively commits apostasy against the Faith. If he includes only Christian religions in his indifference, he commits heresy by denying that the Catholic Church is the one true Church. See **apostasy**, **heresy**, and **indifference**.

thing – a being that is not rational, and thus cannot truly know or love God. See **person**.

Thomas Aquinas, St. – saint known as the Angelic Doctor, who proved the existence of God in five different ways.

three aspects of temptation – the lust of the flesh, the lust of the eyes, and the pride of life. One or more of these three aspects of temptation have been behind all the sins ever committed since the first sin of Adam and Eve. See **sin** and **temptation**.

three sources of temptation – the world, the flesh, and the devil. See **temptation**.

three stages of temptation – the occasion of temptation, the conflict of temptation, and the resolution of temptation. See **temptation**.

threefold mission of the Magisterium – to teach, govern, and sanctify. See **Magisterium**.

tithe – an offering of 10 percent of one's income to God. Under the Old Law, the Israelites were required to pay tithes to God, which were typically in the form of flocks or produce. Under the New Law, we are not required to devote any precise percentage of our income to almsgiving. However, we are still required to provide for the Church, promote social justice, and give to the poor, according to our means. See **almsgiving**.

totalitarian – a type of State in which the government tries to control virtually every aspect of the lives of the people within that State. Examples of totalitarian forms of government include communism, socialism, and fascism. The Church condemns all totalitarian forms of government. Such systems are contrary to the dignity of the human person and his natural right to personal liberty. See **right to personal liberty**, **State**, and **unalienable rights**.

true conscience – a conscience that consistently makes correct judgments about what is morally good and evil. When a person has a true conscience, the voice of his conscience is like an echo of the voice of God in his soul Along with a true conscience, he will have a watchful conscience and a tender conscience. See **tender conscience** and **watchful conscience**.

truthfulness – virtue by which a person is morally upright, true, and sincere in all his words and deeds. Truthfulness includes both honesty and discretion. A person who loves the truth will cultivate other virtues as well, including fidelity and righteousness. Truth, fidelity, and righteousness are essential elements of every society. See **discretion**, **fidelity**, **honesty**, and **righteousness**.

ultimate goal of morality – happiness through union with God in Heaven. See **morality**.

unalienable rights – fundamental rights that belong to every human being and cannot be taken away. Every human being has equal dignity as a person created in the image and likeness of God. Along with this dignity comes certain fundamental rights. These rights are not from man or the State, or even the Church; they are from God. Therefore, they cannot be taken away. See **common good**, **right to personal liberty**, **State**, and **temporal welfare**.

understanding – intellectual virtue that perfects the intellect in its comprehension of first principles. See **first principles** and **intellectual virtues**.

unitive – see **marriage**.

universal destination of goods – principle of the Church which teaches that God has given all of creation to the entire human race, and He intends everyone to have the essential material goods that are needed to live (food, clothing, shelter, etc.). When someone is deprived of even these most basic needs and truly has no way to pay for them, he has effectively been robbed of what is rightfully his. When he appropriates for himself or his family these goods, he is not stealing; he is exercising his right to share in the goods of creation intended for him. Even in such cases, however, he must have the intention of restoring what he has taken to the rightful owner, if he ever becomes able to do so. See **stealing**.

usury – charging excessive interest on loans. Usury is a sin against the Seventh Commandment. See **speculation**.

vandalism – intentionally damaging another's property. Vandalism is a sin against the Seventh Commandment. It is a serious sin if the damage is significant or if it is done with malice.

veneration – profound respect, honor, and devotion. The veneration given to the angels and saints is called *dulia*. The highest form of veneration, *hyperdulia*, is reserved for the Blessed Virgin Mary. Veneration may also be given to sacred images and relics. The adoration given to God alone is called *latria*.

venial sin – any morally evil act that does not separate our soul from God, but that wounds our relationship with Him. There are two main categories of venial sin: (1) sins that do not constitute grave matter, and (2) sins that constitute grave matter but that are not done with sufficient knowledge or consent to be mortal sins. See **mortal sin**.

vice – a morally bad habit due to repeated sins in a particular moral area. See **sin**.

virtue – a firm and habitual disposition to do good; a morally good habit. There are two main *categories of virtues in terms of their source*: natural and supernatural. There are three main *categories of virtues in terms of their type*: intellectual virtues, moral virtues, and theological virtues.

virtuous – consistently doing what is good.

vocal prayer – conversing with God. See **prayer**.

vocation – an invitation by God to serve Him in a particular way, so that we may grow in sanctity and Christian charity. In addition to the general means for cultivating Christian charity and attaining Christian perfection, God has given each of us a specific way to achieve this goal: our vocation (or *state in life*). There are three main vocations: single, married, and religious. The highest vocation is the religious life. See **Christian perfection**, **marriage**, and **religious life**.

voluntary doubt – the willful rejection of a truth that God has revealed or that the Catholic Church teaches. Voluntary doubt is always gravely sinful. See **involuntary doubt**.

vow – a sacred act of devotion in which a person freely and deliberately dedicates himself to God or solemnly promises God to do some good work.

watchful conscience – a conscience that can more readily discern the right path from all the wrong paths placed before it. If a person has a watchful conscience, then regardless of what disguise evil assumes, it will not fool him. See **true conscience**.

will – the faculty of our rational soul through which we decide what we will believe and what we will do. See **free will**.

wisdom – intellectual virtue that perfects the intellect to grasp the highest causes of everything that exists. See **intellectual virtues**.

Word of God – God's revelation of Himself to man, which He has accomplished definitively through Jesus Christ, the Word Incarnate. The Word of God is revealed to us in two ways: orally through Sacred Tradition, and in writing through Sacred Scripture. The Word of God is public revelation, which all Christians are bound to believe. See **public revelation**, **Sacred Scripture**, **Sacred Tradition**, and **supernatural revelation**.

wrath – see **anger**.

Index

E

F

G

H

I

J

K

L

M

T

U

V

W

Bibliography

Aquinas, St. Thomas. *Summa Theologica*. Online ed. by Kevin Knight, New Advent, 2016; www.newadvent.org/summa.

Athanasius, St. *Life of St. Anthony*. Circa 360 A.D. Online ed. by Kevin Knight, New Advent, 2009; www.newadvent.org/fathers/2811.htm.

Augustine, St. *Letter of Augustine to Jerome*. 405 A.D. In *Faith of the Early Fathers*, vol. 3. Translated by William A. Jurgens. Collegeville, Minn.: Liturgical Press, 1970.

Blackstone, Sir William. *Commentaries on the Laws of England*. 1765-1769. Online ed. by Lonang Inst., 2014; www.lonang.com/exlibris/blackstone/bla-002.htm.

Catechism of the Catholic Church. 2nd ed. Translated by United States Catholic Conference, Inc. Citta del Vaticano: Libreria Editrice Vaticana, 1997.

The Catechism of the Council of Trent. 1566. Edited by St. Charles Borromeo. Translated by John A. McHugh and Charles J. Callan. Reprint. Rockford, Ill.: TAN Books and Publishers, Inc., 1982.

Congregation for the Doctrine of the Faith. *Responses to Certain Questions of the United States Conference of Catholic Bishops Concerning Artificial Nutrition and Hydration*. Aug. 1, 2007.

Council of Trent. Session VI. *Decree on Justification*. Jan. 13, 1547. Canons on Justification.

Crean, Fr. Thomas. "Praying with Non-Catholics – Is It Possible?" Feb. 8, 2009. In *Christendom Awake*; www.christendom-awake.org.

The Holy Bible. Revised Standard Version, Catholic Edition. Ft. Collins, Colo.: Ignatius Press, 1994. (All Scripture quotations are from the RSV-CE, except Genesis 3:15 and Matthew 16:18-19, which are from the Douay-Rheims Version. Reprint. Rockford, Ill.: TAN Books and Publishing, Inc., 1971.)

Irenaeus, St. *Against Heresies*. Inter 180/199 A.D. In Jurgens, vol. 1.

Laux, Father John. *Catholic Morality: A Course in Religion, Book III*. Rockford, Ill.: TAN Books and Publishing, Inc., 1990.

May, William E. *An Introduction to Moral Theology*. 2nd ed. Huntington, Ind.: Our Sunday Visitor Publishing, 2003.

Pope Benedict XVI. *Deus Caritas Est* (Encyclical on Christian Love). December 25, 2005.

Pope John Paul II. *Dies Domini* (Apostolic Letter on Keeping the Lord's Day Holy). May 31, 1998.

Pope John Paul II. *Veritatis Splendor* (Encyclical on the Splendor of Truth). Aug. 6, 1993.

Pope Leo XIII. *Immortale Dei* (Encyclical on the Christian Constitution of States). November 1, 1885.

Pope Leo XIII. *Providentissimus Deus* (Encyclical on the Study of Sacred Scripture). Nov. 18, 1893.

Pope Leo XIII. *Rerum Novarum* (Encyclical on Capital and Labor). May 15, 1891.

Pope Paul VI. *Humanae Vitae* (Encyclical on the Regulation of Birth). July 25, 1968.

The Second Vatican Council. *Gaudium et Spes* (Pastoral Constitution on the Church in the Modern World). December 7, 1965.

Thomas à Kempis. *The Imitation of Christ*. Online ed. by Leadership Univ., Cyber Library, 1995; www.leaderu.com/cyber/books/imitation/imitation.html.

United States Declaration of Independence. July 4, 1776.

Notes

Notes

Notes